THE RIGHT TO JUSTICE

THE LOCKE INSTITUTE

Founded in 1989, The Locke Institute is an independent, non-partisan, educational and research organization. The Institute is named for John Locke (1632–1704), philosopher and political theorist, who based his theory of society on natural law which required that the ultimate source of political sovereignty was with the individual. Individuals are possessed of inalienable rights variously defined by Locke as 'life, health, liberty and possession,' or, more directly, 'life, liberty and property.' It is the function of the state to uphold these rights since individuals would not enter into a political society unless they believed that it would protect their lives, liberties and properties.

The Locke Institute seeks to engender a greater understanding of the concept of natural rights, its implications for constitutional democracy and for economic organization in modern society. The Institute encourages high quality research utilizing in particular modern theories of property rights, public choice, law and economics, and the new institutional economics as a basis for a more profound understanding of important and controversial issues in political economy. To this end, it commissions books, monographs, and shorter studies involving substantive scholarship written for a wider audience, organizes major conferences on fundamental topics in political economy, and supports independent research. The Institute maintains a publishing relationship with Edward Elgar, the International Publisher in the Social Sciences.

In order to maintain independence, the Locke Institute accepts no government funding. Funding for the Institute is solicited from private foundations, corporations, and individuals. In addition, the Institute raises funds from the sale of publications and from conference fees. The Institute is incorporated in the State of Virginia, USA, and has applied for non-profit, tax-exempt educational status under Section 501(c)3 of the United States Internal Revenue Code.

Officers of the Institute are listed above. Please direct all inquiries to the address given below.

5188 Dungannon Road • Fairfax, Virginia 22030
(703) 385–5486

The Right to Justice

The Political Economy of Legal Services
in the United States

Charles K. Rowley

Senior Research Associate
Center for Study of Public Choice
George Mason University

and

General Director
The Locke Institute

Research Assistance by:

Amanda J. Davies-Rowley, Sarah L.D. Davies-Rowley,
Judith Hally and Nancy Oliver

Edward Elgar

Published by
Edward Elgar Publishing Limited
Gower House
Croft Road
Aldershot
Hants GU11 3HR
England

Edward Elgar Publishing Company
Old Post Road
Brookfield
Vermont 05036
USA

A CIP catalogue record for this book is available from the British Library

Library of Congress Cataloguing in Publication Data
Rowley, Charles Kershaw.
        The right to justice: the political economy of legal services in
the Unites States/by Charles K. Rowley.
            p.   cm.
        1. Legal aid–Political aspects–United States.   I. Title.
KF336.R68 1991
344.73'03258–dc20
[347.3043258]   91–13344
                                                                                                    CIP

ISBN 1 85278 526 8

Printed in Great Britain by
Billing & Sons Ltd, Worcester

In Loving Memory of

My Mother

Ellen Rowley (née Beal)

January 10, 1901 – December 22, 1985

Mens sibi conscia recti
(A mind true to its knowledge of the right)

and of

Whisky

January 8, 1980 – October 24, 1990

Contents

PART VII   TOWARDS TOMORROW

Tables

Preface

This book was conceived in September 1987 in the midst of a great struggle between the Congress and the White House over the federal program of legal services in the United States, certainly over its direction, even over its existence. The Legal Services Corporation, through its President, John Bayly, commissioned the study on which this book is based, thus financing a major independent program of research which was to draw significantly on the recently developed analytical techniques of public choice and the new law and economics as lenses through which to evaluate the performance of the legal services program. The book was completed in October 1990 in the wake of a decisive victory by the Congress over the White House and at a moment of apparent calm in the legal services bureaucracy reflecting not only the temporary political equilibrium negotiated between the Congress and President Bush, but, ultimately, the supremacy in the legal services market place of those powerful members of the organized bar who exploit the rational ignorance both of their own colleagues and of the wider electorate to pursue their own political agendas through the institution of the American Bar Association.

It is the acknowledged intent and indeed expectation of this book to help to destabilize this equilibrium, which is more fragile than is widely recognized, by exposing the behavior and the consequences of the principal actors to the relentless lens of public choice, by narrowing the range of that rational ignorance on which the special interests ultimately depend for political influence, and by identifying incentives for a regrouping of forces in the market place for legal services into constellations more favorable to the deserving poor. The book will succeed in this mission, not by appealing to some misplaced notion of the public interest, not by tapping, however deeply, into the limited resources of altruism available within the American electorate, but rather by informing and harnessing the forces of enlightened self interest and launching these forces into effective collective action.

Fundamental to this exercise, and indeed the driving force behind the research program, is an unshakeable belief that ideas matter in the shaping of policy, indeed that without ideas would-be political entrepreneurs remain helplessly adrift, enjoying the useless freedom of the boat without the compass. Ultimately, however, ideas are necessary but far from sufficient preconditions for the radical reformation of adverse institutions. Only when good ideas are harnessed into effective political campaigns by skilled entrepreneurs motivated to do well while doing good is there any realistic prospect for institutional reform. The concept of the legal services voucher as a device for restoring to poor Americans their fundamental rights of access to civil justice, as we shall argue, is a good idea whose time has come.

A book of this reach and magnitude could not be researched effectively by one individual. I was fortunate indeed to find the support of an intelligent, enthusiastic and hard working research team who brought joy as well as skill to a demanding task. Amanda Davies-Rowley, Sarah Davies-Rowley, Judith Hally and Nancy Oliver each performed beyond the call of duty in collating and sifting institutional information and commentary, in researching legal services litigation through the Nexis computational system, and even in the first drafting of sections of some of the institutional chapters. I am indebted to them for their assistance.

I am indebted also to Robert Elgin, then of the Legal Services Corporation, for facilitating access to Corporation documents, for his continuing help and assistance on all aspects of the research, for his helpful comments on all chapters in the book, and for his encouragement at times when my own confidence began to flag. It is rare to find a member of a government bureau so refreshingly open minded and so willing to contemplate the prospect for root-and-branch-reform even when such reforms must reach out and perhaps challenge his own job security.

Early drafts of the various chapters were tested out in presentations at universities throughout America, in England, Germany and Austria and I am grateful to the many individuals whose criticisms and comments served to enhance the text. I am particularly privileged in this prospect in my location at George Mason University which serves as the confluence of four mighty research programs vested separately in the Center for Study of Public Choice, the Institute for Humane Studies, the Law and Economics Center and the Center for Study of Market Processes. By blending the separate contributions of these programs and harnessing them into an effective lens through which to evaluate political institutions this book serves as a harbinger of the new political economy which is emergent as an influential program of research in the dying years of the twentieth century.

Although for some time Gordon Tullock has not been located in the Center for Study of Public Choice, his influence upon this book will be evident to all who know him. Rational ignorance, the economics of persuasion, the problem of majority voting, logrolling, rent-seeking, the stability of political equilibrium, the logic of the law, the politics of bureaucracy, the economics of charitable giving, yes, even 'Tullock's' law that everyone is altruistic, but at most five per cent of the time, are really important ideas, bequeathed to us by Tullock, without which public choice literally would not exist in its current form, and without which this book would have taken a quite different form. Tullock read an early draft of this book in its entirety, wrecked my research program, including work on our projected joint book with Arthur Seldon (A Primer on Public Choice), by his insightful comments, and thus helped to shape the final structure of this book. I take this opportunity to thank him for all that he has done to help me.

In addition, the book has benefited from constructive criticism and helpful suggestions from Robert Anthony, James Bennett, Roger Congleton, Mark Crain, Michael Crew, Kathy de Bettencourt, Thomas DiLorenzo, Clark W. Durant III, Harold Elder, David Fand, Kevin Grier, Gail Heffernan, Jerri Joy, Israel Kirzner, William Landes, David Levy, Leonard Liggio, James C. Miller III, Francoise Monceaux, Mancur Olson, Emilio Pacheco, Glen Parker, George Priest, Mario Rizzo, Robert Tollison, Michelle Vachris, Richard Wagner, Walter Williams and Jack Wiseman. I am grateful to each of them.

The research grant provided by the Legal Services Corporation took care of the fundamental research on which this book is based. Additional research support from the Lynde and Harry Bradley Foundation through the Center for Study of Public Choice, facilitated the drafting of the text by the provision of summer release, travel and secretarial support. In this latter respect, I am grateful to Gloria Yeager, who ably typed chapter revisions and references during the final stages to ease the pressure on Helen Rusnak, and who helped to shape the final typescript for despatch to my publisher.

To Helen Rusnak, I must express overwhelming gratitude for three years of dedicated effort to steer this research to its successful completion. From the outset, Helen took this project under her wing, helped to organize my research team, to plan my program of research, to program my travels and to take care of all the complexities of typing and communication that arise in any ambitious venture. Not only is Helen a superb secretary and a skilled typist, but also she is a formidable psychologist who sensed just how and when to lift my spirits when they began to flag. Without her loyal support, the book might not have been completed. I am enormously indebted to her and trust that she is as proud as I am of the final product.

The book was written at home and I am extremely grateful to my wife, Marjorie, and to my daughters, Amanda and Sarah, not only for their loyal support, encouragement and assistance, but also for their generous toleration of my conversion of much of the house into a research laboratory and for their willing accommodations of their own life styles to an activity which became an obsession as the coarse threads of the research were spun and woven into creative scholarship.

I wish also to thank posthumously my cairn terrier, Whisky, who was much less accommodating of my preoccupations, and much more willing to impose his own preferences. Whisky, who was my constant companion throughout the two years that I spent writing this book, sitting at my feet while I wrote, and taking me for walks when he determined that I was tired, died in October 1990, just as this book was completed. Fittingly, the sun was shining on that day for a creature that brought so much sunshine to my life.

The book is dedicated to my mother Ellen Rowley (née Beal) whose steadfast dedication to the principles of classical liberalism on which this book is based made it possible for me to write this book. Her sacrifice in relinquishing a prized place in a grammar school at age 13, upon the untimely death of her father, to work in a Lancashire cotton mill to assist in the private education of her brother, paved the way for the entire family to lift itself out of poverty. Her dedication to 'life, liberty and property', and her devotion to her family are principles that have stood me in good stead. I know that she would have been proud that her life would be remembered in a book which is to be the first publication of the Locke Institute. I know also that she would have been glad to make a small space in her Dedication for Whisky whom she also grew to love.

Prologue

The persons entrusted with the great interests of the state may, even without any corrupt views, sometimes imagine it necessary to sacrifice to those interests the rights of a private man. But upon the impartial administration of justice depends the liberty of every individual, the sense which he has of his own security.

Adam Smith (1776), The Wealth of Nations Book V, Part II

Part I

HISTORY

1　The historical perspective

History, a distillation of rumor

T. Carlyle, *French Revolution*

1　Introduction

This text deals with a political invention of the mid-twentieth century – The Legal Services Corporation – as it plays out a role and exerts an economic and social impact during the closing years of that turbulent century. Yet, the philosophical and political issues that the text confronts find their roots in thirteenth-century England, most notably in the pledge of the Magna Carta extracted from King John in 1215:

> To no one will we sell, to no one will we refuse or delay, right or justice.

From Magna Carta onwards, English justice evolved a principle, albeit one that was not always honored, that free counsel should be provided to litigants too poor to employ their own, a common law development that became a written guarantee in the statute of 1495 enacted by King Henry VII:

> The Justices ... shall assign to the same poor person or persons counsel learned, by their discretions, which shall give their counsel, nothing taking for the same; ... and likewise the Justices shall appoint attorney and attorneys for the same poor person or persons ...

In essence, the right to counsel formed an important element in a social contract or constitution designed to create society from a situation close to anarchy. A guarantee of counsel in court proceedings apparently was required as a substitute for the individual right to take or to protect property by force of arms. The courts, thenceforth, would become the substitute arena for resolving disputes over rights. This historical right to counsel, as a fundamental cornerstone of equality before the law, slowly eroded in the centuries that followed, as the English legal system evolved in terms both of comprehensiveness and of complexity. However, the objective of equal access to justice was never extinguished entirely and the evident gap that slowly emerged was narrowed in 1949 through the enactment by the British Parliament of an almost comprehensive statutory right to counsel, supported, where necessary, by the public finances.

This right to counsel, even in its early embryonic form, was not exported to colonial America. The legal process was much simpler in the colonies than in England, with litigants for the most part proceeding without the assistance of lawyers. Indeed, several colonial legislatures passed statutes that barred lawyers from the lower courts. Legal counsel was not viewed as a necessary condition in the colonies for equality before the law. Thus, the written Constitution of the United States, though it enshrined a commitment to the principle of justice, provided no explicit guarantee of the right to legal aid. The Bill of Rights, designed to protect the individual against government and to ensure due process, only endorsed the right to counsel explicitly in federal criminal cases. For a century after the Declaration of Independence, no formal mechanism existed in the United States to provide the poor with counsel as an aid to litigation, though informal, charitable, mechanisms undoubtedly existed throughout the colonial period and the century thereafter.

The first legal aid organization in the United States, *Der Deutsche Rechtsschutz Verein*, was established in 1876 by the German Society in New York to provide assistance in landlord–tenant disputes, family law and the like and thus to discourage the exploitation of German immigrants by 'runners, boardinghouse keepers and a miscellaneous coterie of sharpers'. This organization, composed largely of lawyers, was viewed as a response to specific legal abuses rather than as a recognition of any generalized right of access to counsel.

The German experiment was the precursor of legal aid societies in the United States. By the 1960s, the New York and Chicago societies had been joined by hundreds of similar organizations as well as by criminal-defence agencies, all supported from charitable donations channelled through private rather than governmental institutions. The services provided were gratuitous, in no sense suggestive of any legal right to counsel, save as prescribed by the United States Constitution and/or as endorsed by the courts.

Section 2 provides a brief history of the legal aid movement over the period 1876 to 1964. Section 3 reviews institutional developments over the period 1964 to 1973 which encompasses the contribution of the Office of Economic Opportunity to the legal aid program. Section 4 reviews developments culminating in 1974 in the creation of the Legal Services Corporation by President Richard Nixon as his final legislative act.

2   The uneven expansion of legal aid in the US: 1876–1964

Charitable legal assistance for the poor developed in the US only on a primitive and piecemeal basis over the period 1876–1964. Indeed, with the important exception of cases taken on a contingency free basis, legal services prior to the 1960s were unobtainable in practice in the civil courts for the great majority of the poor population. E. Johnson Jr (1978) estimated, for example, that in the early 1960s there were perhaps fewer than 400 legal aid lawyers to serve almost 50 million eligible poor persons in the US as a whole. The majority of such lawyers were concentrated in a few areas in the East, although almost every major city had some kind of program. Approximately 157 organizations provided civil legal assistance to the poor, operating with an aggregate budget of nearly $4.5 million.

Until 1920, legal aid was provided by an unorganized collection of independent agencies located in a few of the larger US cities. By 1917, 41 cities were represented by some form of legal aid organization which provided in aggregate an annual outlay of $181 000 in legal assistance to the nation's poor. Working through 62 full-time legal aid attorneys and 113 part-time attorneys, the 41 legal aid agencies handled a total of 117 201 cases in 1917. Against this background, Reginald Heber Smith, whose initial career as an attorney was that of organizer of the newly-formed Boston Legal Aid Society, researched the US legal aid experience and published, in 1919, his influential book, *Justice and the Poor* (Heber Smith, 1919), the first definitive treatment of inequality in the administration of civil justice.

Smith's principal recommendations concerned mechanisms for opening up the courts to the poor and for increasing the flow of financial support to legal aid, central to both of which was his strategy of forming a national association of legal aid offices. His recommendations attracted the interest of the American Bar Association which devoted one entire session of its 1920 Annual Convention to a panel on legal aid and which announced the creation of a Special Committee on Legal Aid, to be chaired by Charles Evans Hughes, a subsequent Chief Justice of the Supreme Court. In 1921, the Special Committee was reconstituted as a Standing Committee on Legal Aid to which Reginald Heber Smith was named Chairman (a position that he retained until 1937).

In 1923, Smith's recommendation bore fruit with the establishment of the National Association of Legal Aid Organizations (later to become the National Legal Aid and Defender Association, NLADA). Shortly thereafter a number of state and local bar associations established committees to promote legal assistance to the poor. As a consequence, financial support for legal aid more than doubled, and 30 new legal aid organizations emerged in the favorable climate of the 1920s.

With the onset of depression, however, enthusiasm for legal aid faltered and financial aid sputtered into decline, despite a burgeoning legal aid case load, which almost doubled from 171 000 new cases in 1929 to 307 000 new cases in 1932. In consequence, the number of cases confronting legal aid societies rapidly outstripped the available supply facilities; and potential clients became disenchanted as the lines lengthened and as the services provided declined in quality. The legal aid case load declined throughout the remainder of the 1930s.

From the outset, legal aid organizers worked through local bar associations to establish legal aid societies, reluctant though many of these associations were to offer support for an activity that might turn out to be competitive to the market interests of their members. In the absence of local bar support, legal aid programs initiated through local charities and community groups failed to prosper. To engage bar association support, legal advocates emphasized lawyer self-interest – the keeping of undesirable, non-paying clients out of private practice offices, the keeping of the poor off the relief rolls, the educating of the ignorant into recognition of the value of attorneys, the provision of training to newly-qualified attorneys, and the public relations benefits to the bar – rather than such moral issues as equal justice and right to counsel. Throughout the 1940s, their messages fell on largely reluctant ears.

The US legal aid movement was stimulated in the 1950s by an outside shock in the form of the British Legal Aid and Advice Scheme (1949). The Act introduced a comprehensive legal aid scheme, funded through the central government, but administered exclusively by the Law Society. The threat of a similar government-financed program in the US galvanized a number of otherwise reluctant state and local bar associations into the creation of private legal aid societies. By 1959, there was an evident breakthrough, with the percentage of large cities without legal aid offices declining from 43 per cent in 1949 to 21 per cent and with support levels advancing to those outlined at the beginning of this section. Yet, according to Dooley and Houseman (1984), legal aid was 'a captive of its principal financial supporters'.

3 The office of economic opportunity (OEO) and the expansion of legal aid: 1964–1973

The early 1960s witnessed the emergence of radically new ideas concerning legal aid for the poor, most notably that legal services could be a component part of an over-all anti-poverty program. In 1964 the US Department of Health, Education and Welfare held a conference in an effort to deal with extending legal services to the poor. By August of that year President Lyndon Johnson successfully manoeuvred the passage of the Economic Opportunity Act, the harbinger and subsequent spearhead of his war on poverty campaign, through a largely complaisant Congress. This legislation encouraged legal aid activists, such as Edgar and Jean Cahn to concentrate their efforts in pursuit of a federal program of legal aid in the US.

Edgar Cahn, a Yale law student and his wife Jean, a Yale Law School graduate both held strong views about urban social service systems. Edgar had written a paper on this issue and Jean had received some notoriety by

working for New Haven's Community Progress, Inc, a non-profit organization (although, not a legal aid society) which offered assistance to the poor
on such matters as education, health services, social workers, and legal
advice. The New Haven program was sponsored by the Ford Foundation, a
non-profit private foundation. William Pincus, an officer of the Foundation,
decided that legal services should be separated from the rest of the Ford anti-
poverty program and thus funded the Legal Assistance Association. This was
one of the first and the largest of the neighborhood lawyer programs and as a
result was influential subsequently in shaping the national OEO program of
legal services to the poor.

By 1964, the Cahns had moved to Washington, DC. Edgar was appointed
Special Assistant to the Director of the OEO, Sargent Shriver who had been
appointed by President Johnson to chair the task force on the war on poverty
campaign. Jean Cahn, prior to working as a Consultant on the Legal Services
Program of the OEO, was Director of the Urban Law Institute at the National Law Center of George Washington University. Throughout the formation years of the OEO, Jean and Edgar Cahn wrote joint papers, attended
meetings and were influential if not instrumental in the establishment of the
Legal Services Program.

There was no reference to legal aid for the poor in the original Economic
Opportunity Act; however, by 1967, legal services was appended to the Act
as a special emphasis program in large part due to the Cahns' persistence.
Thus, federal money became available for legal services to the poor for the
first time. Such an innovation was not achieved without an impressive range
of institutional support, not merely from the leadership of the Office of
Economic Opportunity, but also from the organized bar at the national level
and from local legal aid program initiatives.

The Cahns provided OEO leadership support for the federal program,
convincing Sargent Shriver of the importance of a legal aid package as part
of the overall war on poverty. This leadership support in itself was insufficient, however, since the Equal Opportunity Act was based upon the philosophy of decentralization, with local planning bodies in the form of community action agencies (CAA) deciding how best to address poverty problems
within their respective communities. The CAAs, for the most part, did not
favor the inclusion of legal services in the OEO war on poverty program in
part because they mistrusted the role of professionals in positions of leadership
and in part because of the perceived independence of legal services from the
CAAs and from their local political control.

The OEO would not accept the alternative route of a national earmarking
of funds to legal services without reference to the CAAs in the absence of
solid bar support for such a venture, providing for lawyer control of legal
services at the national level. Bar support, under the facilitating leadership

of Lewis Powell (ABA President), William McCalpin (Chairman of the ABA Standing Committee on Lawyer Referral) and John Cummiskey (Chairman of the ABA Standing Committee on Legal Aid and Indigent Defendants), was unexpectedly forthcoming. The ABA House of Delegates unanimously endorsed the OEO legal services program on the conditions 1) that the organized bar retained a measure of control over the program and 2) that traditional legal ethics were maintained.

The generation of a local service delivery program, in the absence of CAA participation, proved to be the most difficult aspect of the new initiative. The OEO could not initiate local programs; nor was it prepared to deliver services directly. Thus funding proposals had to be drawn from local agencies at best embryonic and for the most part unformed. Even existing agencies, in the form of established legal aid societies and experimental foundations, would find it difficult, if not impossible, to initiate relevant proposals in the absence of some central guidance. To this end, the American Bar Association worked with other bar participants under the guidance of the OEO staff directed by E. Clinton Bamberger, the first director of the OEO Legal Services Program, to evolve a suitable overall design.

A design began to emerge at the National Conference on Law and Poverty, sponsored jointly by the Department of Justice and the OEO during the summer of 1965. It was refined at the 1965 annual meeting of the National Legal Aid and Defender Association (NLADA). It was completed by the OEO staff and the National Advisory Committee, a group representing the organized bar. The design was disseminated as the *OEO Legal Services Guidelines*, supplemented by an OEO staff advisory, *How To Apply For A Legal Services Program*.

The impact of the Cahns on this development was considerable. Throughout, they had remained hostile toward lay involvement in the central program, arguing strongly against any monitoring role for non-lawyer bureaucrats within OEO. They were equally opposed to CAA involvement at the local level, viewing the CAA as a monopoly 'of local services, dedicated ... to its own survival and prosperity, subservient to local political interests ... controlled by social service administrators and local politicians'. Instead, the Cahns envisioned a program which would empower legal services lawyers to assist the poor much in the way that private lawyers assisted non-indigent clients.

From the outset, the Cahns pressed for a dominant ABA involvement, suggesting that it 'could provide just the muscle needed to persuade OEO to affirmatively promote legal assistance for the poor' (Cahn and Cahn, 1964). Jean Cahn's impatience with the OEO bureaucracy led to her resignation as consultant on legal services to Sargent Shriver in 1965, thereby inducing a search for a director of legal services within the OEO. Yet, her influence continued, with Shriver promising that he would not appoint a director without explicit ABA approval. The Bamberger appointment honored this commitment with a former defence attorney spearheading the OEO legal services program.

The OEO Guidelines, developed by Bamberger in association with the ABA, compromised on almost all issues of controversy that separated those who supported client service from those who advocated a root-and-branch war on poverty. The Guidelines, in a genuflect to client influence, required representation of the poor – though not necessarily by poor individuals – on the boards of eligible local programs; they strongly encouraged the establishment of client advisory councils. In deference to local autonomy, the Guidelines refrained from defining national financial eligibility standards; but they excluded fee-generating cases from financial support and provided explicitly for the eligibility of poor persons' organizations.

The Guidelines further required local programs to provide client services in all areas of the law save for criminal defence which was constitutionally guaranteed at the federal level. They encouraged eligible organizations to advocate reforms in statistics, regulations and administrative practices as part of a more collective program against poverty. They identified preventive law and client education as essential elements of an eligible program. They required programs to be easily accessible to the poor, preferably from neighborhood office locations, and to maintain convenient office hours.

It proved to be much easier for the OEO to establish national standards and guidelines than to generate local applications. Proposals emanated principally from existing legal aid societies and progressive local bar associations located in the urban areas of the northeast and on the west coast. Few proposals were received from the south and the southwest. Local bar associations were frequently hostile to the OEO, some fearing competition from publicly supported legal services, others fearing the impact of legal subsidies on the clients of private lawyers. There was a concern lest public subsidies should prove to be a harbinger of public regulation.

A popular reaction among hostile local bar associations was that of advocating OEO funding for judicare programs – a delivery system in which attorneys in separate private practices would be reimbursed for handling the cases of poor persons. The OEO consistently refused to fund such programs, viewing them to be prohibitively expensive and not to be conducive to aggressive advocacy.

The OEO's persistence proved to be slowly successful. By end 1966, 130 legal services program grants had been effected and federal funding for these, together with other national programs to provide training and back-up assistance, was in excess of $20 million. By 1968, 260 programs were in receipt of federal subsidies, with representatives in every state except North

Dakota, where the governor had vetoed grant acceptances. Despite budget cuts on the war on poverty program, the budget for legal services grew from $20 million in 1966 to $71.5 million in 1972, though the rate of growth declined sharply after 1967.

The policy thrust of the OEO, during the term of its second director, Earl Johnson (1967–68), shifted perceptibly away from the concept of individual client service towards that of law reform for the poor. To such an end, Johnson relied not upon regulations alone, recognizing enforcement problems at the local level, but upon the creation of legal services leaders within a national structure of advocacy, support, training, technical assistance and information sharing. This structure was to be the shield against attacks while details of policy were allowed to evolve through decisions in individual cases, with the Guidelines serving as a constitution, the regional legal services personnel as lower court judges and the headquarters office as the appellate court.

Law reform possessed several advantages over client service for those imbued with objectives of societal reform. First, unlike community organization, social reform and similar concepts, law reform had established roots in the ideals even of a politically conservative legal profession. Indeed, the ABA Code of Professional Responsibility, introduced in 1970, imposed an explicit duty of law reform on every member of the legal profession:

> If a lawyer believes that the existence of a rule of law, substantive or procedural, causes or contributes to an unjust result, he should endeavor by lawful means to obtain appropriate changes in the law.

Second, law reform offered the prospect of a much wider political reach in benefiting many of the poor who could not be served directly at legal services offices. A single test case, or legislative change, or modified administrative regulation potentially could benefit many thousands of individuals. Moreover, law reform, rather than social reform directly, is an activity in which lawyers are trained and skilled, and thus at a comparative advantage in terms of any organized opposition.

A major political advantage of law reform was the link that it provided between the goals of the legal aid movement and of the neighborhood lawyer experiments from which strong local organization emanated. Earl Johnson seized upon this link as a focal point of the OEO legal services program, placing the resources of the OEO decisively behind the movement for law reform. By concentrating resources behind this single objective the OEO set about making a major impact on the problem of poverty without dissipating its energies across a wider spectrum of social intervention.

To this end, particular attention was paid to the development of law centers, often initially housed in progressive law schools, specialized in specific fields of poverty law (such as welfare or housing) or in eligible populations (such as Indians or the elderly). These centers were encouraged to engage in national litigation, in legislative and administrative representation relevant to eligible clients while providing support, assistance and training for local programs. In so doing, they mobilized specialized knowledge, both in the law and in techniques of representation, to develop new areas of poverty law and to interact with national movements of the poor (for example, the National Welfare Rights Movement and the National Tenants Organization).

The centers were supported by nationwide publications describing developments in poverty law (Law in Action, Clearinghouse Review and the Poverty Law Reporter), together with national training and technical assistance programs. A number of state support programs were also established, providing coordination of policies in states represented by a large number of local programs. In some cases, state grantees were chosen as basic models for programs elsewhere in the state (for example, Community Legal Counsel in Chicago and Detroit). The OEO also invested in the Reginald Heber Smith Fellowship Program, recruiting high-quality, aggressive lawyers for distribution to local programs.

By 1970, the legal services program as envisioned by Earl Johnson was in place in the form that has continued through the 1980s, distinguished from legal aid by five important characteristics. The first was the concept of service to the poor resident in an area as a whole rather than to individual clients. Second was the concept of legal service as advocacy, the direction of which should be determined by the poor (or their representatives) rather than as an agency to provide services for the poor. Third was a commitment to the redressing of existing inadequacies in the enforcement of legal rights of poor people consequential upon an historical lack of access to rights-creating institutions. Fourth was a commitment to redressing legal problems unrecognized by the poor, through community education and outreach programs. Fifth, was the establishment of a comprehensive range of service and advocacy instrumentation to implement policies deemed to be advantageous to the poor.

4   The creation of the Legal Services Corporation 1971–74

The OEO Legal Services Program remained subject to strong opposition. Conservative critics attacked what they viewed as its interventionist law reform emphasis while liberals lamented the fact that most of the attorneys performed little other than a service function, which they viewed as a classic statement of a judicare program. Typical of this latter lament was the following 1966 complaint by Kenneth Pye, Associate Dean at Georgetown Law School and an advocate of law reform:

> There will be no national offensive against the existing legal economic institutions, because the funds will have been expended to provide emergency relief to the victims of the present system.

Pye exaggerated the limitations of the OEO legal reform initiative, which, in California, was to result in a pitched battle against the policy initiatives of then-Governor Ronald Reagan. The California Rural Legal Assistance Program (CRLA), the largest and most controversial program in the state, had been designated by the OEO in 1968 as one of the best legal services programs in the nation. Although some 80 per cent of the work of the CRLA was dedicated to routine casework for indigent clients, nevertheless a significant agenda of law reform was pursued through which controversial, expensive but successful test cases mandated the state government to enforce costly legislation. For example, in *Morris* v. *Williams* 1967, the CRLA obliged the state to restore $210 million in cutbacks incorrectly imposed upon the 'Medi-Cal' program. Other successes forced the implementation of a minimum wage for farm workers, blocked the importation of cheap foreign farm labor, and generated an expansion in the federal food stamp and school lunch programs.

Political reaction to such a radical agenda was sharp, if relatively unsuccessful. In 1967, Senator George Murphy of California sought to amend the OEO legislation to prohibit legal services lawyers from bringing legal actions against federal, state or local government agencies. The amendment failed in the Senate by a vote of 36 to 52 and was not introduced in the House. In 1969, Senator Murphy submitted a second amendment, designed to provide state governors with an absolute veto over OEO programs, rather than the existing veto power which could be over-ridden by the OEO director. This amendment, widely viewed as an attempt to strengthen the political hand of Governor Reagan in his travails with the CRLA, passed the Senate, despite a muted protest from the Nixon administration, only to fail in the subsequent conference committee, where it was dropped.

The CRLA dispute was the most widely publicized event of the OEO legal reform initiative. It was also reflective of all the major issues that attract attention at the present time in the debate over the future of the Legal Services Corporation. The 1970 Reagan veto of the annual CRLA program grant had been justified by reference to a critical report prepared by Lewis K. Uhler, director of the California Office of Economic Opportunity, itemizing some 150 charges of misconduct, including disruption of prisons and schools, labor organization, criminal representation, representation of ineligible non-poor clients, unethical conduct and the pursuit of frivolous suits. In essence, the Uhler report suggested that legal services monies had been diverted to an activist political agenda far-distant from the original legislative intent.

The OEO, instead of responding directly to the veto, established a commission composed of three justices of state supreme courts to evaluate the charges contained in the Uhler report. The commission rejected the criticisms of the report and found that 'CRLA has been discharging its duty to provide legal assistance to the poor ... in a highly competent, efficient and exemplary manner'. It recommended that CRLA be refunded. The OEO director, Frank Carlucci, used the report to persuade Governor Reagan to withdraw the veto in return for a $2.5 million OEO grant to establish a demonstration judicare program. The refunding imposed conditions to prevent abuses of the kind alleged in the Uhler report.

By 1970, the legal services program appeared to be well established, with 293 legal services projects employing approximately 2200 lawyers and servicing 500 000 clients. The back-up centers were playing a major supportive role, via a range of experimental projects, research activities and volunteer programs, offering group facilities for lawyers to engage in test case litigation and law reform advocacy. All such projects attracted federal funding subject only to a 20 per cent local contribution. The program, though answerable to the OEO headquarters in Washington, was administered and directed by local boards.

Yet underlying weaknesses were increasingly evident as the program expanded and became geographically more diverse. In the absence of any coordinated national strategy, the local programs diverged greatly with respect to client eligibility, wages and working conditions, case loads, and the nature of community participation. The absence of any commitment to long-term funding rendered them insecure and made them vulnerable to special interest political intervention. These weaknesses, widely remarked upon by critics of the legal services program, both left and right in the political spectrum, found their most influential expression in an article entitled 'The Legal Services Corporation: Curtailing political interference' published in the *Yale Law Journal* in 1971.

This article articulated the widespread feeling that the strength and integrity of local legal services was threatened by the evident weakness of central control mechanisms. This weakness served to create the overall effect of a vacuum into which groups and individuals, representing primarily the professional community and the community at large, moved to seize control and exert pressure. The article conceded that offsetting advantages had arisen from the absence of a strong central focus, notably the action orientation of the program, the absence of excessive bureaucracy and a profile sufficiently low as not to provoke a political backlash. On balance, however the weaknesses of the program outweighed the strengths. The article concluded that:

Congress would probably be more inclined to defer to a corporation that defines and enforces policies and develops formulae for allocating control to the competing constituencies.

In this way the concept of a national legal services corporation capable of formulating and implementing a centralized program of legal services for the poor while delegating clearly defined powers to appropriate legal agencies was first etched into the political consciousness. During the following three years, the vision of a national legal services corporation took root and, through a welter of political manoeuvring and logrolling, came to fruition in 1974 just prior to the resignation of the President. It is in a sense ironic that President Nixon, who was never embraced politically by the radicals pressing for a strengthening of the legal services program, was the most effective if not the most steadfast proponent of the Legal Services Corporation.

In 1971, a study committee of the American Bar Association and the President's Advisory Council on Executive Organization each separately recommended the creation of an independent corporation to receive appropriations of funds from the Congress and to distribute them to local legal services programs. The Advisory Council, in particular, was circumspect in its recommendation, viewing the Corporation as a step toward reprivatization and stressing that legal representation of a special group was not a proper permanent and established role of government.

Legislation was introduced in the Congress in February 1971 in an attempt to create a Legal Services Corporation. Known as the Mondale–Steiger bill, it was sponsored by a bipartisan group of representatives and senators. Designed to limit the power of the President over the provision of legal services to the poor, this bill permitted the President to name only a minority of the directors to the board of a newly constituted Legal Services Corporation. The bipartisan bill also provided a broad authorization for legal services without explicit restrictions on the program discretion of the Corporation.

President Nixon countered the Mondale–Steiger bill with a bill designed to provide greater presidential control and less discretionary power for the Legal Services Corporation. The bill gave the power of appointment over all directors to the President and placed explicit restrictions, notably against lobbying, against any assistance in criminal cases, and against group representation and political activity by staff attorneys in the legal services program.

Following considerable debate, notably over the structure of the board, Congress endorsed a compromise bill as part of the reauthorization of the Economic Opportunity Act. The compromise empowered the President to make all appointments to the board (subject to advise and consent by the Senate). However, 11 of the 17 members had to be appointed from lists supplied by various interest groups, such as the American Bar Association, the American Trial Lawyers Association and the National Legal Aid and Defender Association. On December 9, 1971, President Nixon vetoed the Economic Opportunity Amendments bill because it compromised his Legal Services Corporation proposal. Once again, the bifurcation between legal reform and client service is evident in the President's criticism of the vetoed legislation:

> I urge the Congress to rewrite this bill, to create a new National Legal Services Corporation, truly independent of political influences, containing strict safeguards against the kind of abuses certain to erode public support – a legal services corporation which places the needs of low income clients first, before the political concerns of either legal services attorneys or elected officials.

In 1972 the Congress returned to the legal services issue reporting out an Equal Opportunity bill that would have established a Legal Services Corporation with limited Presidential power over board selection. Faced with another veto threat by the President, Action for Legal Rights, a lobbying special interest group for the legal services community, urged the House and Senate conferees to remove the legal services section of the bill rather than to accede to the demand for full Presidential powers over board selection. The lobbyists feared the establishment of a client service, judicare system and the abandonment of legal reform in the event that the President's will should prevail. The bill was recommited with the clauses authorizing the Legal Services Corporation excised.

In January 1973, the President became determined to dismantle the OEO and to terminate the war on poverty. He nominated to the directorship of the OEO Howard Phillips, a critic of both the war on poverty and of the legal services program. Phillips swiftly moved to place the legal services program on month-to-month funding, to cancel law reform as a program goal and to defund the back-up centers. His assault was aborted by the federal court which removed him from office on the ground that his name had not been submitted for confirmation by the Senate. Legal service programs were funded thenceforth on the order of the federal court. In May 1973, President Nixon sponsored a bill to establish the Legal Services Corporation reserving to the Presidency the right to appoint all board members subject to advise and consent by the Senate.

On this occasion, the House legislated on the basis provided by the Administration's bill, notwithstanding its restrictions and prohibitions and the complete absence of affirmative requirements and positive mandates for legal services attorneys to pursue an activist policy agenda. In a 'free-for-all' floor debate, the House introduced 24 restrictive amendments on the behavior of legal services attorneys and on the role of the back-up centers.

The Senate was more supportive than the House and less circumspect concerning the powers of the Corporation, of legal services attorneys and of the back-up or support centers. The Labor and Public Welfare Committee unanimously reported out bipartisan legislation designed to preserve the authority of legal services programs to provide a full range of representation to eligible clients. The Committee negotiated secretly with the White House in the drafting of its legislation, receiving in return the support of the administration for its bill. The only significant restriction addended by the Committee prohibited the application of legal services funding for non-therapeutic abortion litigation.

From the conference committee, a bill emerged much closer to the Senate than to the House bill, allowing legal services programs to continue most of the activities that had been pursued under the earlier OEO legislation. Prohibitions were placed on legal assistance in such areas as non-therapeutic abortions, school desegregation, selective service and some kinds of juvenile representation. However, the conference committee retained the back-up centers together with the authority of legal services staff attorneys to represent clients before legislative bodies and in administrative rule-making. Restrictions were placed on the outside (especially political) activities of staff attorneys and an attempt was made to limit the hiring in of aggressive North-Eastern attorneys to the South and to rural areas by an amendment requiring that preference be shown to attorneys resident in the areas served by a local program. The bill also prohibited programs from utilizing private funds to pursue activities restricted by the legal services funding.

The conference report passed in the House by a vote of 190 to 183, following an abortive attempt to eliminate the back-up centers. Despite Senate support, however, the political struggle continued, with key conservative leaders both in the House and in the Senate making their continued support for President Nixon in the politics of the impeachment process dependent upon his promise to veto the bill if the back-up centers were not eliminated. The President requested that the House provision designed to eliminate such centers (the Green Amendment) be added to the bill in exchange for his support. Finally, the Senate agreed and a comprehensive bill was passed by both Houses. The President signed the bill into law on July 25, 1974, just 14 days prior to his resignation from office.

Part II

THE PHILOSOPHIC DIVIDE

2 Goals

For the man devoted to liberty, there is nothing which makes liberty important.
And he has no reason for his devotion

R. Rhees, *Without Answers*

1 Introduction
The debate over the nature and role of legal services in the US has been
pursued without resolution through three decades of turbulent politics and
volatile attitudes toward public policy, at a level of angst, indeed of outright
rancor, usually reserved for such issues as civil rights and involvement in
foreign wars. At first sight it is difficult to comprehend why such an apparently limited area of policy has drawn such heated intellectual and political
debate, unparalleled in other Western democracies, and which has long
outlived the debate over the Great Society program of which it was but a
part. In a closer perspective, however, the legal services program impacts
sharply upon fundamental issues of philosophy that have divided the United
States throughout the postwar period.

This chapter centers attention on the ethical foundations of five theories
of public policy, namely (i) utilitarian/Paretian, (ii) classical liberal, (iii)
contractarian, (iv) liberal democrat and (v) Marxist, each of which enjoys a
significant presence in contemporary policy discussions concerning legal
services.

2 The utilitarian/Paretian ethic
Classical utilitarianism dates back two centuries and owes much to the
philosophic writings of Jeremy Bentham (1789). It has a lengthy pedigree,
therefore, as an ethical foundation for public policy, and a particularly strong
following among economists despite questionable technical assumptions.

The utilitarian ethic, (Black, 1972; Sen, 1987; Sen and Williams, 1982)
can be separated into three basic parts, namely welfarism, sum-ranking and
consequentialism. Welfarism defines the stock of ethically relevant information in any social situation as a listing of utility levels, one element for each
individual in society. The sum-ranking part asserts that all such utility elements are fully comparable, both for each individual across his/her lifetime
and across all individuals. Since utility is measurable on a cardinal scale, the
sum-ranking principle ensures that the ethical value of any social situation is
simply the sum of the utilities (or the utils) of all individuals relevant to that

situation. Consequentialism then provides the prescriptive component in which all choices that influence social situations are to be determined exclusively by reference to the utility status of the social state that would emerge as a consequence of each such choice. The end-state that maximizes utility must be chosen from all available alternatives.

Of the five views of ethics here under review, only the Marxists would question seriously the welfarist component of the utility ethic. For, in the absence of an organic notion of the state, a society cannot be conceived except as some configuration of its individual membership. Even among utilitarians, however, there is a significant division between those who allow that individuals are the best judges of their own utilities and those who argue for paternalism (Rowley and Peacock, 1975). Among the paternalists, there is a divide between those who argue that some individuals, notably the poor, are generally incapable of making rational choices, whether private or public, and those who argue that such incapacity extends only to a limited range of choices, defined as merit wants.

The principle of welfarism evaluates alternative states by reference to their respective collective utilities calculated at a single point in time without reference to source or to history. As Sen (1987) has commented, the utility of the sadist, achieved through the enjoyment of coercive power, is indistinguishable from the utility of a normal person, achieved perhaps through free exchange of commodities. Similarly, the utility of the masochist, achieved as a consequence of experienced coercion, enters equally into the welfarism social calculus. Thus, end-states based on the principle of slavery will be valued equally with end-states based on the principle of liberty if the calculated collective utilities so dictate.

The sum-ranking component of the utilitarian ethic strongly presupposes that distinctions between individuals are unimportant since utilities are to be added across individuals cardinally as though they can be measured on a single-dimensioned scale. There is no problem of interpersonal utility comparison in this ethic. In consequence, its policy reach is immense. The impartial observer who acts as the judge over alternative social states must show equal concern for each individual and, therefore, equal respect for the preferences of each individual.

Not all utilitarians accept the sum-ranking component as here outlined. Some (for example Mirrlees, 1982) argue that the impartial observer should weigh the preferences of the poor more heavily than the preferences of others in the social welfare calculus. Others, who utilize willingness-to-pay as a measure of utility effectively endorse a positive relationship between individuals' preferences and their respective net wealth (Posner, 1981a).

The most forceful contemporary applications of the utilitarian ethic assert the effectiveness of the measuring rod of wealth in the sum-ranking component and accept the prevailing distribution of wealth and income as the basis for the associated willingness-to-pay criterion. Richard Posner is the arch-exponent of this approach which is the fulcrum of his major jurisprudential contribution to the common law. Posner justifies the use of wealth as a surrogate for utility as follows:

> The things that wealth makes possible – not only luxury goods but also leisure and modern medicine, and even departments of philosophy – are major ingredients of most people's happiness, so that wealth maximization is an important – conceivably the only effective – social instrument of utility maximization. (Posner, 1986, pp. 14–15)

Posner defines wealth as follows:

> Wealth is the value in dollars or dollar equivalents ... of everything in society. It is measured by what people are willing to pay for something or, if they already own it, what they demand in money to give it up. The only kind of preference that counts in a system of wealth maximization is thus one that is backed up by money – in other words, that is registered in a market. (Posner, 1979, p. 281)

Posner's approach has been criticized as presenting a fundamental circularity problem where policy issues raise questions simultaneously with respect to utility (or wealth) and to the underlying distribution of wealth and income (Samuels and Mercuro, 1984). For any choice concerning wealth maximization will impact upon distribution, and vice versa. This is a problem that cannot easily be escaped with respect to legal services policy since legal services, in one viewpoint, is designed to resolve a distributional problem. The existence or absence of legal services, whatever its impact on collective utility, will affect the underlying distribution of wealth and income (Rowley, 1989c). Standard utilitarianism has no answer to this ambiguity, though, as we shall demonstrate, John Rawls (1971) has developed a contractarian solution, if certain rather strong assumptions are accepted.

The notion that utility could be measured cardinally had been challenged by Jevons as early as the 1860s though he suggested a way of approximating it via the assumed constancy of the marginal utility of money. Jevons had also denied the possibility of making interpersonal comparisons of utility. Subsequently, however, Jevons made statements about welfare economics that implied both cardinal measurement and interpersonal comparisons.

It was only during the 1930s with the emergence of a positive economics methodology, and with it a generalized assault upon the relevance of ethics for economics, that cardinal measurements and interpersonal comparisons of utility came under heavy and sustained fire. Robbins led the attack on the untrammeled utilitarian ethic denying the key precepts that confirmed its policy reach. By the time that the positivist attack had made its inroads the

Second World War was over and a 'new' welfare economics embraced the remnants of utilitarianism in the form of the Paretian ethic. In the full triumph of positive economics, the Paretian ethic was suitably modest and its policy reach was correspondingly constrained.

The Paretian ethic is usually portrayed as a minimalist ethic in the sense that it is based on only a very few ostensibly attractive value judgments (Rowley and Peacock, 1975). With cardinal utility and interpersonal comparisons of utility eschewed a social state is described as Pareto optimal if and only if no one person's utility can be increased without reducing the utility of some other person. Any social change which improves one person's utility without diminishing that of any other person is Pareto preferred on this criterion. In essence the Paretian ethic retained welfarism and consequentialism but abandoned the sum-ranking component of the utilitarian ethic rejecting indeed any method of aggregating individual utilities.

Even among Paretians (Sen and Williams, 1982), however, there are major areas of disagreement concerning the relevant thrust of their policy ethic. The social engineers who believe that individual utilities can be mapped by some impartial spectator or benevolent despot into some social choice (Arrow, 1963) are opposed on fundamental grounds by the methodological individualists who reject all policy solutions that are not negotiated by individuals through free exchange (Buchanan, 1959, 1964, 1983). Conservative Paretians who center attention upon efficiency outcomes dependent upon some prior distribution of rights find themselves at odds with radicals who either view the prior distribution of rights as subject to contractarian reassessment or who would impose a prior distribution of rights on the basis of some value judgment not encompassed by the Paretian ethic. In its undiluted form, the Paretian ethic is extremely conservative and highly protective of any existing status quo though it has been employed on the basis of the compensation principle to justify policies that are highly invasive of individual rights and that are vehicles for significant wealth redistribution (Rowley and Peacock, 1975).

The limitations in the policy reach of the full-blooded Paretian ethic with each individual effectively able to veto social change quickly became irksome to its practitioners. Thus restricted, the Paretian ethic could provide only a partial (or quasi) ordering over potential end-states. Most policy alternatives were simply non-comparable by reference to the strict Paretian ethic. To extend policy reach the principle of potential compensation was invoked and developed by Kaldor, Hicks and Scitovsky into an important component of the Paretian policy approach. If the gainers from some policy, in principle, could compensate the losers while still experiencing a net increase in their individual utilities and if such a process could not be reversed subsequently on the same criteria the policy was declared to be a potential Pareto improvement.

The compensation test in its potential form violates the precept of methodological individualism (Buchanan, 1959) since the compensation is not paid. As such it trades off gains and losses between individuals. Nevertheless, it is accepted by many Paretians who pursue policy influence even at a serious cost in ethical inconsistency. Perhaps 90 per cent of policy contributions in the leading journals of economics still employ the Paretian ethic buttressed by potential compensation, by the assumption of near-constancy in the marginal utility of income, and by the assumption that income distribution does not matter. By this device Paretian welfare economics subtly has changed its thrust from providing intellectual justification for conservatism to promoting the liberal democratic cause.

3 The classical liberal ethic
The utilitarian and the Paretian ethic both evaluate individuals' well-being exclusively in terms of end-state utilities. Many classical liberals part company with this approach and emphasize instead freedom of choice as the relevant process criterion for assessing welfare (but see Rowley and Wagner, 1990 for an end-state emphasis).

A basic distinction between negative and positive freedom is the essential point of departure for an understanding of the classical liberal ethic (Berlin, 1969). Negative freedom, the oldest and the most pertinent definition of freedom in the classical liberal sense, implies independence of the individual from the arbitrary will of another individual. In the words of Hayek (1960):

> It is often objected that our concept of liberty is merely negative. This is true in the sense that peace is also a negative concept or that security or quiet or the absence of any particular impediment or evil is negative. It is to this class of concepts that liberty belongs: it describes the absence of a particular obstacle – coercion by other men. It becomes positive only through what we make of it. It does not assure us of any particular opportunities, but leaves it to us to decide what use we shall make of the circumstances in which we find ourselves. (p.19)

Negative freedom thus defined clearly is distinct from positive freedom which emphasizes freedom as power, effective power to achieve specific objectives, and which often is viewed as justifying the exercise of coercive powers by some individuals over others (Berlin, 1969). Positive freedom is a measure of ability to achieve objectives; as such it may be diminished by all manner of constraints, not least by the existence of negative freedom. In essence, positive freedom is the philosophy of the liberal democrats as currently preached in the United States which has developed subtly from a doctrine of freedom into a doctrine of authority and of Marxists who rely upon it as a justification for autocracy. Although frequently confused with true (negative) freedom, positive freedom in reality is its most dangerous enemy. Thus Berlin (1969):

> The freedom which consists in being one's own master, and the freedom which consists in not being prevented from choosing as I do by other men, may, on the face of it, seem concepts at no great logical distance from each other – no more than negative and positive ways of saying much the same thing. Yet the 'positive' and 'negative' notions of freedom historically developed in divergent directions not always by logically reputable steps, until, in the end, they came into direct conflict with each other. (p.132)

To the classical liberal freedom is not a means to a higher political end, but is itself the highest political end (Rowley and Peacock, 1975, p. 80). This is a deontological value judgment which paves the way for an evaluation of the worth of any society. As such it does not require any justification since freedom is valued as an ultimate end and not as a means to some higher political good or as a derivative of some other end. Liberty may be used well or ill without any impact upon its value since for the person devoted to it there is nothing which makes it important (Rowley and Wagner, 1990).

Yet classical liberals remain good democrats accepting as a corollary to equality before the law the requirement that all individuals should have an equal share in making the law (Rowley and Peacock, 1975). Some form of majority voting is essential to such a process. If coercive policies should emanate from the majority vote classical liberals accept the outcome though they will not endorse it and will advocate constitutional limitations on political markets. Classical liberals will not force individuals to be free (Hayek, 1960):

> Liberalism is a doctrine about what the law ought to be, democracy a doctrine about the manner of determining what will be the law. Liberalism regards it as desirable that only what the majority accepts should in fact be law, but it does not believe that this is therefore necessarily good law. Its aim, indeed, is to persuade the majority to observe certain principles. It accepts majority rule as a method of deciding, but not as an authority for what the decision ought to be. (p. 104)

Negative freedom is an absolute goal of classical liberalism; yet it cannot be achieved absolutely. Coercion cannot be avoided altogether because the only way to prevent it is by the threat of coercion (Barry, 1987). Classical liberals, unlike libertarians, are not anarchists. They endorse the conferring of a monopoly in coercion on the state though they press for the constitutional limiting of such coercive powers to instances where it is required to obviate potential coercion of private citizen by private citizen. This notion of the minimal state as referee is central to the classical liberal constitution of liberty (Rowley and Wagner, 1990). More controversial is the view endorsed by Rowley and Peacock (1975) that negative freedoms may conflict with each other and therefore that classical liberals must look to the state to enforce a hierarchy of freedoms. Lockeian classical liberals would emphasize the primacy of property rights and the freedom of contract as discriminants in determining which rights should predominate in the free society. Others would emphasize the primacy of freedom of choice over freedom of contract.

Classical liberalism is thus concerned with preservation of rights designed to protect individuals from coercion by others, not least by transient political majorities. Of course, the utilitarian/Paretian ethic also contains implicit theories of rights, since exchange economies cannot function in their absence. However in this latter ethic rights are viewed entirely as instruments for achieving utility gains. No intrinsic importance is attached to the existence or fulfilment of rights as an end-state value. This divergence of emphasis leads to a serious potential conflict between the two doctrines neatly summarized in an impossibility theorem posed by Amartya Sen (1970, 1976) which demonstrated that even a condition of minimal liberty was potentially incompatible with the weakest form of the Paretian ethic.

Specifically, Sen established that potential conflicts could arise between social choices based upon universal consent and social choices that protected the choices of individuals, even though the same individuals were involved in both approaches to social choice. His proof depends on the existence within a society of meddlesome individuals.

Sen illustrated his theorem by reference to a social choice concerning the book *Lady Chatterley's Lover*, namely whether the book should be read by Mr Lascivious, by Mr Prude, or not at all. Although Mr Lascivious is anxious to read the book, rather than let it go to waste, his first preference is to have Mr Prude read it to relax his rigid moral code. Although Mr Prude's first preference is for the book to go unread, he prefers to read it himself rather than for Mr Lascivious further to debauch himself. Thus, they both agree that the book should be read by Mr Prude and not by Mr Lascivious (the Paretian outcome), even though the former does not wish to read the book and the latter does (the classical liberal outcome).

Of course if rights of ownership of the book existed in the pre-social choice situation the impossibility theorem would be irrelevant. The choice to read or not to read the book would be private and would be determined by individual preferences subject to exchange opportunities. In such a Lockeian world social problems of the kind envisaged by Sen would be much less common, though certainly they could arise not least with respect to such issues as AIDS prevention and the control of drug abuse which are imbued significantly with publicness characteristics. Classical liberals would always give precedence to the condition of minimal liberalism over that of Paretian utility though they would not force that outcome on a reluctant society.

Since this book centers attention upon the legal process it is appropriate to conclude discussion of classical liberalism with an outline of one of its most important precepts, namely the preservation of the rule of law, viewed as an indispensable foundation for the establishment and maintenance of negative freedom (Hayek, 1960). The rule of law constitutes a limitation on the powers and privileges of government including the powers and privileges of the legislature. The rule of law is more than constitutionalism. It requires that all laws should conform to a set of principles which are designed to minimize the probability of arbitrary or discriminatory invasion of individual rights (Rowley, 1978b, 1979).

First, laws must always be prospective and never retrospective in their reach. The intention is to influence the future, not to punish retrospectively. To tolerate retrospective punishment is to expose individuals to arbitrary and/or to discriminatory punishment. Second, laws must be known and certain (to the extent feasible) so that individuals are in a position accurately to predict the decisions of the courts. Third, laws must apply with equal force to all individuals including those in government without exception or discrimination. It is this requirement most especially that makes it improbable that truly oppressive laws will be enacted or will evolve.

The relevance of the rule of law for legal aid is self-evident. Classical liberals are committed to the concept of equal access to the law in areas where rights safeguarding negative freedom are at risk. They are antipathetic to legal services that would destroy negative freedoms in pursuit of social engineering.

4   The contractarian ethic

The defining characteristic of the contractarian approach is the identification of ethical values with the outcomes of particular types of agreements between individuals (Hamlin, 1986). The most radical of the contractarians, Buchanan (1964, 1974a), entirely eschews end-state values and denies relevance to such classical liberal points of departure as the natural rights of John Locke. Instead he has established a process mechanism designed to avoid retreat into empty arguments about personal values that spells the end of rational discourse (Buchanan, 1977a). Other contractarians, such as Nozick (1973) and Rawls (1971, 1980, 1985), do not hesitate to employ arbitrary starting points or in the case of Rawls (1971) even to derive end-state values as part of their contractarian ethic.

All contractarians embrace in some sense the ethical notion that individuals are the best judges of their own well-being. They further embrace the notion that contracts of certain kinds freely entered into are ethically good, indeed are the only indicators of improved well-being. Yet this consensus has not prevented them from adopting radically different models of contractaranism.

Rawls (1971) strips individuals of all their particular interests, desires and special knowledge, so that they are all equally informed about the nature of society without being informed at all about their own particular position or roles within society (Hamlin, 1986, p. 84). They negotiate rules for the basic structure of society in such circumstances behind a veil of ignorance and are hypothesized to reach a reflective equilibrium which is the Archimedean point for a social contract. This hypothetical is utilized to ensure objectivity and to recognize the autonomy of individuals so that real individuals may accept contracts thereby negotiated as just or fair.

Thus, the reflective equilibrium notion serves to ground in real individuals ethical intuitions which are generated from the original position and to obligate real individuals to endorse contracts that satisfy such ethical intuitions. The approach is an ingenious attempt to overcome real-world conflicts which derive from individuals' knowledge of their respective positions in society. Rawls's notion of contractarianism does involve real individuals, each in a state of reflective equilibrium induced by consideration of the original position. Any contract, universally endorsed, in such circumstances satisfies the ethical requirement of justice as fairness.

Nozick (1973, 1974) has pursued a procedural, historic approach to contractarianism in sharp contrast to the end-state approach of Rawls. His search for an Archimedean point is based upon realism rather than the hypothetical, although he also makes use of the reflective concept. Hamlin (1986) designates Nozick's approach as prospective contractarianism since the social contract takes place directly between real individuals in choice situations which are distinguished from day-to-day decision making by an important imaginative step.

Nozick grounds the contractarian ethic in the behavior of real individuals, each viewed as taking an imaginative step dreaming of a world entirely his own. Stable equilibrium, Nozick's vision of Utopia, consists of a real-world outcome.

The bargaining game envisaged by Nozick has characteristics that can be identified with the model of perfect competition in neoclassical economics. Since Nozick analyses the behavior of real individuals, each with their own endowment of skill and energy, Utopia cannot exist unless each individual is guaranteed the value of his/her marginal product. This alone cannot guarantee a determinate outcome since there is no necessary reason why such an allocation would exhaust the social product in an economy possibly characterized by increasing returns to scale. Many possible allocations thus lie within the core of Nozick's Utopia. Further complexities arise where team production prevails and where the marginal products of individual members of the team are nonseparable (Alchian and Demsetz, 1972). Moreover individuals whose skills are in short supply attract quasi-rents (rewards in excess of opportunity cost), leading to divergences between wages and the value of marginal product even under conditions of perfect competition.

Nozick is not prepared however to rely upon the hypothetical contract alone. Property exists at the time of any contract and rights to such property exist prior to such contract. The imaginative step does not apply to the determination of rights to property. In this respect Nozick grounds his starting point squarely on the Lockeian concept of the state of nature (Locke, 1690) in which natural rights are well defined and fully recognized although they may be breached in the absence of enforcement.

Nozick claims that a minimal, night watchman state will emerge from the efforts of private citizens to enforce pre-existing rights through the social contract. The state will become the single dominant protective agency because of the natural monopoly, public good characteristic of rights enforcement through a social contract. The state will be restrained from providing any other goods – even polar case public goods in the sense of Samuelson – since all such provisions threaten redistribution and potentially violate Lockeian rights.

Buchanan (1964, 1975a) has pursued consistently the goal of justifying the contractarian ethic in terms of some Archimedean point though he has varied the basis from which such a point is seen to emerge. Throughout, Buchanan has remained faithful to Knut Wicksell (1896), requiring universal (or near universal) consent as the fulcrum of the contractarian ethic. His approach can be categorized into three phases.

The early Buchanan, in collaboration with his colleague Gordon Tullock (1962), sought out a social contract not through Rawls's hypothetical original position nor through Nozick's imaginative introspection but through the choices of real individuals in real choice situations characterized by uncertainty. Individuals were viewed as universally endorsing constitutional rules which offered a logical foundation for constitutional democracy by minimizing the joint cost of expected externalities and of decision making. Because such individuals could not identify their particular circumstances in a future political process they chose constitutional rules under a strong veil of uncertainty thus avoiding inevitable conflict within unrestrained legislatures where vested interests would be apparent and would dominate the vote motive.

The *Calculus of Consent* (1962) thus rationalized constrained government, posing no ethical judgment on the direction of policy which must simply reflect whatever preferences become paramount in constitutional democracy. For this reason libertarians such as Rothbard are hostile to Virginian public choice, claiming that it has rationalized the coercive state (Rothbard, 1989). Certainly, the *Calculus of Consent* provides an optimistic vision of the state which is viewed as emerging to secure gains from trade and which is seen to engage usefully in production as well as in the securing of property rights.

In 1975, writing in the wake of Vietnam and Watergate, Buchanan (1975a) rationalized government by consent as being driven negatively by the threat of anarchy and the negative sum game of jungle survival rather than optimistically by perceived gains from trade. *The Limits of Liberty* (1975) was a sustained attempt to derive a constitutional basis for ordered anarchy from a pre-contract state of nature much as Thomas Hobbes (1645) had attempted to justify the Sovereign in his book *Leviathan* (1645). As with Hobbes, Buchanan's ordered anarchy views the social contract as an escape route from a prisoner's dilemma situation attractive to the strong as well as to the weak and endorsed by the rich as well as by the poor.

In Hobbesian anarchy, which precedes any notion of society, any concept of property, rights or entitlements, there exists a war of each against all. Buchanan argued that such an environment was more reflective of the 1970s democracies than was a calculus of consent drawn from the more consentaneous relationships of the late 1950s and early 1960s. In anarchy, there is no mine or thine save that which emerges from some truncated process of production and exchange bounded by the continuing urge to predate upon the commodities stock piled by others and the corresponding urge to defend such commodity stock piles as have been accumulated. Even in such a jungle a natural distribution emerges, more or less equal, depending on the relative strength, fortune and ability of individuals and their groupings. This natural distribution is not a structure of rights since it is not based upon consent. Yet costly as it is in terms of deadweight losses of predation and defense of commodities, it offers a basis for mutually advantageous exchange.

In a sense, the rights established by contract out of the natural distribution are not dramatically different from those grounded in the state of nature (Locke, 1690; Rowley, 1988a). The gap between Hobbes and Locke, in this sense, is not completely unbridgeable. For Hobbes and for the Buchanan of the mid-1970s, however, the minimal state of Locke grounded in the notion of a contractarian, night-watchman government is not enough (Buchanan, 1974a). The sovereign (for Hobbes) and the consent calculus (for Buchanan) must be supreme. If market failure offers utility gains from collective action even at the expense of rights then the consent calculus will endorse the productive and the transfer state even, in the limit, state socialism. In this sense contractarianism is neutral with respect to goals and is exclusively rooted in process ethics.

As the 1970s advanced, Buchanan became increasingly dissatisfied with the Hobbesian framework as a basis for contractarianism. The Archimedean point of Hobbes, the initial rights established in the constitution of contract, after all were windfalls, the outcome of jungle conflict (Buchanan, 1974a). Contracts drawn upon the basis of such rights in some sense were fraudulent even those based on the altruism of the rich toward the poor. For Buchanan as for Rawls justice as fairness required universal consent over the initial distribution of rights and not a constrained consent based on Tullock's Law that might is right (Tullock, 1971).

By the late 1970s, therefore, Buchanan more or less had abandoned Hobbes (but see Buchanan, 1977a) and working in tandem with H. Geoffrey Brennan had embraced the philosophy of John Rawls, accepting the hypothetical of the veil of ignorance and the essence of his derived concept of justice as fairness. In so doing, Buchanan resisted the temptation to join Rawls in end-state inferences drawn from the conditions of the original position, though he utilized those conditions to establish a consent-based rationalization of limited constitutional government (Brennan and Buchanan, 1980, 1985).

Justice as fairness, both for Rawls and for Buchanan, is the Archimedean point for the contractarian ethic. As such, it merits close scrutiny since the assumptions that underpin it are by no means uncontroversial. Rawls (1971, 1980, 1985) set out the principles of justice that free and rational persons would establish unanimously were they to deliberate in a hypothetical situation corresponding to the state of nature in traditional social contract theory. In this original position individuals would not know their respective places in society, their class positions, their race, their fortunes in the distribution of natural assets and abilities, even their own concept of the good. Thus, deliberating behind a veil of ignorance individuals would determine their rights and duties. This original contract establishes the principles of justice that govern the basic structure of society and that regulate all subsequent agreements including the kinds of social cooperation that can be entered into and the forms of government that can be established.

Rawls suggests that the conditions of the original position are such as to induce all deliberators to utilize the extremely risk-averse game strategy of maximin or minimax when selecting the principles of justice that will govern the basic structure of society; that individuals whether or not they are risk-averse by nature will find themselves taking up positions that maximize their minimum gains or that minimize their maximum losses. Rawls has never effectively justified this inference (but see Rawls, 1974) which appears to reflect confusion between games between individuals and games between individuals and a benign or at least non-alien state of nature (Rowley and Peacock, 1975).

In games between individuals the expectation that a rival may play an extremely risk-averse strategy does impose a strong pressure even upon a risk-neutral individual to forsake the gambling strategy for a more cautious play in order to avoid a catastrophic loss. Such is not the case, however, when individuals stake out strategies against a non-alien state of nature which essentially categorizes the original position. In such latter circumstances rational individuals should be expected to develop strategies strictly in accord with their attitudes towards risk which will vary from the extremely risk-averse at one end of the scale to the extremely risk preferring at the other (Mueller, 1989).

Buchanan (1972, 1977a) has never embraced the extreme risk-aversion assumption as posited by Rawls, recognizing the unreasonably restrictive assertion about human action that such as assumption implies. Instead he has justified maximin and minimax as a reasonable inference concerning individuals' strategic reactions to a government that they view as essentially malign in the absence of constitutional constraints (Brennan and Buchanan, 1981, 1983). Buchanan is careful not to categorize government as a malignant institution but rather suggests that individuals deciding upon a constitution behind a veil of ignorance would unanimously protect themselves against the worst case scenario of a Leviathan state.

Suppose, however, that justice as fairness is attainable in the sense of Rawls and Buchanan and that risk-averse contracts indeed are forged behind a sufficiently thick veil of ignorance. Even then serious problems remain concerning the process that Rawls and Buchanan designate as justice as fairness. For on this pivot of risk-aversion two principles of justice emerge, the first lexicographically superior to the second. The first principle, of liberty, determines that each person is to have an equal right to the most extensive basic liberty compatible with a similar liberty for others. The liberties thus protected include the economic liberties to hold property and to engage in transactions under the rule of law as well as the political liberties without which economic liberties have little or no substance. This principle which takes precedence over all others is the principle of natural liberty and presumably must embrace some system of rights.

Rawls and the post-1978 Buchanan find this principle alone to be inadequate for justice as fairness since the distribution thus sanctioned reflects the initial distribution of talents and assets which is neither just nor unjust but simply arbitrary. Thus Rawls draws out a second principle which may be labelled the principle of liberal justice from behind the veil of ignorance. Liberal justice reaches out beyond formal equality of opportunity to correct to the extent possible for social and cultural disadvantages. In itself this principle invokes the redistributive affirmative action state reaching well beyond the minimal state endorsed by Nozick.

Even this extension is inadequate if the social contract is to ensure justice as fairness given the arbitrariness of fortune. For the natural distribution of abilities and talents will still largely determine the distributive outcome.

This recognition leads naturally in the original position to a universal endorsement of what Rawls calls the democratic conception designed to nullify the effects of natural differences while acknowledging their intractability. This principle, which may be labelled the principle of democratic equality, falls short of equality of result. Rather, it requires that the scheme of benefits and burdens is so arranged that the least advantaged members of society benefit from its existence.

This difference principle, as Rawls denotes it, deems as just only those social and economic inequalities that work to the benefit of the least advantaged members of society. This principle denies to any individual sole proprietorship of assets or talents but rather treats such advantages as a common asset. It justifies a redistributive state which responds exclusively to those individuals who find themselves the least advantaged as they emerge from behind the veil of ignorance into the real world. There are no inalienable property rights in such a society.

From a practical political viewpoint, therefore, as Sandel (1982) explicitly recognized, the position of Rawls, Buchanan and Nozick are clearly opposed. Rawls the welfare state socialist, Buchanan the constitutional conservative and Nozick the Lockeian classical liberal define between them the clearest alternatives that the American political agenda has to offer with respect to attitudes towards distributive justice. Yet these antagonists are equally committed to the contractarian ethic in its explicitly individualistic form. Each appeals to the precept of Kant (1797) in treating each individual as an end and not merely as a means and in seeking principles of justice that embody this precept. Yet, Rawls and Buchanan arrive at a theory of justice in which social and economic inequalities are permitted only to the extent that they benefit the least advantaged whereas Nozick holds justice to consist in voluntary exchanges and transfers alone, ruling out the redistributive state, whereas Buchanan envisions government as severely constrained constitutionally by citizens who live in dread of Leviathan.

Rawls and Buchanan part company most sharply with respect to the emphasis that they place upon the contractarian process. Concerning process, Rawls applies the difference principle almost exclusively to restrictions on the nature and magnitude of social and economic inequalities whereas Buchanan focuses attention equally exclusively on notions of constitutional constraints designed to protect minorities from the majority vote which he views as likely to produce a Leviathan in the absence of over-riding constitutional constraints. Concerning end-state implications, Rawls derives a policy blueprint which might have been drafted (quite possibly was) by John Kenneth Galbraith, together with other members of the Harvard economics faculty; whereas Buchanan eschews any possibility of drawing end-state pronouncements from the contractarian process.

5 The liberal democratic ethic

The liberal democratic doctrine dominated American political discourse from the start of the New Deal until Ronald Reagan defeated Jimmy Carter in the 1980 Presidential Election. It reached the peak of its influence during the presidency of Lyndon Johnson, reaping its policy fruits in the Great Society Program. Thereafter slowly but continuously its influence waned though its doctrines continue to exert influence over both US federal and state governments. Since 1980 it has been the subject of anxious re-examination as advocates of its doctrine have found it to be an increasing impediment to the gaining or retaining of major US elective offices. The doctrine retains a significant political influence in Western Europe and in some of the newly emerged Eastern Europe democracies. It exerts a dominant continuing influence over the program of legal services funded by the US federal government.

For the most part liberal democrats do not subscribe to socialism in the sense of the widespread public provision of goods and services though they do welcome an extensive role for government in the provision of public goods and as the effective medium of a major program of affirmative action, of regulation of the economy and of social security wealth transfers. Liberal democrats for the most part do not subscribe to the notion that the individual is the best judge of his own welfare. They envision a wide range of so-called merit goods which would be wrongly undervalued in the private welfare calculus and which it is the duty of a wiser government to advance upon its citizenry. They also envision a wide range of demerit goods which would be overvalued in the private calculus and which it is the duty of a wiser government to prohibit or to regulate. The invasion of individual rights inherent in such interventions is justified in terms of an overriding community or public interest.

Liberal democrats for the most part do not attach high priority to the securing of property rights on grounds either of liberty or of efficiency (Dworkin, 1985, 1986; Tribe, 1985). By placing a major emphasis upon justice as an end-state objective they recognize a major role for wealth redistribution through the coercive powers of the federal and state governments. While searching for efficient mechanisms for transferring wealth they recognize constraints in the form of specific in kind transfers and affirmative action policies that reflect worries about the ability of certain individuals to engage in rational choice. Primacy is placed in this doctrine upon the furtherance of positive freedoms, even at some significant cost in terms of sacrificed negative freedoms.

Liberal democrats for the most part do not accept the existing legal system as one that provides for social justice. To rectify weaknesses in the existing legal system they endorse patterns of litigation including widespread recourse to the class-action suit designed to change the law in favor of redistributionist doctrines. Inevitably, liberal democrats have encouraged the development of a legal services program that is a fulcrum for law reform even at some cost to providing poor Americans with an adequate access to justice under the existing law. The doctrine of liberal democracy dominates legal thinking within the US legal services program and is endorsed currently by the Democrat-controlled US Congress.

6   The Marxist ethic

Two themes dominate the modern debate on the Marxian interpretation of ethics, one centering on Marx's discussion of justice and freedom, and the other evaluating exploitation through the debate on the labor theory of value and the institution of private property (Hamlin, 1986).

In the view of Wood (1972), Marx distinguished sharply between justice and freedom. Justice was viewed as a relativistic concept with each form of society, be it feudal, capitalist, socialist or communist, having its own concept of justice which formed part of the superstructure of society and which was dependent upon the underlying mode of production. Freedom was viewed as a more absolute base for inter-societal comparisons. Freedom for Marx, however, is not the negative freedom of the classical liberal ethic, absence of coercion of one individual by another, but freedom from exploitation. Marxian freedom thus is positive freedom with exploitation condemned not because it is unjust but because it is a barrier to freedom viewed as the power over economic resources.

In this perspective, freedom and private property are held by Marx to be in conflict (Gintis, 1972; Roemer, 1982) since private property depends upon some arbitrary or natural fact which itself constrains freedom by facilitating exploitation of those who do not hold such property. Freedom for Marx is not an individualistic concept at all but is community based, existing only when property is communally held. It is important in this perspective to emphasize that most Marxists (Mandel, 1968; Roemer, 1982) now agree that exploitation is not grounded in the labor theory of value but in the institution of private property itself. The inequality of access to the stock of alienable property (capital), which describes the capitalist mode of production, ensures exploitation even in the absence of labor market exploitation.

Nozick (1973), in his discussion of Marxian exploitation, agreed with the property–relation definition but denied the existence of exploitation in voluntary employment markets. For, if the fact of non access to the means of production is the essence of exploitation, it follows that exploitation will be absent in a society in which the workers are not forced to deal with the capitalists. Roemer (1982) rejects this interpretation, arguing that it is not the crucial fact of non access to the means of production which determines exploitation but rather the unequal access to the means of production. Hamlin (1986) provides a compromise interpretation suggesting that Nozick's point establishes voluntary labor markets as just in the sense of Marx, but leaves them exploitative, at least in the sense of Roemer.

It is important to note that absence of exploitation in the sense of Roemer does not imply an entirely egalitarian outcome. Capitalist exploitation arises as a consequence of unequal access to alienable property. However unequal access to inalienable property is sufficient to ensure inequality. The simple endowment of unequal talents across individuals thus results in general in inequality but not in exploitation. In this respect Rawls (1971) is more egalitarian than sophisticated modern Marxists since he places within the common pool inalienable as well as alienable property. Of course, significant differences exist between the route to equality pursued by Rawls and by Marxists, with the former relying upon hypothetical consent behind a veil of ignorance and with the latter relying upon the removal of exploitation through inevitable class conflict and bloody revolution.

The ultimate goal of Marxists (Lindbeck, 1971) therefore, is freedom from exploitation, a process rather than an end-state objective in which individuals fuse their individual interests for the communal good. Such freedom is grounded in solidarity of the species man, which a society divided into antagonistic classes and nations cannot achieve (Marcuse, 1964, 1969). *The First International* is revered from this perspective as the last attempt to realize the solidarity of the species by grounding it in that social class in which the subjective and objective interest, the particular and universal, coincided (Marcuse, 1969).

It follows from this world vision (Rowley and Peacock, 1975) that welfare is not defined by Marxists as the outcome of stable individual preferences or as a vehicle of continuous marginal adjustment. Individual preferences are viewed as being highly dependent on the particular form of society most especially with respect to its modes of production and its patterns of consumption. In such circumstances the preferences of individuals conditioned by a capitalist society are irrelevant to the goal of Marxist freedom, which anticipates the preference transformations that will occur as that society is levered into socialism and then progresses ultimately to the communist ideal. Even within the work environment the disutility of work associated with individuals under capitalism is seen to transform itself into positive utility as workers are released from alienation in the non-exploitative environment of the post-Marxist revolution (West, 1969).

The precise nature of the economic system that will replace market capitalism is not outlined in detail by Marxists. It is defined more by the characteristics that are presumed to be absent than by those that are to emerge. For example, money as a medium of exchange is rejected as is any form of hierarchical organization of production, whether or not the means of production are owned collectively. There also appears to be a strong antipathy towards urban living and culture as manifestations of the capitalist achievement. In the caustic words of Von Mises (1947), an early critic of socialism, 'roast pigeons will in some way fly into the mouths of the comrades'. If they are to do so any guidance offered evidently will be communal in nature and any satisfaction recorded will be registered in the internal organs of the state bureaucracy rather than from the bellies to the brains of the fortunate recipients.

The Marxist doctrine has been advanced within the legal profession most persistently by advocates of critical legal studies (Kelman, 1987; Kennedy, 1981; Unger, 1983) who attempt to advance the socialist if not the Communist cause by converting the legal process itself into a program of constructive dissidence and radicalism. Adherents to this doctrine within the legal profession remain disproportionately active in the US legal services program as they are in US lawschools, even following the demise of communism in much of Eastern Europe.

3   Methods of analysis

The Calculus of Consent was the first attempt to derive what we called an 'economic theory of political constitutions'. It would, of course, have been impossible to make that effort without the methodological perspective provided in economics-as-exchange, or catallactics. The maximizer of social welfare functions could never have written such a book, and indeed, even today, the maximizer of such functions cannot understand what the book is all about.

James M. Buchanan 'The Public Choice Perspective'
Economica delle scelte pubbliche 1, January 1983

1   Introduction

The economic theory of public policy has attracted several important but competing research programs since the end of the Second World War, each offering its own insights into the debate over the appropriate role of the state and the economic consequences of state intervention in predominantly market economies such as that of the United States. Since each such research program has conditioned thinking about the program of federal government expenditures and transfers, of which legal services is a small but not insignificant component, their distinctive characteristics, apparent strengths and weaknesses are briefly outlined in this chapter.

The comparative analysis so provided is particularly important for this book since the research programs predominantly accessed and evaluated are those of the Virginia and the Chicago schools of political economy, both of which are regarded as important but neither of which stands in the recognized mainstream of the current economic policy literature. Because these approaches are still somewhat controversial, their insights are compared throughout the book with those of the mainstream public interest approach (Rowley and Peacock, 1975). Ultimately, of course, scientific testing of the evidence will determine which approach will survive and which will be denied credibility in policy analysis and debate. Suffice it to say that the mainstream is not performing well in terms of the growing empirical literature.

Section 2 outlines the central tenets and research methods of Chicago Political Economy (CPE). The approach of this program which emerged in the early 1970s under the leadership of George Stigler (1971) resembles that of the neoclassical school in its reliance upon Marshallian microeconomics, though it is a good deal more consistent in its reliance upon empirical testing. However, it breaks with the mainstream in its policy thrust by rejecting any organic notion of government and by applying the utility maximization assumption of individual behavior to all actors within the political market place, recognizing that such markets typically transfer rather than create wealth. Surprisingly, for a school that once was viewed as supportive of laissez-faire (Friedman, 1962) Chicago Political Economy typically concludes that all existing economic institutions are efficient whether they are private or public despite the self-seeking objectives of those responsible for their actions. (For the most extreme statement of this view, see Wittman, 1989.)

Section 3 outlines the central tenets and research methods of the Virginia Political Economy research program (VPE) which emerged in the early 1960s under the intellectual leadership of James M. Buchanan and Gordon Tullock. VPE explores the limitations of political markets much more critically than Chicago employing the modern techniques of public choice analysis. Using the techniques of neoclassical economics, VPE denies all relevance to public interest theories of economic policy, recognizes the role of error in institutional development and acknowledges the opportunities for institutional reform that always confront self-interested individuals. Political markets are treated almost exclusively as extremely inefficient transfer mechanisms in this approach.

Section 4 outlines the available methods of resolving the policy disputes that arise from these alternative research programs. Rejecting the notion of McCloskey (1985) that unstifled rhetoric is an appropriate framework for the economic policy debate, in favor of Karl Popper's (1959) logic of scientific inquiry, a conclusion is advanced that disagreements over positive issues concerning policy ultimately can and must be resolved by empirical research. Disagreements over matters of ethics however ultimately cannot be resolved save by persuasion and must be viewed as a legitimate reason for ongoing policy disagreements, always assuming that the underlying value judgments have been clearly outlined.

2   Chicago Political Economy

Since 1945, the Chicago School of Economics arguably has been pre-eminent in the developing scholarship of economics and the single most important influence in reshaping economic science into its present rigorously theoretical and sophisticated empirical form. Blessed with the intellectual leadership of Milton Friedman, George Stigler and Ronald Coase, drawing on the intellectual capital of Frank Knight, Henry Simons and Jacob Viner, and supported by the contributions of such developing superstars as Robert Lucas, Gary Becker, Sam Peltzman, William Landes and Richard Posner, high quality scholarship was inevitable.

Recognition, in the form of Nobel Prizes in Economic Science, for Friedman and Stigler, and with two or three more such prizes surely yet to come, ensures world-wide attention and publicity for the School's various programs. Editorship of three of the world's leading journals, *The Journal of Political Economy*, *The Journal of Law and Economics* and *The Journal of Legal Studies*, guarantees prestigious outlets for its scholarship. Diversity in research programs which span inter alia such fields as monetary economics, rational expectations, labor economics, law and economics, industrial organization and methodology, further ensures the interactive vitality of the School's contributions.

Chicago Political Economy (CPE) is one such research program which has earned for itself an influential niche within the Chicago School of Economics and which has spawned a research literature together with an ongoing research agenda directly relevant to the subject matter of this book. Although CPE constitutes an independent research program, nevertheless it draws heavily upon the central analytical assumptions that identify the Chicago School and interacts significantly with the other major programs that nestle under the School's umbrella.

CPE is a body of literature which analyses government from the perspective of price theory and positive economics (Mitchell, 1989; Tollison, 1989). In essence it is the Chicago version of the modern development of public choice theory. It views the state as a mechanism which is used by rational economic agents to redistribute wealth within a society. Wealth transfers are viewed as the essence of all regulatory and other governmental activity, whether on or off budget in nature. Although governments may produce some real goods and services, in practice such contributions are viewed as byproducts of effective schemes for wealth transfers. CPE thus denies all credibility to the public interest theory of government and instead recognizes the omnipresence of homo economicus, wealth-seeking rational man, in the market place of politics. Yet, by outcome rather than by any explicit public interest design, political markets are viewed as fundamentally efficient mechanisms for achieving the redistributionist preferences of decisive interest groups. In this sense CPE does not represent a theory of government failure such as that which is the hallmark of Virginia political economy. In no sense, however, does it represent a Marxist interpretation in which one class capital systematically dominates another class labor and exploits it for its own benefit. Stigler restricts the 'efficiency' inference to political relationships. Others (notably Wittman, 1989) extend the inference to economic relationships.

Stigler (1985, 1988) is the key architect and now eminence grise of CPE, though certain ideas of Director (Stigler, 1970) can be viewed a precursory to his initiative. The thrust of the CPE research program derives from Stigler's 1971 paper on economic regulation which demonstrated the testability of an interest group theory of the transfer state. Other key contributors to CPE have been Peltzman (1976, 1984, 1985, 1990), Becker (1976, 1983, 1985), Landes and Posner (1975) and Posner (1986). CPE has now established a geographically dispersed following among scholars who have identified with its research methods (McChesney, 1987, 1989, 1991; Wittman, 1989) and who are extending the breadth of its research reach.

CPE is based on the principles and practice of positive economics drawing its methodology from Friedman's famous (1953) essay. Not only is the formulation of testable propositions derived from well articulated theory emphasized but so too is the actual testing of such theory. As Tollison (1989) has noted, the level of empirical analysis utilized by CPE scholars such as Peltzman has become formidable in comparison, say, with that of Virginia political economy, notwithstanding the evident difficulty of confronting CPE theories with data comparable in quality to that readily accessible to the mainstream economics research program.

Drawing upon the methodology applied by Chicagoans in their analyses of private markets, CPE has applied tight prior equilibrium theory (Reder, 1982) in its analyses of transfer politics. The protected core of this theory is the assumption that all actors in political markets are rational utility maximizers and that expected wealth, or some close relative, is the dominant element in each actor's utility function. The thrust of the theory is toward instantaneous and durable equilibrium with political markets clearing so that no actor can raise his expected utility (wealth) without reducing the expected utility (wealth) of at least one other actor. Political agents clear political markets without invading them as principals. They are driven by constraints and not by preferences. There is no role for ideology in the CPE research program.

The auxiliary hypotheses of the CPE research program ensure that equilibrium is not only instantaneous but is also tight, as is the case in Chicagoan models of private markets. First, it is assumed that individuals are price-takers rather than price-makers and can exercise little or no discretionary power in political markets. Second, it is assumed that the prices at which individuals agree to transact are market clearing prices consistent with optimizing behavior. Third it is assumed that such prices reflect all economically revelant information. Fourth, it is assumed that all constraints on economic behavior are economically efficient reflecting utility maximizing behavior on the part of all individuals who create or modify them.

The auxiliary conditions imposed by CPE do not impose equilibria based upon perfect foresight. Random disturbances cannot be accommodated even within a highly efficient information network. Such disturbances pose no threat however to the efficiency of competitive markets. Actors devise methods for dealing with uncertainty which reflect their own attitudes towards risk and a stochastic analogue to the deterministic general equilibrium model takes over. The efficiency characteristics of the deterministic equilibria carry over into their stochastic counterparts.

A particular feature of CPE, as of Chicago economics writ large, is the presupposition that propositions derived from tight prior equilibrium theory are the only valid propositions of the research program. If, for some reason, the propositions do not appear to hold in particular political markets then CPE should step aside and leave the analysis to other research programs. CPE thus appraises its own research, and that of others, by a standard that requires the findings of empirical analysis to be consistent with the implications of standard price theory (Reder, 1982). Evidence of behavior that does not conform to such implications is viewed as anomalous rather than as striking at the auxiliary conditions of the model (let alone the protected core). Ultimately, this prejudice must be viewed as a weakness of CPE, at least from the perspective of Popperian methodology, which as section 6 indicates is the scientific logic adhered to in this book. Admittedly, the prejudice has served CPE well in identifying for itself a unique approach to the study of political markets.

An important implication of this approach is that ideas do not matter and that there is no role for the economist as preacher with respect to economic policy. If all actors in political markets maximize expected utilities subject to the constraints that confront them, which themselves have emerged efficiently, Pareto optimality prevails. Ex post, errors may be apparent as a consequence of random disturbances but since, by definition, such errors cannot be anticipated ex ante (Stigler, 1976), they must be considered irrelevant to rational choice. What is, therefore, is efficient at any instant in unfolding time (Crew and Rowley, 1988, 1989). How and why, in such circumstances, institutional change actually occurs is an issue which CPE does not choose to explore (Mitchell, 1988).

3 Virginia Political Economy

If CPE is a research program identified with the notion of efficient government, Virginia political economy (VPE) is a research program identified with the notion of government failure, designed more or less explicitly (Buchanan, 1989) to displace the market failure presumption of the Paretian approach with a more neutrally balanced presumption in favor of comparative institutions analysis. Viewed from this perspective, VPE has made an immensely powerful impact on the economic policy debate, arguably much more so than CPE, notwithstanding the latter's higher purely technical standing among mainstream economists. In this respect, VPE has been well served by the prodigious scholarship of its intellectual leaders, James M. Buchanan and Gordon Tullock (Rowley, 1987, 1988a; Mueller, 1989; Romer, 1988; Sandmo, 1990), and by others associated at varying points in time with the Center for Study of Public Choice (Mueller, 1985; Breit, 1986; Mitchell, 1988).

VPE, like CPE, analyses government from the perspective of price theory and positive economics, introducing this method some ten years prior to Stigler's original CPE contribution (Buchanan and Tullock, 1962). Like CPE also, though less exclusively, VPE views the state as a vehicle used by rational individuals to redistribute wealth (McCormick and Tollison, 1981; Tullock, 1983a and b). Unlike CPE, however, there is room within the VPE research program for a consentaneous vision of government certainly for the minimal state (Rowley and Wagner, 1990) and even for the limited productive and transfer state (Buchanan, 1975a). This concession does not extend in any sense whatsoever to an acceptance of a public interest theory of the state. Rather, homo economicus is modelled as choosing constraints by unanimous agreement designed to limit his own access to the political market place and thus to canalize short-term political market behavior away from wealth dissipative activities (Brennan and Buchanan, 1980a, 1983).

The protected core of the VPE rescarch program, like that of CPE, is homo economicus, rational utility maximizing man. Unlike CPE, however, homo economicus is not viewed as exclusively, or even in Buchanan's case as predominantly (Buchanan, 1989), to maximize the value of his net wealth. For the most part economic value is viewed as entering the individual utility function only as one among several arguments, albeit as an important argument which renders homo economicus predictably responsive to any change in the structure of economic rewards and costs. Unlike CPE however, the more general utility function utilized by VPE allows political markets to respond also to changes in wealth-unrelated variables in so far as those variables are relevant to individual actors in those markets.

Although the more general nature of the protected core provides VPE, at some cost in terms of focus, with a more comprehensive model of political market behavior, the more important analytical differences between the two programs stem from their auxiliary hypotheses. VPE does not assume that individuals are always price takers in political markets but allows for the possibility of discretionary power. VPE does not assume as generally as CPE that political markets clear instantaneously and completely. VPE does not assume that decision makers in political markets are always fully informed about the present, nor does it assume that uncertainty concerning the future can always be transformed into certainty equivalence by stochastic methods (Knight, 1921). Nor does it assume as readily as CPE that equilibria are perceived to be durable by those who set out to influence political market outcomes. Nor is VPE as resistant as CPE to the notion that human error plays an important role in political markets and that error, once recognized, may be a driving force in political market adjustments.

In combination, these conditions define a diffuse rather than a tight prior equilibrium as the hallmark of the VPE research program. Political markets are not always in equilibrium though they do adjust dynamically towards underlying equilibria. Political markets are not always efficient, even in the subjective Virginian sense of that concept (Buchanan, 1969; 1975c). Institutions do matter and cannot be ignored in favor of black box, neoclassical price theory analytics (North, 1984, 1990). Ideas are important, not in the public interest sense of the Paretian approach, but in their impact upon individuals' behavior. How and why institutional changes occur are issues of central importance to the VPE research program (Rowley, 1991a).

By treating political markets as forums for exchange, while recognizing the problems of achieving contract efficiency under conditions of less than perfect delineation of property rights (Ordeshook, 1986), VPE has set itself at odds with conventional political science which either endorses Platonic idealism or treats all politics from the perspective of conflict and conflict resolution. By replacing the Paretian philosopher king with homo economicus, VPE has parted company unequivocally with conventional welfare economics. By denying ubiquitous efficiency it has separated itself even from its closest neighbor, CPE. Arguably, however, it is the most successful research program in the field of political economy by reference to the most important criterion of all, namely the predictive test of Popper (1959) and of Friedman (1953).

4   The logic of scientific discovery

It might seem, with separate research programs offering such differing insights into political economy, that policy analysis is in a state is disarray, and that science must give way in favor of what McCloskey (1985) calls economic conversations or the use of rhetoric, here defined in its ancient Greek usage to encompass the study of all the ways of accomplishing things with language. McCloskey (1985), in particular, is in favor of the rhetorical approach in policy discussion and is opposed to what he calls economic modernism, which categorizes science as axiomatic and mathematical, which is antihistorical and disinterested in cultural and intellectual traditions and which admits only falsifiable hypotheses to be meaningful.

McCloskey criticizes modernism in economics as supporting a rules-bound methodology which attempts to limit the arguments that scientists can make by restricting their discussions into conformity with a set of arbitrary a priori rules. McCloskey draws upon the critical writings of sociologists such as Feyerabend (1975) and Rorty (1979) to support his conclusions that rules typically are not adhered to by scientists who break new ground in their discipline, but only by those who seek refuge within a sharply-defined research program.

There is an undeniable force to McCloskey's criticisms, especially with respect to such rules-based research programs as the Pareto approach and Chicago Political Economy. The picture that he conjures up of '[m]ethodology strutting around issuing orders to working scientists' (p. 24) is close to the mark for these programs and, indeed, it is not irrelevant that McCloskey himself is an escapee from the Chicago School. For, as Reder (1982) has indicated, graduate students at Chicago are well aware of the hoops through which they must be prepared to jump in order to complete their doctoral studies and of the scepticism that their work will attract if they endorse empirical results that cannot be reconciled in terms of neoclassical price theory.

Yet, there are countervailing benefits from specialization in the logic of inquiry, not least for those who engage in the important puzzle-solving aspects of any research program. Rules constrain, certainly, but also they guide and discipline the organization of inquiry. As long as the rules are derived explicitly from clearly stated objectives, and scholars are free to choose or to reject them without coercion, the open society is not placed at risk. In this respect, Popper (1959, 1962) most especially does not deserve the strictures of McCloskey, since the rules that he urges scientists to observe are derived carefully and systematically from his over-riding objective of falsification of theory. Those who have observed the discipline imposed by Popper's logic arguably have contributed a great deal to scientific inquiry, both in the natural and in the social sciences.

Moreover, it is fallacious to argue on behalf of all scientists an approach, rhetoric, which may be admirable for great intellects but which offers to the less gifted the Trojan horse of the freedom of the boat without the compass. Without rules, potentially creative individuals may waste their talents in an undisciplined lunge in pursuit of knowledge. Humans are a rules-based species, albeit ideally a species which thrives when the rules are freely chosen and not imposed from without. In this book, the methodology of Karl Popper (1959), adjusted to accommodate the relaxations introduced by his student Lakatos, is utilized as the normative basis for discriminating between the conclusions of alternative research programs in political economy. Even with the adoption of this set of rules there is plenty of remaining ambiguity over which economists no doubt will converse and upon occasion, no doubt, will agree to differ.

Popper's major task in his magnum opus, *The Logic of Scientific Inquiry*, was to derive a logical basis for distinguishing science from meta-physics. His solution was to reject the inductive approach in which singular statements, even a single observation, become generalized into a universal verified statement in favor of the deductive approach in which universal statements are tested with the intent to falsify them by exposing their implications to the available evidence. This approach was introduced into economics by Friedman in 1953 and initially was extremely controversial. By the mid-1960s, however, Popper's methodology had become the mainstream set of rules governing economic science discourse.

In the form adopted by Friedman, Popper's falsification test was excessively ruthless, drawn incorrectly from a deterministic view of economics science which suggested that a single refutation was sufficient to destroy an economic theory. This approach has been criticized by Lakatos and Musgrave (1970) as naive falsificationism which fails to give due weight to the unreliability of experimental results and statistical tests and which ignores the stochastic nature of almost all social phenomena. Once the possibility of testing error is acknowledged and the stochastic nature of all uncontrolled experiments is recognized, the single adverse result at best, implies only some probability that the theory is false. Where possible, a sequence of tests heavily weighted with adverse results may be necessary to eliminate a theory as undeniably false; and some theories may live on, suspect but not entirely rejected, simply because of testing limitations.

For these reasons, Lakatos (1970, 1978) rejected the notion that isolated individual theories are the relevant units of evaluation, emphasizing the importance of clusters of inter connected theories, denoted as scientific research programs. In this respect, he provides a broader framework than that advocated by Popper who allows a theory to be rescued from potential falsification only through the employment of non-ad hoc auxiliary assumptions. The avoidance of the ad hoc, for Popper, implies that theoretical adjustments increase the empirical content of theory by augmenting the number of its observational consequences; Lakatos (1970) reinterprets this notion to distinguish between progressive and degenerating research programs.

The history of science, Lakatos hypothesizes, is the history of research programs rather than of theories. All scientific research programs are characterized by their hard core central assumptions, surrounded by a protective belt of auxiliary hypotheses which bear the main brunt of testing. The protected core itself is irrefutable, containing as it does metaphysical beliefs as well as a positive heuristic of hints on how to develop the refutable variants of the research program. By combining the hard core with the protective belt, specific testable hypotheses are derived which become the forcing agents of the entire research program.

In this view, and in sharp contrast to the concept of scientific revolution advanced by Thomas Kuhn (1970), competing research programs may co-exist over lengthy periods, even perhaps indefinitely, as their protective belts adjust to acknowledge adverse research findings. Typically, a research program will only be finally eliminated by rival programs when the latter both explain the previous successes of the displaced rival and supersede it by a further display of heuristic power. Lakatos (1970, 1978) argues that the entire history of science can be explained in these terms. Certainly, this book will adhere to his falsification principles in attempting to discriminate, with respect to legal services policies, between the rival research programs outlined in this chapter.

Part III

LITIGATION, LOBBYING AND THE LAW

4 Litigation and the common law

The efficiency theory of the common law is not that every common law doctrine and decision is efficient. That would be completely unlikely, given the difficulty of the questions that the law wrestles with and the nature of judges' incentives. The theory is that the common law is best (not perfecty) explained as a system for maximizing the wealth of society.

R.A. Posner, *Economic Analysis of Law*, Third Edition, Little Brown, 1986, p. 21

1 Introduction

Two distinct legal traditions underpin and shape the development of late twentieth-century legal systems, namely the common law and the civil law tradition. The common law tradition, much the more recent of the two, originated in England at the time of the successful invasion by the Normans in AD 1066. It has retained its influence over the United Kingdom and has become an important tradition, also, in the United States. This chapter provides an evaluation of the changing nature of the common law in the latter country.

In countries characterized by the common law tradition, judicial decisions are an important source of law. Judges make laws directly through judgments in specific cases; they also interpret and decide the constitutionality of statutes, orders, regulations and rules initiated in other branches of government. In this chapter the rules and the institutions of the US common law system are reviewed to determine whether or not they are vulnerable to sustained litigious pressure by interests opposed to the status quo. Contrary to influential schools of thought, it is argued that the common law successfully has been invaded by anti-utilitarian, anti-classical liberal and anti-contractarian interests, Legal Services attorneys have been active in this invasion.

This chapter will review the hypothesis of Posner (1986) that the common law is efficient. In this view, the common law, in the absence of legislative intervention, is extremely robust against external pressures, and relatively secure against internal insurgency, thus offering little scope for those who would manipulate it away from economic efficiency as an agent of policy activism.

2 The law as croesus: The law of wealth maximization

The new law and economics has exerted a powerful positive impact as a consequence of the scholarship of Posner (and his research collaborator,

Landes) who has stressed the wealth maximizing (efficiency) characteristics of the common law. As a consequence of extensive empirical investigation, the wealth maximization hypothesis currently dominates the new law and economics literature, suggesting that the common law is invulnerable to wealth destructive interventions. In this interpretation, the law of tort, as well as the laws of property and of contract (even the criminal law), equally are enjoined. In a world of conflicting ethics, this is a surprisingly robust positive hypothesis, dependent upon a research program that already has sustained itself against some 15 years of hostile intellectual criticism.

In the view of Posner (1979), three factors lead to wealth maximizing efficiency in the common law:

> (1) Wealth maximization is closely related to utilitarianism, and the formative period of the common law as we know it today, roughly 1800–1950, was a period when utilitarianism was the dominant political ideology in England and America; (2) judges lack effective tools for enriching an interest group or social class other than by increasing the society's wealth as a whole in which the favored group or class presumably will share, and, (3) the process of common law adjudication itself leads to the survival of other rules. (Posner, 1979, pp. 281–306)

The economic analysis of law has investigated the possibility that litigation can improve the common law without the conscious help of judges; improvement being assessed in terms of wealth maximization, objectively perceived. In part, this view is based upon behavioral assumptions, and has been supported by extensive empirical testing. Ultimately it is an 'as if' theory of the common law, which in the view of its many proponents, performs exceptionally well against the predictive test advocated by Popper and by Lakatos.

Posner restricts the term 'common law' to mean the body of principles applied by the royal law courts of England in the eighteenth century (thus excluding equity and admiralty law but including some statutory law) (Posner, 1986, p. 29). He extends this definition to embrace also the fields of law that have been created largely by judges as the by-product of deciding cases, rather than by legislatures, and indeed any field of law shaped largely by judicial precedents.

In the sense of Posner, wealth maximization is confined to those areas of the law characterized by Hayek as 'Nomos' or the law of liberty, which have evolved slowly over time essentially as judge-made; to those areas of the law relatively independent from political intervention. The first, and inescapably the most fundamental of these, is the law of property, without which a capitalist economy could not exist. The robustness of the law of property, as Merrill (1986) has noted, is vested in the fee simple precedent of ancient Anglo-Saxon precedent:

The fee simple is often defined as an estate or interest of 'potentially infinite duration.' This way of speaking suggests that property rights are fixed and permanent – indeed that they last forever. Similarly, property rights are regarded in classical liberal thought as sources of stability and security that foster individual autonomy and protect owners against the vicissitudes of life. This too suggests that property rights are not contingent upon a particular temporal context, but rather are impervious to the passage of time. (Merrill, 1986, p. 661)

And why not? For property rights, thus defined, are the basis of any society whose citizens are not enamored of wealth dissipation, as the socialist countries of Eastern Europe are now painfully aware. Yet, property rights are far from inalienable in US, as Epstein (1986) has acknowledged. Legislative constraints now are widespread, in the form of the rule against perpetuities, the various statutes of limitation, the prohibitions on restraints against alienation, the statutory prohibitions on the creation of fee tails, the title acts that limit the duration of defeasible fees, and the changed circumstances doctrine in the law of servitude.

Epstein (1986) has sought to justify the attack on entitlements within the law of property as a utilitarian contract-based response to problems of generalized market failure:

Politics is doing business with strangers when no one is in the position to choose his trading partners. The cumbersome nature of government becomes more plausible, and even more acceptable, once it is recognized that private agreements go to considerable cost to introduce similar safeguards against opportunistic behavior even when they are less needed. In both the public and private domain, everyone wants some assurance that he will see his share of the gain from the collective enterprise. The question of a constitution is the question of permanent structures of governance over time. (Epstein, 1986, p. 722)

This idealized view of government as based upon consent, which draws much from the vision of Buchanan unfortunately is not reflective of real-politic in the darker vision of public choice. The old saw that 'no man's property is safe when the legislature is in session' unfortunately is much more reflective of the concerns of Hume (1739, 1777) and Locke (1690) than Epstein is prepared to envisage.

Yet, despite all the above mentioned misgivings, the law of property may well be the strongest candidate for Posner's wealth maximizing hypothesis (Rowley, 1986; Rowley and Brough, 1987). For the most part, it deals with relationships that are absolutely essential to wealth creation or dissipation within any economy. By inference, therefore, those economies that are relatively successful in terms of the level and the rate of growth of per capita gross national product are unlikely to be, and to have been, endowed with relatively efficient property laws. Such, arguably is the late twentieth-century experience of Taiwan, Hong Kong, South Korea and Singapore, the Pacific rim success stories of the second half of this century. Such was the nineteenth-century experience of Great Britain and the experience of the US until the middle years of the twentieth century. Such is not the experience, in any sustainable sense, of any socialist economy in the history of mankind.

Contract law also plays an important role in the success or failure, relatively, of any economy, determining how the owners of property, human as well as physical, can or cannot engage in mutually advantageous trade. In the view of Posner (1986), contract law has three functions. First, it maintains proper incentives for exchange to take place, protecting the parties from non-performance and fraud, minimizing the transaction costs of trade. Second, it reduces the complexity associated with trade, by establishing a systematic set of rules. Third, it forewarns individuals of the likely impediments to effective exchange, allowing them to plan exchanges effectively for the future.

Posner argues that each such function is designed to improve efficiency in the exchange process, once the terms of exchange have been agreed. Once again, the issue of time is seen to exercise an important influence. Only where both parties to a contract perform their obligations simultaneously, a relatively rare occurrence, will the exchange process be expected to operate reliably without legal intervention.

Where the simultaneity condition does not hold, two dangers to the process of exchange arise – opportunism and unforeseen contingencies – for which the law offers remedies. The famous doctrine of Holmes is invoked to indicate that the purpose of contract law is not to enforce adherence to contracts but rather to offer the alternative of performance or full compensation for injury in the case of non-tortious contract breach.

However efficient contract law may be from a constructivist rationalist viewpoint, however, recent thrusts have moved it well away from the contractarian efficiency of the methodological individualistic vision. The attack, for the most part, has been anti-institutions in emphasis, sheltering behind the rhetoric of consumer protection, and utilizing doctrines of public policy and unconscionability to oust contractual language especially in consumer situations described, often uncritically, as adhesive (Epstein, 1979; Huber, 1988).

Similarly, legislative interventions designed to foster full disclosure have been adopted aggressively by the courts, in some cases clearly beyond the intent of parties to contracts, in forcing disclosure, both in truth in lending laws and in securities statutes. In all such instances, the social conscience of the judge replaces the contract nexus and, with it, constructivist rationalism substitutes for methodological individualism.

Finally, we come to the law of tort, now arguably the greatest single threat to wealth accumulation confronting the US economy, a growing haven for those who have lost all vestige of the frontier spirit, all notion of being ultimately responsible for their own actions; and a notorious hunting ground for contingent fee attorneys seeking litigation against deep pocket defendants, however far distant they may be from strict liability in the tort opportunity that has been defined. The long-term cost to US citizens, paid in the rising cost of services susceptible to tort law manipulation, even the withdrawal of such services from the market process, plays no role in the private calculus of those who ambulance chase through the law of tort (Huber, 1988; Rowly and Brough, 1987).

Yet, even with respect to tort law, Posner (1986) continues to claim that the wealth maximization principle holds, at least to the extent that the famous formula handed down in the judgment of Learned Hand as the basis for negligence judgments is seen to hold. For, in his 1947 judgment in the case of *United States* v. *Carroll Towing Co.*, a case concerning whether or not the owner of a barge owed a duty to keep an attendant on board when the barge was moved in harbor to obviate the danger of a barge breaking its mooring and damaging other vessels, Hand defined such a duty as a function of three variables: namely P = probability that the barge will break away; L = gravity of consequential damage; and B = burden of precautions adequate to prevent the barge from breaking away. According to Hand, the owner is negligent and liable for damages only if $B < P.L.$

Expressed in its appropriate marginal form, this is the Hand formula of negligence, clearly anticipating the seminal efficiency conclusion by Coase (1960), that liability should lie, in cases of genuine externality, with the least cost avoider and not necessarily with those who might be deemed to be strictly liable for the damages incurred. In short, Hand recognized in the courts, prior to the Coase insight in economics, that externalities are reciprocal in nature and not uni-directional, as the Pigovian approach to social cost more or less explicitly had pre-supposed.

Posner consistently has argued that the common law of tort is efficient in the wealth maximizing sense across its broad range of concerns over civil wrongs that result in personal injury or property damage. He has upheld this view despite the absence of evident exchange relationships in cases of tort. However, in 1987, for the first time, a note of doubt is evident in his (and Landes's) position, as the following passage clearly indicates:

> We make no attempt in this book to evaluate the overall efficiency of any field of tort law, which depends on the actual administration of the law by judges, juries, lawyers, insurance claim adjusters and others. (Landes and Posner, 1987)

Landes and Posner are wise to leave this escape route. For as we shall show in the next section of this chapter, there is a real problem of establishing empirically the efficiency or otherwise of any policy instrument, a problem that has not been resolved despite impressive attempts to do so by Landes, Posner and others. In the final section of the chapter we shall demonstrate further that there are good theoretical reasons to suppose that the common law broadly defined will not turn out consistently either libertarian or wealth maximizing judgments. Least of all can such outcomes be predicted consistently for the law of tort.

If the common law is not that of Croesus it may well be vulnerable to minority pressures, as certain supporters of legal services in its US form have long perceived (Houseman, 1986).

3 Problems in testing the Chicago hypotheses of the common law

American jurisprudence has been influenced powerfully by less than conclusive evidence to the effect that the common law is efficient. Major law schools indeed reflect the efficiency hypothesis in their programs of study to a greater or lesser degree, a few according it the cachet of the dominant jurisprudence. Judges are educated in economics and are introduced to the efficiency hypothesis of the common law, as yet with undetermined consequences for their judgments. Senior scholars of law and economics (most notably Richard Posner and Frank Easterbrook) have succeeded to appellate judgeships often in important divisions, carrying a unified jurisprudence into a profession more usually subdued by stare decisis. Arguably, however, their belief in the efficiency hypothesis outruns the evidence concerning its universality in common law decision making (see Posner, 1984, 1985, 1990) for a more jaundiced perspective on the issue).

To polarize the difficulty of testing for efficiency in the common law, we utilize the subjectivist, contractarian perspective of efficiency advanced by scholars of Virginia Political Economy (Rowley, 1986) though we recognize that most of the scholars of law and economics pursue a more objective standard, notably that of wealth. Although the difficulties are more intractable from the former perspective, they exist and also pose serious problems within the objectivist approach.

If the only source of valuation of assets or resource claims is the revealed choice behavior of parties to actual or to potential exchange, external observers cannot determine whether observed trades satisfy or fall short of the opportunities ex ante available. To do so, they would require access to the choice influencing costs as evaluated by the actors at the moment of choice, information which cannot be available in a subjective world. External observers can only infer, therefore, that, within the existing institutional framework, an absence of exchange demonstrates that the asset or resource concerned remains in its most highly valued use (Buchanan, 1975c, 1986a).

Efficiency in this limited but essentially unchallengeable sense seems almost assured in the absence of coercion or of fraud. Ignorance is no impediment in an approach that recognizes the cost of search and the imperative of rational ignorance. Transaction cost impediments to exchange are merely part of the institutional structure on which efficiency rests. In this sense they do not reflect the presence of market failure, but are irrelevant to the evaluation of efficiency within an institution's specific situation.

Of course, if this concept of efficiency is pressed to the meta-level of analysis, to the level of choices concerning the institutions themselves, it will collapse into tautology. Buchanan (1983) has argued against such an interpretation, allowing that rules and institutions may be inefficient, that transaction costs may often be lowered as a consequence of reforms endorsed through universal consent. The role of the political economist, in such comparative institutions analysis, is ideally restricted to identifying changes in rules and institutions capable of improving exchange efficiency and to subjecting his hypotheses to Wicksell's unanimity test through the vote mechanism (Buchanan, 1959, 1964).

Conventional welfare economics emphasizes the role of transaction costs as a barrier to the attainment of allocative efficiency, although it does not take account of the distinction between decisions over rules and decisions within rules. For this reason, the relevant transaction costs are often ignored, both because institutions are perceived to be too malleable and because they are viewed to be too inflexible with respect to human initiatives. Moreover, conventional welfare economics tends to emphasize an objective measurement of cost and to define market failure against an absolute, nirvana, standard of government intervention. Indeed, a significant contribution from public choice has been the redressing of the theory of market failure by a generalized theory of government failure, thereby providing opportunities for comparative institutions analysis as the basis for policy evaluation.

It is to the great credit of the new institutional economics – 'economics as it ought to be' in the words of Ronald Coase – that it has moved transaction costs to the center of the stage both conceptually and empirically as the basis for comparative institutional analysis. In this approach, the costs of specifying and enforcing all the contracts that underpin exchange are identified, including 'all the cost of political and economic organization that permit individuals to capture available gains from trade' (North, 1984).

Posner, Landes and other pioneers of the economic efficiency of the common law make significant use of this comparative institutions methodology, defining relevant transaction costs to the extent possible in their impressive empirical studies. Yet, their analyses are flawed essentially because they cannot overcome the measurement problems that the Virginia political economy program has identified. Most especially is the inadequacy of transaction cost information evident in attempts to justify the law of tort against the criterion of economic efficiency.

For, as Tullock (1981) has shown, at least four alternative approaches to the law of tort satisfy the efficiency criterion in the absence of relevant transaction costs: contributory negligence, strict liability, strict negligence of the uninjured and strict negligence of the injured party. In essence, this is a restatement of the Coase theorem, but one which is not widely recognized in comparative institutions analysis. If the impediments to bargaining are low, individuals will negotiate efficient settlements whatever the direction of the initial liability.

Transaction costs, therefore, become crucial in evaluating whether or not a particular law is efficient or wealth maximizing in the sense of Posner. Yet such costs are subjective and very difficult to measure for outside observers (Buchanan, 1969). The relevant costs – the choice influencing costs – reflect the most highly regarded legal rule sacrificed in the selection of the rule under consideration. The ex post cost information utilized even by scholars as experienced as Posner and Landes at best is an imperfect measure of the consequences and not the determinants of choice. As such, it has some of the flavor of the wind blowing through the rocks at Delphi as a mechanism for assessing the efficiency or inefficiency of the common law. In such circumstances, it is predictable that arguments from transaction costs tend to be based more on rhetoric than on convincing scientific evidence (Tullock, 1980).

4   The invadeability of the common law
Although there can be no clear-cut statistical test of the efficiency of the common law, a compelling case can be mounted in support of the view that the common law is not immune to invadeability and that the recent drift within the common law is away both from freedom (negatively defined) and efficiency. In this section, the impulses that govern the common law and its development are reviewed to determine the scope available to well-organized interest groups to reunite the common law to their own sectional advantages (Rowley and Brough, 1987, Rowley, 1989c).

The origins of the common law
The common law of England emerged and was consolidated in the years between 1154 and 1307, essentially through the writ system. A writ was an order from the King under the Great Seal founded on some principle of law, regular juris, which gave the right on which the action was founded and which stated the facts of the case. Appropriate writs were created for the protection of every private right or interest recognized by the royal courts, and were collated as registers. The Register of Writs was one of the most valuable sources of legal remedy available of common law, certainly until the nineteenth century. Even now, following the abolition of many forms of

action by nineteenth-century legislation, a knowledge of the old writs remains useful in the understanding of common law principles.

It is important to note that the early evolution of the common law occurred at a time when the royal courts faced strong competition from alternative legal systems (Hogue, 1985). Only in cases involving freehold were Englishmen compelled to present their cases before the king's courts during the twelfth and thirteenth centuries. Otherwise, they could take their cases to the county courts which administered local, customary law; or into the church courts, which administered canon law; or into the borough courts which administered the law merchant; or, in the case of feudal barons, into the courts of a baronial overlord which would apply the rules of feudal custom. Only by the end of the thirteenth century, when much of the common law was already hardened and set, were the royal courts at all secure in their competitive victory over alternative jurisdictions.

The competitive nature of early common law evolution inevitably provided a powerful impulse for the law to reflect the interests of the litigants and, in this sense, to be efficient. For exit, and to a lesser extent voice, were available weapons to those who became disenchanted with the writs and their court interpretations. The royal courts indeed survived two major rebellions by the feudal barons, in 1215 and in 1258, attempting to curtail the authority of the Crown. The royal courts succeeded by providing the best available justice, reflecting not least the preferences of merchants and money lenders attracted to England by the development of foreign trade. The law of property and the early law of contract undoubtedly benefited from the efficiency impulses thus provided.

Only England among the nations and empires of Europe successfully carried the essential elements of the medieval common law into the modern world. It did so, through almost eight centuries of significant violence and disorder, the consequence of repeated attempts to disturb the balance between the prerogative of the Crown, the rising privileges of Parliament and the customary rights of individual citizens. A sequence of fortuitous events ensured its survival and consolidation over time, notably the restoration of order by Henry Tudor in 1485 following the dynastic quarrels between the Houses of York and Lancaster, the break with Rome and Tudor continentalism by Henry VIII in 1534, the initial removal of Stuart continentalism with the defeat of Charles I in the Civil War and his execution in 1649, and the ultimate demise of the House of Stuart following the Glorious Revolution of 1688.

Thereafter, despite the emergence of legislative sovereignty in Parliament during the eighteenth century, despite Blackstone's acknowledgment that parliament was supreme even over the common law, nevertheless the important common law doctrines of stare decisis and of established legal principles survived and were further consolidated. As such, the common law of England became an established feature of the New World prior to the American Revolution and survived the emergence of the United States of America as an independent nation.

Thus, the essential elements of the common law remained unchanged, albeit with adaptations to reflect new conditions, until the slow erosion of laissez faire and the emergence of a more aggressive legislature, from the late nineteenth century onwards. During this early phase, the law of land (now property) and the law of contract evolved largely on efficiency foundations certainly forged within a framework of methodological individualism, and supported by almost all significant holders of property, who had privileged oligarchic access to the British Parliament and effectively vetoed invasive legislation. The drift away from principles thus established (which has occurred during the twentieth century), as the right to vote was extended, is significant, but not overwhelming though the domain of contract law has been eroded. The law of tort, which was a much later common law development with respect to accidents and personal injury, is quite a different story.

Judicial incentives and constraints

No one within the law and economics research program, prior to 1979, had presented a convincing explanation as to why, or through what mechanism, the judiciary should be supportive of wealth-measured efficiency in a largely monopolistic court bureaucracy such as that which characterizes twentieth-century Britain and the US. In essence, they all relied upon the widespread ideology of late eighteenth and early nineteenth-century laissez faire as continuing to permeate the bench in the much changed environment of the twentieth century, together with the binding power of stare decisis to blunt the edge of twentieth-century constructivist rationalism.

Posner (1979), recognizing this lacuna in his efficiency analysis, suggested three reasons why judge-based law might be efficient. First, wealth maximization is closely related to utilitarianism, and the formative period of the common law as we know it today, roughly 1800–1950, was a period when utilitarianism was the dominant political ideology in England and America. Second, judges lack effective tools for enriching an interest group or social class other than by increasing society's wealth as a whole, in which the favored group or class will presumably share. Third, the process of common law adjudication itself leads to the survival of efficient rules. He recognized explicitly that the absence of a theory of judicial behavior weakened the credibility of the efficiency hypothesis.

Landes and Posner (1975) had earlier emphasized the conventional view that the judicial branch of government in general, and the US Supreme Court in particular, were independent from the pressures of public choice and that this independence was ensured by the nature of judicial appointments. They had noted that Article III of the US Constitution provided for the appointment, rather than for the election, of federal judges, that such judges were to have life tenure, and the Congress should not reduce their salaries while they remained in office. In a number of the States, similar arrangements were provided, though the protection was not as extensive as that offered to the federal judges.

The constitutional guarantees enjoyed by federal judges certainly protect them from flagrant political pressure, though a guaranteed nominal salary offers only a limited protection in an inflationary economy, as periodic pay reviews indicate. Even if Landes and Posner are correct in their independence hypothesis, however, this does not guarantee that federal judges will uphold efficiency or liberty. Rational judges will decide cases, in such circumstances, in accordance with their own views on justice. Since they are all screened by the Senate, following nomination by the President, their views are likely to be sympathetic to those who moved them into office. In many cases, therefore, the federal judges will themselves reflect the constructivist rationalism which has tended to dominate many postwar US Senates, and which has conditioned Presidents in their nominations to the federal bench. Only a minority could be expected in such circumstances to uphold the principles of contractarian efficiency or of classical liberalism.

Landes and Posner (1975) have suggested that the federal judges, in essence, enjoy independence so that they will behave in the long-term interests of wealth maximization by members of the US Congress. For Congress to exploit its brokerage role among the special interest groups, it is argued, it must minimize the expectation that current legislative contracts will be repudiated by some future Congress. Procedural rules developed within the Congress itself are designed to facilitate such stability and continuity. By themselves, however, they must be insufficient, since the courts will be called upon to enforce the statutes. If the judiciary were subservient to the current Congress, a change in the balance of the special interests would endanger existing contracts. To avoid the long-term erosion of the congressional contract nexus, therefore, the judicial must be protected from the legislative branch of government.

This hypothesis seems somewhat far fetched in theory and has not stood up especially well to econometric testing. Landes and Posner (1975) admitted that their regression results were inconclusive. Buchanan (1975b), commenting upon them, stated that 'it is possible that, over a sequence of rejected hypotheses, the basic paradigm might be modified' and cryptically rejected their conception of the judicial role:

the modern political science or Warren Court model of a judiciary cannot, by any stretch of the imagination, be made consistent with a 'public capital' conception of law. (Buchanan, 1975, p. 905)

More recently, the economic analysis of judges has shifted focus, in an attempt to improve on the minimal predictive powers of the unlimited judicial discretion model by incorporating institutional constraints on judicial behavior. Higgins and Rubin (1980), in particular, developed and tested a formal theory of such behavior assuming that judges maximized some combination of personal wealth and ideology subject to judgment reversals, political and seniority constraints.

In this theory, judges were assumed to benefit from imposing their values upon society through precedent-setting opinions. They also benefited from increased wealth, which was enhanced by an absence of judgment reversals by superior courts, and by promotion within the judicial system, which enhanced both the opportunity to effect ideology and also to add to personal wealth. However, empirical tests decisively rejected the theory. Judicial discretion appeared to be unconstrained, with age and seniority insignificant, with precedent unimportant and with no evidence of effective policing through appellate review.

Inevitably, the Virginia School is equivocal in its response to this aspect of the efficiency of the common law hypothesis (Buchanan, 1974b), not least because it fails to equate with the self-motivation axiom of judges. Kimenyi, Shughart and Tollison (1985), in particular, stress the importance of individual rather than collective utility functions within the context of judicial behavior and suggest, on the basis of empirical analysis, that judges are influenced in their outputs by personal economic reward. Narrow though this result is, given the diversity of individual judicial preferences, it warns against any constructivist rationalist vision of judicial behavior, and suggests that the presence or absence of incentives to economic efficiency are as relevant to the judicial as to other areas of economic behavior. As we shall argue, these incentives, in post middle twentieth-century America, have been sufficiently loose as to allow individual judicial discretion an almost unlimited free rein.

The litigation process

If the judges cannot be relied upon as an active agent in the promotion of contractarian efficiency, perhaps the process of litigation itself will force the common law into an equilibrium characterized by an efficient set of legal precedents. Such is the view of a number of distinguished proponents of the efficiency hypothesis, notably Posner (1979) and Rubin (1977). Once again, however, this efficiency hypothesis is the subject of keen, unresolved controversy.

At issue in this controversy is the implication of the extent to which potential litigants make use of the courts. If the common law is efficient, and the courts and their litigation procedures are low cost, the large majority of disputes might be expected to be settled either directly in the courts or indirectly in the shadow of court precedents. In fact, such is not the case. The large majority of cases end in out of court settlements, many through private arbitration procedures. Once out of court settlements become the norm, the common law loses its flexibility to adjust precedents as a spontaneous reaction to a changing environment, and thus becomes a weakened vehicle to facilitate contractarian efficiency.

Once again, however, the proponents of common law efficiency have a counter argument. Rubin (1977) has suggested that the courts will be utilized more frequently when the legal rules relevant to a dispute are inefficient and less frequently when the rules are efficient. Once efficient rules have evolved, their existence lowers the incentive for future litigation, thus raising the probability that efficient rules will endure. In this perspective efficiency is the outcome of evolution generated by the myopic utility maximizing decisions of potential litigants and not by any efficiency predilections of the judges. Rubin applies his theory to the most suspect branch of the common law, namely tort law concerning accidental liability, and shows that where both parties to a dispute have an ongoing interest in efficient outcomes (e.g. insurance companies) efficient evolution is a predictable consequence of litigation.

Rubin's result, therefore, is not general. If only one party to a dispute is far sighted with respect to the liability system, precedent will evolve in favor of that party, whether or not such precedent is efficient. Such was the situation of nineteenth century nuisance law, which favored large corporations to the disadvantage of individuals. If there is no far-sightedness, the status quo may persist despite the imposition of significant efficiency losses on parties to a dispute.

Rubin's solution to the litigation issue is not strictly evolutionary since it depends on foresight. Terrebonne (1981) has presented an extreme form, evolutionary model, without foresight, and with a random generation of dispute options, demonstrating, even in such circumstances that selection favors common law rules that promote efficiency, save only when high litigation costs impede litigation on inefficient legal rules. Despite the elegance of Terrebonne's analysis, his result depends upon sleight of hand: the unexplained assumption is that frequently litigated rules have a lower probability of survival than those that are subjected to less frequent litigation. As with Rubin, Terrebonne relies on inefficient rules attracting relatively high rates of litigation, an assumption which is not necessarily justifiable, since litigation usually is not motivated by a group cost minimizing rationale.

Cooter and Kornhauser (1980) model legal evolution as a Markov process, abandoning the troublesome assumptions of Rubin (and later Terrebonne). They determine that blind evolution will not take the legal system to an efficient equilibrium, but rather will settle down to a stable state in which each legal rule will prevail for a fixed proportion of time. The system never settles down to a situation in which the best rule prevails forever, even when bad rules are litigated more frequently than good rules, and even when judges are more likely to replace bad rules by good rules than vice versa. This interpretation has the commendable advantage of corresponding with common sense.

Litigation unaided cannot be relied upon to move the common law to universal efficiency. Where the environment is favorable, notably in the law of property and the classical law of contract, litigation will help to maintain a close correspondence between the law and contractarian efficiency. Even in these branches of the law, however, recent developments have proved to be adverse, with property no longer protected by the takings clause in the US Constitution, with the doctrine of unconscionability invading the law of contract and with tort law massively invading the former terrain of the law of contract.

The law of tort has not been blessed with an environment favorable to efficiency. In consequence, litigation has served throughout the twentieth century to expand the liability of the defendants, with the individual responsibility of defendants for losses imposed a subordinate issue (Huber, 1988). Juries, often selected following psychological testing for malleability to emotional testimony have been persuaded to impose extremely high damage awards upon deep pocket defendants, most spectacularly in product liability and medical malpractice cases. Clients have been stimulated into litigation by attorneys offering contingent fee contracts, anxious to take advantage of increasingly vulnerable defendants, however far distant from the issue of litigation.

5 The gathering crisis in the law of tort

The law of tort has a long common law history, with intentional torts, involving violence or threatened violence to others already actionable in England in the seventh century. This area of tort law has evolved slowly over centuries and has not featured significantly in the gathering crisis which has centered on the law of accidents and personal injury. Albeit, in specific recent cases such as that of *Pennzoil* v. *Texaco*, juries have sent corporations a message in the form of astronomical damage awards.

Until the 1950s, the tradition with respect to the law of accidents and personal injury was to concentrate the attention of the courts on civil wrongs involving strangers, where there could be no advance agreement, nor any advance arrangement specifying who will pay for the damage. In such circumstances, the courts would step in to establish rights and responsibilities. Such interventions were comparatively rare in the wider universe of accidents and injuries which more frequently involved assailants and victims who were acquainted often in the form of a commercial relationship.

In those circumstances, the tradition of the courts was to handle disputes under the broad heading of contract law, searching for understandings between the parties and respecting them where found. The old law treated cases in contract and in tort under essentially different rules which reflected the line drawn between choice and coercion. The line tended to be tightly drawn in favor of contract.

During the 1950s, however, a visionary group of legal theorists (constructivist rationalists in our currency) invaded the law of accidents and personal injury, with consequences well beyond the bounds of their expectations. Huber (1988) refers to them as the Founders of modern tort law, naming as members such distinguished scholars and judges as William Prosser, John Wade, and Roger Traynor.

The Founders were to be joined within a decade or so, following a revolution in tort law, by a second group of scholars specialized in the economic analysis of law and eager to apply the Coase theorem to the law of tort. Notable among the early members of this School were Guido Calabresi, Richard Posner and William Landes. Their contributions set about proving that the new structure of tort law established through the pressures of the Founders was economically efficient, and an appropriate response to market failure. In so doing, they were to claim that the question asked by the old law – how did the parties agree to allocate the costs of the accident? – was wrong. The real question to ask was: How can society best allocate the cost of accidents to minimize all relevant costs and to provide potential victims with the accident insurance that not all of them currently purchase? (Huber, 1988, p. 7)

Such complacency among the second generation of socio-legal analysts was entirely misplaced (Epstein, 1980, 1985). The revolution in the law of tort, which began and ended with widespread repudiations of contract law, was neither a spontaneous order, nor ultimately was it efficient, certainly in any contractarian sense of that term. The revolution was activist, driven by attorneys in search of high expected rents from increased litigation, supported by legal scholars of interventionist predilections and by judges and juries whose social consciences too frequently led to changes in precedents conducive to a flood tide of litigation and to the widespread shift from consent to coercion in the law of accidents and personal injury.

Its principal consequence was the placing into market jeopardy or market demise a whole range of products and services subject to some risk to the client and reducing the availability of such commodities by imposing a significant tax upon consumers levied, without representation through the US courts. For the most part, the new law has created a moral hazard, by encouraging negligence of a contributory nature, which poses a serious threat to the US economy.

The first onslaught came in 1964, predictably from the California Supreme Court, in the case of *Chester Vandermark* v. *Maywood Bell* where the Court explicitly rejected a contractual limitation of the dealer's warranty to replacement without charge of such parts acknowledged by the dealer to be defective and imposed substantial damages for the car accident in favor of Vandermark. The court redefined accident law in the announcement: 'The fact that the dealer restricted its contractual liability to Vandermark is immaterial. Regardless of the obligations it assumed by contract, it is subject to strict liability' (Huber, 1988, p. 19). With that decision, contract rules that had slowly developed from the thirteenth century were sharply curtailed. In a sequence of small but decisive incremental steps the Founders and their successors were to transform the law of accidents and personal injury.

Other courts followed the California lead, denouncing safety disclaimers as unconscionable, contrary to public policy or inconsistent with natural justice and good morals. Within a decade, centuries of law governing contracts had been dismantled. The judges, in the meantime, were faced with the task of replacing the old law with an entirely different jurisprudence. At first they turned to the modest law of tort developed through the common law in the nineteenth century to deal with industrial accidents. This law was fault-based. The person seeking recovery must prove negligence to succeed in the suit. Juries had proved capable of evaluating negligence in terms of the appropriate degree of care required, and also of applying the concept of contributory negligence to limit damage awards to careless plaintiffs.

This approach did not hold for long as the California Supreme Court decision of 1962 in the case of *Greenman* v. *Shopsmith* demonstrated. Strict liability, the court announced, no longer would be rationalized in terms of implied warranties, fictional contracts, etc. Product manufacturers instead would be held strictly liable for accidents caused by a defect in manufacture of their product.

This decision was extended in 1968 by a federal appeals court, in the case of *Larsen* v. *General Motors*, to encompass design faults as well as manufacture faults, dramatically expanding the reach of strict liability while simultaneously increasing the technical complexity of issues argued to the jury. Eventually, by the mid-1970s, drugs and pharmaceuticals despite the existence of regulation by the FDA, were also swept into design defect litigation. In the meantime, highly remunerated expert witnesses were confusing juries with paid for, and naturally, conflicting testimony.

Strict liability came under increasing questioning as juries became increasingly bemused by the conflicting technical assessments to which they were exposed. A short-lived response of the courts was reliance on warnings or their absence attached to the products subject to litigation. All residual hazards should be clearly intimated or the producer would be held strictly liable for those that were omitted. Unlike product designs, warnings should be understandable by the general public. Unfortunately, for the activists, producers became increasingly competent in writing warnings. If the expansion of tort litigation was not to be slowed, alternative processes were essential.

One such process was the class action suit increasingly utilized by environmental lobbyists during the 1970s in nuisance litigation, especially on issues of environmental health risks. Class action suits were also popular among attorneys who stood to gain enormous contingent fees as threatened producers caved in to out of court settlements or succumbed to uncertain (but typically high) jury damage awards. Consent, or its absence, suddenly became of major significance when discussion moved to the victims of pollution! Federal rules of procedure conveniently had been amended in 1966 to permit the common question class action which enables a single class representative to initiate suit for a group while offering individuals the right to opt out.

A second closely related process was that of widening the scope of defendants' liabilities. For the most successful litigation was useless if the defendant had insufficient resources to satisfy awarded damages. Inevitably, this led to a sustained attack on the doctrine of proximate cause designed to limit liability to those who had caused it. The courts succumbed to a range of doctrinal innovations designed to widen the net for potential tortfeasors.

One such development has been an increase in the use of joint and several liability to shift the damage liability to those who are able to pay it. Thus, defendants with only a fractional responsibility for causing injury have been made to bear the full cost of compensation, even in the light of clear evidence of gross plaintiff negligence or of a major single tortfeasor contribution to the injury. Even the insurers of the defendants have been invaded on the joint and several liability doctrine.

Another development has been the use of joint and several liability to establish market share liability for damages for injuries covered by 'generic products' even though the products are not generic and evidence of cause is indeterminate. A yet further development, increasingly common in toxic tort cases, is the use of burden-shifting techniques to force defendants to prove lack of causation in order to avoid liability. Such developments are part of a successful campaign to socialize the risk of accident and injury, not through the legislature, but capriciously through the courts.

The invasion of the twin historic pillars of the law of tort – deterrence and compensation – by notions of societal insurance and risk-spreading and the undermining of fault as a doctrinal justification for limiting tort liability to tort feasors also generated a movement toward no-fault liability which began during the 1960s and accelerated sharply in the 1980s in the US. An inevitable consequence of such a shift has been an increase in moral hazard as plaintiffs claim doubtful exposure to injuries and/or gain from negligence regarding their exposure to injury. It has further lowered the importance of causation and has exposed non-tortfeasors to accident and injury liability.

Finally there came successful pressure for loosening the time constraints on litigation for torts, essentially by reinterpreting statutes of limitations designed to prevent excessively early or excessively tardy litigation. This process was successfully achieved by redefining the date by which an injury was assumed to occur that is, by stopping the clock to assist late litigants. In some cases, indeed, judges ruled that injuries did not exist until discovered by the defendant, a device that opened the door to considerable toxic tort litigation.

If the time restrictions could be released with regard to past torts, surely they could also be released to anticipate injuries not yet established. By recharacterizing injury as the distress and anxiety that a plaintiff might anticipate in anticipation of future harm, a whole new category of suits became ripe for litigation. In 1977 the case of *Laxton* v. *Orkin Exterminating Company* resulted in just such a jury award for mental anguish and opened up the route to anticipating suits. It was not long before cases involving accidents that had not even occurred were moving into the courts.

One outcome of all these endeavors was to ensure that evidence of adequate insurance cover made those who carried it a prime target for successful tort litigation, creating an adverse selection problem that can now only be resolved by the retreat of the law of tort (Huber, 1988).

6   Conclusions

Our evaluation of the common law ends with major doubts as to whether it is utilitarian, Paretian, classical liberal or contractarian. Recent developments in the law, especially the attack on contracts and the socialization of risk through a much expanded law of tort reflect scholarly activism by theoreticians of the Left, with the Tribe's and the Dworkin's taking the baton of the *Founders*, their writings seized upon by rent-seeking attorneys and condoned by left-leaning judges. Certainly, they do not appear to reflect any efficiency thrust as envisaged by Posner. The insurance crisis generated by tort judgments is one indicator of economic damage imposed, as is the withdrawal of otherwise profitable but relatively high risk goods and services from the US but not from the European market place.

Of course, tort law is not a major area of litigation for legal services lawyers. Nevertheless, it is a clear instance of a more general vulnerability of the common law system to sustained litigation with reform intent. The fact that the judicial process is vulnerable to such reformist pressures is important in evaluating the legal services program, for it suggests that if legal services litigation in the hands of reformist, constructivist rationalist attorneys is capable not only of influencing access to civil justice but also of redefining the nature of civil justice for overtly redistributionist ends (Faber and Frickley, 1991).

5 Lobbying and the law of legislation

... the rational individual in the large group in a socio-political context will not be willing to make any sacrifices to achieve the objectives he shares with others. There is accordingly no presumption that large groups will organize to act in their common interest. Only when groups are small, or when they are fortunate enough to have an independent source of selective benefits, will they organize or act to achieve their objectives.

Mancur Olson, *The Logic of Collective Action*,
Harvard University Press, 1965, pp. 166–167

1 Introduction

Modern political theory tends to view the making of legislative law as the chief function of legislative bodies. This view cannot be faulted as a positive statement concerning the behavior of contemporary government. Yet, it represents a far call from the recognized role of parliamentary government in its original English form. The Mother of Parliaments, the English legislature, emerged in a country where the rules of just conduct, the common law, were supposed to exist independently of political authority and where, at most, the legislature periodically might codify existing customs.

Indeed, as late as the seventeenth century, it was still questioned whether parliament could make law inconsistent with the common law. This constraint was embodied in the widely used phrase – the limited constitution – the underlying meaning of which was that of limiting government and of requiring those who governed to conform themselves to laws and rules. The concern of legislatures was seen to be the control and regulation of government whose principal but not exclusive role was that of nightwatchman, assuring that the rules of just conduct were enforced. Legislature was seen to originate from the necessity of establishing rules of organization for government itself.

This chapter is concerned with the law of legislation, its determinants and its predictable·consequences for efficiency, liberty and justice. Section 2 outlines the much more favorable view of legislative law envisioned by the Chicago Political Economy research program. Section 3 reviews the less favorable alternative perspective of the Virginian Political Economy research program.

At first sight, there may seem to be no place for a chapter on interest group lobbying in a book concerned with a program of legal services that explicitly prohibits the application of federally appropriated budgets to the lobbying of the legislature. In reality, however, as subsequent chapters of this book will chronicle, the US legal services program, from its outset, has ignored this prohibition and has allocated a significant part of its annual federal budgets to political lobbying for law reforms exploiting every subterfuge available, to avoid criminal repercussions for its officers, and relying upon its unique statutory protection to fend off the pressures of a periodically hostile legislature and, over the decade of the 1980s, of an avenging US president. Since such lobbying is not an accident of a particular legal services bureaucracy, but rather the predictable consequence of the 1964 and 1974 legislation, it is important to outline and evaluate conflicting theories concerning the relationship between lobbying and legislation.

2 The perspective of Chicago Political Economy

The overwhelming perspective of the CPE research program is that political markets are efficient in effecting wealth transfers and that interest groups play an important and beneficial role in ensuring that the deadweight losses to society are minimized in the wealth transfer process. The key contributors to this research program are Stigler (Leube and Moore, 1986), Peltzman, Becker, McChesney and Wittman, all of whom subscribe to the tight prior equilibrium method of the Chicago School of Economics.

Chicago's formal entry into public choice came a decade later than Virginia (1962) with Stigler's 1971 paper on the theory of economic regulation which challenged the public interest theory of regulation as being theoretically underdeveloped and empirically empty. A central thesis of his paper was that, as a rule, regulation was acquired by an industry and was designed and operated primarily for its benefit, that the basic resource of the state, the power to coerce, was a commodity freely traded in the political market place, and moved to its most efficient margins by competing pressures. Stigler marked Chicago's entry into the field with a typical empirical emphasis that supported his rudimentary theory of economic regulation. His paper initiated the CPE perspective of political markets as trading in coerced transfers rather than as correcting market failures.

Stigler's new theory was extended and formalized in 1976 by Sam Peltzman in a widely cited paper which has played a pivotal role in the developing CPE research program. Like Stigler, Peltzman assumed that what was basically at stake in regulatory processes was a transfer of wealth, not usually in cash form, but rather indirectly in the form of a regulated price, an entry restriction and the like. The regulator was viewed as seeking direct political support, or as vote maximizing, by allocating transfers in response to the competing bids of political coalitions. From this generating assumption, Peltzman formulated a theory of the optimum size of effective political coalitions within the framework of a general model of the political process. As such, his contribution must be viewed not just as the first CPE vote theory but also as the progenitor of the Chicago theory of pressure group lobbying as developed by Becker during the early 1980s.

Even though Peltzman retained Stigler's presumption that the regulator conferred benefits on a single victorious coalition, his theory nevertheless implied that the size of the dominant coalition would be limited (by diminishing returns) and that the winner would not receive the entire transfer since the regulator would have to secure his own position by purchasing marginal votes from the losing coalition. The implication of this insight is that not only will the average level of prices under regulation be below what it would be in pure monopoly, but that the structure of relative prices will depart from that in either pure monopoly or in competition. From this perspective, every identifiable group contains winners and losers, and even where all the winners are in one group, they end up short changed. Yet, the regulatory market is efficient in the sense that the regulatory equilibrium lies within the core and cannot be replaced by any conceivable regrouping of coalitions or by any reallocation of wealth transfers.

Both Stigler and Peltzman acknowledged the excess burdens associated with transfers through the regulatory process, but ignored the inefficiency implications, presumably on the ground that lump sum transfers were not feasible institutionally. They made no reference to the possibility that the rents associated with regulation might attract rent-seeking outlays that would waste additional resources (Tullock, 1967) an insight which is central to the VPE research Program. In a comment on Peltzman's paper, Becker (1976) even rejected the excess burden implication of regulation transfers, asserting that 'voters perceive correctly the gains and losses from all policies' (p. 247).

Becker concluded, on the basis of this premise, that cash transfers must carry deadweight loss and that all marginal deadweight losses will be equated in full equilibrium. Otherwise, votes could be increased by switching to the socially cheaper (cash transfer) method and away from regulatory transfers. This result is then generalized as follows:

> the methods used to accomplish any given end tend to be the most efficient available, in the public as well as the market sector, and the efficiency of methods should not be confused with the attractiveness of the ends themselves ... this approach leaves little room for economists to suggest improved methods in the public sector. (Becker, 1976, p. 248)

In 1976, Becker was willing, along with Peltzman, to rest his public choice analysis on the vote motive, which at that time still dominated the spatial theory of politics. By 1983, this theory had lost ground as a consequence both of important criticisms based on the notions of rational voter ignorance and of vote cycling in large numbers elections, and of a growing recognition that interest groups exerted political influence not only upon elections but also upon elected governments. Becker therefore shifted the emphasis away from the vote motive and instead envisioned politicians, parties and voters as agents whose purpose was mainly 'to transmit the pressure of active groups' (Becker, 1983, p. 372). Interest groups were viewed as competing within the context of rules that translated expenditures on political pressure into political influence and, thus, into access to political resources.

Becker's (1983) paper presented a theory of competition among pressure groups for political influence. Political equilibrium was shown to depend on the efficiency of each group in producing pressure, the effect of additional pressure on their influence, the number of persons in different groups, and the deadweight cost of taxes and subsidies. An increase in deadweight cost was shown to discourage pressure by subsidized groups and to encourage pressure by taxpayers, and vice versa. In Becker's summary, this analysis 'unifies the view that governments correct market failures with the view that they favor the politically powerful: both are produced by the competition for political favors' (Becker, 1983, p. 371).

In essence, Becker rehabilitated the pioneering work by Bentley (1907) which also had viewed the contributions of pressure groups benignly, essentially as information providers and consolidators of underlying political equilibria. Although his paper cited Olson (1965), it failed explicitly to challenge the entirely different perspective offered by that important contribution (see Section 4). Becker's paper, which was extended in 1985 (Becker, 1985), presented a theory of the political redistribution of income and of other public policies based on competition among pressure groups for political favors. Active groups produced pressure to raise political influence. The sum of all influences, given by the budget balance assumption, was zero. Each group maximized membership income on the Cournot–Nash assumption that additional pressure would not influence the political expenditures of other groups.

Efficiency in producing pressure is determined in part by the cost of controlling free riding among members. Efficiency is also determined by the size of the group, not only because size affects free riding, but also, countervailingly, because small groups may not be able to take advantage of scale economies in the production of pressure. The most important variables, in Becker's view, are the deadweight costs of taxes and subsidies associated with and assumed to be an increasing function of the taxes and subsidies implicit in group-induced transfers. An increase in the deadweight cost of a subsidy is seen to discourage pressure by the subsidized group, since it lowers the subsidy available from any given tax revenue. An increase in the deadweight cost of a tax, on the other hand, stimulates pressure by tax payers, since a given tax reduction is less damaging to those whose subsidies will be reduced.

All groups, in this model, favor and lobby for efficient taxes. Efficient subsidies benefit recipients, but harm taxpayers since they tend to abate taxpayer pressure production. Politicians and bureaucrats are assumed to carry out the political allocations resulting from the competition among pressure groups efficiently, although Becker does acknowledge the existence of a principal–agent relationship between those who dictate the pattern of transfers and those who must effect their wishes. In such an environment, lobbying leads to efficient legislation and there is no presumption that federally-supported lobbying agencies such as the outreach programs of the legal services program might impact harmfully upon the law of legislation.

The papers by Stigler, Peltzman and Becker, referred to above, constitute the core of a research program that maintains a universally high regard for the performance of democratic political markets, given the predisposition in favor of wealth redistribution of the vote majority, that emphasizes the efficiency of all political processes, and that rejects categorically the inferences of government failure that emanate equally consistently from the Virginia School. In 1989, in a paper published in Chicago's *Journal of Political Economy*, Donald Wittman pulled together the various strands of the CPE research program to demonstrate, in his view so conclusively as to shift the burden of proof against those who henceforth hypothesize government failure, that democracies produce efficient results.

Wittman's non-empirical all but tautologous paper presumably rang so favorably in Chicogoan ears that the world's most empirically-orientated economics faculty accepted it for publication in its most highly-regarded journal. Wittman's rhetoric of efficiency merits a brief summary here, since it is highly relevant to the policy debate over legal services that is the preoccupation of the remaining chapters of this book. For, in his view, any policy that exists is efficient as long as it emanates from democratic political markets, irrespective of the institutions that influence market equilibria.

In Wittman's world, elected officials are viewed as agents and the voters as their principals. Assuming that the vote motive itself is efficient, the question remains whether opportunistic behavior by agents (shirking, responding to bribes, pursuing goals detrimental to those of their principals) might result in slippages between political outcomes and voters' registered political preferences. Wittman minimizes this prospect claiming that competition, reputation, monitoring, and optimal contact design reduces opportunistic behavior in the political sector and that principal–agent problems may be no more severe than in the private sector.

Candidates for office develop reputations, based on their adherence to past campaign promises, which are important for re-election or for election to higher office. Although such reputations cannot easily be sold, in the manner of the goodwill of a firm, the existence of political dynasties enables the politician to transfer his reputation to designated heirs, broadly construed. This prospect curtails the incentive to shirk during terminal phases in office. Political parties also nurture reputations so that it becomes costly for candidates to shirk on their party's ideology, since the brand name is valuable in attracting and in holding votes.

Within legislatures it is relatively easy to monitor politicians' voting behavior, and to reward loyalty to the party (brand name) by appointment to influential committees. Without party support, a wayward member of a legislature is generally ineffectual in a system that requires a majority coalition. The political party is thus the analogue to a franchise in the private sector, preventing shirking within the legislature and allowing voters to make informal judgments about how the coalition of its members will behave.

Monitoring takes place not only within but also across political parties since competitors gain political advantage by reporting on the shirking behavior of the opposition. The threat of takeover (electoral defeat) thus reduces opportunism in democratic political systems. Wittman views elections as a relatively low transaction cost method of effecting political takeovers since the time period between elections is relatively short, there are no supra-majority requirements for being elected, and the defeated opposition retains a role within the legislature.

Optimal contract design also reduces opportunism. In this respect, Wittman cites the payment of above-market salaries designed to punish those who fail to gain re-election and to enforce costly campaigns to gain or remain in office, and the absence of a mandatory retirement age for legislators, to reduce the severity of the last period problem.

With politicians tightly constrained to fulfil the median voters' preferences, attention shifts to the issue of the extent to which voters are well-informed on politics. Once again, Wittman outlines the optimistic Chicago viewpoint. While acknowledging that search costs may be high for the typical voter and that personal expected benefits may be low, Wittman directs attention to the low cost methods of information acquisition that exist in political markets and that protect against this form of potential market failure. In particular, he notes the returns available to informed political entrepreneurs from providing information to voters, winning office, and gaining the direct and indirect rewards of holding office. In addition, as Downs (1957) originally noted, the development of party brand names and candidate reputations reduces still further the cost of information acquisition to the voter.

Voters will not be perfectly informed by these arrangements, but perfection is not required for efficiency, which must reflect the irreducible costs of search. By identifying with groups specialized in political issues relevant to their interests, individual voters are able at low cost to access information not provided to them directly by would-be politicians and their party organizations. Thus, Wittman views voters as choosing their pressure groups as a means of information acquisition, rather than pressure groups as influencing voter preferences through persuasive advertising. Interest group endorsements are thus seen to serve as market signals, providing strong cues about the policy preferences of selected candidates for public office.

The fact that voters are dependent for information upon biased sources (candidates and pressure groups) is not seen to imply that they make irrational choices on the basis of biased political beliefs. Voters are viewed as being fully competent to discount exaggerated political claims that emanate from biased information sources. To the extent that some individuals under-discount the exaggerations so others will over-discount them, with the law of large numbers likely to yield the correct majority choice. Wittman, in true Chicago style, has no time for a model of public choice that assumes that voters are consistently fooled and that there are no entrepreneurs to cleanse them of their confusions.

Most, though not all, public provisions have some public good characteristics that take the form of non-rivalry in consumption, and this may lead the median voter to select an inefficient outcome, notably one that equates the marginal value of the expenditure to the median voter with his own tax rate, rather than the sum of marginal valuations of the good to all citizens with the sum of their marginal tax rates. Once again, Wittman minimizes the significance of such political market failure, noting that in the case of symmetric distributions (with the median voter's marginal valuation and marginal tax bracket equivalent to that of the mean voter), the median outcome is actually efficient.

Even where such symmetry does not hold, however, Wittman does not concede political market failure. For, if the median voter result were truly inefficient, then there would exist a different tax policy, coupled with an efficient amount of public good supply that would dominate the median. By trial and error, if not by prescience, candidates would locate the optimum and, by appropriate locations in multidimensional policy space, would defeat rivals who located themselves incorrectly at the single dimensioned median of the voter distribution.

Moreover, notwithstanding McKelvey's 1976 result which demonstrated inefficiency in multidimensional political space, Wittman relies upon a probabilistic voting theorem to deny it relevance and to secure all relevant multidimensional outcomes within the Pareto-optimal set. Maximizing the expected vote becomes equivalent to maximizing the sum of the individual probabilities. This result holds even with respect to income redistribution since, on Wittman's assumption, any crumb needlessly left on the table reduces the expected vote of the candidate.

Finally, Wittman challenges a widely held presumption of public choice that the geographical ties of individual members of the US Congress create market failure, most notably in the form of excessive pork-barrel legislation. He suggests that three institutional factors of the Congress combine to ensure that this kind of market failure does not arise, namely the small size of the Congress, the party system and the structure of the Congress.

The small size of the Congress ensures that transaction costs are low and thus facilitates efficiency enhancing trades and bargains. If excessive pork is scheduled for the members' districts, a lean omnibus bill will counteract it as vote conscious congressman scramble to avoid vote losses threatened by the excessive tax liabilities of their electorates. Wittman rejects the assumption of voter asymmetry (which suggests that voters tend to undervalue the tax cost of public expenditures) on the usual rational expectations grounds of the Chicago Political Economy research program.

Against the argument that politicians can take continuing and full credit for pork going to their district but only partial and one time credit for pork elimination, Wittman again invokes rational expectations counter arguments which he claims are reinforced by the existence of political parties. National political parties are viewed as internalizing the negative externalities that might arise from local interests trying to shift costs onto other districts. Through their control over committee assignments and independent access to campaign funds, party leaders are able to restrain the opportunism of individual party members and to enforce a coalition that facilitates Pareto-improving trades.

Wittman further asserts that the committee structure of the Congress is efficiency enhancing, that it bestows political property rights that can be used for facilitating bargains. Although certain of the Congress's committees appear to represent special interests, they are counterbalanced by committees that exercise a more global perspective. Moreover, in his interpretation, the mechanism for making committee assignments, which is ultimately the responsibility of the political parties, is designed to avoid negative sum legislation. Even the agenda setting power of committee chairmen does not lead to inefficient outcomes, since these powers will be traded for the most highly valued outputs, providing the agenda setter and his constituents with increased political wealth.

The CPE vision of the political process offers no prospect of harmful or wealth dissipative lobbying, no possibility that even the most determined lobbyist will succeed in diverting the political market equilibrium from the preferred outcomes of median voters. This vision of the political process is extremely flattering for the federal program of legal services. For even if the legal service outreach should succeed in diverting a significant part of its budget from the individual poor to political lobbying then it must be presumed that such is the wish of the median voter and that the lobbying itself merely serves to consolidate to overall median voter politics.

3 The perspective of Virginia Political Economy

The overwhelming perspective of the VPE research program is one in which political markets, in the absence of enforceable constitutional constraints, are vehicles of wealth redistribution. Unlike CPE, however, VPE perceives such markets to be generally inefficient, dissipating as waste much of the wealth potentially available for distribution and moving much of the wealth that is redistributed in directions that would not be countenanced by those who initially set the political market process into action. Interest groups, rather than individual voters, are viewed as the major actors in political markets. Such groups are by no means equal, but rather are possessed of highly asymmetrical access to political markets, thus biasing political market equilibria away from those that would reflect the median voter preference. Because political markets allocate inefficiently and at high cost, the prevailing vision of the VPE research program is of government failure, save only where individuals protect themselves ex ante by carefully articulated and enforced constitutional constraints.

The approach of VPE is methodological individualism – all organic notions of institutions are anathema – and the method of analysis is that of diffuse prior equilibrium. The protected core of the research program is the assumption of homo economicus, rational self-seeking man, capable variously of great foresight and of great error in establishing the institutions of politics, through which his political goals must be pursued. The presumption of the research program is the notion that ideas are important, that what is is not necessarily efficient and that homo economicus is capable of institutional reform.

If individuals are the only actors, so the present and the future is their only stage. The past is history, choices have been made, and any costs arising from past choices are choice-influenced and not choice-influencing in nature. The concept of efficiency, therefore, is meaningless with respect to the past, since history is set in stone. What has been, is history, and outsiders cannot read the minds of actors from the Shades.

If rational self-seeking individuals interact in choices concerning the future such choices must be in period efficient in terms of the institutions which condition them. In this sense, the CPE and the VPE perspectives on efficiency converge. If transaction costs or information costs prevent superior outcomes they constitute components of the opportunity cost which determines choices. Even if individuals perceive a prisoners' dilemma at the moment of choice, their inability to escape it implies that it is not a prisoners' dilemma from the perspective of methodological individualism. For, by definition, superior outcomes are not feasible.

In itself, this does not imply an absence of reform potential, does not relegate the outsider to the role of impartial spectator, as CPE is led to conclude. The prior equilibrium is diffuse and not tight, and may well be susceptible to improvement through entrepreneurial intervention designed to influence rational individual choices in some meta-level perspective. If political economists, or others, are able to supply inventions which lower transaction or information costs, which pinpoint potential error, or which otherwise change the relevant climate of ideas, and if individuals seize upon such contributions, internal institutional reforms may result and tomorrow may differ significantly from today. The political economist has an important role to play, as the creator and tester of institutional reform hypotheses, not in the role of philosopher king (Buchanan, 1959, 1964).

Public choice scholars seek to explain how real political markets actually function and to compare the outcomes of such markets with the predicted outcomes of private choices effected by individuals through ordinary market process. To this end, the public choice research program, heavily influenced by the VPE research program has sought to develop a logically consistent and empirically supportable theory linking individual behavior to collective action. In so doing, the self-interest postulate, which is the fulcrum of all private market economics, has been extended to the analysis of politics, on the assumption that individuals do not metamorphose their personalities as they move between private and public markets.

In using the concept of rational self-interest, VPE, unlike CPE, infers nothing about the specific arguments that motivate individual behavior, whether they are focused on expected wealth, on power or an ideology, or whether they are driven by solipsism, malevolence or benevolence. Individuals differ and act on a wide variety of impulses in search of diverse goals. The self-interest postulate implies that their behavior nevertheless responds systematically at the margin in response to changes in perceived net wealth and does so irrespective of other arguments in their utility functions. It suggests that if the collective actions of individuals in some sense do not accord with their individual policy goals, they may wish to look to institutional reforms rather than to moral exhortation to close the gap between aspirations and social outcomes.

The principal actors in political markets, all of them individuals, are voters, members of interest groups, bureaucrats and politicians. In the VPE model, politicians provide a brokering function in a political market which primarily, though not exclusively, is concerned with wealth transfers. Voters, special interests and bureaucrats, capable of effective economic organization, 'demand' favorable transfers of wealth. Other voters, special interests and bureaucrats, less well organized and incapable of effective countervailing pressures, 'supply' such transfers, albeit at a political price. The politicians effect market equilibrium, balancing costs against benefits at the margin, thus maximizing their own utilities, weighted variously in terms of expected wealth, expected votes, power and ideology subject to a minimum vote constraint required to ensure re-election. The relevant bureaucrats effect the supply of policies thus brokered.

The concepts of 'demand' and 'supply' in this stylized model require a special interpretation. Demand consists of willingness to pay in votes, lobbying time and/or political action money transfers by those who perceive net transfer returns through political markets. For the most part, such returns represent rent and not profit, since they represent transfers and not wealth creation. The rent-seekers who represent demand encompass not only the direct beneficiaries, but also secondary recipients such as paid lobbyists, consultants, expert witnesses and attorneys, who are essentially parasitic upon the political process.

Supply consists of the inability or unwillingness at the relevant margin of those from whom political transfers are to be extracted to rent protect their wealth by the expenditure of votes, lobbying time and/or political action money transfers. Of course, evidence of effective supply does not imply an absence of rent protection outlays, but rather that such outlays allow for some increment of wealth transfer, given the condition of demand. For this reason, the magnitude of transfers actually effected in political market equilibrium is a treacherous guide to the total amount of wealth dissipation that drives the equilibrium and which should be measured as the total of those rent-seeking and rent-protection outlays.

The vote motive
The extent to which lobbying and political action outlays will occur in political markets is predictably a function of the discretion allowed to vote-seeking politicians by the electoral process. In this respect, early optimism among VPE analysts, who believed that the vote motive rigorously controlled political markets (Downs, 1957), has been eroded as the research program has developed momentum (Rowley, 1984), even to the extent that an influential minority of VPE scholars now deny any significant role for individual voters in political markets (Tullock 1967a).

The early hubris surrounding the vote motive stemmed from the pioneering contribution of Downs (1957) who first presented a behavioral theory of politics in which political parties were assumed to seek votes and to formulate policy to win elections rather than to seek political victory in order to effect policy. From this radically new perspective, Downs offered the highly attractive 'median voter theorem' which indicated that rival political parties would be forced by vote considerations to converge in policy space to a unique and stable political equilibrium which reflected the preferences of the median voter (Rowley, 1984). This equilibrium offered no discretion to political parties, unless they had no aspiration to govern, and it was robust against all outside influences. As such, it reflected an attractive majoritarian solution to policy analysts wedded to contemporary notions of democracy.

Unfortunately, hubris turned to nemesis as the research program demonstrated the stringency and lack of realism of the conditions necessary for the median voter theorem to hold:

1. the election must be contested only by two political parties;
2. the policies at issue must collapse into one dimension of left–right space;
3. voter preferences must be single-peaked over policy space;
4. the political parties must be able and willing to move in policy space;
5. the political parties must be well informed regarding voters' preferences for policy;
6. voters must be well informed regarding the policy positions of the political parties;
7. there must be no abstentions by voters at elections; and
8. voters must punish governments who deviate from their successful electoral manifestoes.

Once these assumptions are relaxed to take account of the realities of political markets, the median solution is seen to be much less dominant (Romer and Rosenthal, 1979). Even the existence of a political equilibrium is placed in doubt and the uniqueness and stability of any equilibrium must be seriously questioned, with cycles a pronounced feature of the political market place (Black, 1948; Arrow, 1951). In consequence, the grip of voter majorities over the election manifestoes of competing parties is seen, for the most part, to be much looser than Downs was willing to acknowledge.

If more than two political parties contest an election there are serious difficulties in predicting the political market equilibrium. As Tullock (1967a) established, convergence may not occur under such conditions since third or fourth parties may rationally space themselves well away from the major parties to identify an independent electoral basis. Coalition prospects jeopardize the control of the majority over political markets and offer the potential for political instability and coalition cycles such as destroyed the Fourth French Republic and paved the way for Gaullist autocracy in 1958. Riker (1962) has suggested that rational coalitions should maximize their rent extraction potential by forming at a minimum winning size. However, the evidence does not generally support this hypothesis.

If policy space is perceived in multidimensional terms by voters and politicians further complications arise. First, if all relevant actors fail to identify commonly perceived issues, the scope for error is large and any tight prior equilibrium theory, such as that of Downs, is unlikely to prove consistently successful. Secondly, even if the issue dimensions are clearly defined, influences of a non spatial nature (the valence of individual candidates) may weaken the political advantage of candidates who locate at the grand median of the distribution, as Ford discovered in 1976 and as Carter discovered in 1980 (Enelow and Hinich, 1984). Finally, even if voters' preferences are single-peaked over each policy issue, instability and cycling is likely across the multidimensioned space (Riker and Ordeshook, 1973). The greater the number of issue dimensions, the more likely is cycling and the more susceptible are elections to agenda manipulation. Downs argued that high information costs induce voters to collapse issues into unidimensional left–right space. Hinich and Ordeshook argue that this is not so. Evidence, as yet, is ambiguous, but leans toward the latter view point (Enelow and Hinich, 1984, 1990).

The assumption, central to Downs, that the competing political parties are mobile over political space has been challenged by Enelow and Hinich (1984). The counter-hypothesis is that political parties are immobilized in the short run by the recent history of their political behavior. Major spatial movements by a party or a candidate are impeded by credibility constraints among the electorate. In such circumstances, parties more frequently advertise to shift the voter preference distribution in favor of their spatial position than to advise the electorate of significant locational adjustments. The CPE program, with its information view of economic advertising, chooses to ignore the persuasion element in political advertising.

Once information is recognized as persuasive and error is acknowledged as an integral component of the political process, the concept of voter preference-based equilibrium itself is suspect. If voters are rationally ignorant and if special interests fund disinformation, the observed political equilibrium will not demonstrate itself in Downsian terms. The political equilibrium, even if it exists, will manifest itself not in terms of underlying but of manipulated preferences (Lee, 1988).

In the absence of mandatory voting, democracies are characterized by voter abstentions, in some elections accounting for 50 per cent or more of the electorate. Such abstentions are not irrational, but rather reflect the nature of political markets, which diverge markedly from those in the private sector. Indeed, the paradox of voting reflects the ironic situation that rational individuals, confronted with a miniscule probability of changing an electoral outcome, have no incentive to vote, given that elections typically impose significant costs upon those who vote. This paradox of voting is a serious, unresolved problem for those who rely upon the vote motive as the basis of majoritarian democracy.

The probability of an individual vote determining an election is very low – less than one in ten million in postwar US Presidential elections – implying that the expected benefit to any individual from the victory of one party, however large the absolute individual benefit, is minute. Even if civil duty compels the vote, therefore, it may not induce the informed vote, since rational ignorance must be widespread among the electorate. In such circumstances, voters may vote their superficial preferences, while operating elsewhere among the interest groups to pursue their underlying political objectives.

Potential voters may abstain as a consequence either of indifference or of alienation. Abstentions through indifference, if evenly matched, are unlikely to disturb the underlying median voter solution, though they may weaken the stability of the equilibrium. Abstentions through alienation, however, exert an altogether more powerful influence, especially when the voter preference distribution is skewed across issue space and abstention threats lie in the extended tail of the distribution. In such circumstances, political equilibrium may be pulled away from the median, towards the mean as the threatened party eases back toward its distribution tail to avoid voter alienation. If the abstention threat pervades both tails of the distribution, equilibrium may not exist, and parties may be immobilized some distance from each other in policy space for fear of alienating extremist support.

Elections are discrete events in a continuous political market process and the vote motive, therefore, is only as influential as are elections and election prospects in controlling the behavior of incumbent legislatures. There are several reasons why political markets are less susceptible to electoral control than are private markets to the sovereignty of consumers. The first is a direct consequence of significant differences in the nature of private and of public choice, namely the bundle purchase nature of political markets. Voters cannot simply shop around among alternative political brokers picking and choosing within the bundle of issues on offer. In consequence, the parties have some discretion to full line force relatively unpopular policies as part of an otherwise popular bundle, much in the manner of a powerful multi-product monopolist in the private sector.

Secondly, political parties can rely upon voter memory decay to protect them from subsequent electoral damage should they deviate from policy manifestoes at an early stage of the incumbency. As the incumbency proceeds so they may excuse as responses to unanticipated external shocks policy slippages that cannot be shrouded in the mists of time. They can always rely upon ongoing rational ignorance when deviating from policies that gained the electoral support of the many to provide specific and highly valued transfer benefits to the few (but not vice versa).

For these reasons, the vote motive cannot be relied upon as a consistent control mechanism in political markets, and the median voter equilibrium must be viewed as an occasional rather than as a dominant feature of democracy.

The special interests

A special interest issue is one that generates substantial personal benefits for a small number of constituents while imposing a small individual cost on a large number of other voters (Gwartney and Wagner, 1988). As Madison recognized in The Federalist Papers, a majoritarian system of representative democracy is biased toward the adoption of special interest policies, even when such policies are wealth destructive or seriously invasive of individual freedoms. The separation of powers was written into the US Constitution to curtail this bias, but arguably parchment has failed to achieve this objective (Wagner, 1987), with special interests successfully invading the executive and the judicial as well as the legislative branches of the Federal and State governments.

Special interests emerge to take advantage of rational ignorance among the electorate by offering political gains to vote-seeking politicians who support the intense, concentrated interest of the few rather than the weak, diffused interest of the many. They do so by offering firm electoral support as well as financial contributions and other forms of assistance to politicians receptive to their interests and by opposing those who are not. In a pluralist democracy with weak party allegiances, such as the US, the special interests are largely responsible for the high incumbent success ratios in congressional elections and for raising entry barriers into the legislature.

Special interests may be viewed as rent-seekers or as rent-protectors whose principal objective is that of creating or maintaining rents through the political process and of securing such rents through transfers from the general interest to their own constituents. Since rents, by definition, are returns in excess of opportunity cost, special interest groups typically do not engage directly in productive activity. Indeed, contrary to the CPE view, rent-seeking takes place in institutional settings where the pursuit of private gain generates social waste rather than social surplus, as competing interest groups expend resources in a once for all or ongoing battle over the distribution of already created wealth.

VPE shares with CPE the notion that the law of legislation is an important vehicle for rent-seeking and rent-protection which is not limited to the domain of fiscal politics. It does not share the judgment of Becker (1983, 1985) that regulations, taxes and subsidies are near perfect substitutes, in particular because regulation is viewed as a much less transparent mechanism for transferring wealth (Crew and Rowley, 1988, 1989). Neither does it share Becker's judgment that competing interest groups generate efficient political equilibria. The reasons for Virginian dissent lie in the logic of collective action (Olson, 1965) and in the rent-seeking insight (Tullock, 1967).

In contrast to Becker, Olson's (1965) logic of collective action predicts that competition among interest groups introduces significant bias into political markets. Such bias is a consequence of unequal access to political influence, reflective of the differential impact of the free-rider problem on the formation and effective mobilization of various kinds of interest groups. Unlike Becker, who viewed free-riding as being related negatively to the overall magnitude of the benefits available, Olson emphasized the importance of being able to privatize such benefits to individual members of the group, thus excluding non-performers from the benefits that are won, and/or the ability to coerce members into active rent-seeking, as means of controlling free-riding in the group interest.

In such a perspective, if the common objectives of a potential interest group have pronounced publicness characteristics, the free-rider problem will hinder group formation and weaken group pressures. Predictably, this is a serious problem for large groups of individuals in the absence of membership coercion. For large pressure groups to be effective politically, they must be organized basically for private purposes which provide selective benefits to the membership, and must attach their political objectives to the private interest essentially as a by-product. The by-product theory explains the existence and the relative success of organizations representing agriculture, labor and the professions. Consumer groups find it much harder to organize on this basis.

Smaller organizations may engage successfully in collective action, without recourse either to coercion or to selective benefits, by utilizing their special interest advantages of limited publicness in group objectives. Olson predicts, on this basis, that small, well-defined interest groups in search of rents that are significant to individual members, will be differentially successful in the political market place. Even within such groups, however, there will be a systematic tendency for the larger demanders of public policies to bear a disproportionate share of the burden of collective action. Organizations representing business interests typically owe their existence and success to special interest factors.

Olson's theory suggests that interest groups introduce significant policy bias into political markets, even where the conditions necessary for the median voter theorem to hold otherwise exist. In such circumstances, campaign contributions are designed either to shift politicians' attention away from votes in favor of wealth or to provide the opportunity for politicians to manipulate rational ignorance within the electorate and to shift the voter distribution itself. Where political equilibrium does not exist, or is not unique, or is unstable, the opportunity for interest group distortions predictably will be more pronounced. The logic of collective action implies that political equilibria rarely reflect the preferences of the median voter.

Olson, writing in 1965 prior to the rent-seeking insight, incorrectly emphasized the costless transfer nature of political markets. Tullock's (1967) contribution suggested that this judgment is overly-optimistic and that rent-seekers waste resources in pursuit of rents. Subsequent empirical analysis has indicated that the dissipation of wealth as a consequence of rent-seeking in political markets is several orders of magnitude larger than any losses through allocative inefficiency (Laband and Sophocleus, 1988, Gwartney and Wagner, 1988). Rent-seeking theory suggests that the empirical studies may understate the actual magnitude of the losses thus imposed on society (Tullock, 1989).

Judgments differ concerning the degree to which rents are dissipated in the process of interest group competition, with some scholars claiming total dissipation (McCormick, Shughart and Tollison, 1984) and with others claiming that the magnitude of rent-seeking waste appears to be surprisingly small (Tullock, 1989). It is important not to restrict measures of dissipation to first order effects. For example, campaign contributions are largely transfers to political brokers, in the first instance, but subsequently are wasted largely in costly electioneering. Indeed, the US political system, by securing significant transfers from rent-seekers to politicians, while providing little control over campaign expenditures may be particularly vulnerable to rent-seeking waste.

Rent-seeking does not always manifest itself in an active legislative agenda. For, as McChesney (1987, 1989) has demonstrated, politicians not infrequently extract rent transfers in return for a promise not to legislate or as payment for repealing earlier legislation. In this perspective, the political brokers became the active principals and the special interests the more passive agents in the rent-seeking process. Fundamentally, however, lobbying activities remain center-stage as the raison d'être of interest groups' existence.

The bureaucracy

The bureaucracy of government is located in the Executive Branch and is composed of public sector organizations in which employees cannot legally appropriate any residual as personal income, and in which a significant part of recurring revenues derive from appropriations other than from the sale of output at a unit price. Following Tullock (1965), Downs (1967) and Niskanen (1971), the senior bureaucrats who exercise control over their budgets are assumed to be self-seeking and to maximize their respective utility which is defined as some balance of expected wealth, ideology, patronage, discretionary power and ease of management. Budget maximization is employed as a plausible proxy for these objectives.

Bureaucrats operate both on the demand and on the supply side of the political market. On the demand side, they operate as special interests, unconstrained by free-rider considerations and differentially well-informed on the likely responsiveness of the legislature to specific initiatives. Bureaucrats predictably favor non-transparent policies, not only to conceal special interest allocations from electoral scrutiny, but also to maximize their own discretionary power in the provision and distribution of commodities subject to their control. In Niskanen's (1971) theory, bureaus typically dominate the legislature and, by offering a total output in return for an overall budget, they extract the total consumers' surplus from the government. Typically, bureaus obtain excessive appropriations from the legislature and supply an excessive output.

From the perspective of supply, bureaus are agents of government and of the legislature. Despite the existence of executive branch monitoring and of congressional committees, designed to provide surveillance over bureau supply, a significant principal–agent problem persists, in part because of attenuated property rights within the legislature and in part because of the multiplicity of principals required by the separation of powers (Rowley and Vachris, 1990).

Senior bureaucrats, in consequence, exercise discretionary power, and are vulnerable to special interest lobbying and bribes, to offers of post governmental employment in favored corporations, as well as to their own ideological preferences. In such ways, bureaus may frustrate the vote motive by their behavior on both sides of the political market, without necessarily bearing the political cost.

The invadeability of the Constitution

The US Constitution was conceived as a parchment that would contain the powers of majoritarian government and provide an impenetrable foundation for economic prosperity and personal liberty. Throughout the first century and a half of its existence, despite the Civil War and other major external wars, it largely succeeded in this ambition, albeit assisted latterly by US adherence to the rules of the Gold Standard. In consequence, public sector spending in 1920 accounted for less than 10 per cent of the US gross national product, testament indeed to the effective reining in of a government of only derived powers. Thereafter, however, the constitutional limits were 'rent asunder again and again' (Gwartney and Wagner, 1988 p. 29) with public sector spending rising to more than 35 per cent of gross national product by the early 1980s. This takes no account of the massive non-budgetary extensions of governmental power achieved through the law of legislation (Bennett and DiLorenzo, 1984).

In the view of Gwartney and Wagner (1988), the major growth in government reflected, to a large degree, an important change in the American concept of government, from that of a consensual arrangement designed for the mutual betterment of all, to one of an agency through which to pursue objectives favored by a transient legislative majority. Adherents of this latter concept have jettisoned notions of negative freedom enshrined in the Constitution and have translated consent of the governed to mean majority rule even in the legislative manoeuvring around unequivocal constitutional safeguards.

The case of so-called entitlements – transfers of income or in-kind benefits from taxpayers to various segments of the population through coercive legislation – highlights the nature of the resulting invasion of negative by positive freedoms. Entitlements, indeed, are often legislated on the basis of minority support within the Congress supplemented with logrolling between minorities. Off-budget invasions of individual freedoms are also a major feature of the US economy, exemplified in the plethora of regulatory agencies that now exist to redistribute wealth and to impede wealth creation.

The US courts are charged with interpreting the Constitution. Clearly, they were viewed by the Founding Fathers as an important check on the legislature as well as on the executive. Since 1937, however, even the Supreme Court has shown reluctance to intervene (judicial restraint) where the issues raised are construed as political questions. In consequence, the invasion by statutes of the eminent domain clause of the US Constitution, which protects individuals from public takings of their property without full compensation, is one of many examples of unconstitutional legislation condoned by the judiciary (Epstein, 1985).

As Gwartney and Wagner (1988) have noted, the very idea of constitutional government is that the authority of government is limited to the boundaries prescribed by the constitutional contract. Yet, unless government is designed with in-built incentives capable of holding it within constitutional bounds, there is no inherent reason for government to comply with the constitutional contract in the real world. Majoritarian legislative processes, even supra-majority processes, are no protection against unconstitutional behavior in the unconstrained environment of post-constitutional opportunism. Even a constitution as internally consistent as that of the United States has not prevented interest groups from invading contract and enforcing takings in a manner proscribed by written parchment:

> just as the social dilemma model indicates, it is one thing to incorporate substantive provisions against takings and quite another to constrain the ordinary legislative process within the constitutional boundary. Despite the internal consistency of the U.S. Constitution and the apparent clarity of key limitations on taking activi-

ties, the constitution has failed to control legislative bodies intent on the support of plunder in the guise of public policy. (Gwartney and Wagner, 1988, p. 39)

The US Constitution has failed as a bulwark against legislative invasion of individuals' rights essentially for three reasons. First, the judiciary has proved vulnerable to politicization and thus itself has become an agent of powerful special interests. Second, the appellate courts have proved to be unwilling to resist the powers of Congress which itself brokers the special interest market in the law of legislation. Third, the legislature has proved to be adept at circumventing substantive restraints where these have been honored by the courts, not least in the arena of fiscal politics where off budget activities abound (Bennett and DiLorenzo, 1984). In such circumstances, the US Constitution is essentially invadeable by special interests.

4 Conclusions

An important issue evaluated in this book is the extent to which federal monies appropriated to the Legal Services Corporation to enable poor Americans to obtain legal advice and/or to litigate to support their civil rights have been and are diverted into lobbying the legislature in pursuit of law reforms. The issue is especially important if one accepts the thesis advanced compiled by the VPE research program that legislative lobbying leads to resource misallocation and wealth destruction.

In contrast, if one subscribes to the logic of the CPE research program, legal services lobbying is to be viewed as an efficient outcome of the political process, given the transfer predilections of the US electorate. In such a vision, lost liberties are seen to be voluntary sacrifices in return for more highly valued individual goals and any apparent loss of wealth to be more than recompensed by increased individual utilities.

Part IV

THE PURVEYORS
AND BROKERS OF
CIVIL JUSTICE
FOR THE POOR

6 The nature and role of the Legal Services Corporation

to preserve its strength, the legal services program must be kept free from the influence of or use by it of political pressures.

Legal Services Corporation Act of 1974, Sec. 1001 (5)

1 Introduction

The market in civil justice for the poor is not a market in the ordinary sense of that term at all. It is a market in which suppliers do not sell, customers do not buy, and those who finance the product are rationally ignorant of its content, even of its existence. Under these conditions, the VPE research program predicts that the economic market will not clear, but will be characterized always by the condition of excess demand, which itself is not at all an indicator of under-provision of the service, but rather is a symptom of pricing a scarce commodity as though it were non-scarce.

The VPE research program further predicts that political equilibrium in such a market will be diffuse and not tight, reflective of rational ignorance on the part of many voters and of effective lobbying by well organized interest groups as well as of bounded rationality on the part of those who broker policy. In brief, the political equilibrium will be shot through with government failure, a predictable result, and not an aberrant outcome, of the institutions of politics.

Part IV of this book concentrates on the market in civil justice for the poor reviewing the principal instruments that purvey and broker legal services through the powerful lens of the VPE research program. The general presumption of this program is that the federal program of legal services is riddled with institutional failure. In this chapter, the Legal Services Corporation is analysed as a government bureau the senior management of which pursue objectives of their own, both narrowly selfish and ideological, which well may result in behavior that is at odds with its statutory duties. This presumption runs counter to the arguments both of the public interest and the Chicago research program that infer respectively that the bureaucrats either will freely seek to honor their statutes or that they will be conditioned to do so.

2 The 1974 statute and its instruments

The Legal Services Corporation Act of 1974 was signed into law on July 25, 1974 by President Richard Nixon following a bumpy passage through the

Congress. The Act declared that there is a need to provide equal access to the system of justice in the United States for individuals who seek redress of grievances; that there is a need to provide high quality legal assistance to those who otherwise would be unable to afford adequate legal counsel; that providing legal assistance to those who face an economic barrier to adequate legal counsel will best serve the ends of justice; that for many US citizens, the availability of legal services has reaffirmed faith in the US as a government of laws; and that, to preserve its strength, the legal services program must be kept free from the influence of or use by it of political pressures.

This Declaration of Purpose unequivocally established an approach to legal services and to the right to justice compatible with methodological individualism. The Act expressly set out to enable indigent Americans to obtain a reasonable individual access to civil justice, given the constraint of the Corporation's annual budget appropriation. Nowhere in the Act is there support for the use of Corporation monies to reform the common law or the law of legislation through organized litigation or political lobbying. Indeed, the Act expressly forbids the use of political pressure and in this matter reflects the Hatch Act which makes it illegal to utilize federal monies to lobby the federal government. The Corporation itself, as a non-federal organization, is not subject to the Hatch Act.

The Corporation was established by Section 1003 (a) of the Act of 1974 as a private, non-membership, non-profit corporation, located in the District of Columbia, for the purpose of providing financial support for legal assistance in non-criminal proceedings or matters to persons financially unable to afford legal assistance.

The Governing Body of the Corporation is a Board of Directors consisting of 11 voting members appointed by the President with the advice and consent of the Senate. No more than six such members can be of the same political party and a majority must be members of the bar of the highest court of any state. No member can be a full-time employee of the United States. The 1977 amendment further requires that Board membership should include eligible clients, be representative of the organized bar, of attorneys providing legal assistance to eligible clients and to the general public. The distribution of so many constituencies across such a small Board would tax the ingenuity of the most harmonious appointment mechanism. Under the less than harmonious circumstances of the 1980s, as we shall show, the process of effecting Board appointments was to encounter significant difficulties.

The term of office of each member of the Board is set at three years. Members appointed to vacancies arising within a term of office are appointed for the remainder of that term. No member can be reappointed to more than two consecutive terms immediately following an initial term of office. The chairman of the Board is elected annually from among the voting members of the Board. Board members may be removed by a vote of at least seven members, only for malfeasance in office, for persistent neglect of or inability to discharge duties, or for offenses involving moral turpitude.

The Governor of each State appoints an advisory council for that State to the Board, consisting of nine members. A majority of such members are appointed, following recommendations from the State bar association, from among the attorneys admitted to practice in the State. Such memberships are subject to annual review. The advisory council is charged with notifying the Corporation of any apparent violation of the statute.

All meetings of the Board, of any executive committee of the Board, and of any advisory council, are open and subject to the relevant requirements and provisions of the United States code relating to open meetings. The Board must meet at least four times during each calendar year.

It is the responsibility of the Board to appoint the President of the Corporation, who must be a member of the bar of the highest court of a state. The President is a non-voting, ex-officio member of the Board. Other officers may be appointed as the Board determines to be necessary. All officers serve at the pleasure of the Board and may receive remuneration from any source other than the Corporation only at the authorization of the Board. The President, subject to the general policies established by the Board, may appoint and remove employees as he determines to be necessary. No political test or political qualification is to be used in any aspect of the Corporation's activities, including employment policies.

The Act explicitly determines that the officers and employees of the Corporation are not to be considered federal employees, and that the Corporation is not to be considered a department, agency or instrumentality of the Federal Government. However, Federal Government rules concerning compensation for work injuries, retirement, life insurance and health insurance are applicable. Moreover, the Office of Management and Budget retains authority to review and submit comments upon the Corporation's annual budget request at the time it is transmitted to the Congress. In essence, the Legal Services Corporation is a quasi-governmental organization and not a part of the Executive Branch of the United States Government.

The Act authorizes the Corporation to provide financial assistance to qualified programs furnishing legal assistance to eligible clients and to make grants to and contracts with: (i) individuals, partnerships, firms, corporations, and non-profit organizations, and (ii) State and local governments where in the Board's view the services will not be provided adequately through non-governmental organizations. Such grants and contracts must be for the purpose of providing legal assistance to eligible clients and/or must otherwise be necessary to carry out the purpose and provisions of the Act. In addition, the Corporation is authorized to undertake research, training and technical assistance, and to act as a clearinghouse for information either directly or by grant or contract, in areas relating to the delivery of legal assistance. The Act establishes no priorities over these varied responsibilities.

The Corporation is enjoined by the Act to allow attorneys providing legal assistance to the poor full rights to carry out professional responsibilities as established in the Canons of Ethics and the Code of Professional Responsibility of the American Bar Association. Nor can the Corporation deny to attorneys in supported programs the authority of a State or other jurisdiction to enforce generally applied standards of professional responsibility. This enjoinment is evidently designed to protect individual attorney–client relationships from adverse political or bureaucratic pressure. To receive compensation under the Act, attorneys must be admitted, or otherwise authorized, to practise law.

The Act specifically requires the Corporation to ensure that its employees and all recipients of legal assistance monies do not engage in political activities:

> The Corporation shall insure that (A) no employee of the Corporation or of any recipient ..., while carrying out legal assistance activities under this title, engage in, or encourage others to engage in, any public demonstration or picketing, boycott, or strike; and (B) no such employee shall, at any time, engage in, or encourage others to engage in, any of the following activities: (i) any rioting or civil disturbance, (ii) any activity which is in violation of an outstanding injunction of any court of competent jurisdiction, (iii) any other illegal activity, or (iv) any intentional identification of the Corporation or any recipient with any political activity prohibited by section 1007 (a) (6)

The Corporation is prohibited by the Act from participating in litigation on behalf of any client other than itself. Nor must it undertake to influence the passage or defeat of any legislation by the Congress of the United States or by any State or local legislative body, except for communications requested by such legislative bodies in connection with legislation or appropriation directly affecting the activities of the Corporation. Nor may the Corporation, or any recipient, contribute corporate funds, program personnel, or equipment to any political party or association, or to the campaign of any candidate for public or party office, for advocating or opposing any ballot measures, initiatives, or referenda.

In an evident attempt to restrain individual attorneys from engaging in social engineering, the Act directs that no class action suit, class action appeal, or amicus curiae class action may be undertaken, directly or through others, by a staff attorney, except with the express approval of a project director of a recipient. The Act prohibits employed attorneys, with minor exceptions, from providing legal assistance without reasonable compensation. Finally, employees of the Corporation and its recipients are denied the right intentionally to identify the Corporation or the recipient with any partisan or non-partisan political activity associated with a political party or association, or the campaign of any candidate for public or party office. Nor may staff attorneys be candidates in a partisan political election.

The Corporation is required to ensure the maintenance of the highest quality of service and professional standards, the preservation of attorney–client relationships, and to protect the integrity of the adversary process from impairment in furnishing legal assistance to eligible clients. In consultation with the Director of the Office of Management and Budget, and with the governors of the several states, the Corporation is required to establish maximum income levels (taking into account family size, urban and rural differences, and substantial cost-of-living variations) for individuals eligible for legal assistance.

The Corporation is further required by the Act to ensure that eligibility of clients for legal assistance is determined by recipients on the basis of factors that must include (i) the liquid assets and income level of the client, (ii) the fixed debts, medical expenses and other factors which affect the clients' ability to pay, (iii) the cost of living in the locality, and (iv) such other factors as relate to financial inability to afford legal assistance (e.g. unwillingness to work).

The Corporation must further ensure: (i) that recipients adopt procedures, consistent with the goals of the Corporation, for determining and implementing priorities in the provision of assistance; (ii) that appropriate training and support services are provided to those significant segments of the population with special difficulties of access and/or special legal problems (e.g. the elderly and the handicapped; (iii) that grants and contracts are effected so as to provide economical and effective legal assistance to individuals both in rural and in urban areas; and (iv) that attorneys employed full time in legal assistance activities refrain from any compensated outside practice of law and any uncompensated practice except where the Corporation so authorizes. These requirements are designed to ensure that recipient programs and their employees will be monitored effectively by the Corporation.

The concern of the legislature that legal service monies might be diverted into political action is strongly evident in the clauses of the Act requiring the Corporation to monitor and prevent diversions of this kind. Such funds are not to be used to influence federal, state or local executive orders, or congressional, state or local legislation or state proposals by initiative petition save where individual clients request assistance concerning relevant legal rights, or relevant agencies request recipients to testify, draft or review measures, or if measures would affect directly the activities of participating recipients.

The Corporation is enjoined to ensure that all attorneys engaged in legal services activities supported in whole or in part by the Corporation should refrain from any political activity, from providing transportation to the polls or from any voter registration activity other than in the form of legal advice and representation. The Corporation must also ensure that all such attorneys refrain from the persistent incitement of litigation; from any other activity prohibited by the Canons of Ethics and Code of Professional Responsibility of the American Bar Association; and from personal representation for a private fee in any cases in which they were involved while engaged in legal assistance activities.

Section 1007 (b) (5) and (6) of the Act prescribes the Corporation itself from funding training programs for the purpose of advocating particular public policies, encouraging, political or labor-related activities, boycotts, picketing, strikes and demonstrations or from making grants to or contracts with any private law firm which expends 50 per cent or more of its resources and time litigating in the broad interests of a majority of the public. These restrictions reflect fears within the legislature that legal services monies might be subverted away from legitimate litigation on behalf of individuals in favor of political activism by special interest groups.

The Act establishes a range of safeguards designed to ensure the integrity of the recipient programs. The Corporation is required to ensure that any recipient organized solely for the purpose of providing legal assistance to eligible clients is governed by a body of at least 60 per cent of which consists of attorneys who are members of the bar of a state in which the legal assistance is to be provided. Waivers are available only for carefully defined demographic reasons. Any attorney serving on such a board is denied compensation from any recipient.

The Corporation is mandated by the Act to monitor and to evaluate, and to provide for independent evaluations of, programs supported in whole or in part under the Act to ensure that all provisions, bylaws, rules, regulations and guidelines stipulated by the Act or arising from the Act are carried out.

The Corporation is entitled under the Act to terminate or to suspend financial assistance and to deny refunding applications provided that reasonable notice is given together with an opportunity to show why such action should not be taken via a timely, full and fair hearing. Upon request, such a hearing, to be conducted by an independent hearing examiner, must be held prior to any decision by the Corporation to terminate financial assistance or to deny funding. Hearing examiners are appointed by the Corporation.

The Act of 1974 authorized an appropriation to the Legal Services Corporation of $20 million for fiscal year 1975, $100 million for fiscal year 1976 and such sums as may be necessary for fiscal year 1977. The 1977 Amendment authorized an appropriation of $205 million for the fiscal year 1978, and such sums as may be necessary for each of the two succeeding fiscal years. Appropriations can be made for not more than two fiscal years at a time and are to be paid to the Corporation in annual instalments at the beginning of each fiscal year in such amounts as may be specified in Acts of Congress making appropriations. The funds thus appropriated remain available across fiscal years until fully expended. A maximum of 10 per cent of the amount appropriated is available for research, training and technical assistance.

Non-Federal funds received by the Corporation, and funds received by any recipient from a source other than the Corporation, must be accounted for and reported as receipts and disbursements separate and distinct from Federal funds. Any such funds so received for the provision of legal assistance must not be expended by recipients for any purpose prohibited by the Act.

3 Towards a theory of bureaucratic behavior

The early theories of bureaucracy tended to be dominated by Weberian notions of impartial, efficient service by government officials concerned to serve the public interest as interpreted by their elected government (Weber, 1947). Economists who preached market failure and demanded government intervention were only too happy to rely upon government servants effectively to implement, as neutered eunuchs, the public policies that their recommendations support.

Early challenges to this public interest model stemmed from Parkinson (1957), Tullock (1965) and Downs (1967) who both analyzed the internal organization of bureaucracy, noting the inevitable loss of information (control loss) associated with such command structure forms of economic organization (Breton and Wintrobe, 1975, 1982). However, it was only in 1971 that Tullock's student, Niskanen, subjected bureaucracy to a comprehensive economic critique which encompassed both its internal organization and its external environment, and which raised serious questions concerning predictable allocative and technical inefficiency in bureaucratic supply.

Although subsequent research (Rowley and Elgin, 1985) has indicated that Niskanen may have underestimated the ability of the legislature to control bureaucratic behavior, thus eroding the principal–agent problem implicit in Niskanen's model, this chapter will focus attention upon those features of the theories of Downs and Niskanen which are directly relevant to the behavior or the Legal Services Corporation, namely the role of ideology within the bureau and the attitude of the bureau towards its budget determination.

A bureau is defined, in the sense of Niskanen (1971), as a public sector organization in which no individual can appropriate any part of the difference between revenues and costs as direct personal income, and in which a significant part of the recurring revenues derive from other than the sale of output at a per-unit price. In such circumstances, self-seeking senior bureaucrats will evidence an interest in any surplus of revenues over costs only if such surpluses can be utilized in ways that augment their individual utilities and are not subject to mandatory confiscation by the government. Since they supply output in markets predictably characterized by excess demand they will evidence little concern about satisfying the detailed preferences of their customers. In contrast, they may well evidence considerable interest over the composition of factor inputs, most particularly labor, not in pursuit of technical efficiency, but rather to augment their respective utilities by indulging non-market-related personal preferences (Orzechowski, 1977; Peacock, 1979b).

If bureaucrats are not the neutered eunuchs of Max Weber's vision, attention shifts to their personal motivations as an indispensible prerequisite for predicting their responses to the reward–cost structure that confronts them in their bureaucratic environments. Although there are differences in emphasis on this issue between Downs and Niskanen, a synthesis is here provided that emphasizes the rational self-seeking postulate of the VPE research program without relying exclusively upon the narrow goal of expected wealth maximization.

All the agents in the VPE theory of bureaucracy are assumed to be utility maximizers, rationally pursuing their own individual objectives. The implications of this axiom for behavior, once the components of an individual's utility are identified, are ambiguous only where there is a conflict between short- and long-run self-interest and where it is not possible to predict a priori which time horizon will dominate his behavior. Otherwise, it is predictable that individuals will respond positively or negatively to any adjustment (downwards or upwards respectively) in the price of an act measured in the relevant coinage of each and every argument in his utility function.

Almost all individuals have multiple goals, and there is no reason a priori to assume otherwise in the case of bureaucrats, though the fact that they have chosen government over free market employment is indicative of a mind-set that differentiates them as a species from other agents. Among the wide range of motives that are conceivable the following are likely to play an important role:

1. Power (both inside and outside the bureau);
2. Money income;
3. Security (defined as a low probability of loss of power and income);
4. Perquisites of office (particularly important because of inability to divert surplus into money income);

5. The easy life (ability to evade the work ethic as well as ease of management);
6. Patronage (used to pursue objectives (1–5);
7. Desire to serve the public interest as individually perceived;
8. Commitment to a specific program of action.

Although the temptation is to categorize motives (1–6) as purely selfish and motives (7–8) as altruistic (Downs, 1967), this is unacceptable in VPE analysis. All goals pursued by individuals are selfish, including those that have the appearance of altruism. The inability of the public interest research program to recognize this fundamental aspect of rational behavior has been a principal cause of its failure as a predictor of non-market decision making. The CPE research program avoids the problem by collapsing utility into wealth maximization alone, which is an excessively narrow approach.

Although eight different motives have been identified as potential components of a bureaucrat's utility function, not all officials are influenced, either absolutely or at the margin, to the same degree by each motive. Five particular combinations can be identified, each typical of a certain kind of bureaucrat, and each signalling a particular set of predictable responses to changes in the external environment (Downs, 1967). The distinctions between these categories turn out to be particularly important in reviewing the behavior of senior bureaucrats within the Legal Services Corporation and in conditionally predicting future behavior in the absence of major institutional reform.

Two categories (labelled climbers or conservers) are identified by reason of their strong preference for some combination of motives (1–6) over the lower valued motives (7 and 8). Climbers consider power, income and prestige as almost exclusively important in their value structures. Conservers consider security perquisites of office, the easy life and patronage as particularly important and seek to conserve rather than to extend existing power and money income.

Mixed motive bureaucrats (labeled zealots, advocates or statesmen) pursue goals that combine motives (1–6) with motives (7) and (8). Such bureaucrats are distinguished by the breadth of the wider values to which they are loyal. *Zealots* are loyal to relatively narrow policies or concepts. They seek power both for its own sake and to effect the policies to which they are loyal. These policies are designated by Downs as sacred policies. *Advocates* are loyal to a broader set of functions or to a broader organization than are zealots. They also seek power in order to influence significantly policies and actions concerning such functions or organizations. *Statesmen* are loyal to society as a whole and seek power in order to influence significantly national policies and actions. They seek utility for themselves by augmenting the general welfare as they conceive it and adjust the behavior of their bureaus to the extent feasible in support of this objective.

All the officials in this theory of bureaucracy are either climbers, conservers, zealots, advocates or statesmen. This classification will be utilized as an effective lens for reviewing the changing bureaucracy of the Legal Services Corporation since its inception in 1974. It will be contended that the institutional structure of the Corporation has exposed it to more than a customary share of zealots and advocates, and has inhibited climbers and statesmen from seeking it out as a vehicle for their goals. As always in bureaucracy, conservers have played a role, though not acting decisively to exert a major impact on program direction. Conservers lack the entrepreneurial drive to seek out new directions but rather consolidate an existing and well-established policy direction.

Economists, for the most part, center attention upon narrow self-interest as the principal motivating force in individual behavior, paying little attention to ideology, even categorizing it as irrational (Barzel and Silverberg, 1973). The VPE research program takes issue with this viewpoint, at least for political market analysis, and recognizes an important role for ideological preferences which are viewed as rational and as responsive to economic signals (Kalt and Zupan, 1984). Given the discretion frequently available to actions in political markets, as a consequence of imperfect information and rational ignorance, ideological preferences predictably will influence the nature of equilibrium in political markets, not least, it will be argued, in the market for legal services.

An ideology is defined as a consistent set of beliefs held by an individual and/or a consistent set of such an individual's normative statements, concerning preferred or best states of the world. Such beliefs or statements amount to political ideology when they are held to be applicable to all members of society rather than to the individual who holds or utters th n exclusively (Kalt and Zupan, 1984). In both cases, ideology is an exclusively selfish motive. Those who profess to care for others do so because such caring augments their own utilities.

A bureaucrat may be motivated by political ideology for a variety of underlying reasons. First, the successful promotion of such ideology, if the cost is not excessive in terms of foregone narrowly selfish objectives, provides direct utility in the knowledge that his vision of the good has been visited on others. Second, even the unsuccessful promotion of ideology, again if the cost is not excessive, may imbue the bureaucrat with utility gain derived from the knowledge of having 'done the right thing'. This second utility gain may hold even when pursuit of ideology from the outset was anticipated to be a lost cause. In all such cases, ideological pursuits are entirely rational given the utility functions of bureaucrats thus defined.

There are important reasons to suppose that ideology will play a more important role in individual action in political markets than in private markets, even ignoring the self-selection bias evident in the choice by an individual to specialize in the one or the other environment.

First, if individuals are successful in achieving political objectives the publicness characteristics of such outcomes typically assure them of the apparatus of government to monitor and enforce their ideological preferences. By hijacking policy, successful ideologues can often require outsiders to finance benefits delivered to the group(s) that they target. Political objectives may be difficult to attain but the expected returns to those skilled in political action may well be very high. Because bureaus are privileged with protection from competition such rents may not be transient but rather may remain as significant stimuli to internal rent-seeking within the bureau.

Second, although the pecuniary gain associated with collective action is often low, eroded by the publicness characteristics of successful policy initiatives, ideological returns retain almost strictly private good characteristics. In itself, this will bias behavior in bureaus towards ideological and away from pecuniary objectives, given the constraints imposed upon them.

Bureaucrats are constrained in their behavior by the legislation which defines the scope of their bureau, and by the monitoring of that legislation achieved by their principals in the legislative and executive branches of the federal government. They are also constrained by the size and composition of their budget. Since senior bureaucrats can influence the nature of this latter constraint in their negotiations with the relevant appropriations committees of Congress, it is predictable that the annual budgetary process will preoccupy a significant proportion of their energies.

Ignoring the role of ideology, momentarily, it can be argued that the principal components of a senior bureaucrat's utility function – power, money income, security, perquisites of office and patronage – are all positive monotonic functions of budget size and that an additional component – the easy life – is a positive monotonic function of the budget's rate of growth (Niskanen, 1971). In such circumstances, narrowly selfish bureaucrats, despite widely differing motivations, will coalesce with each other in seeking out a large and rapidly growing budget, though, as we shall demonstrate, they may not always seek the maximum size or rate of budgetary growth available, given the preferences of their principals in the legislature (Niskanen, 1975).

At issue in this tension over budget policy is the precise balance struck among members of the top-level bureaucracy between those seeking money income, security and the easy life, which rest predominantly on budget size and rate of growth, and those seeking power, perquisites of office and patronage which rest predominantly on the discretionary budget that remains once the total cost of the bureau's output has been accounted for. Furthermore, since all bureaucrats are rational, the balance between budget size and budget discretion ultimately pursued by their bureau will depend not only upon the distribution of underlying preferences, but also upon the particular reward/cost environment within which they act.

To illustrate, let us suppose that the utility function of each senior bureaucrat takes the form

$$U = \alpha_1 \, Y^{\beta_1} \, P^{\gamma_1} \tag{6.1}$$

where Y is the present value of personal income, security and the easy life, P is the present value of power, perquisites of office and patronage, and where β_1 and γ_1 differ according to individual predisposition, though the common reward structure predictably leads the set of bureaucrats to have a relatively high preference for P.

Further suppose that the reward structure confronting such bureaucrats takes the form

$$Y = \alpha_2 \, Q^{\beta_2} \, (B-C)^{\gamma_2} \tag{6.2a}$$

and

$$P = \alpha_3 \, Q^{\beta_3} \, (B-C)^{\gamma_3} \tag{6.2b}$$

where Q is the output of the bureau (measured for example in the case of legal services as the number of cases closed), B is the maximum budget that would be approved by the legislature, C is the minimum cost of producing the output of the bureau and B–C is thus the discretionary budget.

A specific theory of bureaucrats' budgetary behavior must be based on the characteristics of equations 6.1 and 6.2. For example, a bureaucrat's reward structure is characterized by a relatively low value of γ_2 since the budget residual cannot be diverted into personal income. The parameters β_2, β_3 and γ_3 however, tend to be relatively high. If the β terms are low throughout the three equations and the γ terms are relatively high, the senior bureaucrats will opt for a budget size that maximizes the discretionary budget and which falls well short of the maximum budget technically available. In contrast, if the β terms are high and the γ terms are low, the maximum budget will be pursued, in the limit, at the sacrifice of all budgetary discretion. In the case of the demand-constrained bureau (Niskanen, 1971), bureaucrats face a genuine choice between budget size and budgetary discretion, with their choices determined by the precise nature of equations 6.1 and 6.2. In the case of the budget-constrained bureau, there is no ultimate choice available since the only feasible budget excludes discretion and imposes a bureau output at which total revenue equals total cost. Predictably, bureaucrats lobby the legislature to avoid the budget-constrained scenario.

If ideology becomes important within the top bureaucracy, as arguments (7) and (8) above (p. 99) are activated within their utility functions, the budgetary policy of the bureau will shift. For example, if bureaucrats are imbued with a strong preference for the output of the bureau, they may forego budgetary discretion, even where they place a positive value upon it, and seek a maximum budget that provides a net utility gain. Alternatively, if ideology demands that non-output-related budgetary outlays be made, budgetary discretion becomes yet more important and constrained outcomes will be avoided. Finally, if ideology requires that the bureau's entire activities should be curtailed, senior bureaucrats may pursue policies of budgetary reduction, even of bureau elimination, notwithstanding the negative implications of such ideological pursuits for the narrowly selfish arguments in their utility functions. The pursuit of ideology by bureaucratic agents in defiance of the reward structure established by the legislature may raise serious principal–agent problems. These problems will be exacerbated when the agents reflect the ideological preferences of the executive branch which itself is in conflict with the legislature (Weingast, 1981; Rowley and Vachris, 1990). The problem of multi-principal conflict, which manifested itself in legal services throughout the period 1980–1988, has been only recently researched in the public choice literature (see Chapter 7).

4   The predictable behavior of legal services bureaucrats
The Legal Services Corporation was established as a private, non-profit corporation in 1974 following a protracted political debate which centered upon alleged misbehavior, if not actual malfeasance, by its forerunner, the Office of Economic Opportunity. The OEO legal services program obtained federal funding by committing itself to a program of legal aid for poor Americans. Its bureaucracy, motivated for the most part by liberal democratic ideology, tainted by Marxism at the fringes, became 'dominated by a desire to be something different from traditional legal aid' (Houseman, 1986). Specifically, senior bureaucrats responsible for program development saw 'an important need to capture a piece of the movement for social and economic reform' (Houseman, 1986, p. 2).

Thus, whereas legal aid was viewed at that time by the American Bar Association as the lawyers' Red Cross, and supported by that body on the basis of Judge Learned Hand's admonition: 'Thou shalt not ration justice', legal services came to be viewed by its major purveyors as a central element in the war on poverty. As Attorney General Katzenbach observed as early as 1964, when the OEO program was in its infancy, a new breed of lawyers was emerging dedicated to using the law as an instrument of orderly and constructive social change. In fact, many of those lawyers were Marxists who invaded the legal services program in disproportionate numbers, accentuating the reformist thrust initiated by the senior bureaucrats, and channelling legal aid monies into a carefully constructed program of social engineering targeted against the family, capitalism and ultimately Madisonian republicanism itself. By 1967, the second Director of OEO legal services, Earl Johnson, himself an activist, defined the primary goal of his program as being:

> to bring about changes in the structure of the world in which the poor people live in order to provide on the largest scale possible consistent with our limited resources a legal system in which the poor enjoy the same treatment as the rich. *Law reform can provide the most bang for the buck ...*

For reasons chronicled in Chapter 1, the first era of activist law reform, fuelled by the successful movement for civil rights, had over-reacted by the early 1970s, and had alienated itself from a growingly conservative legislature. The 1974 Legal Services Corporation Act was designed to curtail significantly, if not entirely to eliminate, social engineering within the legal services program and to re-emphasize in unambiguous language the primacy of pursuing equal access to justice for the poor to the extent possible given budgetary limitations.

Let us imagine that the Legal Services Corporation would have been manned by a public interest motivated senior bureaucracy dedicated to the pursuit of its legislative responsibilities throughout the period 1975 to 1988. Its behavior predictably would have been sharply at variance with that revealed in this book, and there would have been none of the political market upheaval that its aberrant behavior in fact invoked.

First, the Corporation unequivocally and unwaveringly would have pursued policies of extending access to civil justice to poor Americans, and would have dedicated its total budget, other than minimal office maintenance expenditures, to this clear-cut objective. Second, it would have eschewed all financial and propaganda support to interest groups involved in law reform, whether through lobbying or sustained litigation and would have closed off all contracts to grantees that illegally lobbied for law reform. Third, it would have subjected to close and critical scrutiny, with a view to contract termination, all grantees seen to utilize the class action suit, the class action appeal or amicus curiae class action suits as a principal rather than as a secondary form of legal services instrument.

Fourth, it would have instituted effective monitoring techniques designed to foreclose quickly on low quality or inefficient grantees. Fifth, it would have established contracts designed to ensure equal access to all poor Americans, disciplining programs that discriminated instead in favor of privileged minorities. Sixth, it would have honored the Green Amendment, rather than lobbying for its removal, and would have foreclosed quickly on all national support centers as illegitimate breeding grounds for illegal lobbying behavior.

The evidence outlined in this book unequivocally falsifies this public interest theory bureaucracy. The reasons for this failure are to be found in the particular characteristics of the Legal Services Corporation. The organization structure, and the reward system, established by the 1974 Act and by the US Congress, was conducive neither to public interested pursuit of statutory goals nor to acquiescence to the priorities of the legislature by the legal services' top bureaucrats. In both regards, policy distortions were entirely predictable in terms of the VPE theory of bureaucracy.

The Corporation itself, at the insistence of an American Bar Association alarmed by the dismantling of the OEO program by the Nixon White House, was established independently from the executive branch of government, which was provided only with minimal rights of commenting on its budget recommendations. Its independent status protected it from the Hatch Act, which renders it illegal to utilize federal monies to lobby the federal government and the legislature, and from other legislation designed to expose non-statutory behavior to criminal proceedings. These provisions alone marked out a predictable window of opportunity for illegal, aberrant bureaucratic behavior.

If statutory independence offered the opportunity for deviance, the employment characteristics of the senior LSC bureaucrats provided predictable incentives for such behavior. The Board of Directors of the Corporation is composed exclusively of part-time bureaucrats remunerated for Board duties at rates of pay significantly below those that can be commanded even by mediocre attorneys in private practice or by middle management career executives. Payment, moreover, is made on the basis of time allocated to Board responsibilities, without any bonus for good performance and without any penalty for deviance or sloth. In terms of narrowly selfish motivations, the more highly remunerated Board members will minimize their contributions to LSC activities, whereas those who are poorly remunerated elsewhere (notably the minority and consumer representatives) will attempt to stack up hours served in order to claim attractive rates of reimbursement.

Given the system of remuneration, individuals who are highly talented and narrowly selfish in their goals will simply refuse to serve as LSC directors unless such positions can be utilized to secure lucrative post-LSC careers either within public interest law firms or elsewhere. By self-selection, therefore, the LSC Board of Directors will be a prime hunting ground for the ideologue and the rent-seekers, to the extent that the ideologies involved do not run aground on the political rocks of the nomination and advice and consent route to office. If ideology and rent-seeking are thus the dominant motives of those who join the Board of Directors, this does not preclude a potential role for a reward structure targeted at more narrow self-interest, for individuals respond to incentives on all margins, not only on those that loom especially large in their utility functions.

Since the members of the Board serve part-time, the President of the Corporation, who is appointed by and serves at the pleasure of the Board as a full-time appointment, predictably exercises significant authority, inevitably over matters of day-to-day administration, but even over policy, though he serves as a non-voting member of the Board. The President, who must be a member of the bar of the highest court of a state, is relatively poorly remunerated with a salary that cannot exceed level V of the Executive Schedule specified in section 5316 of title 5, United States Code. Predictably, therefore, individuals available for this position will be either of mediocre calibre or motivated primarily by ideology.

The President of the Corporation is endowed with considerable managerial discretion, which tends to be widened by the part-time nature and infrequent meetings of the Board of Directors. In particular, he is authorized to make grants and to enter into contracts, to monitor and evaluate supported programs, to initiate and to respond to independent audits of such programs, and to initiate defunding procedures against non-compliant programs. In the hands of a climber or a conserver, and under the surveillance of a statesmanlike Board, such discretionary power would pose little threat to the statute and its mission. In the hands of advocates or zealots, however, the threat to the statute is evident, as experience during the years 1981 and 1982 unequivocally demonstrated.

7 The two ends of the avenue

> Then everything includes itself in power,
> Power into will, will into appetite;
> And appetite, an universal wolf,
> So doubly seconded with will and power,
> Must make, perforce, an universal prey,
> and last, eat up himself.
>
> William Shakespeare

1 Introduction

The purpose of this chapter is to model the relationship between the Legal Services Corporation, the United States Congress and the United States Presidency. These relationships have become important, and indeed controversial, because of the perceived political importance of the Legal Services Corporation as a purveyor of legal services policy to impoverished US citizens.

This perceived importance is no figment of the imagination of those who inhabit the two ends of Pennsylvania Avenue, but rather is the inescapable consequence of the peculiar nature of the Corporation as a quasi-governmental organization. First, the Corporation is the largest organization in the US representing legal action on behalf of the poor. The attorneys supported by its grants and contracts widely are viewed as experts, specialized in the law of poverty. For this reason alone, the Corporation is viewed as an important institution in the debate on poverty and its resolution, a debate which attracts significant constituencies that exert their own influence on the Congress and the Presidency.

From its inception, the Legal Services Corporation was viewed by influential advocates as catering for 'an economic class of poor people and not just individuals who happen to be poor' (Houseman, 1986). Clinton Bamberger, a former Vice President of the corporation, described legal services as 'voice for the poor in the community' (Houseman, 1986). This philosophy inevitably implied that Congress and the Presidency would be lobbied by constituencies both hostile to and supportive of the poor; and that they, in turn, would respond by accentuated surveillance of the Corporation and its programs.

Second, the attorneys employed on grants and contracts dispersed by the Legal Services Corporation, by their choice of cases to litigate, are in a position not only to ensure that the existing law is or is not applied with respect to poor individuals, but also to reform the law itself, by establishing or shifting precedents. In this respect, the lawsuit does not merely clarify the meaning of the law, remitting the parties to private ordering of their affairs, but itself establishes a regime ordering the future interaction of the parties and absentees as well. The class action suit, the class action appeal and the amicus curiae class action suit have become powerful weapons utilized to such ends by legal services attorneys.

The Legal Services Corporation, therefore, is a bureau capable of enforcing, establishing and reforming the law of poverty. Acting ostensibly on behalf of the poor, the Corporation, nevertheless, is free to follow its own criteria in determining what is right and best, from the particular perspectives of its senior bureaucrats. Its grant and contract recipients are also relatively unfettered in the criteria that they establish for litigation, despite increased monitoring efforts since 1982 by the Legal Services Corporation and other government agencies. It is a matter of no surprise, in such circumstances, that the Congress and the Presidency eye the Corporation with more than a paternal interest, since they are the principal recipients of electoral and constituency pressures that are both proactive and reactive with respect to legal services activities.

The Legal Services Corporation was established by the 1974 Act as a private, non-membership, non-profit corporation, exempt from taxation under section 501 (a) of the Internal Revenue Code. As such, it was entirely independent of the executive branch of the United States Government, except only that the President exercised the right to nominate individuals to serve on its Board of Directors. The President's Office of Management and Budget has no authority over the Corporation's annual budget request to Congress, but can provide its own comment on such budget requests. The Corporation is also required to publish an annual report to be filed both with the President and with the Congress detailing a description of services that it has provided. The audited accounts of the Corporation must be filed with the General Accounting Office and must satisfy rules established by the Comptroller General of the United States, who must report the audit to the Congress and the President.

The Act authorizes the Congress to appropriate funds to the Corporation to enable it to carry out it statutory duties for fiscal years 1975 through 1980. Although authorizing legislation lapsed in 1980 and has yet to be re-enacted, the Corporation has received annual appropriations from the Congress throughout the period of its existence. The Act stipulates that funds appropriated remain available to the Corporation until expended, and that unexpended surpluses, therefore, are not returnable annually to the US Treasury. The Congress has the authority to attach spending instructions to its appropriations bills, and thus to intervene directly in the affairs of the Corporation. The President, in contrast, can only intervene indirectly through his powers of nomination to the Corporation's Board of Directors and through the moral suasion powers of his office.

The Judiciary Committee exercises oversight authority with respect to the Legal Services Corporation in the House of Representatives and the Subcommittee on Courts, Civil Liberties and the Administration of Justice was responsible for appropriations recommendations prior to the 101st Congress, when such responsibility switched to the Subcommittee on Administrative Law and Governmental Relations. The Committee on Labor and Human Resources exercises oversight in the Senate and the Subcommittee on Commerce, Justice and the State, the Judiciary, and Related Agencies is responsible for appropriations.

2   Towards a theory of the behavior of the US Congress

In this section, a VPE theory of the relationship between the US Congress and its electoral constituency on the one hand and between the US Congress and the Legal Services Corporation on the other is set out. In this perspective, the Congress is analysed primarily as the broker of policies that are developed elsewhere, though it is acknowledged that the ideologies of influential members of the Congress periodically may be visited upon specific aspects of the legal services program. Overall, the relationships thus analysed are predicted to result in government failure with respect both to the distortion of voters' preferences and to loss of control over the behavior of the Legal Services Corporation. The VPE theory, in these important respects, is sharply at odds both with the public interest theory of government and with the CPE research program.

The relationship between Congress and the median voter

A general VPE theory of the relationship between Congress and its electorate was sketched out in Chapter 5. In part because the vote mechanism does not conform to the necessary conditions for the median voter theorem to hold, and in part because voters themselves are viewed to be rationally ignorant concerning the affairs of politics, the median voter equilibrium was seen to be only an occasional and transient feature of political markets. The Congress itself was not viewed as exercising significant discretionary power as a consequence of this failure of the vote motive, but rather was seen to be controlled by the lobbying of those interest groups that most effectively were able to overcome the publicness characteristics of their outputs and/or to avoid the associated free-rider problem within their memberships.

The logic of collective action which underpins the VPE theory of interest group behavior establishes a strong presumption of policy distortions away from median voter preferences as politicians respond to asymmetric lobbying pressures that favor the small, well-organized professional and producer groups and which disadvantage the large, diffuse, amorphous consumer interests. In such circumstances, the nexus between the voters and their legislative representatives predictably is marred by a serious principal–agent problem which existing governance structures do not effectively resolve.

The interest-group approach to politics implies that the behavior of politicians within given political institutions is most effectively analysed by application of the self-interest axiom. The important difference between the market and politics in this perspective does not lie in differences in individual motivations, but rather in the different constraints that confront self-interested agents (McCormick and Tollison, 1981). The market setting is a proprietary setting where individuals bear the consequences of their actions directly in terms of changes in their net worth. The political setting, in contrast, is a non-proprietary setting where individuals do not bear the full economic consequences of their decisions. Behavioral differences in the two settings reflect these significant differences in institutional constraints.

The principal–agent problem manifest in the relationship between voters and politicians is predictably far more serious than that between stockholders and managers of private firms precisely because of the absence of effective property rights in the former setting. The means available to voters to contain shirking by politicians are minimal and costly to implement, in sharp contrast to those through which stockholders control the management of private enterprise (McCormick and Tollison, 1981). Predictably, shirking, which manifests itself primarily in the asymmetric political influence wielded by powerful interest groups, is a pervasive feature of politicians' behavior.

The VPE research program analyses the behavior of politicians as brokers in the market in wealth transfers (and not in wealth creation). Legislators essentially are viewed as brokers matching the demanders and suppliers of wealth changes, embodied respectively as relatively strong and relatively weak interest groups, operating within the area of discretion opened up by rational ignorance within the voter population. Given the limited strength of the charitable impulse (Tullock, 1971, 1983a and b, 1986), the existence of a political market in wealth transfers must be predicated on the existence of certain information and transaction costs. In the absence of such costs, wealth would not be given up willingly by some individuals as transfers to others, nor would they accede willingly to the potential coercion of wealthy minorities implicit in majority vote or plurality vote systems of government.

The individual confronts two important types of information cost in seeking to promote or to prevent transfers. He must determine the effects of a political issue on his personal wealth; and he must identify and enjoin other individuals to concerted action on the issue. Several possibilities are relevant in this situation: (1) the winners and losers on an issue are well identified and know who each other are; (2) the winners and losers are not easily identified, either to themselves or to each other; (3) winners can be identified easily but losers cannot; (4) losers can be identified easily but winners cannot. The VPE prediction is that political transfers will occur disproportionately among categories (3) and (4) and that political brokers will have incentives to search for this type of issue. The legal services program is a perfect example of a type (3) issue.

Individuals who have organized themselves for reasons unrelated to lobbying enjoy a comparative advantage in seeking transfers, since organization costs, once borne, do not affect the marginal cost of lobbying. Groups that are characterized by such jointness in production and are able to produce political lobbying as a by-product of some other function will tend to be particularly successful in procuring transfers. If such groups exercise coercive powers over their memberships, as a consequence of legislation, and thus are able to avoid the free-rider problem associated with most forms of collective action, they must be viewed as formidable operators in the transfer market.

Politicians will expend resources in brokering a particular wealth transfer market in return for a brokerage fee which typically will take the form of some mixture of cash and promised votes. Once the market is in equilibrium, the brokerage fee will be paid continuously until some event dislodges the equilibrium, in which case politicians may be voted out of office, their policy platforms may change, and so forth, until a new political equilibrium emerges.

The VPE research program predicts that individuals from certain occupational backgrounds have a comparative advantage in political brokering in that they have a low reservation wage because they can combine legislative service efficiently with their primary employment. Predictably, such individuals will be the first to be hired (elected) into the legislature. Foremost among such occupational groups is the legal profession, despite the fact that its members may have high opportunity costs for serving, because they have a unique ability to internalize the outside returns from passing laws (McCormick and Tollison, 1981).

Rent-seeking agents of special interests groups can influence the lawyer–legislator because legal avenues to compensate lawyers exist that are not cheaply available to other occupations. Lawyer–legislators can maintain residual claims in their law firms while serving in the US Congress. Therefore, the congressman's law firm becomes a suitable avenue of compensation protected from close outside scrutiny by the tradition of attorney–client privilege. Furthermore, outside payments to lawyer–legislators may be paid for private legal services at rates well in excess of market norms without provoking questions of conflict of interest that would automatically be levelled at non-lawyer–legislators. Finally, lawyer–legislators can influence the

pattern of legislation to destabilize existing laws, thus creating for themselves or for their partners lucrative litigation opportunities at an insider
trading advantage over rivals who have not shared in the legislative process.

Conventional labor market theory, therefore, predicts that lawyers will be
represented disproportionately within the legislature both at the federal and
the state levels. The evidence amply sustains this prediction. Fully 47 per
cent of all members of the US Congress are attorneys, a proportion which
has varied only marginally throughout the postwar period. Lawyers further
comprise approximately 22 per cent of all state legislators (McCormick and
Tollison, 1981, p. 82).

VPE rejects the superficially attractive hypothesis that lawyers are elected
to legislatures as representatives of a special interest group (the American
Bar Association). While lawyers as an occupational class benefit from the
passage of many laws, all lawyers are free-riders in this context. Special
interests typically find it more efficient to organize and to lobby for their
rents than to try to elect a majority of their members to the legislature.
Despite predominance of lawyers in the US Congress, the American Bar
Association is no exception to this special interest lobbying rule. In the
particular case of legal services, however, as Chapter 14 will demonstrate,
the coincidence of a powerful ABA lobby and of lawyer domination of the
oversight and appropriations committees has proved to be highly protective
of a technically inefficient mechanism of wealth transfer.

McCormick and Tollison (1981, pp. 86–97) tested the theory that lawyer--
legislator representation is enhanced by low legislator pay and not by special
interest penetration of the legislature, utilizing 1975 data for all state legislatures. The results strongly supported their theory and thus also the VPE
perspective that the brokerage function is separable from the special interest
lobbying function in the political market place. This separation is maintained as a working hypothesis throughout the remainder of this book.

In a representative democracy, society has selected a method of choosing
political agents (approximating to one man–one vote) that does not lead to
efficient outcomes in the same sense that such outcomes are achieved in
private competitive markets. There is an evident principal–agent relationship problem between voters and politicians that is exploitable by interest
groups. Even the relationship between interest groups and politicians retains
similar, though less accentuated, problems as a consequence of the nature of
elections.

First, the right to run the government is not auctioned off to the highest
bidder. It is granted in a voting process, the characteristics of which vary
from country to country. As public choice has shown (McCormick and
Tollison, 1981) not only will the size of bids from potential political agents
to voters be important, but their distribution among voters will be crucial in

determining the outcome of majority voting processes (Liebowitz and Tollison, 1980). Therefore, the highest bidder will not necessarily win the contract.

Second, voters have no way between elections to liquidate their ownership rights in the output of government. They cannot extract payment from the politicians prior to productive activity, but must wait for in kind payments after the fact of production. As is well known, inalienability of property rights has serious inefficiency implications for the maintenance of productive activity (Alchian and Demsetz, 1972).

Third, politicians do not run separately issue by issue in electoral competition, but rather bundle policies, thus forcing voters to exercise indivisible choices. Such bundling presents opportunities for full-line forcing of policies which allow for the protection of unattractive programs by attaching them to highly attractive programs, save only where the conditions necessary for the multidimension median voter outcome hold in an unusually robust form (Rowley, 1984).

The relationship between Congress and the dominant interest groups
The CPE research program acknowledges the potential existence of principal–agent problems between interest groups and politicians in the determination and brokering of policy but suggests that such problems are eliminated by the development of a cost minimizing governance structure (Wittman, 1989). Since interest groups are viewed as minimizers of dead-weight social losses in an efficient transfer process, (Becker, 1983, 1985) the governance nexus that exists between such groups and politicians guarantees efficiency measured in terms of opportunity cost and also reflects the preferences of median voters.

The VPE research program rejects categorically the implications of Chicago's tight prior equilibrium modelling. As section 2 (a) has indicated the relationship between the median voter and his political agents at best is weak, in part as a consequence of rational ignorance, but in part also as a consequence of governance structures that leave considerable discretion to well-organized interest groups. The relationship between interest groups and their political agents, though markedly stronger, yet remains incomplete. Thus, although the VPE research program acknowledges the research of political scientists, working broadly within the Rochester research program (Mitchell, 1988b) and the work of economists working, broadly, within the transactions cost research program (Williamson, 1985b), both of which point to the emergence of governance structures to contain agency discretion, it rejects any notion that such structures are efficient.

Interest groups access the political market only with variable facility and at significant social cost measured in rent-seeking resource dissipation. Moreover, their grip upon the brokerage function itself, though undoubtedly strong, is loosened as a consequence of the imperfect property rights system that exists in the political market place (Rowley and Vachris, 1990). Furthermore, their methods of accessing representative government create monopoly in the brokerage function, by guaranteeing subservient incumbents continuation rights, and thus ensure a high cost legislature.

The governance structure resolution of the principal–agent problem between interest groups and the US legislature is a hypothesis that merits critical evaluation. In this hypothesis, legislative institutions provide an efficient nexus between principal and agent, designed to minimize transaction costs, based on three important characteristics of the United States Congress.

First, members of Congress represent the politically effective interests located within their district together with geographically dispersed interests prepared to finance their campaign expenditures. In this respect, rational ignorance underpins interest group advantages in targeting selected politicians. The lack of complete fungibility of votes, in a geographically segmented legislature, implies that legislators are particularly advantaged in attracting support from interest groups located in their district.

Second, it is relevant that political parties place few constraints on the behavior of individual party members. This is especially relevant since the late 1960s when party organizations began to lose control over the pattern of new entry, over positions of legislative authority, as distributors of legislative benefits and in the application of the party whip over vote divisions. Individual members now operate through committees paying at most a minor regard to party considerations (Weingast and Moran, 1983).

Third, although it is recognized that proposed bills must command, at the minimum, the support of an absolute majority of the vote in the legislature, in order to become law, the open and continuous nature of voting provides for such majorities to be logrolled form minority positions as the typical, rather than the unusual, legislative outcome. In such circumstances, the ambitious legislator must engage in exchange and cooperation to provide significant benefits to powerful constituent interests. The institutions of Congress have evolved to ensure the delivery of such benefits and to protect incumbents from outside electoral competition.

If all bills and their payoffs were known in advance, and if there were no random or unforeseen future events that might influence outcomes or payoffs, if the time dimension was suppressed and the enforcement of agreements over time unquestioned, there would be no need for an intricate governance structure to facilitate the market in logrolling. For this is the world of classical contracting, absent are all the problems of bounded rationality, opportunism and asset specificity that signal potential contract failure (Williamson, 1985b). This was the environment assumed by early equilibrium models of logrolling (Buchanan and Tullock, 1962) in which votes explicitly were bought and sold at prices that determined vote trades and the passage and failure of those bills that achieved legislative scrutiny. This model applies particularly well to pork-barrel politics in its crudest form, but much less well to the more complex politics of redistribution and regulation, where problems of non-contemporaneity and non-simultaneity are more pronounced (Ferejohn, 1974).

Suppose that two tradeable bills arise simultaneously in the Congress, but offer a non-contemporaneous flow of benefits, one a pork-barrel set immediately available and the other establishing an agency designed with a future flow of benefits in mind. A serious problem of opportunistic agency renegement arises once the immediate benefits have been received. In the absence of suitable governance facilities, trades across such margins would be predictably suboptimal.

Suppose, alternatively, that two potentially tradeable bills do not proceed to a vote simultaneously and that the potential logroll cannot be salvaged by packaging the legislation into an omnibus bill containing all elements of the trade. In the absence of an effective market in IOUs, sufficiently specific to encompass all contingencies, ex post opportunism must pose a fundamental threat to efficient ex ante trades, even in markets where repeat trading offers incentives to cooperate. Where repeat trading is less pronounced, as in much of the regulation field, non-cooperation would lead to unresolved prisoners' dilemmas in the absence of an effective governance structure.

The legislative committee system of the US Congress has been explained as a governance response to precisely such problems of potential political market failure (Weingast and Moran, 1983). As such, it facilitates logrolling solutions under conditions that seriously jeopardize classical contracting possibilities. In essence, the committee system establishes property rights that militate against opportunism in markets characterized by bounded rationality and asset specificity.

Committees are composed of a number of seats, each held by an individual legislator. Each committee is delegated by a specific set of policy issues over which it exercises jurisdiction. Within that jurisdiction, the committee possesses a monopoly right to bring policy proposals to a legislative vote. Such proposals must command a majority vote to become law. The seniority system is an important, truncated property right designed to regulate committee behavior. A committee member holds such a position as long as he chooses, subject to his re-election to the Congress, and cannot be removed. Leadership positions within the committee (notably chairmanship and ranking minority membership) are allocated (though with recent exceptions) by seniority, that is, by the length of continuous service on the committee. Rights to committee positions cannot be traded (at least openly) to others.

Should a committee seat become vacant, a bidding system assigns the vacancy to another member of Congress.

Such a system provides powerful constraints against opportunistic behavior in situations of non-contemporaneous or non-simultaneous legislation, by limiting the potential for coalition formations. Since only the committee with jurisdiction can bring a renegement proposal to the floor for a vote, that committee has a veto power over the proposals of other legislators. If a pork-barrel committee, having won its benefits, wished to renege on a legislative deal, it would be able to succeed only by persuading the agency committee to revoke legislation on which its own expected returns depend. In the absence of a significant new logroll such an outcome cannot be predicted. The agenda power of each committee also serves as an effective substitute for outstanding IOUs with uncertain contingencies, and thus resolves the problem of contract failure with respect to non-simultaneous legislation.

The committee system facilitates the forging of contracts between effective interest groups and suitably motivated members of Congress by providing a bidding mechanism to assign members to committee positions. Since a congressman's electoral success depends on obtaining benefits for his constituents, and since constituent interests differ, legislators seek assignment to those committees which offer the greatest expected marginal impact.

The committee system has important effects on coalition formation, reducing the feasible set of policies that can be implemented and extending the durability of those that are successfully enacted (Crain, Shughart and Tollison, 1988). The agenda power exercised by committee members implies that successful coalitions must include a majority of members of the relevant committee (Crain, 1990). Policies that provide benefits only to a non-committee majority are unlikely to become law. In this respect, trades among committee members are more likely to succeed that those across committees, since there is a much reduced risk of renegement, indeed in some cases a single up or down vote on a package of proposals. The incumbency rights of committee members enhances legislative durability, especially in response to small changes in political circumstances (Crain and Tollison, 1979a). Would-be revolutionaries must bid for seats on the committee as they become available and await an achieved committee as well as a legislative majority.

Committees are influential, decentralized agencies of the legislature composed of those legislators with high stakes in their respective jurisdictions. Their separate authority presents a threat of moral hazard which the legislature, as coordinating agent, is concerned to control, not least through its own majority rule requirement. Any committee that attempts to seize excessive surpluses, measured in political currencies, will invoke censure from the floor of the relevant chamber, reflected in a denial of their bill proposals. If committee agendas, once hidden from the legislature, become exposed to legislative debate, jurisdictional changes may result designed to curtail the political damage imposed by an errant agent of the Congress.

The committee system thus protects interest groups from the full impact of small changes in their political influence, reflected in changes in the balance among the competing coalitions within the legislature. In consequence, legislation is rendered more durable, to the mutual benefit of principal and of agent. The interest groups gain by reason of the extended time horizon of their flow of benefits. Predictably, incumbents in the legislature are able to extract larger brokerage fees which can be utilized to augment both their private wealth (which includes pension rights) and their grip on office. The committee system is essential to this mutual gain (Coker and Crain, 1990).

The temptation is considerable to follow the lead of CPE and to categorize this governance structure as efficient at least in its matching of interest group demands with legislative responses. Many even among those not associated with CPE indeed have edged in this direction (Weingast and Moran, 1983; Weingast and Marshall, 1988). The temptation, however, is misleading and ignores significant property right imperfections that permeate the political market governance relationship (Rowley and Vachris, 1990).

Untruncated property rights provide individuals with clearly defined authority to use their resources as they wish, and to transfer their resources to whomsoever they wish, whenever they so choose, either through voluntary exchange or as gifts and bequests. Such rights, to be fully effective, must be enforceable through a well-functioning, non-invadable legal system. In such circumstances, it is predictable that property rights will lead to highest-valued resource use, regardless of the initial assignment of such rights.

The best example of such a right in capitalist economies is that of stock ownership in a publicly quoted corporation (Jensen and Meckling, 1976). For such stocks are highly divisible, clearly define rights of exclusive ownership and are freely transferable through an efficient market. In consequence, one of the most widely supported hypotheses in financial economics is that of the efficient capital market, in which stock prices are viewed as reflecting all publicly available information economically relevant to the performance of each quoted corporation. In such circumstances, rational behavior ensures that resources move to their highest valued uses and that emerging principal–agent problems will be swiftly eliminated either by internal reorganization or by external acquisition. The marketability of stock enables risk-averse stockholders to diversify their stock portfolios and to rely upon market specialists to monitor and control the behavior of corporate management.

Property rights in political markets are much more attenuated than those in corporate stock, to the disadvantage both of individual voters and of special interests. Individual members of congressional committees are bought out by the special interests that they purport to serve, indeed must be so if the have a long-term interest in their incumbencies. However, those rights in policy brokerage are strictly non-transferable, since committee seats are not openly marketed, at least at the present time. Nor do such seats readily capitalize, even as non-transferable assets, the flow of future income that the committee member may broker for his client. For periodic elections do present a threat to committee composition and to the durability of legislation, introducing inescapable myopia into the political market place (Lee, 1988). Nor can interest groups diversify their portfolio of political property rights in the manner of the corporate stockholder, without sacrificing the specific value of such rights. Nor can they trade their entire existing portfolios among themselves without rendering meaningless the specific rationales for their existence (Kau, Keenan and Rubin, 1982).

Congress indeed may be bought and sold at any point in time, both during and in between elections. Predictably, however, it is not bought and sold completely. Agency discretion is a residual of attenuated property rights in the US Congress. Politicians can purvey as well as broker policy within the strict limits of this discretion.

The relationship between Congress and its bureaus

The public interest research program views senior bureaucrats as policy eunuchs, neutered by the nature of their contracts of employment and by their concern for the commonweal into upholding efficiently and impartially the policy preferences of their political masters. In this perspective there is no conceivable principal–agent problem. The CPE research program, in contrast, acknowledges a potential principal–agent problem between the politicians who broker wealth transfers and the wealth maximizing senior bureaucrats hired to carry out their policies. However, CPE methodology requires potential principal–agent problems to be resolved at least cost by efficient governance procedures. In this perspective, median voter preferences, conveyed to the politicians by deadweight loss minimizing interest groups, are implemented effectively and at least cost by tightly constrained bureaus.

The VPE research program casts doubt upon the CPE predictions, while utilizing the behavioral assumptions from which these predictions are derived. In particular, the self-seeking nature of senior bureaucrats is endorsed by VPE, though with reservations concerning exclusive reliance upon wealth maximization. Despite early emphasis by Niskanen (1971) on the predictable dominance of bureaus over the legislature in budgetary bargaining, VPE now acknowledges the superiority of the principal–agent model, following contributions by Weingast and Moran (1983), Muris (1986), Rowley and Elgin (1988) and Grier (1990). Nevertheless, efficient governance is not predicted by the VPE research program in view both of the significant attenuation of property rights inherent in political markets and of a serious problem of multiple principals that emanates both from within the Congress and from the separation of powers between the Congress and the President required by the United States Constitution (Rowley and Vachris, 1990).

Superficially, the notion that Congress controls the behavior of the federal bureaucracy as part of its brokering of interest group policies runs counter to a great deal of case study evidence that indicates infrequency of oversight hearings, infrequency of congressional investigations and policy resolutions, the perfunctory nature of confirmation hearings of agency heads, the absence of congressional interest in or knowledge concerning the actions and policy consequences of the bureaus and their grantees, and the casual, unprofessional nature of the annual appropriations hearings (Weingast and Moran, 1983). Such evidence had influenced Niskanen in 1971 to hypothesize that bureaus systematically outmanoeuvred their congressional committees in bilateral bargaining over their budgets and fundamentally were free from congressional control.

By 1975, however, Niskanen had modified his views concerning the relationship between the Congress and its bureaus. In Niskanen's revised theory, congressional committees (and subcommittees) tend to be dominated by legislators with a high demand for bureau services, relative to the tax costs in their constituencies, given that legislators, with some exceptions, tend to access the committees of their choice (Benson, 1981). Relative to the preferences of the median voter, therefore, congressional committees predictably under-monitor the output growth of their bureaus and approve excessive budget appropriations.

A high-demand committee, however, has the same incentives to control production inefficiency as would a randomly-selected committee. Given the cost of control devices to reduce oversupply and to reduce inefficiency, therefore, a high demand committee will use relatively more control devices to reduce production inefficiency. This prediction weakens if the bureau uses some of its discretionary budget to purchase high cost factor inputs in the constituencies represented in the review committee. Overall, under-monitoring is predictable given that the monitoring function is a public good in that its benefits accrue to the whole population as a function of their tax costs. This creates a free-rider problem internal to the legislature which it is the function of the committee system to counteract, and of the party leadership, such as it is, to resolve.

The congressional dominance approach adopted, though with reservations, by VPE, assumes that congressmen on the relevant committees possess sufficient rewards and sanctions to create an incentive system for agencies

(Fenno, 1973). Notwithstanding agency mandates, rewards are directed to those agencies that pursue policies of interest to the current committee members; those agencies that fail to do so are confronted with sanctions (Weingast and Moran, 1983). If the incentive system is effective, agencies will pursue congressional goals even though they remain on a loose leash from their overseers. In the absence of fire alarms, congressmen will gauge the success of programs at low cost through constituent reactions rather than by high cost agency monitoring. The threat of ex post sanctions and the promise of ex post settling up creates ex ante incentives for the bureau to serve the congressional clientele and avoids the high cost of direct and continuous monitoring of inputs. High cost monitoring predictably will reflect a failure of the incentive mechanism.

A number of factors interact in the incentive system through which Congress seeks to control bureaucratic behavior. First, advantage is taken of a budgetary process designed to set agencies in direct competition with each other for annual appropriations. In stark contrast to the Niskanen notion of the monopolistic bureau, the reality is that up to 2000 federal agencies confront only 13 subcommittees of the Appropriations Committee, each of which develops a single bill, which, as amended, becomes the actual federal budget appropriation. Inevitably, self-seeking committee members, pursuing constituency interest, favor those agencies that provide good service to those markets.

Second, oversight plays an important role in sanctioning errant agencies. This includes new legislation designed to narrow agency discretion, prohibitions of specific agency activities, and other interventions that serve to harass and to embarrass agency heads, to damage future career opportunities and to foil pet agency projects. Once the fire alarm has sounded, congressional committees predictably meddle and intervene at the basest levels of agency affairs, not only to re-establish control but also to signal elsewhere the high cost of ex post sanctions.

Third, the Senate committees exert significant control over the appointment and reappointment of agency members, even though many of the confirmation hearings may appear perfunctory. If the hearings are typically brief, that is because the long arm of the Senate has reached back to the selection process and has influenced the President's nominations to its own advantage. Where such influence fails, the hearings are aggressive and protracted and the veto over nominations is a not infrequent outcome (Fiorina, 1977; Weingast and Moran, 1983). Once again, high cost governance occurs only in the fire alarm situation.

The congressional dominance model (Fiorina, 1977) is grounded on the generative assumption that each congressman responds to the well-organized interests in his own district, and acts to maximize his political support function. Because interests are not distributed uniformly across districts, the bureaus relevant to the electoral fortunes of one congressman differ from those relevant to another. The committee system is the mechanism for dividing the federal budget across the bureaus avoiding direct inter-bureau conflicts while maximizing political support for incumbents within the legislature. The committee system is also the pivot on which congressional surveillance and monitoring of bureau behavior is focused. The rules of the US Congress confirm this committee function, though Weingast and Moran (1983) overstate their effectiveness (Rowley and Vachris, 1990).

The hub of the efficient governance hypothesis is the assumption that congressional committees exercise near-monopoly jurisdiction over a well-defined set of policy issues, thus defining property rights that encourage and enable the committees to police agencies that fall within their jurisdictions. To this end, committees are vested with the power to make proposals that alter the status quo, subject to majority rule approval, typically logrolled, by the entire legislature. They are vested also with an effective veto power over proposals relevant to their jurisdictions that emanate from outside the committee.

Given that members are assigned to committees largely on the basis of self-selection (Shepsle, 1978), the near-monopoly power that they access implies that they obtain leverage over precisely those issues relevant to their individual political support and, hence, to their potential for re-election to Congress. Each legislator thus can specialize in overseeing agents most closely associated with his constituency, in return for sacrificing any interest in other agencies. This approach yields two testable implications for policy, namely (1) that specific oversight committees should be observed to have more influence that the rest of Congress over a particular agency and (2) that if the interests reflected in committee membership change, then so also will the policy-relevant behavior of the agency. Empirical testing so far has not refuted either of these hypotheses (Weingast and Moran, 1983; Grier, 1990).

The VPE research program views this efficient governance hypothesis as overly optimistic, derived from an exaggerated emphasis upon the monopoly characteristics of the congressional committee system. A major theoretical weakness is located in the assumed one-to-one nature of the principal–agent relationship, which ignores important realities of the US Congress.

Multiplicity of principals arises from at least four sources, namely: (1) the jurisdictional overlap of many oversight committees within each chamber of the legislature; (2) the duality of oversight inherent in the bicameral legislature; (3) jurisdictional conflict between the oversight and the appropriations committees within each chamber; and, (4) the competing jurisdictions of the Congress and the Presidency. Each of these sources of multiplicity will be addressed in turn.

The first problem is that of jurisdictional overlap within each legislative chamber. The efficient governance literature ignores such overlaps by centring attention on the relationship between the oversight committee and the bureau. In practice, however, legislative committee jurisdictions are not always aligned with the defined domains of the bureaus. In consequence, most bureaus, though not as it happens the Legal Services Corporation, are subject to oversight by two or more standing legislative committees.

This overlap was seen to be enough of a problem in the House of Representatives to warrant, in 1975, formal procedures to deal with the referral of bills to more than one committee (Davidson, Oleszek and Kephart, 1988). When a bill falls under the jurisdiction of more than one committee, it can be referred simultaneously to each committee (joint referral), it can be divided among the committees (split referral), or it can be referred to each committee sequentially. Some 23 per cent of the workload of a typical House committee involves multiple referrals (Davidson, Oleszek and Kephart, 1988, p. 10).

The second problem is associated with bicameralism, which involves separate oversight by committees of the House and of the Senate. Inevitably, this weakens property rights within any given committee, significantly so if the interests represented are materially different. If legislation differs and cannot be resolved by the amendment process, a compromise bill must be forged in yet another committee, the conference committee, before the bill can be sent forth for Presidential review. The conference committee combines the senior members of each committee, though any member of the legislature may attend as a non-voting participant, as well as senior bureaucrats from the agencies themselves.

Shepsle and Weingast (1981) view the conference committee process as providing an ex post veto power for the oversight committee, and thereby extending its agenda power. They downplay the fact that power becomes dispersed as a consequence of two committee participation and of third party intervention in the conference proceedings. The weakening of committees' agenda powers implicit in multi-principal bargaining inevitably opens up windows of discretionary opportunity for experienced bureaucrats, thus exacerbating the agency problem that confronts the US Congress.

A further attenuation of each oversight committee's property rights is located in the congressional budgetary process. For each bureau's budget must be approved by a subcommittee of the Appropriations Committee of each chamber of the Congress and then must be approved by the full chamber before exposure to potential conference committee reconciliation. Congressional control over agency budgets constitutes a powerful monitoring weapon. But it also presents additional problems of principal multiplicity, not least because the self-selection process does not apply to Appropriations subcommittee appointments (Shepsle, 1978, p. 146).

Finally, the efficient governance literature ignores or downplays the independent role of the Presidency with respect to bureau monitoring and control. Yet, the President appoints the Cabinet members who serve as Department heads and the Commissioners who head the independent agencies. The President has a direct input into budgetary allocations to the separate bureaus and exercises an ultimate veto power over the overall budget. The power struggle that may occur between President and Congress, fought out precariously across the separation of powers, opens up potentially a window of opportunity through which senior bureaucrats can give rein to their own preferences within the disturbed political market place.

3   Toward a theory of presidential conflict with Congress over bureau governance

In the public interest research program, the President and the Congress are viewed as a single important entity responding impartially and effectively to public policy advice (Nelson, 1984) and ensuring that public-spirited bureaucrats are well-informed in purveying the policies that are enacted (Fisher, 1984). In the CPE research program, the President is viewed as a non-player in bureaucratic politics and is ignored in favor of a theory of efficient congressional governance (Wittman, 1989). Even within the VPE research program, the President is not accorded much of an independent role, but rather is viewed as exploiting the separation of powers to increase the returns from congressional policy brokerage by exercising veto authority to extend the durability of legislation (Crain and Tollison, 1979b). In this section, however, the VPE approach is amended to allow an independent role for the President (Weingast, 1981; Davidson, 1984; Carter and Schap, 1987; Rowley and Vachris, 1990).

Potential differences in the interest group constituencies of the Congress and the President stem in part from their different bases of representation. The specific state and district bases of members of Congress, specialized through the committee governance system, differ markedly from the national basis of the presidency and provide asymmetrical access to distinct coalitions of special interest. Differences are a consequence also of variations in the degree of transparency in relevant political markets. The less transparent the market, the more effective will be the small specialized interest groups that benefit from the logic of collective action (Olson, 1965). The more transparent the market, the better the prospects for generalized interests which suffer from the organizational problems endemic in the logic of collective action (Crew and Rowley, 1988, 1989). Usually, though not always, presidential politics are more transparent than congressional politics.

Where the Congress and the Presidency are at odds with each other, especially concerning fundamental goals or underlying visions of society, it is by no means clear which branch will dominate. Madison (Federal Paper No. 53), envisaged the legislature as the dominant branch, and worried about its likely manipulation by effective special interests. Subsequent experience, however, suggests that dominance will vary, partly in response to the individual personalities concerned, partly with respect to the competing constituencies involved. Even the notion that the President proposes and the Congress disposes appears superficial in view of the complex interactions of the two branches on almost all issues of significant policy concern.

A compound republic interpretation of the relationship between Congress and the Executive suggests that the Constitution was designed to support the durability of legislation (Crain and Tollison, 1979b; Landes and Posner, 1975). In this view, the US Constitution was written to reflect interest group concerns that hard-won legislation should not be vulnerable to low cost renegements. Majority voting, bicameralism, even the committee system itself, contribute to such durability. By themselves, however they are less than adequate. The independence of the judiciary (allowing for the striking down of legislation as unconstitutional) promotes such durability (Landes and Posner, 1975). The veto power of the President, linked to the two-thirds majority legislative over-ride requirement, however, is regarded as crucial to legislative durability (Crain and Tollison, 1979b).

In this view, the US Constitution provides not a separation, but a collusion of powers taking the form of a legislative-executive-judicial compound nexus analogous to a vertically integrated seller of long-term legislation to special interests. The veto power is a device for rendering legislation durable under conditions of changing legislative coalitions (Crain and Tollison, 1979b).

Given the differing constituencies of the President and of members of Congress, this collusion theory, in our view, is too extreme, or at least, is relevant only when both long-term constituency interests are in conflict with the short-term interests of the transient Congress. An alternative hypothesis, which is consistent with the evidence is that the presidential veto power enables the President to enter the legislative logrolling process as a third chamber of government. The hypothesis that gubernatorial veto power over deficits is utilized in such a fashion at state level was tested and supported by Rowley, Shughart and Tollison (1986).

In the absence of a presidential line-item veto, the veto threat is a blunt logrolling weapon. Congress is adept at the compilation of omnibus appropriations bills that impose high costs on a presidential veto, notably the threatened temporary closure of the federal government. This imbalance of legislative power encourages presidents at odds with Congress to compromise on legislative policies.

An important source of potential conflict exists between the President and his federal agencies emanating from his central agenda setting responsibility. The optimal presidential agenda, given constituency interests and congressional constraints, almost always compromises the individual goals of the bureau chiefs, despite the fact that they owe their original nomination to their President. Heclo (1977) characterized the executive branch as a 'government of strangers' – strangers both to the President and to each other – loosely linked through political appointees who are closer in ideology and more intense in their loyalty to the President than are the career bureaucrats. Political appointees, by nature of their brief tenure in office, however, are more dependent on the career bureaucracy than is ideal from the viewpoint of presidential governance.

Weingast (1981) is almost alone among the major proponents of congressional dominance in his recognition of the destabilizing influence potentially available to an effective president. In general, Weingast views bureau policies as reflective of a structure-induced equilibrium in which a wide variety of political actors interact, namely the Congress (especially members of the key committees), the President, the courts, the interest groups and the agencies themselves, each playing an appropriately specialized role. Agency policy equilibrium, typically dominated by the Congress, is a consequence of low, intermittent presidential interest, clear court precedents with little expectation of change, stable patterns both of public opinion and of relative balance among the interest group constituencies.

The President may destabilize such an agency equilibrium by entrepreneurial initiative under propitious circumstances. First, the intervention must be a high presidential priority, especially when it affects an ongoing program rather than a new program initiative. Second, the policy change must reflect a significant change in broadly-based public opinion or in the relative composition of active interests, sufficient for the nomination of sympathetic and effective political appointees to survive the potential congressional veto. Third, the presidential constituency must be resilient to powerful counter pressures exerted through the Congress and through the public agencies by those whose well-established privileges are threatened.

If these conditions hold, and if the President is popular within the broadly-based electorate as well as highly skilled in policy-making, even a robust political market equilibrium, lobbied by powerful interest groups and brokered by a sympathetic Congress, is vulnerable to destabilization (Ordeshook and Shepsle, 1982). Inevitably, however, the process of attempted destabilization, especially if it involves a protracted conflict across the separation of powers, opens up opportunities for discretionary behavior that will be exploited by zealots and advocates within the federal bureaucracy. It may also result in technical inefficiency within the embattled federal agency especially if conservers join forces with zealots and advocates to take personal advantage of Austrian market dis-equilibrium.

4 The scope for bureaucratic discretion

The efficient governance hypothesis of the CPE research program is highly dependent on the assumption that congressional committees enjoy near-monopoly rights in the properties of the federal agencies that they oversee. Recognition by the VPE research program that oversight rights are both seriously attenuated and relatively widely dispersed across a range of principals calls into question the CPE hypothesis. Where ownership is diffuse and attenuated, shirking behavior is predictable within the monitoring function, opening up opportunities for agency discretion (Alchian and Demsetz, 1972). Where the senior bureaucrats of a federal agency are neither climbers nor statesmen, such monitoring deficiencies will be systematically exploited, unless internal bureaucratic constraints replace the external monitors.

Within the capitalist firm, the outside labor market is seen to provide an effective internal monitoring mechanism, should capital market governance ever fail (Fama, 1980; Faith, Higgins and Tollison, 1984). Within bureaucracy, despite the far greater probability of governance failure among a bureau's principals, the outside labor market will exercise minimal internal impact upon a potentially rogue bureau (Rowley and Elgin, 1985).

Senior bureaucrats move only with extreme difficulty from one bureau to another, not least because of the complex procedures of the political appointment process. Moreover, the complexity of measuring and evaluating a bureau's outputs is reflected in ambiguity in the criteria by which a top bureaucrat is evaluated. In such circumstances the relationship between inside performance and opportunity wage is nebulous.

Furthermore, the internal incentives to efficient bureau monitoring are relatively low. There is no equivalent to the private enterprise stock option that can be offered to senior bureaucrats to provide them with political equity in their public agency. Salaries and promotions within a bureau are strongly linked to level and seniority rather than to assessed performance. Even merit pay bonuses are vulnerable to non-performance distortions in organizations that are not accountable to the profit criterion. In such circumstances, the performance qualification that can be easily measured and most probably will be rewarded, in kind if not by salary adjustments, is that of raising the budget of one's bureau. In this sense, Niskanen's (1971) judgment of a top bureaucrat's motivation is worthy of serious general consideration.

The potential for bureaucratic discretion identified by the VPE research program is not such as to lead to a reversion to the Niskanen bilateral bargaining approach of bureau dominance and certainly does not support Breton and Wintrobe's (1982) pessimistic dependence on a network of trust. Nevertheless, the issues presented in this chapter certainly cast serious doubt on the CPE hypothesis of efficient governance and leave open the possibility that federal agencies may run out of control. Chapters 11 and 12 evaluate the hypothesis that the Legal Services Corporation became ungovernable over the period 1981 to 1982 with adverse consequences, as yet largely unmitigated, for the right to civil justice of poor Americans.

Part V

THE MARKET IN CIVIL JUSTICE FOR THE POOR

8 Producers who do not sell

Public services are never better performed than when their reward comes only in consequence of their being performed, and is proportioned to the diligence employed in performing them.

Adam Smith, *The Wealth of Nations*, Book V, Part II

1 Introduction

The Legal Services Corporation was created in 1974 as a private, non-membership, non-profit corporation for the purpose of administering federal funds to support legal services for poor persons in civil matters. The Corporation itself cannot and does not directly represent clients. Rather, it provides funds to legal services programs in all 50 states, as well as Puerto Rico, the Virgin Islands, Micronesia and Guam. The majority of funds appropriated by Congress under the 1974 Act are distributed by grant or contract to some 284 basic field offices that provide legal assistance to clients. The Corporation is responsible for ensuring that its grantees provide services efficiently and effectively to their clients in compliance with the rules and regulations that it promulgates from time to time.

The Corporation is responsible for maintaining the highest quality of service and professional standards, the preservation of attorney–client relationships, and the protection of the integrity of the adversary process from any impairment in furnishing legal assistance to eligible clients. The Corporation is required by law to continue funding each of its grantees at the same level each year unless it determines that such funding should be denied or reduced. The Corporation may deny funding for a recipient only under carefully defined circumstances:

1. Denial is required by or will implement a provision of law, a corporation rule, regulation, guideline, or instruction that is generally applicable to all recipients of the same class, or a funding policy, standard, or criterion approved by the board.
2. There has been significant failure by a recipient to comply with a provision of law, or a rule, regulation, guideline, or instruction issued by the corporation, or a term or condition of a current or prior grant from or contract with the corporation.
3. There has been significant failure by a recipient to use its resources to provide economical and effective legal assistance of high quality as

measured by generally accepted professional standards, the provisions of the act, or a rule, regulation, or guideline issued by the corporation.

4. The corporation finds that another organization, whether a current recipient or not, could better serve eligible clients in the recipient's service area.

Refunding of a grantee, contractor, person, or entity receiving funds from the corporation, however, may not be denied without first providing reasonable notice and opportunity for a timely, full and fair hearing to enable the grantee to show cause why such action should not be taken. Any hearing to dispute refunding must take place prior to any final decision by the Corporation to terminate financial assistance or to suspend or to deny funding.

Each recipient of legal services funds is an independent private organization governed by a locally selected board of directors whose major concern is to ensure that the money appropriated by Congress for its use provides direct delivery of civil legal services to the poor while upholding professional standards. According to Legal Services Corporation regulations, at least 60 per cent of a governing body must be attorneys admitted to practice in a state in which a recipient is to provide legal assistance, and who have interest in, and knowledge of, the delivery of quality legal services to the poor. In addition, at least one-third of a governing body must be eligible clients at the time of their election to the board.

Because grantees provide legal services at zero price, but from a restricted budget, they cannot address all the legal problems presented to them. In consequence, they are required to establish priorities for the allocation of resources in the most efficient and economical manner in accordance with the purposes of the 1974 Act and the regulations of the Corporation. It is a responsibility of the grantee's governing body to establish procedures that assure its clients and the Corporation that cases accepted comply with the priorities that it has adopted.

In establishing priorities, local legal services programs are required to appraise the needs of eligible clients in the geographic areas served by the recipient, and their relative importance, based on information received from potential or current eligible clients. Such appraisals are expected to include advice from the recipient's employees, governing body members, the private bar and other interested persons.

In setting priorities, recipients must also take into account the population in the geographic areas served characterized by special legal problems or special difficulties of access to legal services, the availability of other sources of free or low cost legal assistance and the susceptibility of particular legal problems to solution through legal processes. A determination of the priorities thus established must be reported on an annual basis to the Legal Services Corporation.

The Legal Services Corporation is required by statute to ensure that attorneys employed full time in the staff attorney delivery program refrain from any compensated outside practice of law and from any uncompensated outside practice of law except when authorized to do so by the Corporation. It is required to ensure that all field programs solicit recommendations from the organized bar in the community that is served before filling any staff attorney vacancy. In such appointments, preference must be given to qualified attorneys who reside in that community. It must also ensure that staff attorneys refrain from persistent incitement to litigate and from any other activity prohibited by the Canons of Ethics and the Code of Professional Responsibility of the American Bar Association. Issues of governance failure and the consequential emergence of agency discretion are not addressed explicitly in the 1974 Act.

The Legal Services Corporation places certain restrictions on its grantees. Grantees are not allowed to use their funds to provide legal assistance with respect to criminal proceedings unless such assistance is required as part of an attorney's responsibilities as a member of the bar, or arises out of a civil action. Nor are recipients allowed to offer legal assistance to persons who seek

Table 8.1   LSC and non-LSC funding of the Legal Services Program 1976–88

Year	Non-LSC Funds $Million	LSC Funds
1976	$0	$79 750 871
1977	$30 697 000	$110 931 855
1978	$44 316 000	$178 203 506
1979	$38 429 000	$234 565 510
1980	$37 662 000	$266 505 111
1981	$48 143 503	$295 745 606
1982	$50 000 000	$223 879 759
1983	$51 956 051	$223 689 759
1984	$63 692 116	$255 519 809
1985	$81 450 358	$280 833 823
1986	$90 994 694	$279 244 888
1987	$123 154 565	$295 679 477
1988	$124 856 499	$295 679 477

Legal Services Corporation Fact Book 1987–1988.

Table 8.2 Private sources of legal services support 1988

State	United Way	Foundation grants	Bar Association	Iolta	Carryover	Other	Total
Alabama	$0	$0	$0	$0	$0	$0	$0
Alaska	0	0	0	0	184 951	300 000	484 951
Arizona	183 341	0	3 750	1 324 900	111 892	39 951	1 663 834
Arkansas	0	0	0	80 000	72 169	27 000	179 169
California	679 147	1 706 463	269 851	10 345 586	1 496 864	2 652 218	17 150 129
Colorado	485 432	149 000	29 500	359 500	161 220	89 650	1 274 302
Connecticut	372 645	47 500	11 166	201 500	125 412	301 060	1 059 283
Delaware	197 950	0	0	293 710	26 920	34 930	553 510
Dist. of Col.	0	786 000	128 000	0	3 340	676 147	1 593 487
Florida	103 710	0	11 000	2 068 804	631 932	269 792	3 085 238
Georgia	243 000	77 289	275 000	50 000	74 259	0	719 548
Guam	0	0	1 500	0	0	37 000	38 500
Hawaii	107 450	0	0	2 000	39 193	5 000	223 643
Idaho	0	0	0	88 000	20 000	19 150	127 150
Illinois	416 167	271 000	48 000	301 000	682 195	526 950	2 245 312
Indiana	105 898	0	0	0	0	31 200	137 098
Iowa	143 098	44 500	14 823	174 003	4 166	3 800	384 390
Kansas	167 839	34 278	83 625	0	0	73 314	409 056
Kentucky	250 525	13 200	26 460	0	33 979	2 800	326 964
Louisiana	17 050	0	16 000	0	10 280	4 250	47 580
Maine	45 377	19 500	0	151 022	0	0	215 899
Maryland	321 024	0	0	724 550	106 000	30 000	1 181 574
Massachusetts	924 402	273 392	19 000	593 558	758 394	1 066 052	3 634 798
Michigan	657 534	16 000	79 441	0	139 698	58 963	951 636
Micronesia	0	0	0	0	0	0	0
Minnesota	150 453	119 158	11 500	925 622	457 416	104 789	1 768 938
Mississippi	0	0	0	134 772	5 897	0	140 669

Missouri	539 647	42 400	1 000	351 786	162 418	59 900	1 157 151
Montana	0	0	0	0	60 263	580	60 843
Nebraska	54 088	17 700	4 500	128 900	107 494	128 800	441 482
Nevada	75 500	2 500	0	28 900	121 391	36 500	264 791
New Hampshire	177 500	8 000	0	589 542	45 539	13 523	834 104
New Jersey	351 700	7 350	10 349	0	278 525	323 344	971 268
New Mexico	0	0	0	68 950	24 458	3 411	96 819
New York	394 489	703 500	12 665	1 203 485	317 144	2 749 068	5 380 351
North Carolina	249 855	164 900	0	1 179 393	69 174	101 902	1 765 224
North Dakota	0	95 000	0	0	39 048	24 360	158 408
Ohio	1 001 076	149 578	8 000	2 862 558	2 558 636	560 422	7 140 270
Oklahoma	156 987	0	27 047	93 480	0	10 100	287 614
Oregon	239 110	0	4 000	285 400	522 135	106 304	1 156 949
Pennsylvania	31 250	25 542	95 000	0	93 388	765 807	1 010 987
Puerto Rico	0	0	0	0	0	0	0
Rhode Island	69 447	51 308	0	390 000	0	0	510 755
South Carolina	8 000	308	0	161 925	13 276	21 900	204 409
South Dakota	0	0	3 600	22 300	28 968	29 200	84 068
Tennessee	192 248	25 000	0	38 081	13 988	94 700	364 017
Texas	64 437	0	8 500	285 478	63 854	44 129	466 398
Utah	0	0	0	20 000	0	5 000	25 000
Vermont	0	0	0	150 000	0	16 770	166 770
Virgin Islands	15 000	0	0	0	0	0	15 000
Virginia	189 836	750	0	530 935	117 764	61 870	901 155
Washington	208 932	0	4 000	1 736 502	145 289	314 170	2 407 893
West Virginia	4 000	1 300	0	0	14 970	30 250	50 520
Wisconsin	16 380	0	0	744 998	29 560	7 700	798 638
Wyoming	0	0	0	0	12 000	14 000	26 000
TOTALS	$9 611 524	$4 852 416	$1 207 277	$28 810 140	$9 985 459	$11 877 726	$66 344 542

Legal Services Corporation Fact Book 1987–1988.

to attack collaterally a criminal conviction, or to any person who is an alien, unless the person is an eligible alien as defined in the Corporation's regulations. Nor are they allowed to offer legal assistance to procure non-therapeutic abortions or to compel individuals or organizations to facilitate abortions contrary to their religious beliefs or moral convictions. Recipients are prohibited by statute from using LSC funds to pay for legislative, administrative or grass roots lobbying. Funds received by LSC grantees from private sources also become subject to these specific and general prohibitions.

Non-LSC funding for legal services field programs rose steadily during the 1980s, reaching $81 million, or about 22 per cent of total funding in 1985 and $124.8 million or 30 per cent in 1988. Some 30 per cent of non-LSC funds is derived from federal sources, 38 per cent from private sources, 25 per cent from state and local sources, and 7 per cent from attorney fee awards. An important and growing component of private funding, controversial in nature – 9 per cent of the total in 1985 – is derived from interest on lawyers trust accounts (IOLTA). By November 1987, 45 states and the District of Columbia had adopted IOLTA programs which take interest earned in trust funds handled by private attorneys for their clients, without the latter's permission, and forward the moneys thus accumulated to the state bar association. Table 8.1 traces the history of LSC and non-LSC funding of the legal services program. Table 8.2 provides a detailed analysis of non-LSC funding by source and state.

The problems that local legal services programs address for their clients fall into ten broad categories: family, housing, income maintenance, consumer/ finance, individual rights, employment, health, juvenile, education, and other problems (Besharov and Tramontozzi, 1990). By far the most common among these are family matters which accounted, in 1984, for over 29 per cent of the 1.2 million cases closed by legal services attorneys. Within this category are adoption, child support, custody and visitation, divorce, separation and annulment, guardianship and conservatorship, name change, parental rights termination, paternity, spouse abuse and other family problems.

Approximately 19 per cent of all cases closed involved housing, including matters of federal and other public housing, home and property ownership, and landlord and tenant disputes. Nearly two-thirds of housing cases closed involved landlord and tenant disputes. Approximately 3 per cent of all cases closed involved employment problems, notably concerning job discrimination and wages. Approximately 2 per cent involved matters of individual rights, including immigration and naturalization, prisoners' rights and rights of the physically disabled. A further 2 per cent concerned matters of health, most notably Medicaid and Medicare. Approximately 2 per cent concerned the problems of juveniles, including delinquency and neglected or abused dependents. Approximately 12 per cent involved other problems such as education, incorporation and dissolution, Indian and tribal law, licenses, torts and wills and estates. Table 8.3 summarizes the pattern of case closures for the top five categories of cases handled.

Table 8.3   The top five categories of cases handled by legal services attorneys 1980–1987

	1980	1984	1987
Category		%	
Family	30.3	29.2	26.7
Housing	17.6	19.1	21.3
Income Maintenance	17.2	18.2	17.7
Consumer	13.7	12.4	12.0
Miscellaneous	11.7	10.5	8.7

(Average Cost Per Case Closed (Mean) in 1987: $194.32).

Legal Services Corporation Fact Book 1987–1988.

2   The organization of industry

The Legal Services Corporation funds 284 basic field legal services programs. Thirty-two recipients receive special grants to provide services to Native Americans and 42 receive grants to provide services to migrant farm workers. Each recipient is an independent private organization governed by a locally selected board of directors whose major concern is to ensure that the money appropriated by Congress for its use provides direct delivery of civil legal services to the poor, while upholding professional standards.

Table 8.4 outlines the level of LSC program support in fiscal year 1988 and subdivides such funding in terms of individual state and dependency as well as by the average level of support made available to the poverty population (as assessed by the US Census). The States of Alaska and Wyoming, the District of Columbia and the dependencies of Guam and the Virgin Islands received significantly higher per capita funding than the average, which amounted to $8.86 per poor person in 1988.

The field program reached its peak in terms both of funding and of scale in 1981, prior to the budget cuts imposed by President Ronald Reagan. At that time, 5944 attorneys, 2540 paralegals and 5961 support staff worked in 1331 neighborhood legal services offices. By 1984, following budget reductions, the field program had stabilized at a lower activity scale, with 4654 attorneys, 1919 paralegals and 4884 support staff in 1310 local offices.

Local legal services providers supplement their full-time salaried staff with the services of private attorneys on a voluntary or partially compensated basis. Indeed, the LSC requires all local recipients to allocate an

Table 8.4   Funding of the field program 1988

State	1980 Census poverty population	Per cent of National poverty population	1988 basic field funding by state	1988 LSC funding per poor person	1988 projected LSC derivate	1988 projected non-LSC funds	Total 1988 projected funding per poor person
Alabama	719 905	2.44%	$6 347 798	$8.82	$754 445	$0	$9.87
Alaska	55 898	0.19	1 038 208	18.57	156 265	1 645 756	50.81
Arizona	308 525	1.05	2 677 317	8.68	135 829	1 601 382	14.31
Arkansas	495 999	1.38	3 720 346	9.16	256 638	187 169	10.26
California	2 626 580	8.91	25 122 882	9.56	2 067 652	15 130 002	16.11
Colorado	284 429	0.97	2 682 464	9.43	368 942	1 584 330	16.30
Connecticut	242 650	0.82	2 372 604	9.78	91 265	3 672 594	25.29
Delaware	68 408	0.23	582 112	8.51	82 560	1 114 710	26.01
Dist. of Col.	113 356	0.38	1 516 575	13.38	204 000	121 000	16.25
Florida	1 287 056	4.37	10 952 097	8.51	942 441	4 782 259	12.96
Georgia	884 393	3.00	7 560 835	8.55	231 633	1 710 821	10.75
Guam	16 571	0.06	170 979	10.32	7 019	108 500	17.29
Hawaii	116 575	0.40	991 985	8.51	94 284	1 319 292	20.64
Idaho	116 808	0.40	993 968	8.51	111 400	173 150	10.95
Illinois	1 230 541	4.18	10 471 187	8.51	1 495 629	2 617 424	11.85
Indiana	516 190	1.75	4 392 476	8.51	506 527	376 111	10.22
Iowa	286 173	0.97	2 707 599	9.46	262 098	448 181	11.94
Kansas	231 718	0.79	2 077 438	8.97	28 000	932 082	13.11
Kentucky	626 240	2.13	5 580 621	8.91	553 739	614 908	10.78
Louisiana	751 442	2.55	6 835 032	9.10	430 713	75 466	9.77
Maine	140 996	0.48	1 199 794	8.51	116 853	367 899	11.95
Maryland	404 560	1.37	3 442 570	8.51	126 500	4 220 002	19.25
Massachusetts	532 458	1.81	5 313 019	9.98	411 173	7 354 226	24.56
Michigan	945 915	3.21	8 055 141	8.52	220 710	1 782 117	10.63
Micronesia	113 713	0.39	967 631	8.51	76 261	264 500	11.51

Minnesota	374 956	1.27	3 209 606	8.56	235 619	3 638 853	18.89
Mississippi	587 450	1.99	5 591 907	9.52	259 177	286 327	10.45
Missouri	582 252	1.98	5 175 746	8.89	422 510	1 740 159	12.60
Montana	88 284	0.30	751 245	8.51	4 600	160 843	10.38
Nebraska	162 413	0.55	1 517 012	9.34	108 575	682 038	14.21
Nevada	68 266	0.23	595 955	8.73	390	576 596	17.18
New Hampshire	75 364	0.26	641 304	8.51	3 096	830 967	19.58
New Jersey	714 781	2.43	6 208 827	8.69	435 502	4 649 073	15.80
New Mexico	197 001	0.67	1 812 305	9.20	231 621	83 200	10.80
New York	2 298 922	7.80	19 759 021	8.59	1 504 796	12 596 002	14.73
North Carolina	839 258	2.85	7 458 913	8.89	604 974	2 094 346	12.11
North Dakota	76 605	0.26	739 212	9.65	71 799	356 649	15.24
Ohio	1 088 962	3.70	9 266 516	8.51	606 796	8 755 091	17.11
Oklahoma	393 866	1.34	3 432 400	8.71	500 619	592 515	11.49
Oregon	273 743	0.93	2 352 332	8.59	193 625	2 221 636	17.42
Pennsylvania	1 184 529	4.02	10 163 529	8.58	799 611	10 462 487	18.09
Puerto Rico	1 983 201	6.73	16 875 885	8.51	3 127 740	0	10.09
Rhode Island	93 959	0.32	799 536	8.51	127 000	569 369	15.92
South Carolina	500 363	1.70	4 454 471	8.90	324 425	273 742	10.10
South Dakota	102 036	0.35	895 469	8.78	78 092	142 088	10.93
Tennessee	736 471	2.50	6 445 499	8.75	665 794	554 516	10.41
Texas	2 053 426	6.97	17 541 714	8.54	1 228 739	1 262 048	9.76
Utah	145 295	0.49	1 236 376	8.51	25 000	206 000	10.10
Vermont	59 059	0.20	533 039	9.03	14 500	1 348 456	32.10
Virgin Islands	31 958	0.11	435 000	13.61	52 000	184 329	21.01
Virginia	611 310	2.07	5 447 605	8.91	307 841	2 779 067	13.96
Washington	394 891	1.34	3 419 893	8.66	445 846	3 030 575	17.46
West Virginia	286 995	0.97	2 759 612	9.62	213 904	53 520	10.55
Wisconsin	397 813	1.35	3 391 461	8.53	198 310	983 421	11.50
Wyoming	34 901	0.12	362 455	10.39	21 945	48 500	12.40
TOTALS/AVERAGES	29 465 419	100.00%	$261 046 525	$8.86	$22 550 022	$113 367 294	$13.47

Source LSC Fact Book 1987–88.

amount equivalent to a minimum of 12.5 per cent of their LSC grants to stimulate the involvement of private attorneys in the delivery of legal services to eligible clients. Such private involvement includes pro bono representation, reduced fee judicare systems, contracts with private attorneys, organized referral mechanisms and cooperative support arrangements.

In addition to basic field legal services programs, the LSC, through its Office of Field Services, is responsible for funding a network of national support centers designed to provide legal assistance to eligible clients and support and advice to local recipients and state support centers on major areas of the law, including specialized assistance to project attorneys in representing clients. The national support centers are responsible for the provision of library and resource material, training and communication and for the development of manuals and materials, technical assistance and strategies for use by local program staff.

In addition, the centers provide support by engaging in (i) litigation, including serving as counsel for eligible clients and as co-counsel with local program staff, (ii) undertaking legislative and administrative representation on behalf of eligible clients and client groups before Congress, state legislatures and administrative agencies, and (iii) coordinating and establishing networks with local program staff, other support projects, other advocates

Table 8.5   LSC support for the National Support Centers: Fiscal year 1987

National Housing Law and Community Development Project	$716 451
Center on Social Welfare Policy and Law	669 050
National Consumer Law Center	653 926
National Health Law Program	609 820
National Center for Youth Law	605 073
National Senior Citizens Law Center	589 512
Center for Law and Education	582 148
Migrant Legal Action Program	547 649
National Employment Law Project	504 031
National Legal Center for the Medically Dependent and Disabled	432 000
National Economic Development and Law Center	410 058
National Social Science and Law Center	306 902
Indian Law Support Center	249 108
National Center on Women and Family Law	244 846
National Committee for Immigrants' Rights	164 410
National Veterans Legal Services Project	91 308
Food Research and Action Center	60 553
Total Support	$7.44 million

Legal Services Corporation Fact Book 1987–1988.

and advocate organizations representing the poor. The centers are located primarily in Boston, Washington, DC, New York, Los Angeles and San Francisco, and their boards of directors are appointed mainly by the respective state bar associations. In fiscal year 1987, the LSC disbursed $7.4 million in grants to 17 national support centers. Table 8.5 outlines the nature of these disbursements.

The Legal Services Corporation is also responsible for the funding of state support centers or units which provide legal assistance to eligible clients and support to recipients on particular issues unique to their states. Support provided by the state support centers generally falls into one or more of the following categories: legislative monitoring, consultation with legal services attorneys, representation of eligible clients, information dissemination and networking or training.

Sixty-seven recipients receive funds from the LSC for state support activities, which encompass litigation assistance, training, research, legal advice lobbying, and relations with the organized bar. Table 8.6 provides an overall outline of LSC funding support by category of recipient for fiscal year 1987.

3   Producers who do not sell

The average starting salary of a staff attorney employed by a legal services local field program or national support center is low, typically lying between one-third and one-half of the starting salary of private attorneys employed in major city offices (Table 8.7). The working conditions, with a few exceptions, are correspondingly poor. The promotion and career prospects within the program are minimal. The clientele overwhelmingly are depressing to work with, poor, occasionally dirty and smelly, inarticulate and not infrequently socially alienated.

Predictably, therefore, budding masters of the universe are not readily attracted from the major law schools into the staff offices of the legal services program, unless their motivation is weighted more significantly in the direction of social engineering than of expected wealth. Predictably, also, those who are motivated by expected wealth, as well as by social engineering, will concentrate on litigation directed at precedent breaking law reform, rather than upon mundane legal assistance to poor individuals, as a means of securing future employment in major public interest law firms. In addition, those attorneys who are only marginally qualified for their profession and who end up in legal services offices to avoid reliance on the welfare rolls will seek out in terms of power over the poor the recognition denied to them by the market.

The scope for social engineering through selective litigation and lobbying is considerable for any staff attorney in a legal services office. At a zero

Table 8.6 LSC funding by recipient category and state in 1987

State	Basic field	Native American	Migrant	State support	National support	Supplemental field	CALRS	Training centers	State Totals
Alabama	$6 347 797	$0	$0	$181 885	$0	$0	$0	$0	$6 529 682
Alaska	1 038 208	439 257	0	27 390	0	0	0	0	1 504 855
Arizona	2 677 317	2 551 817	272 953	116 530	0	0	0	0	5 618 617
Arkansas	3 720 348	0	0	109 561	0	0	0	125 765	3 955 674
California	25 122 884	717 579	1 305 060	1 237 241	3 095 324	261 276	21 738	48 366	31 809 468
Colorado	2 682 464	23 181	180 678	106 824	249 108	0	0	164 458	3 406 713
Connecticut	2 372 603	12 714	59 982	90 364	0	0	0	0	2 535 663
Delaware	582 112	0	0	0	0	0	0	0	582 112
Dist. of Col.	1 516 575	0	0	0	1 006 412	107 012	0	0	2 629 999
Florida	10 952 096	0	889 729	243 230	0	0	0	0	12 085 055
Georgia	7 560 836	0	305 893	208 564	0	0	0	0	8 075 293
Guam	170 979	0	0	0	0	0	0	0	170 979
Hawaii	991 986	103 775	0	0	0	0	0	0	1 095 761
Idaho	993 968	52 768	215 539	63 923	0	0	0	0	1 326 198
Illinois	10 471 187	0	253 232	201 079	865 000	0	157 012	0	11 947 510
Indiana	4 392 476	0	118 882	77 605	434 000	0	0	130 595	5 151 558
Iowa	2 707 598	0	13 632	0	0	0	0	0	2 721 230
Kansas	2 077 438	0	57 254	0	0	0	0	0	2 134 692
Kentucky	5 580 621	0	5 549	190 292	0	0	0	0	5 776 462
Louisiana	6 835 032	0	79 067	145 135	0	0	0	0	7 059 234
Maine	1 199 794	52 351	197 350	47 951	0	0	0	0	1 497 446
Maryland	3 442 570	0	100 492	68 329	0	0	0	0	3 611 391
Massachusetts	5 313 020	0	0	448 194	1 236 074	159 098	105 343	154 780	7 416 509
Michigan	8 055 142	116 603	447 793	408 630	0	0	0	0	9 028 168
Micronesia	967 632	0	0	0	0	0	0	0	967 632
Minnesota	3 209 607	194 103	324 005	87 731	0	0	0	0	3 815 446
Mississippi	5 591 906	67 515	0	187 618	0	131 666	0	0	5 978 705
Missouri	5 175 747	0	10 905	0	0	0	0	0	5 186 652
Montana	751 245	108 332	109 967	65 973	0	0	0	0	1 035 517

Nebraska	1 517 013	26 848	28 174	0	0	0	0	0	1 572 035
Nevada	595 954	108 004	5 543	40 280	0	0	0	0	749 691
New Hampshire	641 304	0	5 550	58 232	0	88 054	0	0	793 140
New Jersey	6 208 825	0	123 327	195 509	0	0	0	0	6 527 661
New Mexico	1 812 304	376 556	98 863	109 366	0	0	0	0	2 397 089
New York	19 759 021	0	253 090	722 097	1 417 927	50 000	17 364	0	22 219 499
North Carolina	7 458 913	113 096	279 035	219 695	0	0	91 958	0	8 162 697
North Dakota	739 212	158 258	0	86 283	0	0	0	0	983 753
Ohio	9 266 519	0	279 812	395 488	0	0	117 029	0	10 058 848
Oklahoma	3 432 401	294 708	87 246	33 770	0	0	0	0	3 848 125
Oregon	2 352 331	149 937	290 949	65 737	0	0	0	0	2 858 954
Pennsylvania	10 163 529	0	55 438	170 933	0	0	0	0	10 389 900
Puerto Rico	16 875 081	0	398 566	0	0	0	0	0	17 274 447
Rhode Island	799 537	0	5 550	79 162	0	0	0	0	884 249
South Carolina	4 454 472	0	109 967	129 753	0	0	0	0	4 694 192
South Dakota	895 469	758 366	5 550	0	0	0	0	0	1 659 385
Tennessee	6 445 499	0	0	181 549	0	83 874	0	0	6 710 922
Texas	17 541 714	25 420	1 716 675	365 785	0	0	0	0	19 649 594
Utah	1 236 376	36 274	39 989	30 486	0	0	0	0	1 343 125
Vermont	533 039	0	5 550	50 112	0	119 020	0	0	707 721
Virgin Islands	435 000	0	0	0	0	0	0	0	435 000
Virginia	5 447 604	0	71 125	219 492	0	0	0	0	5 738 221
Washington	3 419 892	196 163	451 682	100 430	0	0	0	0	4 168 167
West Virginia	2 759 611	0	12 725	121 941	0	0	0	0	2 894 277
Wisconsin	3 391 461	111 268	111 694	88 958	0	0	0	0	3 703 381
Wyoming	362 456	140 354	46 349	52 024	0	0	0	0	601 183
NATIONAL TOTALS	$261 046 525	$6 935 247	$9 430 321	$7 831 131	$8 301 845	$1 000 000	$510 444	$623 964	$295 679 477

Table 8.7 Average salaries by position and years of experience 1987

Years of Experience	Program Director (01)		Deputy Director (03)		Director of Litigation (05)		Managing Attorney (07)		Supervising Attorney (09)		Staff Attorney (11)		Paralegal (13)		PAI Coordinator (15)	
	NBR	Average Salary	NBR	Average Salary	NBR	Average Salary	NBR	Average Salary	NBR	Average Salary	NBR	Average Salary	NBR	Average Salary	NBR	Average Salary
1 YEAR OR LESS	8	$36 582	3	$26 010	0		30	$23 820	9	$30 548	537	$19 731	209	$14 896	13	$13 865
2 YEARS	0		0		0		17	24 157	4	22 052	348	20 923	144	15 137	6	19 446
3 YEARS	0		2	30 079	0		23	25 470	13	24 691	299	22 087	124	15 578	9	18 895
4 YEARS	7	31 862	2	33 080	0		41	25 032	18	25 655	244	23 996	100	16 018	11	21 101
5 YEARS	4	39 425	1	25 500	2	32 992	40	27 054	24	28 034	195	25 674	110	17 112	8	23 318
6–7 YEARS	19	34 925	5	33 051	1	35 000	115	30 613	58	29 846	334	26 918	170	17 743	22	22 063
8–9 YEARS	40	34 773	10	39 192	14	36 309	138	31 784	73	33 564	225	29 736	221	18 636	13	22 534
10–14 YEARS	125	43 028	29	42 250	58	41 214	259	35 900	110	37 914	300	33 804	413	19 997	30	23 155
15 YRS OR MORE	131	48 704	21	43 020	16	41 065	87	39 207	47	43 244	111	36 682	180	21 987	13	26 356

Years of Experience	Training respon. Person (17) NBR	Average Salary	Management Professionals (19) NBR	Average Salary	Law Clerk (21) NBR	Average Salary	Senior Aid (23) NBR	Average Salary	Administrative Assistant (25) NBR	Average Salary	Secretarial/ Clerical (27) NBR	Average Salary	Other (99) NBR	Average Salary
1 YEAR OR LESS	0		21	$21 094	62	$9 978	0		16	$18 116	243	$11 558	32	$13 831
2 YEARS	2	$19 870	10	18 696	7	17 145	0		11	17 631	154	11 925	20	15 689
3 YEARS	3	25 483	19	25 074	5	6 208	0		16	16 135	153	12 858	13	12 769
4 YEARS	0		18	23 389	0		0		11	18 610	145	13 663	14	16 537
5 YEARS	3	26 877	12	23 968	0		2	8 153	15	18 335	154	13 855	12	17 422
6–7 YEARS	6	23 099	46	25 277	1	16 235	1	8 450	54	18 794	282	15 196	26	21 968
8–9 YEARS	4	31 959	45	24 992	0		0		46	18 256	330	15 619	25	17 047
10–14 YEARS	9	28 851	117	27 462	0		2	19 381	105	19 694	647	16 438	62	18 789
15 YEARS OR MORE	4	31 516	165	28 452	2	19 882	0		140	22 453	593	17 512	65	22 894

price, his services are sought out by an inexhaustible queue of potential customers among whom he is free (more or less) to pick and choose. Since rationing is inevitable, discrimination becomes socially acceptable, offering to the petty bureaucrat the satisfaction of exploiting the power to offer and to deny service and, thus, to control the lives of others. Such an exercise in power leads to some loss of humility, even to some delusion of omnipotence, that serves further to fuel the drive to social engineering within the staff attorney office (Buchanan and Devletoglou, 1970).

By institutional circumstances, therefore, legal services attorneys are forced to make subjective or personal choices among potential customers instead of relying upon the objective, impersonal character of the price mechanism. By pre-selection, those who participate in such a non-market will be more likely than the average attorney to be predisposed to enjoy the power that they must exploit. They would be irrational if they failed to select clients and to service their needs in ways that best advanced their own subjective goals.

Since the queue of customers is almost unlimited in the zero price situation, and since there is no objective way in which to determine its optimal length, staff attorneys confront an additional opportunity to over-indulge their leisure preferences, that is, to shirk in the provision of legal services. Such shirking will manifest itself not only in frequent absences from the office in working hours, excessive breaks for refreshment and the like, but also in a preoccupation with litigation and lobbying targeted at law reform, leaving the tedious work of client counseling to paralegals or even to unqualified office personnel.

The low quality of client service predictable in the bureau mode of product delivery will not provoke customer resistance in the degree to be expected in a normal market. Many clients, seduced by the zero price of legal services, given their low opportunity cost of time wasted in the queue, will have only a minimal interest in the service that they seek. Producer and client, not unusually, will be equally indifferent in their non-market transactions, punctuated by not infrequent unscheduled absences on the one side or the other of the relationship and not unusually by an abortion of the negotiations. A low frequency of cases closed is predictable in this environment. Many of the cases closed would be poorly evaluated in any independent peer review process.

The poor clients who are genuinely concerned about legal problems that loom significantly in their overall list of priorities, have no bargaining power with the local legal services office, no purchasing power to withhold and no alternative source of supply to which they might turn. They have 'Hobson's choice' in the matter of access to civil justice (Brough and Elgin, 1984).

9 Consumers who do not buy

Justice, however, never was in reality administered gratis in any country. Lawyers and attorneys, at least, must always be paid by the parties; and, if they were not, they would perform their duty still worse than they actually perform it.

Adam Smith, *The Wealth of Nations*, Book V, Part II

1 Introduction

Only poor individuals satisfying the prescribed conditions of US citizenship or legal residence are eligible for legal services. To determine an operational measure of poverty, the Legal Services Corporation, in consultation with the Director of the Office for Management and Budget and the governors of the states, has established maximum income levels permissible for individuals to qualify for legal assistance under the 1974 Act. Account is taken within this measure of family size, urban and rural differences, and substantial variations in the cost of living. Grantees are free to set their own maximum income levels, though these may not exceed the ceiling established by the Corporation. In a number of instances, local programs operate on maximum income level criteria below the established ceiling.

According to LSC regulations, unless specifically authorized by the Corporation, a recipient of legal services shall not establish a maximum annual income level that exceeds 125 per cent of the current official Federal Poverty Income Guidelines. For a family of four in all states except Alaska and Hawaii, the maximum annual income level (in 1989 prices) would be $13 750. Income limits in Alaska and Hawaii are higher, $17 188 and $15 813 respectively.

The local programs are allowed some discretion in their interpretation of the eligibility requirements for potential clients. A program must take into account the following factors: (i) the liquid assets and income level of the client; (ii) the fixed debts, medical expenses, and other factors which affect the client's ability to pay; (iii) the cost of living in the locality; and (iv) such other factors as relate to the financial inability to afford legal assistance, which may include evidence of a prior determination that such individuals' lack of income results from refusal or unwillingness without good cause to seek or accept an employment situation.

In addition, local programs must determine eligibility according to criteria that give preference to the legal needs of those least able to obtain legal assistance, as well as to afford sufficient latitude to consider local circumstances and their own resource limitations. In establishing its own maximum income ceilings the governing body of the local program may take into consideration: (i) the cost of living in the locality; (ii) the number of clients who can be served by the resources available to the program; (iii) the population who would be eligible at and below alternative income levels; and (iv) the availability and cost of legal services provided by the private bar in the area.

A person who fails to satisfy the requirements for eligibility still may qualify for free legal services if he or she can satisfy certain authorized exceptions. For example, an exception may be made where a client is seeking legal assistance to secure benefits provided by a governmental program for the poor. All such exceptions must be documented by the program and must be included in the client's file for future reference.

A person whose gross income exceeds the maximum income allowable, but does not exceed 150 per cent of the national eligibility level, may still be eligible for legal assistance on the basis of one or more of the following factors: (i) current income prospects of a client, taking into account seasonal variations in income; (ii) medical expenses; (iii) fixed debts and obligations, such as unpaid federal, state and local taxes from prior years; (iv) child care, transportation, and other expenses necessary for employment; and (v) expenses associated with age or physical infirmity of resident family members.

Local programs may provide legal services to persons who are ineligible if the assistance provided is supported by funds from a source other than the Corporation. They may provide assistance to a group, corporation, or association, if it is composed primarily of persons eligible for legal assistance under the Act and if such a body can demonstrate that it lacks, and has no practical means of obtaining, funds to retain private counsel. Programs must discontinue representation of any client who becomes ineligible unless such discontinuance would violate an attorney's professional responsibilities.

In implementing their eligibility guidelines, local legal services programs are expected to adopt a simple form and procedure to obtain information on client eligibility. If there is substantial reason to doubt the information provided by a client, however, the program must make efforts to verify it in a manner consistent with the attorney–client relationship. The responsibility for ensuring that such procedures are maintained resides with the Legal Services Corporation.

2 The nature of the clientele

The local legal services programs handle a wide range of cases for a diverse population of poor clients. The Legal Services Corporation provides only limited information concerning the market served, and none on the incomes of the clients who receive legal assistance.

In 1987, the basic field program served 1.37 million poor persons throughout the United States. Of these, 54 per cent were Caucasian, 25 per cent were black, 17 per cent were Hispanic, 1 per cent were native American and 1 per cent Asian or Pacific Islander. Group representatives accounted for almost 2 per cent of the total cases. Approximately 2 per cent of the clientele were under the age of 18 years and 15 per cent were aged 60 or over, leaving a very large majority, 83 per cent, between the ages of 18 and 59 years. Table 9.1 provides further details on the ages and ethnicity of the clients served.

Table 9.1   Ages and ethnicity of Legal Services customers in 1987

Basic field program

(1)	(2)	(3)	(4)	(5)	(6)
Client age and ethnicity	Under age	Age 18–59	Age 60 and over	Group	Total
Caucasian	15 133	619 692	109 517	0	744 342
Black	7 486	295 237	35 233	0	337 956
Hispanic	7 722	201 125	22 975	0	231 822
Native American	226	12 526	1 506	0	14 258
Asian or Pacific Islander	278	11 056	2 177	0	13 511
Other	156	271	29	0	456
Group	0	0	0	25 362	25 362
Total	31 001	1 139 907	171 437	25 362	1 367 707

Legal Services Corporation Fact Book 1987–1988.

The service provided to clients by the basic field programs typically fell well short of litigation. In 1987, 34 per cent of all cases were limited to counsel and advice and 21 per cent to brief service, whereas only 13 per cent were concluded by negotiated settlements following litigation or by court decision. Some 11 per cent of the cases handled were abandoned either because the client withdrew or failed to return or because the local program determined that there was insufficient merit to proceed. Table 9.2 provides further details on the reasons for case closure.

3   Consumers who do not buy

The number of customers served by legal services programs, measured by the imperfect standard of 'cases closed,' increased ten-fold between 1917

Table 9.2 The reasons for case closure in 1987

		Reasons for case closure									
(1)	(2)		(3)		(4)		(5)		(6)		(7)	
Type of case	Counsel and advice		Brief service		Referred after legal assessment		Insufficient merit to proceed		Client withdrew or did not return		Negotiated settlement without litigation	
	Total	%	Total	%	Total	%	Total	%	Total	%	Total	%
Consumer finance	70 710	42.28	34 015	20.34	16 214	9.69	3,664	2.19	12 961	7.75	8 519	5.09
Education	1 687	8.96	14 416	76.60	489	2.60	174	0.92	513	2.73	773	4.11
Employment	13 851	37.38	8 331	22.48	5 786	15.61	1 593	4.30	3 525	9.51	879	2.37
Family	124 880	30.29	55 397	13.43	49 664	12.04	5 868	1.42	59 945	14.54	5 893	1.43
Juvenile	3 090	13.64	1 322	5.83	1 054	4.65	263	1.16	861	3.80	1 027	4.53
Health	13 458	36.13	11 796	31.67	1 656	4.45	1 074	2.88	1 958	5.26	1 981	5.32
Housing	117 067	39.62	83 587	28.29	18 007	6.09	5 213	1.76	19 193	6.50	14 777	5.00
Income maintenance	73 961	30.11	52 341	21.31	15 209	6.19	10 389	4.23	17 894	7.29	13 402	5.46
Individual rights	12 504	38.93	7 201	22.42	3 777	11.76	706	2.20	1 693	5.27	721	2.24
Miscellaneous	44 163	36.74	29 140	24.24	17 870	14.86	1 882	1.57	6 910	5.75	2 547	2.12
Total Cases	475 371	34.23	297 546	21.42	129 726	9.34	30 826	2.22	125 453	9.03	50 519	3.64

Reasons for case closure

Type of case	(8) Negotiated settlement with litigation		(9) Administrative agency decision		(10) Court decision		(11) Change in eligibility status		(12) Other		(13) Total cases closed	
	Total	%	Total	%	Total	%	Total	%	Total	%	Total	%
Consumer finance	5 000	2.99	958	0.57	9 194	5.50	876	0.52	5 146	3.08	167 257	100.00
Education	104	0.55	304	1.62	104	0.55	24	0.13	231	1.23	18 819	100.00
Employment	534	1.44	949	2.56	507	1.37	119	0.32	983	2.65	37 057	100.00
Family	11 824	2.87	1 997	0.48	75 696	18.36	2 961	0.72	18 214	4.42	412 339	100.00
Juvenile	1 993	8.79	167	0.74	11 948	52.72	110	0.49	826	3.65	22 661	100.00
Health	513	1.38	3 531	9.48	383	1.03	77	0.21	822	2.21	37 249	100.00
Housing	15 790	5.34	2 907	0.98	11 656	3.94	1 001	0.34	6 273	2.12	295 471	100.00
Income maintenance	3 234	1.32	45 637	18.58	8 216	3.35	618	0.25	4 714	1.92	245 615	100.00
Individual rights	893	2.78	1 624	5.06	1 594	4.96	181	0.56	1 228	3.82	32 122	100.00
Miscellaneous	2 105	1.75	1 283	1.07	6 464	5.38	464	0.39	7 390	6.15	120 218	100.00
Total Cases	41 990	3.02	59 357	4.27	125 762	9.06	6 431	0.46	45 827	3.30	1 388 808	100.00

Legal Services Corporation Fact Book 1987–1988.

and 1984 and then stabilized in the region of 1.37 million per annum. The American Bar Association claims that cases closed account only for the tip of the iceberg of the number of cases that should be handled. On the basis of dubious statistical projections (see Chapter 14), the ABA estimated that some 3.53 million civil legal problems of poor individuals are dealt with each year outside the legal services program but that a further 19 million cases per annum are not dealt with at all. By reference to these statistics, the ABA has mounted a political campaign, so far without success, to increase substantially the annual federal budget appropriations to the Legal Services Corporation (see Chapter 14).

In the case of a marketed commodity, in the absence of regulation, such excess demand would not exist, and if it threatened to emerge, would be eliminated by an upward price adjustment. The market would clear and there would be no frustration of demand in terms of the willingness to pay criterion. In the case of legal services, apparent market disequilibrium is a predictable consequence of the zero price of commodity provision, with potential needs choked off only by the opportunity cost of queuing.

There are two means of limiting demand in a situation where pricing is not allowed. The first is to allow the available facilities to become congested, permitting the quality of service to decline. In the case of legal services, this implies the use of unqualified staff to deal with consumer problems, the shortening of the service contribution to counseling rather than to case preparation, and the litigating of cases with inadequate preparation by counsel. Quality failure in such circumstances is not necessarily a fault, but quite possibly an efficient supply response to market disequilibrium imposed by statute.

Congestion is less likely to occur, however, even in the absence of pricing, in a market for personal services, since such congestion tends to be distasteful to those who effect supply. Here, direct rationing, which offers discretionary power to producers who do not sell, is much the more attractive solution, as Chapter 8 explains. There can be no expectation that direct rationing will reflect in any degree the relative intensity of preferences of those customers who stand in line, qr even their willingness to sustain the opportunity cost of queuing. The preferences of the staff attorneys and their program directors, influenced by their bar-dominated boards of local directors, will determine the case portfolios of the field (Buchanan and Devletoglou, 1970).

Those customers who gain access to legal services confront a zero priced service, and this also has predictable behavioral consequences. Specifically, the client will tend to treat the legal services office and its staff as if no scarcity value attaches to them. There is no incentive for such a client to economize in his requests or to treat the program with the respect that a market price evokes. In many cases, the consumer will place a lower value upon legal services at the margin than the cost of its provision, regardless of where this cost will be borne. In such circumstances, consumers will allow themselves readily to become the pawns of the producers, to be moved across the chess board of the legal system in pursuit of the grandiose objectives of those who do not sell their services in the constrained environment of a real market (Alchian, 1968; Alchian and Allen, 1968).

Even in the case of inframarginal consumers, who do value the service that they receive above its marginal cost, the absence of competition in supply, and of any requirement that legal services offices should satisfy prescribed standards of service or be closed, minimizes their ability to discipline inefficiency. Those who become disillusioned and seek a resolution of their legal problems in the deregulation of the legal process, and in self-help kits on legal matters, find themselves hostage to the bar cartel which manipulates the legislatures to secure attorney rents from competition (see Chapter 14).

10 Owners who do not control

The abuses which sometimes creep into the local and provincial administration of a local and provincial revenue, how enormous soever they may appear, are in reality, however, almost always very trifling in comparison of those which commonly take place in the administration and expenditure of the revenue of a great empire. They are besides, much more easily corrected.

Adam Smith, *The Wealth of Nations*, Book V, Part III

1 Introduction

The local field offices and the national support centers of the United States legal services program whose principal source of funding derives from grants and from contracts with the Legal Services Corporation, are private, non-profit organizations. Such organizations are dependent on government grants, largely federal, but also state and local in nature, tax privileges and private funding. In the case of legal services, their ability to secure independent finance from fee income is tightly constrained by Legal Service Corporation regulations. They are proscribed, at least in principle, from engaging in political activities such as lobbying, both by reason of their non-profit status and by the wording of the 1974 statute. They may not lawfully pay out any surplus of revenue over cost as profit to anyone associated with the organization.

Non-profit organizations may act differently from private firms because they confront radically different behavioral constraints, most particularly with respect to the prospect of profit distribution. They may act differently also because the motivations and goals of managers and directors differ with respect to the two categories of organization, as a consequence of self-selection, given the perceived constraints that are available to them. These issues will be explored in Section 2 with particular reference to the predictable behavior of the legal services offices.

Although formally, they are private, non-profit organizations, the legal services offices form the essential conduit through which federal monies for legal services are channelled into the provision of access to civil justice for poor Americans. In such circumstances, the nature and effectiveness or otherwise of the governance relationship between the taxpayer/voter donors, the Legal Services Corporation and the local legal services office recipients cannot be ignored in an evaluation of the program as a whole.

Chapters 5, 6 and 7 have explored the weakness of the governance relationship between taxpayer/voters, the Congress and the Legal Services Corporation. Section 3 of this chapter extends the analysis of governance to embrace the relationship between the Corporation and its grant recipients in a market in which owners do not control. In this analysis, due recognition is given to the fact that some 16 per cent of legal services funding in 1988 derived from entirely private sources and that an additional 16 per cent derived from non-LSC public sources (Tables 8.1 and 8.2).

2 Constraints and preferences in the federally funded non-profit organization

Views concerning non-profit organizations tend to be firmly held and yet sharply divergent. For many observers, they are viewed as being guided by public-spirited altruists who seek only to serve the public interest. For others, they are viewed as being manipulated by shrewd entrepreneurs who have discovered in non-profits an uncontroversial mechanism for lining their own pockets and permeating their own political agendas (Bennett and DiLorenzo, 1989). In reality, non-profit organizations are a varied set of institutions that behave in conformity with the constrained preferences of their managements (Weisbrod, 1988). Like all institutions, they are subject to economic constraints, that condition performance, though the absence of stockholders is also an important characteristic.

Non-profit organizations are viewed by many as being less susceptible than for-profit firms to opportunistic behavior under conditions of informational inequality and bounded rationality, because their management cannot extract profit and make it their own. However, even when informational inequality is substantial, as some argue to be the case with legal services, proprietary firms are not necessarily inferior to non-profit organizations. Competition among suppliers will drive out harmful opportunism as long as clients can discriminate between efficient and inefficient service. The characteristic of poverty does not imply, necessarily, any failure in judgmental capacity. Undoubtedly, certain categories of the poor – notably those whose indigence is a consequence of senility, chemical dependance, exceptionally low intelligence or psychological illness – may lack the basic facility for rational choice. In almost all other circumstances, however, it is a misplaced social engineering presumption to assert that the condition of poverty implies an absence of the capacity of an individual to choose rationally. It is an interesting sociological phenomenon that many of those who purport to support the poor, evidence contempt for their individual abilities. Given the opportunity of competition in supply, the potential clients of legal services would discriminate among them as effectively as they discriminate among other suppliers of their needs.

Competition in supply, unfortunately, is unavailable to the potential clientele of legal services who must seek assistance from the local program monopoly that services their locality. Nor are the local programs well endowed with high quality personnel dedicated to the effective deliverance of contractual obligations. In this respect, low remuneration exerts a predictable toll. As Table 8.7 underlines, the salary scales for program directors and staff attorneys are low by comparison with private practice remuneration for attorneys even of only average ability. Prospects for promotion within a program are limited and opportunities for advancement by relocating among the programs are restricted by the preference in favor of local applicants imposed by the 1974 Act.

Predictably, those who join the local programs tend to be less well-qualified than those who enter private practice, they tend to move on, if at all successful, to other fields and they tend to be more motivated by ideology than their peers who pursue careers in private practice. In the absence of effective governance from above, therefore, individual clients will not be well served in their search for civil justice through the legal services program.

3   The failure of governance

Manifestedly, the ultimate locus of control over the supply of any commodity rests with those individuals who finance it. In the case of legal services the route back to this ultimate locus is extensive and tenuous, moving as it does through the Legal Services Corporation, through the US Congress to the voter/taxpayers who legitimize and finance the program. At each staging point on this route, serious problems of governance are manifest, not as a consequence of accidental circumstance, but rather as a predictable implication of the institutions that surround it (Buchanan and Devletoglou, 1970).

The taxpayer-voters who ultimately determine the existence, size and composition of a legal services program are unlikely ever to agree unanimously upon these matters. As Chapter 7 explains, political markets are vehicles for wealth redistribution and not for achieving gains from trade. In such circumstances, significant conflict is inevitable with some taxpayer-voters imposing their will upon others through the vote mechanism. Given the nature of the vote mechanism, (Chapter 5), the large majority of voters will remain rationally ignorant concerning all aspects of a legal services program, which impacts but minimally upon the average US household. Among the rationally ignorant are those whose votes and pressure secure the wealth transfer as well as those whose minority votes and pressure fail to deter the transfer.

Among the voters who are not rationally ignorant two categories are seen to be especially important for legal services. The first, smaller and yet potentially important at the margins of the appropriation, comprises those directly affected, on the one side the poor who are concerned to gain and/or to maintain access to civil justice, and on the other side those who fear that legal services will be targeted against their wealth. Such voters will know the issues and will follow closely the governance relationship that runs from Congress through to the local delivery programs. Insofar as the vote motive is active in the governance of the legal services program, these are the active players.

The second category, predictably much larger and in terms of vote effectiveness, therefore, more influential, views the right to civil justice in some sense as an amorphous public good, characterized by a zero opportunity cost in consumption, to be protected against the excludability implications of the willingness to pay criterion by government support and public provision. For such voters the financing of legal services is akin to charitable giving, albeit of taxpayers' dollars that are not exclusively their own, with government employed to coerce contributions to counter free-riding propensities (Hochman and Rodgers, 1969).

The concept of legal services financing as a moral act, as an expression of Kantian goodwill, has significant implications for governance. If the voting of tax dollars to legal services is motivated by a belief that the act itself is good, regardless of its predicted consequences for the right to justice in any specific situation, such taxpayers will evidence little interest in the use that is made of the appropriation (Ireland and Johnson, 1970). For such taxpayer-voters, neither rational ignorance nor irrational behavior explains their failure to establish a governance procedure to control the use made of appropriations to the legal services program. As Tullock (1971) explains in his analysis of charitable institutions, when that which is valued is the act of giving, the giver has little interest in the consequences of the gift, may indeed by discomforted when attention moves to outcomes rather than to initiatives.

If the right to justice is assigned strong publicness characteristics by those taxpayer-voters who are concerned, nevertheless, it is a strictly private good from the perspective of those influential interest groups that fill the vacuum left by rational ignorance and Kantian goodwill in the vote motive. As Chapter 14 demonstrates, it is such interest groups that dictate the level and composition of federal appropriations to legal services and that shape the organization of the bureaus that serve as the instrument of supply. If such groups are to be able to invade the program in pursuit of the self-serving goals of their memberships without disturbing the rational ignorance or the naive goodwill expectations of voters, it is essential that any governance relationship between Congress and the local programs should allow avenues of discretion and, in particular, should not foreclose completely on highly valued prospects for self-serving law reform.

Nevertheless, in 1974, when legal services legislation finally worked its way into the statute book, such was the concern of President Nixon, and of the conservative caucus within the Congress upon which he relied for protection against arraignment, that governance machinery designed to control the local programs, to restrict the politicization of legal services and to prevent the diversion of federal appropriations into law reform adventures, was written explicitly into the Act. The Legal Services Corporation was to be the custodian of the right to civil justice for poor individuals in the United States, a bulwark against weaknesses in local program contracting that threatened to undermine the expressed intent of Congress.

Governance is seen to be necessary when the conditions conducive to classical contracting are threatened by specific characteristics of the contracting environment. If individuals are subject to bounded rationality (Simon, 1972), whence behavior is intendedly rational, but only limitedly so and are given to opportunism (or self-seeking with guile), the preconditions for contract failure exist (Williamson, 1985a, 1988). In such circumstances, if the contract relationship is lengthy and circumstance specific, as is the case with legal services, there is a high probability that classical contracting will fail and some form of governance arrangement, therefore, becomes necessary if the transaction itself is not to be undermined.

Contracts fail in such circumstances because planning necessarily is incomplete (because of bounded rationality), promise predictably breaks down (because of opportunism) and the pair-wise identity of the parties matters (because of asset specificity). In a well-ordered system, the governance structure that emerges organizes transactions so as to economize on bounded rationality while simultaneously safeguarding against the hazards of opportunism. Such a structure is necessary where individuals are neither omniscient nor imbued with honor and where transactions are indivisible with respect to time.

Bounded rationality, which plays an important role in the marketing of legal services to the poor, requires careful definition. Its presence does not challenge the assumption of rational behavior. All individuals are viewed as rational expected utility maximizers but are variously limited in information and in cognitive abilities as they pursue this objective.

If information and ability are scarce resources, then economizing on claims against them is plainly warranted. Recognition of this simple but important point makes sense of many organization forms that otherwise are extremely difficult to justify, not least with respect to legal services where human actors encounter problems that are often complicated in relation to their cognitive abilities and which have ramifications that extend over time intervals so lengthy that unforeseen contingencies are almost inevitable. It is important to note that bounded rationality falls well short of organic rationality (or blind evolution) in which agents stumble without purpose in an environment characterized by complete ignorance (Nelson and Winter, 1982).

Opportunism is the strongest of three levels of self-interest-seeking discernible in human action, with open or simple self-interest-seeking the semistrong behavioral assumption on which neoclassical economics relies and with obedience to rules the weakest of the levels so distinguished. Opportunism embraces not only the most blatant forms of lying, stealing and cheating, but also more marginal and subtle forms of deceit which involve the incomplete or distorted disclosure of information calculated to mislead, disguise, obfuscate or confuse. As such, it complicates problems of economic organization by compounding the sources of uncertainty.

Opportunism poses a problem for economic organization whether it is universal among individuals in a society or whether it is present only variously among members of the contracting population, exposing those who are obedient to rules to the guiles of those who are not. Once opportunism is present, behavior can be rule-governed only to the extent that rationality is not bounded so that guile can be anticipated and aborted by explicit contracts. Uncertainties contingent upon opportunism disappear if individuals are fully open and honest in their efforts to realize individual advantage, as is assumed in neoclassical economics. Equally, they do not exist in the robot world of the public interest research program characterized by full subordination, self-denial and obedience of the individual to the dictates of some philosopher king.

Transaction cost economics (North, 1984, 1990) thus rejects the notions of unrestricted cognitive competence and honesty in human nature, which tend to dominate neoclassical economics and replaces economic man with organization man who is cognitively less competent and motivationally more complex. In such latter circumstances, the principal dimensions of transactions, from the viewpoint of the viability of classical contracting, are asset specificity, uncertainty and frequency. The most important of these dimensions is asset specificity.

Asset specificity refers to durable investments undertaken in support of particular transactions in the prior expectation that the opportunity cost associated with such investments will be low, once the commitment of resources has been effected. At issue in this definition is the potential redeployment of assets and the salvageability of resources once sunk should the transaction itself then sour. If assets are specific in this sense their owners are vulnerable to potential manipulation if dealing with opportunistic agents within an environment of bounded rationality, even where contracts set out explicit rules to which all parties must adhere.

Uncertainty poses important problems of economic organization within the transactions cost perspective, most particularly with respect to its behavioral origins in the strategic non-disclosure, disguising or distorting of information. Such behavioral uncertainty is akin to what Mises (1949) referred to as case probability, which views human actions as a sequence of unique events which cannot be compiled into frequency distributions amenable to the classical probability approach to decision making under risk. In such circumstances, even full knowledge of the particulars of a contract does not preclude surprise.

For governance to counteract contractual failure that is endemic in the transaction cost environment of legal services, it must be devised so that individuals are vested with property right incentives to monitor and to control. As Chapter 6 indicates, such is not the case of the Legal Services Corporation. A private, non-profit corporation, significantly dependent upon federal appropriations, parked uneasily in the no-man's land between the legislature, the executive and the private market place, has few incentives to effect strong governance and yet is sufficiently footloose to wreak its own havoc upon the legal services program should it ever run out of control.

Part VI

THE EVIDENCE

11 The battle over the budget

As much as legislators and founders of states ought to be honoured and respected among men, as much ought the founders of sects and factions to be detested and hated; because the influence of faction is directly contrary to that of laws. Factions subvert government, render laws impotent, and beget the fiercest animosities among men of the same nation, who ought to give mutual assistance and protection to each other. And what should render the founders of parties more odious is the difficulty of extirpating these weeds when once they have taken root in any state. They naturally propagate themselves for many centuries, and seldom end but by the total dissolution of that government in which they are sown.

David Hume, *Essays Moral, Political and Literary*,
Essay VIII Liberty Classics, Indianapolis 1985, p. 55

1 Introduction

The 1974 Act itself as amended authorized to be appropriated, for the purpose of carrying out the activities of the Legal Services Corporation, $90 million for fiscal year 1975, $100 million for fiscal year 1976, and such sums as may be necessary for fiscal year 1977. It further authorized to be appropriated $205 million for fiscal year 1978 and sums as may be necessary for each of the two succeeding fiscal years. The Act specified that appropriations should be made for not more than two fiscal years at a time and should be paid to the Corporation in annual instalments at the beginning of each fiscal year. Funds thus appropriated were to remain available to the Corporation until expended.

Non-federal funds received by the Corporation, and funds received by any recipient from a source other than the Corporation, were to be accounted for and reported as receipts and disbursements separate and distinct from federal funds. Such funds were not to be expended by recipients for any purpose prohibited by this title. Not more than 10 per cent of federal appropriations was to be allocated by the Corporation to research, training and technical assistance or to serve as a clearing house for information.

The Legal Services Corporation was established as an independent non-profit organization, located outside the Executive Branch of the US Federal Government. As such, the process of its budget determination was further removed than usual from the influence of the President. Nevertheless, since its budget remained an integral part of the annual budget the President, through the Office of Management and Budget, retained the authority to comment on the Corporation's annual budget request to Congress and of course the authority to sign or to veto the ultimate budget appropriation by Congress.

Section 2 of this chapter reviews the roles of the principal actors who engage in the determination of the annual budget appropriation to the Legal Services Corporation and briefly assesses their relative importance in the budget process. Section 3 outlines the nature of the giant jigsaw puzzle of Congress as it impacts on legal services. Section 4 details the annual budget appropriation experience of the Corporation over the period 1976 through 1988, and reviews the respective positions adopted by each significant actor on this issue. Section 5 surveys the changing pattern of legal services budget negotiations over the period 1976 to 1989, and reviews the battle between President Reagan and the Congress over the period 1981 to 1988. Section 6 assesses the implications of this battle for the Virginia political economy research program.

2   The principal actors

Earlier chapters of this book have depicted the political market place as a market in wealth transfers brokered by politicians and bureaucrats in response to demand and supply pressures of voters and special interest groups. Once the relevant wealth transfer institutions are in place, the annual appropriation of funding to such institutions by Congress becomes the principal manifestation of market equilibrium, which in the view of many scholars of public choice, is structure-induced (Shepsle and Weingast, 1981). The executive branch is perceived to influence the budgetary equilibrium by disturbing structure through its budget proposal and veto powers.

According to Census Bureau statistics, some 13.5 per cent of the United States population falls within the definition of poverty. Chapter 13 suggests that this estimate is excessive, that some 7 per cent of the US population is currently poor and that a significant proportion even of that fraction confronts only transient and not permanent poverty. Few even among the long-term poor are entirely destitute. In such circumstances, even a well organized poverty vote would make only a marginal impact upon congressional elections, more notably in the inner city House constituencies than statewide in the Senate. Moreover, the poor tend to be affected more frequently by rational ignorance than the average US voter and to be characterized by relatively high abstentions both in presidential and in congressional elections. The direct poverty vote is insignificant, therefore, as a determinant of the legal services budget appropriation.

The legal services program is one of the less publicized of the various federal anti-poverty programs and, as such, is not clearly identified by the large majority of the general electorate. Even those non-poor voters who are imbued strongly with a Kantian goodwill towards the poor, therefore, typically target their political concerns on such issues as Headstart, food stamps, medicaid, housing shelter programs, rent-control and minimum wages legislation rather than on the right of access to civil justice. In such circumstances, the vote motive offers only a weak and flickering political market signal, even in election years. In non-election years even that weak signal fails and dies, leaving the market place vulnerable to well organized special interests – the detested factions of David Hume – and to the media, the fourth estate of the US political process.

Olson (1965) has reasoned that interest groups will overcome the logic of collective action only if they are small, or if they are large but engage in lobbying as a byproduct of some private purpose, or if they can subdivide their members in pursuit of separable and clearly defined special interests, or if they are the creations of government subsidized by tax dollars to lobby for special privileges. Such interest groups will enjoy asymmetric access to the political market place and will wrest wealth transfers away from voters who cannot organize themselves effectively into countervailing interest groups.

Chapter 14 chronicles the triumph of the special interests in the battle over legal services – a battle which initially was fought over the survival or death of the program and which subsequently shifted to issues of budget provision and program composition. Dominant among the special interests that engaged in this battle was (and is) the American Bar Association, whose rationally ignorant members are skilfully manipulated by the ideologically motivated executive of the Standing Committee on Legal Aid and Indigent Defendants (SCLAID) and by a sequence of rent-seeking presidents. The ABA has received predictable support in its wealth transfer endeavors from the organized legal services field program the regional and local legal services offices and from left-leaning law schools (funded by legal services tax dollars) as well as from the loose 'rainbow coalition' of special interests whose members expect to feed at the legal services trough. The poor are conspicuously absent from the interests groups that effectively control the legal services program.

If the special interests dominate the political market in legal services, they have received unremitting support throughout the 16 years since the passage of the 1974 Act from influential elements within the media, most notably the major Eastern establishment daily newspapers, the *Washington Post* and the *New York Times*. As the copious references in this book to articles published by these newspapers confirm, information has been selectively chosen (or suppressed) and columns have been written extensively to persuade rather than to inform readerships on legal services issues that are viewed to be of value to the liberal democratic establishments whose wealth interests and ideological predilections these newspapers openly court and unashamedly support.

As Tullock (1967a) has noted, media persuasion plays an influential role in an environment in which individuals are rationally ignorant. Predictably, journalists with strong policy agendas invade such outlets in an attempt to impose their own preferences disproportionately upon the polity. Although conceivably the contestable nature of the media market place should result in evenly balanced debate, such is not the case in many major US cities, especially on the Eastern Seaboard, where the liberal democratic viewpoint is disproportionately fostered and portrayed.

Foremost among the brokers of the legal services program are members of the US Congress who submit the relevant authorization and appropriations bills for the signature of the President. These brokers, like their counterparts in private markets, pair demanders and suppliers of legislation (Tollison, 1987), linking those who most desire a law or a transfer with those who object the least. Following Olson's (1965) logic, of collective action, such brokers will concentrate on legal arrangements that benefit well organized and concentrated groups for whom the pro rata benefits are high, at the expense of diffuse interests, each of which is taxed a little to fund the transfer or the legislation. By efficiently pairing demanders and suppliers of legislation, the political brokers establish an equilibrium. If they fail to do so, they expose themselves to defeat in some ensuing election.

The nature of the legislative equilibrium, together with the level of cost of the brokerage function, will depend on the particular structure of the legislature, its committee and subcommittee subdivisions and its voting rules, in conjunction with the structure of the interest groups with which the brokers must interact. Although individuals certainly matter, it is the structure of the institutions, the constitutional rules of the Congress, which largely determine the total cost of any brokered equilibrium. From this perspective, the independent judiciary can be viewed as an effective enforcement mechanism for brokered legislation, increasing and sustaining its durability and, thus, raising the margins of the legislative function (Landes and Posner, 1975).

The Legal Services Corporation, through its senior bureaucrats, and despite the anti-lobbying provisions of the 1974 Act, plays an active role on the demand side of the budget negotiations as well as exercising its prerogative to present a budget proposal to the Congress. Following Niskanen (1971) the Corporation will press for a high rate of budget growth as a means of satisfying growth related objectives of its senior bureaucrats. Such, evidently, was its behavior throughout the period 1976–1982. As Chapter 6 indicates, however, the role of ideology cannot be ignored in a bureau which is especially vulnerable to the hiring of advocates and zealots (Downs, 1967) into executive office and whose Board of Directors is politically appointed on the basis of presidential nomination and of advice and consent by the US

Senate. In such circumstances, an expressed preference for budget reduction on the part of the bureaucrats themselves is entirely compatible with the axioms of rational choice, though it denies general validity to Niskanen's theory of bureaucracy.

3 The giant jigsaw puzzle of Congress and the political market in legal services

Chapter 7 emphasized that the primary role of the US Congress is to broker legislation and to appropriate funds to authorized programs in conformity with the supply and demand pressures of voters and (especially) of special interests. Although members of the Congress, initially, may have been attracted by the prospect of pursuing personal ideological agendas, as well as by the prospect of amassing personal wealth, the constraints on such behavior are tight unless a congressman's personal ideology is compatible with his constituency interests. With a Senate seat in a moderately contested election priced at $4 million in 1988, and with a seat in the House of Representatives fetching $1/3 million, many members of the Congress find themselves completely bought and sold, working the political action committee treadmill for the major part of their working hours, and voting on roll calls like zombies to maintain their ADA or ACU ratings at levels expected by those who have bought them out. In notorious instances, indeed, congressmen have been known to vote both ways on a single roll call issue to hold their ratings in some appropriate balance (for example, Senator Paula Hawkins, Republican, Florida). Although votes without roll call offer opportunities to indulge individual ideologies, such opportunities are constrained by the ease with which roll calls can be required by those present in the chamber.

Though the scope for ideology is a topic of unresolved public choice research, with Kalt and Zupan (1984) prepared to grant it relevance but with Peltzman (1984, 1985, 1990) able to detect only minimal deviations by congressmen from their constituents' interests, properly defined, it is clear that ambitious politicians either locate themselves with constituencies sympathetic to their personal agendas or adapt their personal agendas to their constituents' interests. This self-serving process of identification has been characterized as the giant jigsaw puzzle (Shepsle, 1978), most particularly in the House of Representatives with its range of jurisdiction specific committees and subcommittees which lend themselves to special interest brokers.

It is instructive to outline the committee assignment process in the House of Representatives, which culminates in separate House resolutions. The first, moved by the majority leader, establishes committee sizes and apportions committee seats between the majority and minority parties. The second and third resolutions, moved by the chairman of the Democratic and Republican Committees on Committees respectively, determine how committee seats are to be distributed among party members. Typically, these resolutions are passed without objection to create the committee structure for a new Congress.

Central to this process, however, is a complex set of interactions among a variety of interested parties, coordinated by explicit institutional rules and by implicit informal practices. The rank-and-file members of the House seek out good committee assignments, defined as assignments from which they can service the interests of highly valued constituents. Their preferences in the search are influenced by expected values, i.e. they are conditioned by the probability of obtaining any particular assignment, which in part depends on seniority and party affiliation. The party leaders, engaged in the coalition-forming activities required of partisan leadership, are concerned to accommodate member requests while taking a more particular interest in the money committees (Appropriations and Ways and Means) and in the agenda committees (Rules). Committee positions are treated as currency and are used by the party leaders to induce member loyalty on issues of overall party importance. Members of the Committee on Committees are interested primarily in chamber influence. Their activities on behalf of members, party leaders and interested others are calculated to elicit specific quid pro quo behavior and more general forms of reciprocity (Shepsle, 1978).

Unless they are overly ambitious, congressmen generally slot into committee assignments from which they can serve relevant constituents and, once there, they gain property rights of possession which are disturbed typically only by choice or by loss of their seat in Congress. In this way, the giant jigsaw puzzle settles into place as the basis for brokering special interests policy preferences in a Congress that is all but bought and sold.

In reviewing the relevance of the giant jigsaw puzzle for legal services, one fact of considerable significance deserves center-stage attention. McCormick and Tollison (1982) have explained why legislatures are especially attractive to attorneys. In the case of the United States Congress, their predictions are undeniably correct. Fully 47 per cent of all members of the Congress, both in the House of Representatives and in the Senate, are attorneys, presumably with some loyalty to their profession, to the American Bar Association and to their respective state and local bar associations.

Many of these members will maintain an eye on some post-congressional career, perhaps in a judgeship, perhaps in private practice of the law, in which the goodwill of their respective bars will play an important role. In brokering policies relevant to these interests, therefore, such congressman may tip the scales in the direction of such interests unless such behavior should threaten re-election prospects to the relevant chamber. This does not imply that the legal special interests have invaded the legislative function – it is still lower cost to specialize – but rather that the brokering of justice tends to be less even-handed than that of policies further distant from an attorney-congressman's profession.

Given the numerical presence of attorneys within the US Congress, it is predictable that they will dominate the membership and control the chairmanship and ranking minority positions of all committees and subcommittees dealing with policies of direct relevance to the judiciary and to the legal profession. It is further predictable that congressmen with some earlier associations with the legal services program – Bruce Morrison in the House and Warren Rudman in the Senate – will manoeuver themselves onto the committees and/or subcommittees responsible for the oversight of and for the budget appropriations to that program.

The House committee which exercises oversight authority over the legal services program – and the Legal Services Corporation – is the House Judiciary Committee. Despite the Democratic caucus resolution of the 94th Congress, banning discrimination on the basis of a representative's prior occupation or profession, the Judiciary Committee continues to impose a de facto occupational requirement of membership: non-lawyers need not apply. In the 100th Congress, as in all recent others, attorneys represented 100 per cent of the total membership of the Committee. Discrimination is now rationalized by reference to the technical nature of this committee's legislative responsibilities.

The subcommittee responsible for House appropriations to legal services, prior to the 101st Congress, was the Subcommittee on Courts, Civil Liberties and the Administration of Justice. As a subcommittee of Judiciary, this body was also characterized by 100 per cent representation. Following reorganization, the responsibility for legal services budget appropriations has shifted to the Subcommittee on Administrative Law and Governmental Relations which is also a subcommittee of the Committee on the Judiciary, with a very similar membership composition to that of its predecessor.

The Senate committee which exercises oversight authority over legal services is the Committee on Labor and Human Resources. The Chairman of this committee is traditionally an attorney and the committee itself has a disproportionate attorney membership (75 per cent in the 100th Congress for example). The subcommittee with responsibility for legal services budget appropriations is the Subcommittee on Commerce, Justice and State, the Judiciary and Related Agencies. This subcommittee also has a disproportionate attorney membership (82 per cent in the 100th Congress).

Under normal circumstances, where congressmen have been assigned to committees on which they wish to serve, with staffs attuned to the preferences of the special interests that make claims upon them, and where the senior bureaucrats responsible for the purveying of policy are in full sympathy with the deals brokered by the committees, a cozy little triangle syndrome provides a set of subgovernments which interact to create self-serving legislation (Shepsle, 1978). Such subgovernments, inhabited by executive agency decision makers, interest group lobbyists, and members of relevant congressional committees and subcommittees, are arenas in which specialized policy is hammered out. The growing weakness of central leadership both in the House and in the Senate, has accentuated the strength of such subgovernments' agendas.

If elements within the cozy little triangle fail to gel, however, the internal equilibrium is threatened and a sequence of threats, counter-threats, Mexican stand-offs or even outright war may ensue. In such a situation, the Congress through its committees will attempt to discipline it aberrant agent, using such oversight and budget appropriation powers as are available.

4   The phase of legal services budget expansion 1975–1981
Over the period 1975 to 1981, despite periodic changes in the composition of the US Congress, and notwithstanding a major shift from the conservative Republican administrations of Nixon and Ford to the liberal Democratic administration of Carter, the legal services program experienced continuous budget expansion within the 'cozy triangle' that comprised its subgovernment.

Table 11.1   Federal appropriations for the Legal Services Corporation 1976–1988 (Millions of current dollars)

Fiscal Year	Appropriation	Rate of change (per cent)
1975	90	–
1976	92	+2
1977	125	+36
1978	205	+64
1979	270	+32
1980	300	+11
1981	321	+7
1982	241	–25
1983	241	0
1984	275	+14
1985	305	+11
1986	305	0
1987	305	0
1988	305	0

Source: Budget of the United States Government.

Table 11.1 outlines the annual appropriations of budget to the Legal Services Corporation throughout the period 1975 to 1988 in nominal terms. On this basis, the budget increased more than threefold over the period 1975 to 1981, fell by 25 per cent in 1982 only to increase thereafter through 1988 without regaining its 1981 high point. Table 11.2 recasts this budgetary experience in real 1987 dollars, without substantially revising this budget history. The LSC budget more than doubled in real terms between 1976 and 1981, fell back almost 30 per cent in 1982, and increased, albeit only by 8 per cent, between 1982 and 1987, as an overall consequence of intermittent years of budget growth and budget decline.

Table 11.2   Federal appropriations for the Legal Services Corporation 1976–1988 in real terms (millions of 1987 dollars)

Fiscal Year	Appropriation	Rate of change (per cent)
1976	184	–
1977	236	+28
1978	359	+52
1979	421	+17
1980	411	–2
1981	401	–2
1982	284	–29
1983	275	–3
1984	303	+10
1985	321	+6
1986	318	–11
1987	305	–4

Source: Budget of the United States Government.

Roger Cramton, the first Chairman of the Legal Services Corporation, conformed fully with Niskanen's 1971 perspective of the budget-maximizing senior bureaucrat, and set the early pace for the Corporation's budget expansion. Strongly opposed to law reform within the context of the legal services program, and to any notion that legal services attorneys should manufacture law suits or organize client groups, Cramton urged the adoption throughout the program of client standards evident in private practice, and strongly supported a philosophy of ready access.

As an effective technique for expanding the legal services budget, and for upholding the objectives of the 1974 Act, Cramton pressed the case for universal effective entitlement of legal services for the poor, offering as a target the provision of two legal services attorneys for each 10 000 poor persons in the United States. Cramton is arguably the only climber and statesman (Downs, 1967) ever to be associated with the Legal Services Corporation, a body which more typically has attracted conservers, zealots and advocates attracted to the organization by its pivotal position within the law reform movement and/or by the security of an independent budget.

Most of the initial energies of the Corporation were expended on budget-augmenting initiatives focused on the minimum access issue. To this end, the Community Services Administration (formerly the Office of Economic Opportunity) commissioned a study of funding levels of local legal services programs relative to the poor populations that they serviced. This study determined that more than 40 per cent of poor Americans lived in areas largely uncatered for by local programs and that of the 17 million poor individuals residing in areas where programs were available, almost 6 million enjoyed only token access, with fewer than one attorney for every 10 000 poor. A further 10 million poor were catered for by programs with between one and two attorneys for every 10 000 poor. Only 1.2 million poor resided in areas endowed with at least two legal services lawyers per 10 000 persons.

The target of two attorneys per 10 000 persons was immediately adopted by the Legal Services Corporation as the basis for its minimum access plan, and was associated with a budget request to Congress of at least $7 per poor person per annum in 1974 dollars. This target was eventually achieved in fiscal year 1981 when the Corporation's annual budget appropriation crested at $321.3 million. By that time, the phase of Cramton's leadership had ended and minority activists had captured the program with the LSC President, Dan Bradley, a noted gay rights zealot who later succumbed to the AIDs virus, openly flouting the 1974 Act.

To facilitate the minimum access initiative, local legal services programs were divided into three categories according to their respective funding levels at the outset of the plan. Those which were already funded at the minimum access level or better, for the most part had their budgets frozen in real terms or even received annual increases at below the annual inflation rate. Programs funded initially below the minimum access level benefited from injections of 'equalization money' designed to move them to their planned targets. New staff were hired, new offices were opened, and physical facilities were upgraded. The third category involved entirely new programs, or new components of existing programs, delivering legal services typically into rural and often politically conservative regions, often encountering hostility from local bar associations and from local politicians.

The program expansion itself sowed seeds of resistance that eventually gave credibility to President Reagan's attack on the legal services budget, and that irritated those congressmen who found themselves the targets of resentful constituents. As the local programs advanced, complaints arose increasingly over alleged representation by legal services attorneys of ineligible clients (illegal aliens and criminals), over class action and other suits targeted systematically against government agencies and over failures to negotiate with opposing parties prior to filing suit. Other complaints focussed on the political activism of the staff attorneys and on their pursuit of lobbying activities expressly prohibited by the 1974 Act. Once President Carter had appointed activists to the Corporation's Board of Directors, there was no point in seeking redress from within the Corporation. Pressures for improved governance of legal services predictably shifted to a reluctant Congress.

Legislative representation (lobbying) within legal services was a major source of unease for the Congress during the late 1970s. The 1974 Act permitted such representation only where legal services staff were providing legal advice or assistance to eligible clients or were responding to requests from a legislator. In 1978, even this exemption was narrowed by the Moorhead Amendment to an appropriations Act, which prohibited the use of LSC funds for publication or propaganda purposes designed to support or defeat legislation pending before Congress or any state legislature. This Amendment was re-enacted annually, but was ignored by the LSC and by its grantees until late 1982 when the Board of Directors moved into a Reagan recess-appointed majority.

In 1979, the Appropriations Committee of the House of Representatives investigated the lobbying activities of legal services staff and issued a report highly critical of the lax interpretations and the lack of enforcement of the 1974 Act by the Legal Services Corporation. The report was ignored. In April 1980, Representatives Railsback and Moorhead visited California in conjunction with staff from the appropriations subcommittee to review the lobbying activities of the California Rural Legal Assistance Program and of other activist LSC grantees. They found serious violations of the 1974 statute. Once again, their adverse findings were ignored.

In the absence of governance responses by the Corporation, and given the reluctance of the Congress to revise the 1974 Act, aberrant grantees could not be disciplined. The 1974 Act, by constituting the Corporation and its employees as an independent non-profit corporation, had placed it beyond the reach of the Hatch Act, which prohibits the use of federal resources for political lobbying and of the battery of Federal reprisals that can be meted out to deviant federal agencies. The Internal Revenue Service appears to have condoned the lobbying of the grantees, whose 501(c) (3) status should have been withdrawn.

A second source of congressional unease concerned the treatment of illegal aliens. Illegal aliens were excluded from access to legal services by the 1974 Act. Following growing evidence that this prohibition was being ignored, an explicit restriction was attached to the 1979 Appropriations Act, and was extended annually through 1982, prohibiting the Corporation and its grantees from undertaking any activity or representation of known illegal aliens in the United States. The Corporation interpreted this order as being relevant only with respect to aliens against whom final orders of deportation were outstanding.

A third source of annoyance within the Congress was the growing dissension within the legal services program over the division of the growing budget. Faced with competing internal pressures, the LSC initially experimented in the use of discretionary supplements but eventually retreated into a formula-driven entitlements program in response to pressure from the organized field, and in particular from the Project Advisory Group (PAG).

More serious was an attempt by legal services attorneys and staff to unionize as a means of diverting budgetary resources to themselves. This trend became widespread during the late 1970s. In some areas, strikes occurred, following clashes between program directors and their staff, disrupting the delivery of legal services to the poor and keeping the more seriously afflicted programs in continuous turmoil (Dooley and Houseman, 1984). The left-leaning National Lawyer's Guild played a prominent role in encouraging such self-serving rent-diversion on the part of legal services attorneys and staff.

By 1980, the Congress was sufficiently alienated by the behavior of the LSC and its grantees that it declined to re-authorize the program. With the Congress subject to internal bickering, and with the triangle between itself, its constituents and the senior LSC bureaucrats no longer cozy, with the Republican Party gaining control of the Senate and with the former Governor of California, who despised legal services, now in the White House, the political equilibrium on legal services no longer appeared to be robust.

5   The battle over the legal services budget 1982–1989

The opposition of Ronald Reagan to the federally funded program of legal services was long standing, stemming from his term of office as Governor of California during the late 1960s and early 1970s. During that term, Governor Reagan, Counselor Meese and Executive Secretary Clark had encountered continuous political opposition to their radical policy programs from the California Rural Legal Assistance Program (then funded by the Office of Economic Opportunity). Legal services lawyers repeatedly filed fair hearing appeals with the State's Department of Welfare, winning a sequence of awards on behalf of Chicanos and farm workers. In 1967, the CRLA successfully brought a suit against the Governor to prevent him from subsidizing cheap labor through the bracero guest worker program. These suits were appar-

ently also designed to support Cezar Chavez's attempts to unionize California farm workers.

By 1971, Governor Reagan had become sufficiently alienated from the
California legal services program as to veto the grant appropriated to the
CRLA by the Office of Economic Opportunity. The CRLA initiated a
statewide propaganda campaign against the Governor's action and litigated
to overturn the veto, which eventually was withdrawn. Governor Reagan
vowed to do away with the program (Denton, 1985, p. 28). Nine years later,
Reagan reinvoked this pledge as part of his policy manifesto during his
successful 1980 presidential campaign. Legal services thus was moved from
a position of relative obscurity to the center stage of policy debate as a
popular president set out to fulfil his campaign promise, forging his former
California colleagues into an effective White House cabinet strongly committed to a populist program of overhaul, reform and reduction in the size of
the federal bureaucracy.

By the summer of 1981, it was evident that the White House following
recommendations by its transition team would opt for a policy of outright
confrontation with those special interests that supported legal services and
would attempt to persuade the Congress to shut down the federal legal
services program. David Stockman the Director of the Office of Management and Budget announced that the top aides of the President had committed themselves to eliminating the entire budget appropriation to the Legal
Services Corporation. The individual states then should decide for themselves whether or not to finance legal services from the reduced federal
block grant funding that would be made available. In retrospect, this policy
was mistaken since it galvanized the special interests into an organized
reaction to counter any attempt by the Congress to broker the presidential
pledge.

Throughout 1981, however, the outcome of this response was by no
means clear, and the President appeared to hold the advantage, not least
because of the Republican majority in the US Senate, Orrin Hatch's chairmanship of the Senate Committee on Labor and Human Resources, and
Jeremiah Denton's chairmanship of the Senate Subcommittee on Family and
Human Services. If sufficient evidence of wrong-doing within the legal
services program could be marshalled – and plentiful evidence undoubtedly
existed – the political equilibrium feasibly might tilt in favor of outright
abolition. In such circumstances, conservative southern Democrats in the
House of Representatives would be under considerable political pressure to
join with Republicans in brokering the demise of a tainted institution.

The President underestimated the commitment of the American Bar Association to a legal services program which had eased the collective guilt of
the legal profession with respect to its neglect of its pro bono responsibilities

and which had already created lucrative private practice opportunities by its sustained attack on important legal precedents. Although legal services was not universally popular among the local bar associations, rational ignorance ensured that highly motivated legal activists would penetrate the decision-making committee structure of the ABA and would access control of those standing committees – most notably the Standing Committee on Legal Aid and Indigent Defendants (SCLAID) – best positioned to launch a counter-offensive in defense of the federally funded program of legal services.

The counter-revolution was well organized and effectively targeted. Acting on legal advice, the Legal Services Corporation diverted the White House by naming the Secretary of Health and Human Services, Richard Schweiker, and the Attorney General, William French Smith, as defendants in separate law suits filed by legal services. Simultaneously, the American Bar Association launched a massive lobbying campaign, pursuing key members of the Congress, the White House, and the Office of Management and Budget, urging support for the existing legal services program and pleading that a past personal grudge should not dictate presidential policy. This campaign blunted the spear-head of the President's attack throughout his first year of office.

Reagan, in pursuit of his policy of eliminating the legal services federal program, declined to nominate in 1981 replacements for six members of the Carter-appointed Board of Directors whose terms had expired with the Carter presidency. With the benefit of hindsight, this must be viewed as a mistake. Reagan's decision against appointing replacements sacrificed an early opportunity to gain control of the 11 member Board and left the Legal Services Corporation under the direction of an activist Board which endorsed the survival program launched by LSC President, Dan Bradley. A new Board of Directors was confirmed by the Senate only in June 1985, well into Reagan's second term. Throughout the period January 1982 to May 1985, the Legal Services Corporation was governed by a sequence of recess-appointed Boards.

From 1982 onwards, a long drawn-out battle was fought out between the general interests that had vaulted Ronald Reagan into the White House and those special interests that controlled the legal services program through domination of the congressional brokering mechanism. Table 11.3 outlines the lines that were drawn by the major participants in this struggle and charts the progress of the battle, clearly identifying the victory won by the special interests and the defeat imposed on President Reagan.

Table 11.3 outlines the responses to the LSC annual budget appropriation process of each principal actor, namely the Corporation, the President, the House of Representatives and the Senate. The final appropriation by the Congress, as approved by the President, is also outlined. Although the President formally plays no role in presenting and negotiating the LSC budget,

Table 11.3   The budgetary history of the Legal Services Corporation
                $ (millions)

Fiscal Year	LSC Request	President's Recommendation	Approved by House	Approved by Senate	Final Appropriation
1976	96.466	71.5	-0-	96.466	92.33
1976(Adj.)[1]	27	24.63	n/a	n/a	24.63
1977	140.97	80	110	130	125
1978	217.053	90[2]/175[3]	217	195	205
1979	304.032	255	285	255	270
1980	337.5	291.8	305	291.8	300
1981	353	321.3	321.3	300	321.3
1982	399.637	347[4]/0[5]	241	241	241
1983	265	-0-	241	241	241
1984	251	-0-	-0-	257	275
1985	325	-0-	-0-	297.55	313
1986	305	-0-	305.5	306.4	292.363[6]
1987	305.5	-0-	305.5	305.5	305.5
1988	305.5	-0-	305.5	310	305.5
1989	250	250	-0-[7]	308.5	308.5

Source: Legal Services Corporation 1989.

Notes: [1] Fiscal year changed from July 1 to October 1
  [2] Recommendation by Ford
  [3] Recommendation by Carter
  [4] Recommendation by Carter
  [5] Recommendation by Reagan
  [6] Funding reduced from $305.5 million by Gramm-Rudman sequestration
  [7] House Appropriations Committee would not appropriate funding without a current Authorization Act.

because of the Corporation's independence from the executive branch of government, he makes known his views through the Office of Management and Budget. He also retains a veto power, though this is blunted by the omnibus nature of the appropriations bills presented to him by the Congress.

The years prior to Reagan were characterized by an underlying equilibrium between the Congress, the White House and the LSC concerning the budget, with each actor playing a predictable role. Throughout his presidency, President Ford reflected a conservative approach by recommending budget appropriations significantly below the levels finally appropriated. The Corporation behaved as a predictable budget-maximizing agency, consistently requesting budget appropriations significantly in excess of final appropriations. The Congress consistently brokered compromise bills that were equally consistently signed into law by the President.

The shift in the Presidency from Republican to Democrat signalled some spatial relocation in the median of the general (voter) interest with respect to the level of LSC funding (Enelow and Hinch, 1984). This shift was reflected in the sharply differing budget recommendations of Ford and Carter for fiscal year 1978. Ford's outgoing recommendation of $90 was almost doubled by his successor. The Congress understood the message and advanced the Corporation's budget by 52 per cent in real terms. Even this significant augmentation of its budget failed to satisfy the Corporation's new Board.

Throughout the Carter presidency, a similar budget equilibrium can be discerned, with the President's recommendation usually falling below the final appropriation, but with the Corporation consistently dissatisfied. The rate of budget growth declined in fiscal year 1979 to 17 per cent in real terms, and became negative for 1980 and 1981, though still rising in nominal terms. This less favorable budgetary experience reflected a growing recognition within the Congress of general interest alienation induced by the excesses of the special interests, evidenced in growing legal services activism, as well as growing unease over the inflation rate.

The election of Ronald Reagan to the presidency in 1980 reflected a change in attitudes towards legal services and a wrenching apart of the cozy triangle that had ensured equilibrium throughout the earlier life of the Corporation. The general interest, revolting against law reform activism, signalled a desire for retreat into a more conservative, even classical liberal, era of legal services governance. For the better part of the 1980s, President Reagan remained faithful to this philosophy, focusing the heavy artillery of the White House on a legal service program that had moved beyond the control of the Congress, and had committed itself to litigation warfare on the family, capitalism and even on republicanism.

The lines of battle were quickly drawn, as Reagan marked down the 1982 budget recommendation of Carter from $347 million to zero, urging the closure of the federal legal services program and its replacement at state level, if the individual states so desired, funded out of the block grants appropriated by the federal government. In the changed climate, the congressional budget process unfolded more warily than in the recent past, but in resolute opposition to the President. The Senate version of the first Concurrent Budget Resolution, despite Republican control, appropriated $100 million for the Legal Services Corporation. The House version was significantly higher, appropriating $241 million.

In November 1981, the Senate agreed to elevate its appropriation to $241 million in return for restrictions designed to narrow the law reform activism of the LSC (the Chiles restrictions). The Republican leadership in the Senate then withdrew the bill. A Continuing Resolution was finally agreed within the Congress in December 1981, appropriating to the Corporation $241 million, without restrictions, for fiscal year 1982. The appropriation was only 60 per cent of the $399 budget requested by the LSC, and represented a real cut of 29 per cent in the budget appropriated in fiscal year 1981.

The deadlock continued throughout 1982 as the President struggled to gain programmatic control. In the absence of an appropriations bill, with the President recommending a zero budget appropriation, and with the Corporation lowering its request to $265 million, a Continuing Resolution, enacted in December 1982, held the legal services budget constant at $241 million (a real cut of 3 per cent). On this occasion, the Congress attached two restrictions. The first, targeted against the representation of illegal aliens, legislative representation (lobbying) and class action suits against government agencies, reflected the growing hostility to legal services activism, which had been energized by White House information gathering. The second, targeted against the remuneration of LSC board members, and designed to prohibit the defunding of existing legal services programs, was a response to heavy special interest lobbying against the Reagan reform initiative.

In 1983, the President reiterated his zero budget recommendation, and the LSC Board further reduced its budget request to $251 million. In view of the failure to re-authorize the Corporation, the House made no budget recommendation. The Senate approved a budget appropriation of $257 million which was increased in conference to a final appropriation of $275 million. With the budget appropriated in excess of the Corporation's own budget recommendation, not much credibility remained for Niskanen's (1971) concept of the budget maximizing bureau in the ideologically charged environment of legal services.

Responding to heavy special interest lobbying, the Congress attached affirmative riders to its fiscal year 1984 appropriations bill, requiring the refunding of all existing grantees and contractees at enhanced levels of budget and prohibiting the Corporation from implementing other grant adjustments. Such line item monitoring by the Congress was designed to obstruct the Reagan Board from imposing budgetary discipline over those local legal services programs that failed to satisfy standards of conduct set out in the 1974 Act.

For fiscal year 1985, the Corporation increased its budget request, despite the President's zero recommendation, and the Congress appropriated $305 million, a budget level that was to hold steady throughout the remaining years of the Reagan presidency. This newly-established equilibrium, associated with tightened congressional control over the budgetary discretion of the Corporation, reflected a clear victory for the special interests. For fiscal years 1987 and 1988, Warren Rudman spear-headed the rejection by the Senate of a proposed restructuring of the Corporation's budget that would have financed a more aggressive pursuit by the Board of its statutory responsibilities under the 1974 Act, including the attempted defunding (at approximately $1 million per grantee) of delinquent local programs. In the Senate debate over the fiscal year 1988 budget, Warren Rudman engaged in acrimonious debate with Philip Gramm in a successful defence of the national support centers against an LSC bid to close them down. The appropriations bill further tightened the line item control by the Congress over the Corporation's budget. Table 11.4 outlines the nature of the line-itemed budget appropriated to legal services for fiscal year 1989, at the end of the second Reagan presidential term. Table 11.5 traces the expansion in the LSC management budget from 1982 to 1986, and its curtailment thereafter by the Congress.

Table 11.4   Fiscal year 1989 Appropriation to the Legal Services Corporation

Total Appropriation	$ million
	308.555
of which:	
Basic Field programs	264.349
Native American programs	7.022
Migrant programs	9.698
Law School clinics	1.100
Supplemental field programs	1.000
Regional training centers	0.624
National support centers	7.228
State support	7.843
Clearinghouse	0.865
Computer assisted legal research regional centers	0.510
Corporation management and administration	8.316

Source: Public Law 100–459, 1 Oct. 1988.

For fiscal year 1989, the White House abandoned its bid to liquidate the Legal Services Corporation. Instead, the President recommended a budget appropriation of $250 million in return for the abandonment by legal services programs of all political lobbying, the imposition of effective accountability on the local programs, the introduction of competitive bidding for Corporation contracts, and the total defunding of the national support centers. The Legal Services Board embraced these reform proposals as part of its own $250 million budget request.

Warren Rudman in the Senate and Bruce Morrison (a former legal services attorney) in the House led the congressional attack on this initiative. The fiscal year 1989 appropriation bill was confirmed at $318 million, confirmed funding for the national support centers, and delayed any movement

Table 11.5 *The management and administration budget of the LSC 1976–90 ($ million)*

Fiscal year	Management & Administration	% of Final Appropriation
1976	1.72	1.47
1977	2.61	2.09
1978	3.81	1.86
1979	4.57	1.69
1980	4.81	1.60
1981	5.14	1.50
1982	5.28	2.19
1983	4.99	2.07
1984	5.55	2.02
1985	7.75	2.47
1986	7.75	2.54
1987	11.74	3.84
1988	10.52	3.44
1989	10.10	3.27
1990*	10.70	3.47

Note * FY 1990 estimated.
Source: Legal Services Corporation, 1989.

towards competitive bidding on contracts until a new Board of Directors could be appointed by a new President. Although Reagan was presented with a sufficient number of signatures from members of the House and the Senate to guarantee that his veto could not be over-ridden, nevertheless, he signed the bill into law thereby signalling the failure of his bold and long-sustained attempt to eliminate the Legal Services Corporation and to reform and decentralize the program of legal services.

6 Implications and consequences

It is not easy to determine the efficiency of political institutions, given the subjective nature of the efficiency concept (Buchanan, 1986a) and the absence of competitive markets which offer some a priori support for the notion that survivorship implies efficiency. For this reason it will never be possible to determine indisputably the relative standing of Virginia and Chicago political economy by reference to the predictive test. Nevertheless, the budgetary experience of legal services over the period 1976 to 1989 offers insights which should not be ignored by the two research programs under scrutiny.

First, there is evident a distinct change of emphasis in the attitude of the LSC Board towards its budget. Prior to 1982, the Corporation behaved like a budget maximizing bureau (Niskanen, 1971). From 1982 onwards, the Corporation assumed a much less aggressive budget stance, even requesting, for fiscal year 1983, a budget less than that finally appropriated. Evidence outlined in Chapter 12 will suggest that ideology played a major role in this change in Board policy. A wealth seeking Board would behave in such fashion only if post-Corporation career rewards for such behavior were high. There is no evidence that the part-time Board members benefited privately from budget abstinence.

Second, there is evident a major battle over the legal services budget between the Congress and the President. As Madison predicted in the Federalist, victory in this battle went to the Congress, despite the high priority accorded by President Reagan to his campaign against the federal legal services program. Was the presidential attack responsible for the once for all budget reduction in fiscal year 1982? Or was that reduction a congressional response to a change in the balance of supply and demand with respect to legal services policy? Even if the latter view is taken, by scholars of Chicago political economy, what is left of the compound republic hypothesis that the separation of powers facilitates legislative brokering by supporting the durability of legislative contracts?

Third, President Reagan's attack on legal services was not simply one example out of many confrontations with Congress reflective of a fundamental difference in budgetary perspective. President Reagan was complacent with regard to the budget deficit, presiding over the largest increase in real national debt per capita ever recorded in the US. This achievement occurred during a period of world peace and of United States economic growth. As Tables 11.6 – 11.10 indicate, the President's overall budget by and large was legislated by a Congress that comprised a Republican Senate and a relatively conservative House of Representatives throughout the period 1982 to 1986. Legal services, agricultural subsidies and the environment were major exceptions to a more general fiscal harmony between the President and the Congress.

If legal services was indeed the exception, what factors other than ideology accounted for its exposure? Was the driving force in the dispute simply a consequence of radically differing perspectives concerning the location of the median voter? Was it a consequence of blind vengeance on the part of once Governor and now President Ronald Reagan? Or was it a set battle between the median voter and the dominant special interests, with the latter defeating the former, irrespective of the underlying balance of social advantage, as Virginia political economy predicts. The fact that agricultural subsidies and the environment joined with legal services as the other major

Table 11.6   The federal budget fiscal year 1982 (outlays in $ billions)

Budget Function	(a) President's Request	(b) House Resolution	(b) Senate Resolution	Actual Outlays
050 National defence	188.9	188.8	188.8	185.3
150 International affairs	11.2	11.2	11.1	12.3
250 General science, space and technology	6.9	6.9	7.0	7.2
270 Energy	8.7	4.2	6.9	13.5
300 Natural resources and environment	12.0	11.9	12.8	13.0
350 Agriculture	4.5	4.4	4.6	15.9
370 Commerce and housing credit	3.1	3.1	4.8	6.3
400 Transportation	20.0	19.7	21.0	20.6
450 Community and regional development	8.1	8.1	9.2	8.3
500 Education, training, employ- ment and social services	25.8	25.7	27.4	27.0
550 Health	73.5	73.3	73.4	74.0
600 Income security	241.4	241.2	238.2	263.7
700 Veterans benefits and Services	23.6	24.1	23.9	24.0
750 Administration of justice	4.4	4.4	4.5	4.7
800 General government	5.0	5.0	4.8	4.5
850 General purpose fiscal assistance	6.5	6.4	6.4	6.4
900 Net interest	82.6	81.8	89.5	85.0
920 Allowances (d)	1.8	.7	0	–
950 Undistributed offsetting receipts	–32.1	–32.0	–33.5	–26.1
Total Outlays (c)	695.5	688.8	700.8	745.7
Receipts	650.3	657.8	650.3	617.8
Deficit/Surplus (–/+)	–45.2	–31.0	–50.5	–127.9

Notes: (a) Submitted by President Reagan, 10.3.1981
(b) First Budget Resolutions, as passed
(c) Sum of function outlays may not equal total due to rounding
(d) Projected allowances are accorded a budget function for legislative purposes; actual outlays are apportioned among other functions.

Source: Budget of the United States Government.

Table 11.7   The federal budget fiscal year 1983 (outlays in $billions)

Budget Function	(a) President's Request	(b) House Resolution	(b) Senate Resolution	Actual Outlays
050 National defence	221.1	214.0	215.3	209.9
150 International affairs	12.1	22.1	12.1	11.8
250 General science, space and technology	7.6	7.2	7.6	7.9
270 Energy	4.2	3.8	5.0	9.4
300 Natural resources and environment	9.9	10.6	11.4	12.7
350 Agriculture	4.5	· 9.0	10.1	22.9
370 Commerce and housing credit	1.6	1.9	3.9	6.7
400 Transportation	19.6	20.1	19.9	21.3
450 Community and regional development	7.3	7.8	7.7	7.6
500 Education, training, employ- ment and social services	21.6	26.2	27.0	26.6
550 Health	78.1	77.8	77.7	81.2
600 Income security	261.4	269.8	273.0	293.3
700 Veterans benefits and Services	24.4	23.8	23.2	24.8
750 Administration of justice	4.6	4.5	4.9	5.1
800 General government	5.0	4.7	4.8	4.8
850 General purpose fiscal assistance	6.7	6.5	6.5	6.5
900 Net interest	112.5	112.3	115.5	89.8
920 Allowances (d)	−1.3	−2.8	−2.0	−
950 Undistributed offsetting receipts	−43.5	−43.2	−39.3	−34.0
Total Outlays (c)	757.6	765.2	784.3	808.3
Receipts	666.1	665.9	668.4	600.6
Deficit/Surplus	−91.5	−99.3	−115.9	−207.8

Notes: (a) Submitted by President Reagan, 8.2.1982
 (b) First Budget Resolutions, as passed
 (c) Sum of function outlays may not equal total due to rounding
 (d) Projected allowances are accorded a budget function for legislative purposes;
   actual outlays are apportioned among other functions.

Source: Budget of the United States Government.

Table 11.8   The federal budget fiscal year 1984 (outlays in $ billions)

Budget Function	(a) President's Request	(b) House Resolution	(b) Senate Resolution	Actual Outlays
050 National defence	245.3	235.4	241.6	227.4
150 International affairs	13.2	13.2	12.7	15.9
250 General science, space and technology	8.2	8.4	8.2	8.3
270 Energy	3.3	4.3	4.1	7.1
300 Natural resources and environment	9.8	12.5	12.5	12.6
350 Agriculture	12.1	14.7	11.4	13.6
370 Commerce and housing credit	.4	2.3	1.8	6.9
400 Transportation	25.1	26.2	25.9	23.7
450 Community and regional development	7.0	8.6	8.1	7.7
500 Education, training, employ-ment and social services	25.3	32.7	27.3	27.6
550 Health	90.6	96.0	93.1	87.9
600 Income security	282.4	284.7	280.4	290.9
700 Veterans benefits and Services	25.7	25.6	25.6	25.6
750 Administration of justice	5.5	5.5	6.0	5.7
800 General government	6.0	6.1	5.7	5.1
850 General purpose fiscal assistance	7.0	7.6	7.0	6.8
900 Net interest	103.2	96.2	95.9	111.1
920 Allowances (d)	.9	1.3	.6	–
950 Undistributed offsetting receipts	−22.8	−17.4	−18.1	−32.0
Total Outlays (c)	848.5	863.6	849.7	851.8
Receipts	659.7	689.1	671.1	666.5
Deficit/Surplus (−/+)	−188.8	−174.5	−178.6	−185.3

Notes: (a)   Submitted by President Reagan, 31.1.1983
        (b)   First Budget Resolutions, as passed
        (c)   Sum of function outlays may not equal total due to rounding
        (d)   Projected allowances are accorded a budget function for legislative purposes; actual outlays are apportioned among other functions.

Source: Budget of the United States Government.

Table 11.9   The federal budget fiscal year 1985 (outlays in $ billions)

Budget Function	(a) President's Request	(b) House Resolution	(b) Senate Resolution	Actual Outlays
050 National defence	272.0	255.9	266.0	252.8
150 International affairs	17.5	14.6	14.1	16.4
250 General science, space and technology	8.8	8.6	8.5	8.6
270 Energy	3.1	4.2	4.1	5.8
300 Natural resources and environment	11.3	12.0	12.2	13.1
350 Agriculture	14.3	16.5	16.4	25.9
370 Commerce and housing credit	1.1	2.0	2.0	4.0
400 Transportation	27.1	27.1	27.0	25.9
450 Community and regional development	7.6	8.2	8.2	8.1
500 Education, training, employ- ment and social services	27.9	29.9	29.9	28.4
550 Health	32.9	34.2	34.2	33.5
570 Medicare (e)	69.7	65.4	65.4	65.8
600 Income security	114.4	111.2	111.2	129.0
700 Veterans benefits and Services	26.7	26.3	26.4	26.4
750 Administration of justice	6.1	6.1	6.0	6.3
800 General government	5.7	5.7	5.5	5.4
850 General purpose fiscal assistance	6.7	6.5	6.5	6.4
900 Net interest	116.1	133.3	133.8	129.2
920 Allowances (d)	.9	.4	1.0	–
950 Undistributed offsetting receipts	−35.3	−33.1	−33.2	−32.9
Total Outlays (c)	925.5	916.2	933.1	946.0
Receipts	745.1	742.7	743.8	734.1
Deficit/Surplus (−/+)	−180.4	−175.5	−189.3	−211.9

Notes: (a) Submitted by President Reagan, 1.2.1984
   (b) First Budget Resolutions, as passed
   (c) Sum of function outlays may not equal total due to rounding
   (d) Projected allowances are accorded a budget function for legislative purposes; actual outlays are
   (e) Medicare is a separate function (previously included with Health) beginning with this fiscal year
   (f) Social security is a separate function (previously included with Income security beginning with this fiscal year.

Source: Budget of the United States Government.

Table 11.10   The federal budget fiscal year 1986 (outlays in $ billions)

Budget Function	(a) President's Request	(b) House Resolution	(b) Senate Resolution	Actual Outlays
050 National defence	285.7	267.1	273.1	273.4
150 International affairs	18.3	18.6	17.8	14.5
250 General science, space and technology	9.3	8.9	9.0	9.0
270 Energy	4.7	5.8	5.1	4.8
300 Natural resources and environment	11.9	13.0	12.5	13.5
350 Agriculture	12.6	15.8	14.5	31.2
370 Commerce and housing credit	2.2	4.6	3.4	4.3
400 Transportation	25.9	26.5	26.1	28.1
450 Community and regional development	7.3	8.2	7.9	7.5
500 Education, training, employ- ment and social services	29.3	31.2	30.3	29.7
550 Health	34.9	35.6	35.3	35.9
570 Medicare (e)	67.2	68.3	68.3	70.2
600 Income security	115.8	121.8	116.6	120.7
650 Social security (f)	202.2	200.8	194.9	198.8
700 Veterans benefits and Services	26.8	26.8	26.1	26.6
750 Administration of justice	6.6	6.8	6.7	6.6
800 General government	4.8	5.3	5.2	6.8
850 General purpose fiscal assistance	2.8	5.7	6.5	6.4
900 Net interest	142.6	141.0	142.3	135.3
920 Allowances (d)	.4	−4.4	−1.6	−
950 Undistributed offsetting receipts	−37.5	−39.8	−35.0	−33.2
Total Outlays (c)	973.7	967.3	965.0	989.8
Receipts	793.7	794.1	793.6	769.1
Deficit/Surplus (−/+)	−180.0	−173.2	−171.4	−220.7

Notes: (a)   Submitted by President Reagan, 1.2.1985
        (b)   First Budget Resolutions, as passed
        (c)   Sum of function outlays may not equal total due to rounding
        (d)   Projected allowances are accorded a budget function for legislative purposes; actual outlays are
        (e)   Medicare is a separate function (previously included with Health) beginning with this fiscal year
        (f)   Social security is a separate function (previously included with Income security beginning with this fiscal year.

Source: Budget of the United States Government.

battlefield between the President and Congress, with a similar political outcome, strengthens the inference that the special interests triumphed over the common good (see Chapter 14).

Fourth, there is evident an unwillingness on the part of Congress to fund the post-1985 monitoring drive by the LSC designed to weed out inefficient and politically charged local programs. Indeed, Warren Rudman and Bruce Morrison (in harness with Barney Frank) explicitly moved to pare down the administrative budget of the Corporation in order to constrain its monitoring programs. How can such actions be reconciled with the efficient, wealth-maximizing governance model expounded by Wittman (1989)?

If the implications for public choice of the battle over the legal services budget are ambiguous, the consequences for expansion of the non-federal budget conform precisely with the predictions of economic theory. As the margins available for mining the federal budget narrowed, so the legal services programs became more active in fund raising through non-federal channels. As the restrictions placed upon the use made of federal dollars by legal services programs tightened, so the search for less circumscribed monies intensified in the knowledge that money is fungible and that the particular source of funding for a proscribed activity cannot easily be identified. Grantees that receive funds from sources other than the Corporation are required to treat such funds as separate and distinct from any federal funding. These funds may not be used in any manner that violates applicable LSC rules and regulations. Nevertheless somewhat different rules govern their use.

During the Reagan administration, non-LSC funding for legal services field programs rose significantly. In fiscal year 1979, such funding totalled $38 million, or about 13 per cent of total funding. By fiscal year 1985, non-LSC funding was $81 million, or about 22 per cent of total funding. Adjusted for inflation, such funding increased 44 per cent over the period 1979 to 1985. During this period, both the level and the proportion of LSC funding from other federal sources declined (Besharov and Tramontozzi, 1990).

In fiscal year 1979, 77 per cent of non-LSC funding came from federal programs, 17 per cent from private and miscellaneous sources, and 6 per cent from state and local sources. In fiscal year 1985, only 30 per cent of such funding came from federal sources, 38 per cent from private and miscellaneous sources, 25 per cent from state and local sources and 7 per cent from attorney fee awards. This adjustment in funding proportions reflected a decline of 13 per cent in real non-LSC federal funding a real increase of 370 per cent in private and miscellaneous funding, and a real increase of 600 per cent in state and local funding, the preferred method of President Reagan for funding legal services (Besharov and Tramontozzi, 1990).

The $25 million of non-LSC funding from federal sources in fiscal year 1985 was composed of 42 per cent from appropriations under the Older Americans Act, 40 per cent from Social Services Block Grants, 14 per cent from Community Development Block Grants, 2 per cent from revenue sharing, and the remainder from a range of other programs. The $20 million of such funding from state and local government sources in 1985 was composed of 71 per cent from state grants and 29 per cent from local grants (Besharov and Tramontozzi, 1990).

The $31 million of non-LSC funding from private and miscellaneous sources in fiscal year 1985 was composed of 25 per cent from United Way, 18 per cent from carry-overs from fiscal year 1984, 10 per cent from foundations, 9 per cent from interest on lawyers' trust accounts and 2 per cent from bar associations (Besharov and Tramontozzi, 1990).

A significant long-term impulse in favor of increased outside funding is the growth of the interest in Lawyers' Trust Accounts (IOLTA). This program was first implemented in Florida in 1981 as a means of supplementing the funding of legal services. IOLTA funds are generated from the interest earned on trust funds handled by private attorneys for their clients that, if held in separate accounts, would fail to draw interest in excess of service charges. Such funds are pooled in a lawyer's unsegregated trust fund accounts, on which interest is accumulated and forwarded to the state bar association.

By November 1987, 45 states and the District of Columbia had adopted IOLTA programs. At that time, the cumulative total income generated by these programs was $111 million, of which $81 million had been distributed to legal services programs. In 1987 alone, an estimated $32 million was generated through IOLTA accounts of which almost $27 million was distributed to legal services programs.

As Chapter 16 suggests, the emergence of non-federal LSC funding since 1979 as an important component of legal services support is to be welcomed, not least because it decentralizes initiatives in assisting the poor to access the civil justice system. This additional source of finance has not abated the pressure from powerful special interests to maintain and to augment the federal legal services budget. The continued, high level pressure by special interests on a constrained federal budget does not fit well into a public interest theory of the political process. To the extent that it appears to be a high cost method of wealth redistribution, as Chapter 13 demonstrates, it does not fit well into the Chicago research program. Virginia political economy, which does not view special interest rent-seeking either as public-spirited or as efficient, has no difficulty in accommodating such observed behavior into its research program.

12 The hubris of ideology

Is our constitution so excellent? Then a change of ministry can be no such dreadful event; since it is essential to such a constitution, in every ministry, both to preserve itself from violation, and to prevent all enormities in the administration. Is our constitution very bad? Then so extraordinary a jealousy and apprehension, on account of changes, is ill placed; and a man should be no more anxious in this case, then a husband, who had married a woman from the stews, should be watchful to prevent her infidelity. Public affairs, in such a government, must necessarily go to confusion, by whatever hands they are conducted; and the zeal of patriots is in that case much less requisite than the patience and submission of philosophers.

David Hume, *Essays Moral, Political and Literary*, Liberty Classics, 1985

1 Introduction

Whether or not ideology exerts influence upon political markets and if so, in what manner, is an issue of considerable significance for each of the major research programs under review in this book. The public interest research program is grounded on the notion that the legislature and its bureaucracy are both amenable to well researched advice by economists who establish a case for efficiency-based institutional reforms, at least where such reforms can be made compatible with ruling distributional concerns. The Chicago Political Economy research program eschews all notions of public interest but yet infers that political markets are universally efficient, with efficiency defined both politically and economically in terms of expected wealth maximization. Wider notions of ideology are denied relevance.

The Virginia Political Economy research program rejects the public interest in favor of a public choice interpretation of the behavior of political markets. Unlike Chicago, however, it recognizes the potential relevance of ideology in political markets and the threat that such ideology poses for wealth maximization even when the median voters are motivated predominantly by wealth-seeking objectives. Should adverse ideologies prevail when median voter preferences are predominantly wealth-seeking, political markets must evidence some combination of the limitations outlined in Chapters 5, 6 and 7 of this book. It is relevant to note that weakness is defined, not by reference to social engineering judgments but in terms of perceived deviations of policy from the preferences of the median voter.

The behavior of the US Congress, the Legal Services Corporation and its outreach programs is evaluated in this chapter to determine the extent to which economic efficiency and wealth maximization have been subverted by incompatible ideologies, the extent to which such subversions have been endorsed by the median voter, and the extent to which they are a reflection of the abuse of discretionary power by actors in the political market place for legal services.

Sections 2 and 3 explore the concept of ideology as it is employed in political market analysis and review the sharply divergent interpretations of this concept in the public interest, the Chicago and the Virginia research programs. Section 4 relates the concept of ideology to the political market in legal services. Section 5 evaluates the conditional predictions of Virginia political economy concerning ideology in the US federal program of legal services with respect to the initial phase of that program, 1964 to 1974, under the auspices of the Office of Economic Opportunity. Section 6 extends this analysis to the phase of legal services expansion, 1975 to 1980. Section 7 takes in the period of illegality within the federal program of legal services, 1981–1982, triggered by the election victory of Ronald Reagan, and by the threatened termination of federal funding. Section 8 takes in the extended battle between the US President and his Board of Directors of the Legal Services Corporation, on the one side, and the US Congress, the legal services outreach program and the American Bar Association, on the other, over the period 1982 to 1988. Section 9 concludes by assessing the costs in wealth dissipation imposed by such a conflict and the damage to the goal of individual access to civil justice that ideology has imposed.

2   Politics, ideology and the strait-jacket of Chicago Political Economy

The term ideology is employed in this book to denote the purported social rather than the more narrowly self-centred objectives of actors in the political market place. An elaborate definition of ideology is not attempted. The definition by Downs (1957), 'a verbal image of the good society and of the chief means of constructing such a society', is deemed to be sufficient. It is important to emphasize that ideology, so defined, is embedded, if at all, in the individual and not in any group or other organization.

The political ideology of an individual thus may be viewed as more or less consistent sets of normative statements as to best or preferred states of the world (Kalt and Zupan, 1984, p. 281). Such statements are moralistic and altruistic in the sense that they are viewed by the individual to be applicable to everyone, rather than merely to the individual who enunciates them. Accordingly, political ideologies are to be viewed as statements about how government can best promote their proponents' conceptions of the public interest.

Economics has attracted criticism for its emphasis upon the wealth-seeking motivation of individuals in society. Even in private markets, it is argued by critics, individuals are motivated by concerns broader than their private interests. Few deny, however, that private interest is the dominant motive in most market choices and most allow, however grudgingly, that it is an acceptable theoretical assumption, when investigating traditional economic behavior, justified by its explanatory and predictive power. There is much greater resistance to the assumption of private interest, as it is employed in public choice, as the dominant motive in political market behavior (Lee, 1988).

Most scholars (indeed most economists) whose work concerns public policy tend to assume, if only implicitly, that actors in political markets and most notably individuals within the government and its bureaucracy are motivated by the desire to promote the interest of the general community. In the words of political scientist, Steven Kelman (1987): 'There is the elementary fact that political decisions apply to the entire community. That they do so encourages people to think about others when taking a stand. This is in contrast to making personal decisions, when people think mainly of themselves.'

According to this perspective, the private interest assumption misses the essence of political decision making and public choice, in consequence, is interpreted as being irrelevant to an understanding of the political process. Once again, Kelman (1987) offers a forthright judgment: 'instead of trying to mix self-interest and altruism into every decision, the individual might try to reserve certain decisions to self-interest and others to altruism'. Kelman leaves no doubt that individuals tend to give the greater weight to altruism in making political choices. If his judgment is accurate, and if social efficiency, appropriately trimmed by equity considerations, is reflective of all individual choices in political markets, there would be little division between the public interest, the CPE and the VPE research programs, in predictions, if not in assumptions. Such evidently is not the case.

In contrast to the public interest research program, CPE, most eloquently in the writings of Stigler (1971, 1988), but also in the contributions by Becker (1983, 1985), by Peltzman (1976, 1984, 1990) and by Wittman (1989), denies any relevance to ideology in the political market place. CPE does not deny that intellectuals, with notable exceptions, tend to expose attitudes toward policy that are fundamentally hostile to laissez-faire capitalism. Rather, it rationalizes such attitudes as emanating from self-interest on the part of individuals, many of whom are only marginally employable within a capitalist system, and whose expected wealth, in consequence, is dependent on the expansion of government expenditures. In the view of CPE, such intellectuals influence few outside their own circle on issues of policy, and exert no more impact on political markets than would any other interest group of comparable size. Political markets broker policies in response to votes and to lobbying outlays, not to ideas or ideology.

For Stigler (1988), the notion that ideology plays a role in political behavior analogous to that played by tastes in the ordinary behavior of individuals is unsatisfying, not least because political activity is conducted by organized coalitions. In his judgment, 'politically effective groups have used the state to foster their ends in all periods of history' (1988, p. xiii). Political intermediaries – parties, legislators, administrators – are not believed to be devoid of influence, 'but in the main they act as agents for the primary players in the construction and administration of public policy' (p. xv).

Among the primary players in the construction and administration of public policy within a democracy are the voters themselves. As early as 1976, Becker expressed scepticism concerning any theory of public policy that assumed that 'most voters are systematically fooled about the effects of policies ... that have persisted for a long time' (p. 246). In his view, voters held unbiased expectations, at least concerning policies that had persisted, overestimating the dead weight loss from some such policies and underestimating it from others. More forcefully, he endorsed an even stronger assumption: 'namely, that voters perceived correctly the gains and losses from all policies' (p. 247). From such a rational expectations perspective, ideology might be predicted to occur within the political market place only when endorsed by some decisive-voter set, usually viewed as the median voter by CPE scholars (Wittman, 1989). In true CPE style, Peltzman (1990) placed this rational expectations theory of the voting market to the empirical test. Utilizing an extensive US dataset for the period 1952 to 1988, embracing income and inflation statistics and details of voter behavior in Presidential, Senate and Gubernatorial elections, Peltzman concluded that 'one would be hard put to find non political markets that process information better than the voting market' (Peltzman, 1990, p. 63) and that '[i]f all voters are rationally ignorant, whence comes efficiency in the voting market?' (ibid, p. 63).

Notwithstanding Peltzman's ongoing research program, Becker (1983) came to accept that voter preferences were not the driving force in political behavior. 'Voter preferences' can be manipulated and created through the information and misinformation provided by interested pressure groups, who raise their political influence partly by changing the revealed 'preferences' of enough voters and politicians (Becker, 1983, p. 392). Becker, in effect, acknowledged the Virginia insight (Tullock, 1967a) that rational voters do not invest in political information, and do not concern themselves much about for whom or what they vote, should they choose to vote at all.

Becker's recognition that the individual voter was rationally ignorant in no sense implied that political markets were prone to ideology. Wealth maximization remained alive and well in political markets in the safe and conserving hands of members of special interest groups (Becker, 1983, 1985). Becker presented a theory of the political redistribution of income and of other public policies that built on competition among pressure groups for political favors. Active groups produced pressure to raise their political influence, where all influences were jointly determined by the pressures produced by all groups. The political budget balance between the total amount raised in taxes and the total amount available for subsidies implied that the sum of all influences was zero.

In Becker's theory, each group is assumed to maximize the income of its members on the Cournot–Nash assumption that additional pressure does not affect political expenditures of other groups. Equilibrium expenditures on pressure and the equilibrium incomes of all groups are determined from these maximizing conditions and from the political budget equation. Political equilibrium is shown to depend on the efficiency of each group in producing pressure, the effect of additional pressure on influence, the number of persons in different groups, and the deadweight costs of taxes and subsidies.

Efficiency in producing pressure is determined, in part, by the cost of controlling free-riding among the members. Greater control over free-riding raises the optimal pressure by a group and thus increases its subsidy or reduces its taxes. Efficiency is also determined by the size of a group, not only because size affects free-riding, but also because small groups may not be able to take advantage of scale economies in the production of pressure.

The most important variables in Becker's model, driving the efficiency implication of pressure group behavior, are the deadweight costs of taxes and subsidies that result from their effects on the allocation of time between work and leisure, investments in human and non-human capital, consumption of different goods, and other behavior. Deadweight costs are viewed as increasing, generally, at an increasing rate as taxes and subsidies increase. An increase in the deadweight cost of a subsidy discourages pressure by the subsidized group because a given revenue from taxes then yields a smaller subsidy. An increase in the deadweight cost of a tax, on the other hand, encourages pressure by taxpayers because a given reduction in their taxes has a smaller effect on the amount available as a subsidy.

All groups, in this model, favor and lobby for efficient taxes because these improve the welfare of subsidized as well as taxed groups. Efficient subsidies raise subsidies and benefit recipients, but harm taxpayers. Overall, Becker infers that policies that raise efficiency – including regulations and quotas as well as explicit taxes and subsidies – are likely to win out in the competition for influence, because they produce gains rather than deadweight costs, so that groups benefited have an intrinsic advantage compared with groups harmed. 'Consequently, this analysis unifies the view that governments correct market failures with the view that they favor the politically powerful by showing that both are produced by competition among pressure groups for political favors' (Becker, 1983, p. 396).

If the pressure groups effect efficient policies, politicians and bureaucrats must implement and enforce them. Becker relies upon the pressure groups to eliminate from office or to repudiate the actions of such individuals through elections, recalls or impeachments when they deviate excessively from efficiency. He acknowledges, however, the problem posed by the separation of ownership and control and urges the necessity for more general analysis to incorporate this principal–agent relation between bureaucrats, politicians and pressure groups into the determination of political equilibrium.

Peltzman (1984) takes up this challenge in an extensive empirical review of the relationship between constituent interest and congressional voting utilizing a simple principal–agent model in the manner suggested by Becker. He concludes that the tendency for legislators to shirk serving their constituents' interests in favor of their own preferences (ideology) 'seems more apparent than real' (Peltzman, 1984, p. 210). Although ideology variables appear to explain much legislative voting behavior statistically, they turn out to be proxies for something more fundamental: liberals and conservatives tend to appeal to voters with systematically different incomes, education and occupations, and to draw contributions from different interest groups. These systematic differences, in Peltzman's view, go far towards rationalizing voting patterns (of the legislators) without relying on explanations that involve shirking behavior.

When Peltzman classifies issues by degree of wealth redistribution, the economic variables fare best, and ideology fares worst, on issues involving the greatest redistribution of wealth. On run-of-the-mill economic issues, economic variables retain above-average explanatory power. Only on social issues, where the wealth states are unclear, does ideology play a prominent role. If shirking is at all important, then, in Peltzman's view, it is subject to the law of demand: less is bought the higher the price, measured as the wealth gain or loss to principals. On this basis, Peltzman concludes that economists could 'shift their major analytical energies toward a simple principal–agent model and relegate shirking to a sideshow, just as profit maximization rather than managerial shirking remains the main analytical engine for understanding firm behavior' (Peltzman, 1984, p. 216).

3   Politics, ideology and the power of Virginia Political Economy

In contrast to the CPE notion that ideology is only minimally relevant as an influence over political market equilibria, the Virginia Political Economy research program allows it much greater scope albeit within a self-seeking individualistic model of political market behavior. Indeed, the particular power and attraction of the VPE program, in this respect, is its ability to reconcile evidence of ideological influence with the universal presence of homo economicus in all stages of the political process (Lee, 1988). Ideology exerts an influence in part as a direct and efficient reflection of voters' preferences, which are not viewed to be as universally focused on expected wealth as CPE suggests. For the most part, however, ideology is let loose on policy as a consequence of political market failure; the result of an imperfect nexus between median voter preferences and ultimate political action.

Pure ideology, if it exists at all, is the manifestation of altruism in the political sector (Kalt and Zupan, 1984). The returns from the furtherance of ideology come in several forms. First, the successful promotion of an ideology may provide individuals with the satisfaction of knowing that they have improved the lot of others. Second, it may be rewarded either by reciprocal favors by those who benefit, or by psychic returns in the form of their elevated esteem. Third, even if the pursuit of ideology has no ultimate effect, those involved may derive satisfaction from having done the right thing, and also may benefit from the warm regard of those who share their failed vision. Such tastes, if they exist, will influence behavior, most particularly where expected individual wealth is not adversely influenced by ideological action. As with all preferences, ideology is responsive to economic pressure; more will be provided as its cost declines.

From this perspective, ideology will be more evident in political than in private markets. First, as Kalt and Zupan (1984) have noted, altruistic ideological preferences, that depend upon outcomes and net effort, encounter significant publicness constraints. Government coercion is a classic Samuelson solution to the free-rider problem that must restrain strictly private actions. Moreover, government can often be manipulated into financing the altruists' programs by seizing the wealth of third parties who do not share the ideology but who cannot organize to avoid coerced supply.

Second, in much political activity, the individual has no meaningful prospect of influencing outcomes. If the paradox of voting (Downs, 1957) does not result in voters' abstaining, it may result in symbolic voting in which voters indulge ideological preferences harmful even to their own expected wealth, secure in the expectation that their vote is indecisive (Brennan and Buchanan, 1983; Lee, 1988). Tullock (1971) relied on the indecisiveness of individual votes to explain why individuals vote for poverty programs which, if enacted, would cost them far more than if they had contributed through charity.

If voters respond to rational ignorance and to the paradox of voting by making many political market decisions primarily on the basis of low cost ideology, special interest groups typically organize around much more narrowly motivated economic concerns (Olson, 1965; Lee, 1988). Since special interests exert a more decisive influence over political outcomes, the cost of casual ideological expression becomes prohibitively high. In such circumstances, members of special interests groups utilize the language of ideology to reinforce the vote motive in favor of legislative action, but invade the details of the unfolding legislation and comb the language of the statutes for exploitable rent-seeking opportunities of a much more wealth-orientated kind (Crew and Rowley, 1988).

Unlike voters, who quickly forget the legislation for which they have cast votes, the affected special interests are unrelenting in their efforts to subvert the statutes to their own pecuniary advantage. Such opportunities explain the existence of large public interest lobbying groups which, at first sight, should not be able to overcome the logic of collective action (Kau and Rubin, 1982).

Virginia Political Economy recognizes additional opportunities for legislators to indulge ideological preferences even to the disadvantage of constituent interests (Rowley and Vachris, 1990). The institutional attributes of the public sector lend themselves to such activity as a consequence of separation of ownership from control and the ultimate failure even of a skilfully contrived governance structure to eliminate the principal–agent problem.

First, the market for control is characterized by significant indivisibilities. Constituents are typically presented with all or nothing choices between a small number of large bundles of issues. The market in which voters' choices are registered is achieved only infrequently, limiting the opportunities for rebundling that a continuous market might provide.

Second, the voters have no greater incentive to inform themselves over legislators' behavior than they have to inform themselves over elections, given the indecisiveness of their individual interventions. Furthermore, since political ownership is non-transferable, even the ownership rights of special interest groups are attenuated, leading to shirking in the monitoring of the legislature.

Third, the political market is subject to less than perfect competition, indeed, is duopolistic in nature. Since the rival parties are constrained by strict capacity limits, at least between elections, competition will follow the Cournot rather than the Bertrand model with significant margins of political discretion available to those who choose to indulge personal ideologies (Tirole, 1989). Moreover, the legislature in the United States is non-contestable, as a consequence both of rational ignorance among the electorate, which renders it vulnerable to high spending election campaigns, and of high sunk cost advantages of incumbents which make them particularly attractive to the political action committees (Crain, 1988). Particularly important among such sunk cost advantages are the membership and seniority of incumbents on key congressional committees that service special interests.

Legislator shirking certainly is not without cost (Kalt and Zupan, 1984). Monitoring does occur both from the voting booth and from the political action committees, as well as from the governance structures of the US Congress (Weingast and Moran, 1983; Weingast and Marshall, 1988). Such monitoring is less effective, however, than that which controls the behavior of senior management in capitalist enterprise (Rowley and Vachris, 1990). The implication of imperfect monitoring is a degree of discretion available to representatives at the expense of their constituents. As Tollison (1988) observed, the issue 'is not whether ideology matters at all to political behavior, but how much and under what conditions' (Tollison, 1988, p. 353).

Finally, the VPE research program, in contrast to its CPE counterpart, recognizes the opportunities available to senior bureaucrats to shirk in their statutory duties in the implementation of public policies in favor of indulging their own ideological preferences. When senior bureaucrats are advocates or zealots (Downs, 1967) such shirking is to be expected, given the limitations of the congressional governance machinery (Rowley and Vachris, 1990).

The attenuated property rights of members of congress, even of those with seniority as members of important committees, given the non-transferability of committee offices and the absence of intergenerational linkages, weakens monitoring incentives by comparison with stockholders in capitalist enterprise, and encourages myopia within the monitoring mechanism (Lee, 1988). The multiplicity of principals overseeing any single bureau further encourages shirking by monitors who must share in the political surplus. Any conflict between the Congress and the President over the appropriate function of a specific bureau opens up ideological opportunities which will be exploited by zealots and advocates.

If the legislature cannot monitor the federal bureaus effectively, the outside labor market for bureaucrats will not close the gap (Rowley and Elgin, 1985). Senior bureaucrats move only with extreme difficulty from one bureau to another, not least because of the high cost of advice and consent. Complexities in measuring and evaluating the output of bureaus are far greater than in capitalistic enterprise where the profit yardstick exists. Salaries and promotions within a bureau are based far more on seniority than on merit. Tenure is more prevalent than in competitive capitalism. There is no loyalty equivalent within a bureau to the stock option of the joint-stock corporation. In such circumstances, ideological shirking may assume significant proportions.

Virginia Political Economy thus outlines an analytical framework in which ideology in politics is consistent with the universal presence of homo economicus. Indeed, the power of the VPE research program rests upon its ability to explain why ideology is more important in political than in market choices (Lee, 1988).

The VPE insight is yet more precise. It suggests that ideology is more important than narrow economic interest in providing general direction to legislation; but less important in determining the details of legislation and its translation into effective policy. This hypothesis is here evaluated, with respect to legal services policy over the period 1964 to 1988.

4 Ideology, self-interest and the market in civil justice for the poor

The political market in civil justice for the poor lends itself admirably to the intertwined forces of ideology and narrow self-interest defined by the VPE research program. Moreover, it does so in a manner closely analogous to that outlined in Section 3 above.

The rhetoric of the American Bar Association, dedicated to persuading the rationally ignorant voter to endorse the federally-funded program of legal services, is the rhetoric of community values, stressing the public good characteristics of charitable giving, and emphasizing the paternalistic case for providing legal services in kind rather than allowing the poor to redirect cash transfers to more highly valued uses. No doubt some members of the organized bar believe this rhetoric. Many view it as a potentially profitable method of raising the level of litigation within the United States. Others view it as a cynical means of fostering, at low cost to themselves, a social agenda reflective of their own ideologies but unattainable directly through the lobbying of the legislature. Few of these latter are sufficiently motivated by ideology as to divert significant resources within their law practices from fee-based to pro bono services (see Chapter 14). The large majority of the US bar is rationally ignorant of the true nature of the legal services program.

Those rationally ignorant voters who are persuaded by the rhetoric of the organized bar to endorse legal services legislation and to support its funding at current and/or at augmented projected levels do so for a variety of reasons. Some, a small minority, share the ideology of social activism, acquaint themselves thoroughly with the 1974 Act and follow closely the litigation paths of the legal services staff attorneys. This group is minuscule, as a small test of my own elicited. In four public choice classes at George Mason University, held over the period 1988 to 1990, comprising some 160 college juniors and seniors specialized in economics, only five students had heard of legal services, and none could outline its organizational form within the United States. All those students were of voting age, though a small minority was foreign.

Other voters, swayed by the importance of the access to civil justice argument, but unwilling or unable to review the details of the legal services program, vote for legal services essentially as a moral act, an expression of Kantian goodwill, approved because the gift itself is viewed as good rather than because the envisaged practical consequences of the gift are assessed to be desirable (Ireland and Johnson, 1970). Such voters, predictably, do not monitor the legal services program.

Yet other voters, the majority of those who dissect the policy bundles presented by the politicians, to determine the legal services component, vote their casual conscience on the issue, secure that their vote is indecisive, and that they do not individually impose upon themselves the tax consequences of the electoral outcome (Lee, 1988). Such voters pay only a negligible regard to the actual performance of the legal services outreach program.

The large majority of the electorate is rationally ignorant of legal services, neither knowing nor caring about the existence or absence of a program which is well outside its area of interest, as it is beyond the individual's ability to influence or to control. It is the ignorance of this majority on the details of policy that really opens up the sluice-gates for ideology and for minority-based legislation which rent-seekers adjust to their narrow self-serving advantages.

5   Star Wars: Legal services and the Office of Economic Opportunity 1966–1974

The Economic Opportunity Act was signed into law in August 1964 by President Lyndon Johnson, as the fulcrum of the Great Society Program. In 1966 legal services was introduced as a special emphasis program as a result of skilful lobbying by Edgar and Jean Cahn, supported by the House of Delegates of the American Bar Association, by the ABA President, and by a range of other interest groups.

In the 18-month period, January 1966 to mid 1967, the investment in legal services for poor Americans increased eight-fold under the impetus of OEO grant support. During that period, 300 legal services organizations, many of which were newly-established, were awarded grants from an annual federal budget of $42 million. More than 800 new law offices and almost 2000 new attorney positions were funded in this exercise. In one burst of federal expenditure, the OEO was able to construct a system of law offices and of lawyers approximately equal in size to the United States Department of Justice, together with all its attorneys' offices (Johnson, 1978). This network was established by an agency that was equipped neither to monitor the performance nor to discipline the transgressions of the outlets that it funded.

The 1964 Act provided broad discretionary powers to the OEO which might provide or withhold funding to local legal services programs for almost any reason. In practice, the OEO tended to defer to local community action agencies, allowing them to set their own priorities and to design their own solutions to poverty:

> The reluctance of the staff of OEO to establish strong national policies was derived from the local orientation of the community action concept. Some OEO

officials held an almost religious revenue for the preferences of local Community Action Agencies. This stance often was taken at the expense of the poor (who usually were outvoted in the councils of local AA's) and the effectiveness of the anti-poverty effort. (Johnson, 1978, p.105)

The OEO rejected the 1967 recommendation in the McKinsey Report that controls should be tightened over the local legal services program through a policy of regionalization. Instead, under the direction of Earl Johnson, the OEO reaffirmed the semi-autonomous nature of the local programs and signalled to them the priority of law reform over access to the right to justice. The American Bar Association was actively involved in this major change in legal services:

> Law reform and all its techniques – test cases, legislative lobbying, advocacy before administrative agencies and the rest – are commonplace to the major firms out of which the ABA leaders came. … Thus it was easier for this type of lawyer to conceive law reform as a natural part of equal justice than it was for the typical private attorney who spent his time handling personal injury cases and drafting wills. Whatever the cause, the leaders of the American Bar Association and other national leaders of the organized bar were seen far ahead of most local agency board members and remained so at least through 1972. (Johnson, 1978, p. 170)

In the absence of central governance, the more activist local programs allowed ideology a loose rein, to the advantage of legal services staff attorneys who had been professionalized in law reform activism while holding Reginald Heber Smith fellowships. The outcome was a swathe of law reform activity which manifested itself in a sustained legal services attack on state governments, in test case and class action litigation and in the lobbying of the federal and state legislatures. Legal services staff attorneys may even have incited race riots during the late 1960s. By 1972, hubris had turned to nemesis in the OEO legal services program and the American Bar Association had to call upon its most powerful lobbying reserves to protect legal services from more general collapse.

6   The Empire strikes back: The Legal Services Corporation as an agent of law reform 1974–1980

The Legal Services Corporation, as a consequence both of ABA lobbying and of skilful legislative drafting by Alan Houseman, a legal services activist, was created as an independent, non-profit corporation, outside the scope of executive branch governance and distanced even from congressional monitoring and control. In such circumstances, its policies would depend significantly upon the philosophies of its Board Chairman and its President, and their willingness and ability to withstand or to succumb to the predictable law reform lobbying of the American Bar Association, the organized legal services field, and the egregious coalition of special interests now loosely referred to as the Rainbow Coalition.

Throughout the initial transition phase, 1974–1976, relationships between the Corporation, whose Board and senior officers had been appointed by President Ford, and an activist legal services field concerned to re-establish the reformist momentum of the Great Society Program, remained tense. In particular, the major field interests – the Project Advisory Group (PAG), the National Legal Aid and Defender Association (NLADA), and the National Client Council (NCC) – lobbied successfully to loosen the governance powers of the Legal Services Corporation:

> While LSC was more bureaucratic and there was far more written policy, LSC, like OEO, de-emphasized its regulatory role in favor of incentives, encouragement and a form of partnership. LSC was not much more willing to be a policeman than OEO. To those who saw as the main role of LSC the enforcement of prohibitions in the Act, the Corporation would be a major disappointment. That disappointment would ensure that controversy would never really go away. (Dooley and Houseman, 1984, p. 5)

The initial policies of the Corporation were developed through the promulgation of regulations. The ABA and the organized field formed an umbrella group, which pressured itself into co-equal status with the Board and staff of the Corporation, promulgating regulations designed to minimize the central governance powers of the Corporation (Dooley and Houseman, 1984).

An early issue of concern for the organized field was the future of the staff attorney model of legal services provision, without which law reform activism would be difficult to maintain. The 1974 Act required the Corporation to evaluate alternative and supplemental methods of delivery of legal services to eligible clients, including judicare, vouchers, prepaid legal insurance and contracts with law firms. This study, which was to be completed by July 1977, was hijacked by special interests, extended into a $13 million four-year evaluation, and ultimately skirted inconclusively around the judicare model of legal services delivery which was the major potential rival to the staff attorney model.

A second area of concern was the issue of legislative representation (lobbying) within the federal program of legal services. The 1974 Act permitted such representation only where program staff offered relevant legal advice or assistance to eligible clients or responded to requests from legislators or their staffs. From the outset, these restrictions were ignored, most particularly by the national support centers which provided the front line of the law reform movement. In 1978, the Moorhead Amendment tightened the restrictions on lobbying by prohibiting the use of LSC funds for publication or propaganda purposes designed to support or defeat legislation pending before Congress or any state legislature. This amendment was also ignored. In 1979, the House Appropriations Committee investigated legal services lobbying and issued a critical report on the laxity of enforcement of the 1974 Act. In April 1980, Representatives Railsback and Moorhead reported serious violations of the lobbying law by CRLA and other LSC grantees; but all to no avail.

The Corporation itself was preoccupied throughout the period 1976–77 with its minimum access plan and it was generally hostile to law reform activities that threatened congressional support for budgetary expansion. With the departure of Roger Cramton from the chairmanship and with re-authorization of the Corporation in 1977 by a more liberal Congress, however, the climate changed. The new Board of Directors, appointed by President Carter, redirected the legal services programs into law reform.

The Carter-appointed Board differed from its predecessor in three important respects. First, a majority of its members had served in the legal services program, retained close links with the organized field, and were networked into the American Bar Association's political branches. In this way, the activists accessed the governance structure of the program. Second, the two client members of the Board, Romano Shump and Josephine Worthy, were themselves activists, focusing Board attention on minority group, rather than poor individual, issues. Third, many of the Board viewed themselves as representatives of specific constituencies – native American, Hispanic, migrant farm workers, etc. – and became advocates of law reform for these groups. The new Board appointed as President, Dan Bradley, a law reform zealot, earlier associated with the Great Society Program, who pursued rather than condoned ideological behavior within the Corporation and its outreach programs. In consequence, the legal services program alienated lay congressional brokers by upsetting constituent interests. In 1980, a deeply-divided Congress refused to re-authorize the Corporation, exposing it to the reform agenda of President Reagan.

Ideology within the local programs
In the absence of strong central governance, the local programs found it low cost to engage in opportunistic law reforms, relying on the bounded rationality of the electorate as a protection against legislative reaction. In this respect, the staff attorneys were on a loose rein, since the local programs are governed by part-time boards, 60 per cent of whose members must be attorneys and 30 per cent eligible clients. The local bar association, law schools, civil rights and anti-poverty organizations dominate the selection of board members, and typically confirm law reform activists into office. Such boards are established, not to manage or to direct, but rather to guide and to facilitate the staff attorneys in their reformist ventures.

Throughout the late 1970s, the majority of staff attorneys within the legal services program was left-leaning, with the National Lawyers Guild alone claiming no fewer than 1000 members (Isaac, 1985). Such attorneys used the rhetoric of right to justice to advance social and economic policies that could not be brokered through the legislature. Bennett and DiLorenzo (1985b, pp. 114–115) chronicled the following major abuses of staff attorney discretion:

1. Local legal service organizations in Montana (1979), Iowa (1980) and Connecticut (1981) sued to force state governments to use taxes for sex change operations. In the Connecticut case, the suit sought between $7000 and $10 000 to relieve the 'frustration, depression and anxiety' caused by a 'gender identity situation'.

2. California Rural Legal Assistance sued the University of California to arrest research designed to improve agricultural productivity. This Luddite suit argued that the development of labor-saving farm machinery would benefit 'a narrow group of agri-business interests with no valid public purpose' and contribute to agricultural unemployment and the demise of the small family farm.

3. A Texas lawsuit brought by a grantee established the constitutional right to free public education for illegal aliens.

4. In Tampa, Florida, the Bay Area Legal Services successfully sued to obstruct implementation of state-wide functional literacy tests as a prerequisite for high school graduation because the high failure rate among black students was allegedly attributable to past discrimination.

5. A grantee in Ann Arbor, Michigan, sued to require the school board to adopt a plan designed to make teachers responsive to problems of students who speak 'Black English' and to require teachers to use knowledge of dialect in teaching students to read.

6. In Youngstown, Ohio, the East Ohio Legal Services sued a US Steel Corporation to require the company to sell its mill to a community organization that received tax subsidies.

7. Grantees in Maine, Colorado, Massachusetts and South Carolina sued to reclaim large expanses of land for Indian tribes. In Maine, it was claimed that two-thirds of the state should revert to the Passamaquoddy and Penobscot Indians, and that 350 000 residents should be forcibly displaced from such land.

8. Grantees sued to obtain Supplemental Social Security benefits for alcoholics.

9. Grantees sued to require the upgrading of Armed Forces discharges on grounds of homosexuality, and to obtain disability payments for homosexuality.

In many such ventures, the class action suit was employed by legal services attorneys, as a means of magnifying policy impact. Frequently, such suits by their nature, tended to downgrade the particular problems of specific individual clients. Indeed, in a number of class action suits, it is doubtful whether all the listed plaintiffs were even aware of the case that was brought allegedly on their behalf. For example, in *Simer* v. *Olivarez*, a September 1979 class action suit brought in the federal district court in Chicago, three of the plaintiffs subsequently stated that they had no knowledge of the suit and others claimed that they had been steered into the action by public interest law firms (Bennett and DiLorenzo, 1985b, p. 115). Legal services lawyers were allowed to initiate suits, even where no client had asked for assistance if they considered that such a suit promoted the public interest.

The local programs, not content with reforming the law through judicial litigation, in certain instances resorted to illegal behavior in the form of political lobbying relying upon a compliant Legal Services Corporation to refrain from the disciplinary action required by the 1974 Act. As Bennett and DiLorenzo (1985a) noted, it is impossible to chronicle the full extent of illegal political behavior since the Freedom of Information Act does not apply to LSC grantees. Moreover, congressional scrutiny over such activities has been muted by the fact that the Hatch Act does not extend to non-federal programs even though such programs are financed by federal tax dollars.

One example of such illegal lobbying was unearthed in 1980 following a staff investigation by the Committee on Appropriations of the US House of Representatives. The inquiry was directed into the activities of an LSC-funded task force in its attempt to defeat California's Proposition 9, which sought to reduce the state's rate of personal income tax. The inquiry determined that California Rural Legal Assistance, which was located in San Francisco, maintained a permanent office in Sacramento with five attorneys who were all registered lobbyists, active in the legislature or in administrative advocacy. Moreover, the Western Center on Law and Poverty Inc., which was located in Los Angeles, shared office space with the CRLA and employed four registered lobbyists also in legislative and administrative advocacy in Sacramento. Alan Rader, an attorney at the Western Center, and a coordinator for the Task Force, received $61 655 from the LSC to finance its activities. Thirty local legal services programs throughout California also participated by supplying staff to work with the media and to register votes in welfare offices. All such funding and support was prohibited by statute.

Among the more blatant misuses of LSC funding by grantees, eventually reported to Reagan's appointees of the LSC, was that of legislative advocacy funded through the law in neighborhood and community services grants (LINCS). Bennett and DiLorenzo (1985a) outline the typical range of such abuses (pp. 311–312):

1. The Office of Kentucky Legal Services reported that its client advocacy included legislative advocacy with clients and client groups around a broad range of issues including Medicaid cuts, child care, etc.
2. The New Mexico Legal Support Project responded that it had engaged in Legislative and Administrative Advocacy Training and the Development of a State Advocacy Network.
3. The Texas Legal Services Center reported that it had conducted a Texas People's Leadership Development Conference, had begun Multi-Form Advocacy Training and set up a statewide Advocacy Task Force.
4. The Friends Committee on National Legislation, in Washington, DC, indicated that it had engaged in legislative advocacy against budget cuts in human services programs.
5. The Raleigh Tenants Association of North Carolina had lobbied to pass state laws improving tenants' rights.
6. The Client's Council of Legal Services of Southeast Nebraska had developed a welfare-rights orientated client group and had instigated legislative advocacy by clients.

Ideology within the national support and training centers
The national support (or back-up) centers were established by the Office of Economic Opportunity as an instrument of the law reform strategy implemented by the second director, Earl Johnson, over the period 1967 to 1968. The OEO invested heavily in these back-up centers, which offered national programs housed initially in law schools, organized around substantive policy areas such as welfare or housing, or around a particular segment of the relevant population, such as Indians or the elderly. These centers engaged in national litigation as well as in legislative and administrative representation, while providing support, assistance and training to local programs.

The centers offered a specialized representation and a specialized knowledge that became indispensable in opening up new areas of poverty law. They also provided leadership on key substantive issues working closely with national movements such as the National Welfare Rights Movement and the National Tenants Organization. They were supported by national training and technical assistance programs which played an important coordinating role among programs and linked local advocates into a national network. By the early 1970s, the back-up and training centers had become principal vehicles for law reform and, as such, were threatened with defunding in 1973 by Howard Phillips who had been appointed by President Nixon to dismantle the Office of Economic Opportunity. The attack on legal services, and with it the bid to defund the centers, was blocked by the federal court which enjoined Phillips from acting as OEO director because his name had not been submitted by President Nixon for confirmation by the US Senate.

Nevertheless, the national support centers, widely viewed as a major source of legal services activism, remained a bone of contention throughout the controversial legislative struggle that culminated in the 1974 Act. Congresswoman Edith Green, who viewed the centers as 'the cutting edge of social change', succeeded in amending the House Bill to ensure that they would be eliminated once the LSC was established. The Green Amendment was endorsed reluctantly by the Senate in 1975 in order to ensure the ratification of the compromise bill by the beleaguered President Nixon. In the event, the purpose of the Green Amendment was thwarted by poor draftsmanship in the 1974 Act.

Under the Green Amendment, research, training, technical assistance and other clearing house activities became the direct responsibility of the LSC and could not be effected by grant or contract. The intent had been to include also direct advocacy for clients, a central function of the back-up centers, but the language failed to reflect that intent effectively. In consequence, the LSC was required to take over only some of the functions of the national centers, leaving an escape route open for retaining the centers to supply the remaining functions.

At the initiative of Alan Houseman, the LSC Board, in 1975, commissioned a study of the future role of the centers in the light of the Green Amendment. The Polikoff Report adopted a compromise position concluding that client representation, including the research normally conducted by a lawyer for a client, fell outside the terms of the Green Amendment. The LSC President, Tom Ehrlich, decided to evaluate each center and to continue those that delivered services allowed under the Green Amendment. On the basis of this evaluation all the substantive area centers were refunded, and only the training centers were terminated. Most of the activities of the terminated centers were continued through LSC's Office of Program Support and the Office of Field Services. The Green Amendment was repealed – except for restrictions concerning broad generalized research – as part of the 1977 re-authorization Act.

Nevertheless, the Green Amendment, and reactions to it, exerted a powerful impact on the structure of the legal services program, stimulating the creation of two separate divisions, the Office of Program Support (OPS) and the Research Institute (RI). The OPS concentrated on training both at the national and at the regional and local levels, greatly expanding the resources devoted to this task. The Research Institute produced a series of publications on the subject of poverty law and sponsored conferences to evaluate and to disseminate its works. The support centers were retained by the Corporation, though at low levels of funding until the Corporation could introduce a coherent policy late in 1978.

The new policy, which was not fully implemented, mandated: (1) increased national support through existing and additional support centers; (2) the extension of state support ultimately through increased funding; (3) the decentralization of training from national to state and local levels; and (4) the targeting of technical and management assistance to specific program problems. The prospect of an expanded role for the national centers failed to enthuse the Congress which placed a much higher priority on the minimum access plan for clients. Indeed, both in 1980 and 1981, the House appropriations committee attached an appropriation rider specifically requiring that the minimum access priority rating be upheld by the LSC.

Despite lack of congressional enthusiasm, the national support centers slowly grew, many of them opening offices in Washington, DC in order to make representations before the Congress and relevant federal agencies. New centers were funded to cover family law, immigration, access to federal courts, veterans issues and mental disability law. Substantial growth also occurred during the late 1970s in state support for back-up centers with state-wide responsibilities. The existing programs in some states, notably the south and southwest, pooled resources to establish joint ventures specialized in training and in legislative and administrative advocacy. In 1979, the LSC decided to fund state support centers throughout the nation.

The greatest increase in centralized support during the late 1970s occurred in training, as the Office of Program Support gave high priority to a series of national and regional training events for attorneys and paralegals. Tensions quickly developed between the centralist aspirations of OPS and the desire for decentralized training facilities at the regional and local levels. Following the 1981 budget crisis, the LSC created regional training centers and shifted training from the LSC to independent programs.

7   Let all the poisons that lurk in the mind hatch out: Illegalities at legal services 1981–82

President Reagan's election in 1980 and the prospect of a major political attack upon legal services, galvanized the Corporation and its grantees into a spate of illegal political activity. The President of the Corporation, Dan J. Bradley, appointed Alan Houseman, then Director of the Research Institute on Legal Assistance, to head a survival task force in response to the political threat. On December 1, 1980, Houseman unfolded his strategy in a memorandum entitled: 'Coalition Building and Strengthening Presence in Community', designed to ensure the survival of an aggressive legal services program.

For Houseman, such a program implied 'the survival of aggressive advocacy (i.e. advocacy which utilizes the full scope of representation including legislative and administrative representation, litigation and community education); advocacy which seeks all possible remedies; and advocacy which is not restricted in what defendants can be sued' (Senate Committee on Labor and Human Resources, 1983, p. 67). To this end, he constructed a survival strategy consisting of three elements, namely (1) an outside entity to lobby on behalf of the Corporation; (2) a grass-roots lobbying campaign directed at members of the Congress; and (3) a 'corporation in exile' to wage ideological war with the Reagan presidency.

The campaign was initiated in 1981 by Joseph Lipofsky of Legal Services of Eastern Missouri and was coordinated through the LSC-funded Coalition for Sensible and Humane Solutions. The Coalition was established to publish a handbook for the People's Lobbyists, to conduct a People's College of Law designed to train community activists, to research and to publish a 'People's Alternative' to budget cuts on a state and local level and to develop a bimonthly statewide publication on ways to impact on budget and tax questions. Another such organization was the Coalition for Legal Services formed with LSC participation as a coalition of PAG, NCC, NLADA and other interested parties to lobby and coordinate survival activities on behalf of the legal services community. All participating bodies were significant recipients of LSC monies proscribed from lobbying by the 1974 Act.

The second component of the survival campaign was a carefully orchestrated program of grass roots lobbying coordinated from the headquarters of the LSC. Each regional office designated an individual to coordinate survival activities within its region; each local affiliate was to appoint its own survival coordinator; and statewide coordinators were also appointed. Dan Bradley, the president of the LSC, gave the 'Call to Battle' speech at the LSC's Chicago region meeting held at St Louis in December 1981, citing the Proposition 9 task force in California as an excellent example of what a concerted political effort could achieve. Strategies were to be developed for the media and for the political community, governing local officials, congressmen, state officials and other individuals who made or influenced decisions.

In May 1981, the General Accounting Office reported critically on illegal lobbying evident throughout the LSC organization. The comptroller-general concluded: 'There is little question that (these activities) ... constitute "lobbying" as the term is used in the applicable restrictive legislation.' Far from restricting the behavior of the Corporation, this criticism stimulated its third strategy of developing a 'corporation in exile.'

The LSC had already explored the possibility of establishing 'mirror corporations' to further its survival battle. Its consultant, Gregg Krech, 1981 had recommended the establishment of a sister corporation which would provide services on a fee-for-service basis to ineligible clients and which would donate all its profits back to the legal services program. He had also recommended the establishment of public interest law firms and social welfare organizations able to provide a wider range of services to poor people with fewer legal restrictions.

As Bennett and DiLorenzo noted (1985a, pp. 124–125) there is evidence that this 'mirror corporation' strategy was implemented. In 1982, for example, the New Haven Legal Assistance Association (NHLAA) transferred its annual grant of $543 000 to the South Central Connecticut Legal Services Corporation. The NHLAA continued to operate funded through alternative funding sources, free of all congressional restrictions. However, South Central handled no cases, merely screening and referring cases to the NHLAA, and paying the latter a set fee for each case. In a similar manner, Texas Rural Legal Aid transferred $760 000 in January 1982 to Texas Rural Legal Foundation Inc. to provide legal services to eligible clients. TRLF was active politically not least in opposing, albeit unsuccessfully, the special senatorial election in Texas won by the Republican congressman, Philip Gramm.

The mirror corporations came to play another more far-reaching role in placing the LSC beyond the reach of the Congress and the Executive, namely that of hiding accumulated fund balances from potential control of retrenchment. This strategy was referred to as 'saving the rubies' – a reference to the alleged action of Czar Nicholas of Russia in sending the Russian Crown Jewels to Switzerland for safe keeping when the Bolsheviks were climbing over the palace walls in 1917 (Denton, 1985, p. 64). In LSC circles, this strategy was also known as the 'Phoenix Project' or the 'Government in Exile.'

The Phoenix Project sought to protect the political elements within the LSC from anticipated attack and to assure their survival during the Reagan 'inter-regnum.' To this end, national support, state support, training and technical assistance were to be disentangled from the Corporation with respect to control, operation and funding, each element retaining an important role in maintaining a program of law reform within the umbrella of federal legal services.

The national support centers were viewed within the Corporation as the fulcrum of poverty law reform development and as the basis for a national lobbying network. As such, they were foremost among the 'rubies' to be saved, as Dooley, a legal services lawyer, recognized in his July 1981 paper, entitled 'Legal Services in the 80s', which emphasized the importance of the national centers for political advocacy but which warned that: 'Increasingly our work will be behind the scenes.' Dooley also predicted that the proposed system of block grants to the states for legal services would shift the fight on many legislative issues from the national to the state support centers.

The national support centers, which came under the direction of Alan Houseman at the Research Institute, organized a formal lobbying presence in Washington as a basis for advocating legal services policies before Congress and the Executive. Equally high priority was the movement of unexpended federal tax dollars from LSC headquarters to the national centers, monies that in many instances were to be held in reserve as unrestricted interest-bearing investments to fund activities that later might be restricted by Congress.

The monies so transferred were substantial. In summer 1981, LSC officials divided $0.5 million among seven national support centers to establish and nurture national networks of lobbyists within their respective fields of interest. In Houseman's view: 'If the national support centers are eliminated it will be the function of this network to contrive providing national advocacy' (Houseman, June 26, 1981). The national centers also received $0.532 million in expansion training contracts and $0.5 million in special, one-time funds, in large part from the Corporation's 1980 appropriation carry over. By hoarding these transfers, LSC activists assured themselves of a survival fund to maintain political campaigns even should the LSC be completely defunded in compliance with President Reagan's 1982 budget recommendation.

The leadership of the LSC also established a system completely outside the Corporation to manage and oversee political activities that would be carried out under the guise of state support (Denton, 1985, pp. 69–73). Two large grants totalling in excess of $1 million were awarded in the fall of 1981, to the Legal Aid Society of Albuquerque and to the Western Center on Law and Poverty in California, to coordinate the work of a new cadre of state-level legislative advocates. Most of these funds were dedicated to anti-block grant lobbying as well as to training in an overt effort to abort President Reagan's reform strategy. The 'apostles' successfully insulated themselves, by the judicious use of such unrestricted balances, as an independent power base, free to engage in activist law reform policies that were threatened by the Reagan reform agenda.

If the Phoenix project was to succeed as an integrated whole – if constructivist rationalism was to survive the anticipated Reagan onslaught – a source of leadership was required from outside the LSC as well as a source of funding to keep that leadership alive. This requirement was satisfied through the segregation and protection of the last of the four 'rubies' – technical assistance. Originally, technical assistance had been viewed as a contingency resource, a source of loosely-controlled funding available to assist field programs in dealing with unexpected problems. Now it was to become a source of unrestricted savings, to fund elements of the survival campaign, drawn from the 'one-time' funds, amounting to $3–$4 million, unexpended within the legal services program by the end of fiscal year 1981. The 'one-time' funds were deliberately withheld from poor would-be litigants for such a purpose at a time when the LSC was pressing the Congress for a budget increase to satisfy unmet client demands.

In Fall 1981, technical assistance was transferred from the LSC to the National Legal Aid and Defender Association (NLADA) together with other major project funds under the control of Clinton Lyons, then director of LSC's Office of Field Services. Lyons then moved to NLADA to supervise the transferred fund, which was in excess of $2 million. The transfer was endorsed by Dan Bradley, President of the Legal Services Corporation, at a time when the Senate was approving a major reduction in the fiscal year 1982 budget appropriation for legal services. The LSC's Board was never asked to confirm these transfers; the Congress was not even advised of this major reallocation of its federal tax dollars. Thus it was that the hubris that had fired legal services during the late 1970s was followed by the nemesis of 1981–1982 as an alarmed rump of Carter-appointed LSC officials abused their offices, even transgressed the law, to protect a seriously threatened but still widespread program of law reform:

> The 'estate' – the funds and functions of LSC – was not theirs to give. It did not belong to them. It did not belong to employees or officers of the Corporation. It did not belong to the Board of Directors. The 'estate' which was given away belonged to the individual client who was turned down so that the 'poverty' lawyers could invest their time in activities prohibited by law. The 'estate' was squandered, and the damage done thereby to the concept of legitimate federally-funded legal services may never be repaired. (Denton, 1985, p. 87)

8 The return of the Jedi: The struggle to restore governance in legal services 1982–1988

Once a governance structure has been dismantled, no matter how flimsy its original form, it is extremely difficult to re-establish, however determined the upper echelon of the weakened hierarchy. For opportunism feeds not only on the absence of effective governance but also on the betrayal of trust and its aftermath of suspicion and deception that accompanies hierarchal disruption and decay. This aftermath typically weakens the principal-agent relationship at every link in the bureaucratic chain by eroding team-playing and effective monitoring of performance both in the upward and in the downward directions. The incentive-cost structure in such an afflicted organization commonly encourages opportunism and narrow self-seeking behavior which reflects itself in myopic decision making and in client disaffection.

Such, in an extreme form, was the experience of the Legal Services Corporation following the battle for survival which raged throughout the first two years of Reagan's presidency. The jaundiced legacy was a set of relationships between the Congress, the Board of Directors, the President and the staff of the LSC which would have threatened the viability of any commercial enterprise and which left activists within the federal program of legal services with a licence to misbehave which was not wasted.

The weakened authority of the Board

The protracted conflict between the Congress and President Reagan over the period 1981–1985, concerning the composition of the LSC Board of Directors, severely damaged the trust relationship between the Congress and the Board, which is essential to the development of an effective hierarchy capable of imposing managerial authority over a heterogeneous and often opportunistic network of legal services suppliers. This breakdown of trust (Breton and Wintrobe, 1982) was the outcome of a sequence of unbecoming squabbles that permeated the first term of Reagan's presidency and which stimulated a climate completely alien to the good conduct of business and to the maintenance of professional ethics and personal integrity. Ideological conflict was the root cause of this disintegration.

Throughout 1981, the battle for survival at the LSC was fully engaged as conservatives attempted first to eliminate the federal program of legal services in its entirety, and then, when this strategy had appeared to fail, to seek to weaken law reform activism through reductions in funding, substantial restrictions on who could be represented, the substitution of judicare for staff attorney provision, and the elimination of the central and regional support and training infrastructures. During this initial phase, no appointments were made to the Board of the LSC. By year's end, the LSC had survived, though its budget had been lowered, and its formal reauthorization had been denied. But the scars ran deep, with a president reluctant to expose board nominees to Senate scrutiny and with a vengeful Congress actively seeking out misbehavior on the part of the recess appointed Reagan board.

The recess board set the combative tone of its tenure early in 1982 with an ill-informed, ill-advised and unsuccessful bid to defund the legal services program without obtaining prior consent from the US Congress. Its move to freeze all fiscal year 1982 grants and contracts to the field had been anticipated by the LSC President, Dan Bradley, who had earlier disbursed the funds in accordance with established LSC criteria. When Bradley left the Corporation in March 1982, the Board confronted a suspicious if not hostile staff and quickly worked its way through two acting presidents, Gerald Caplan and Clinton Lyons, by which time, Fall 1982, it was in a state of internal turmoil and essentially at war with the staff of the Corporation (Dooley and Houseman, 1984, p. 17).

The Board itself divided over the choice of a new president, with the majority siding with Chairman William Harvey and William Olson and overruling the reservations expressed by Howard Dana, head of the presidential search committee, in favor of Donald Bogard in October 1982. Harvey and Olson then proposed, unsuccessfully, a controversial regulation that would have prohibited legal services attorneys from filing any class action suit against federal, state or local governments where a successful suit would result in increased government expenditures, and/or where the prior consent of all parties to the suit had not been obtained. The proposal was condemned by David Landau of the American Civil Liberties Union as amounting to 'invidious discrimination' against poor people and as virtually abolishing class action suits in favor of the poor (*Washington News*, November 18, 1982).

Congress, the organized bar and other legal services supporters reacted adversely to this provocation, and the Senate, in December 1982, indicated that it would confirm only six of the nine proposed members and, in particular, that it would refuse to confirm the two most conservative of the nominees, Harvey and Olson. The President responded by withdrawing the complete list. A House Judiciary Committee subcommittee hearing, shortly afterwards, disclosed that members of the Board had been reimbursed for their services by fees well in excess of those received by their predecessors. Following a typical Washington hue-and-cry, Congress overruled the proposed restrictions on class action suits, affirmed that all existing programs must be funded during the lifetime of the recess Board, and imposed strict limits on payments to members of the Board. Even the subsequent exoneration of Board members from the charge of excessive remuneration – by the General Accounting Office, the watchdog of Congress – failed to ease the ill-will and mistrust that had developed between the Congress and the LSC Board.

The Board was alerted early in its tenure to the illegalities that had engulfed the LSC and its delivery programs following Reagan's 1980 electoral success, both in the form of survival lobbying and of the Phoenix project, which had successfully 'saved the rubies' by the time that Reagan could use the recess to effect control over the Board. The LSC Board initiated an investigation in 1983 at the instigation of Senator Orrin Hatch (then Chairman of the Senate Committee on Labor and Human Resources) and Senator Jeremiah Denton (then Chairman of the Senate Subcommittee on Family and Human Services).

This investigation demonstrated that the official LSC budget statement significantly underestimated the actual funding available to the Corporation (in 1983 the actual funding available was $320 million as compared with a fiscal year budget appropriation of $241 million). Thus alerted, the Senate Committee launched a wide-ranging investigation of the entire legal services program and of the allegations against it. On the basis of this investigation, the Committee concluded that:

1. Throughout the early 1980s, former Corporation officials had systematically violated the law which prohibits the use of federal funds for partisan political activities and which bars their involvement in orchestrating grass roots political campaigns;

2. Corporation officials had diverted federal funding away from traditional legal services, denying eligible clients the right to justice in order to finance training programs designed to create political organizations that would fight President Reagan's economic initiatives and to abort the proposal to provide block grants to the states in lieu of a federal legal services program;

3. Corporation officials had destroyed or removed documents following Reagan's election in an attempt to cover up illegalities. Moreover, individuals critical of the Corporation's political agenda had been harassed and intimidated;

4. Officials of the National Clients Council had used legal services monies to pay for their personal expenses, including exorbitant hotel bills and salaries. These transfers were not repaid.

This evidence was turned over to the Department of Justice and to the General Accounting Office with a request that they review it and, where necessary, conduct their own investigations. In September 1983, the GAO's preliminary report confirmed that the LSC had behaved illegally, engaging in political activities at a training session in Denver in January 1981, and lobbying in California in 1980 and in Oregon 1981. In July 1984, the Criminal Division of the Department of Justice terminated its investigation of the LSC with the following damning comment:

> the unauthorized activities of the Corporation, and many of the people associated with it, are uniquely reprehensible and beyond the scope of the LSC's original mission ... not withstanding these inappropriate, misguided, and abusive activities, 18 USC Sec. 1913 as well as federal theft and fraud laws – for technical reasons – were not violated by the lobbying activities involved here. (S. Trolt, July 5, 1984)

There was no federal government redress against those who violated Congressional prohibitions concerning the legal aid program. The Corporation alone was empowered to ensure that its employees and its grantees were in compliance with the Act and no third party had standing to sue. The recess Board showed no stomach to pursue Bradley, the field programs and the support centers through the federal courts. No other individual or body could do so. This signal – *rex non potest peccare* – brought its predictable response among activists within the legal services program.

In August 1985, the General Accounting Office concluded its investigation into the deviant behavior of the LSC during 1981 and concluded that two of three grant recipients under review – Texas Rural Aid, Inc. and South Central Connecticut Legal Services Corporation had created alternative corporations with the intent and the effect of circumventing restrictions in the

LSC Act and regulations. The GAO recommended that the alternative corporations should be brought into compliance with the law by the LSC and should be treated as single entities together with the grantees with which they were associated. Representative Bruce Morrison, an unwavering protagonist for legal services activists in the House of Representatives, pleaded (unsuccessfully) with the GAO to reconsider its adverse conclusions (Morrison, May 30, 1985). It is noteworthy that Texas Rural Aid Inc. and South Central Connecticut Legal Services Corporation were not defunded as a consequence of the 1985 Report.

Evidence of illegal lobbying by LSC grantees accumulated throughout 1983 as the Senate Labor and Human Resources Committee held hearings on the issue and produced its own series of 'horror stories' (*Washington Post*, July 26, 1983). One such involved a grant to a Citizens League in Wadley, Georgia, which turned out to be a front organization for a candidate for mayor, in which the monies were deployed for door-to-door canvassing and for producing and distributing leaflets under the guise of citizenship education. Another was a grant made to a St Louis group and used to organize and train community activists to lobby against proposed federal budget cuts. The *Washington Post* was moved to criticize such activities in the following terms:

> Any fair reading of this discussion makes it clear that these were not borderline cases, on which reasonable people could disagree over whether the law was violated. Nor does this seem to have been an isolated incident ... Legal Services is not the first agency with officials convinced that their program is so important, so imbued with the public interest, that they are entitled to use public money to ensure its perpetuation. It's sad that, of all people, the custodians of a program justified by principles of fair play failed to understand this. (*Washington Post*, September 23, 1983)

Yet, the Congress, responding to ABA and other lobbying pressures, refused the recess board the authority to control the aberrant centers and field programs. The 1984 Appropriations Act indeed strengthened the affirmative rider by (1) providing a clear formula for funding legal services programs and prohibiting LSC from altering those grant levels, and (2) refunding all current grantees and contractors with a required increase unless contrary action was taken by a confirmed LSC Board by January 1, 1984. These provisions were continued under the 1985 Appropriations Act, with specific protection for the Western Center on Law and Poverty which the LSC had attempted to defund in 1984. Warren Rudman in the Senate and Bruce Morrison and Barney Frank in the House were particularly active in hamstringing the LSC in its attempts to establish governance and to penalize illegalities.

Senator Rudman and other moderate or conservative supporters of LSC took the steps they did because they understood how lawyers functioned. They were outraged by the illegality and arbitrariness of many LSC actions during 1983 and 1984 and by the failure of the White House to propose a set of board candidates that could achieve confirmation. In the House, two key members played increasingly important roles, Barney Frank and Bruce Morrison. Before he was elected to Congress in 1982, Morrison had been director of New Haven Legal Assistance and was one of the key leaders of the legal services community. He and Frank understood what legal services was and what it was designed originally to do and were committed to its fundamental purposes. (Dooley and Houseman, 1984, p. 15)

In June 1985, the Senate confirmed 11 members of the LSC Board of Directors, providing an effective reformist majority of six to five in favor of President Reagan's reform initiative. This confirmation signalled, however, only the termination of phase one of the conflict between the Congress and the Executive. The LSC Board continued to be the focal point of criticism and attack by a Congress that had come to view its role as that of micro-manager of a program that, by statute, was independent of both branches of government.

Under the leadership of Warren Rudman in the Senate and of Bruce Morrison in the House – important congressional mouthpieces for 'Bar Leaders for the Preservation of Legal Services for the Poor' which is headquartered in Rudman's New Hampshire constituency – the 'independent' Board was to be subjected to unremitting, hostile surveillance and criticism by the House and Senate committees responsible for budget appropriations.

The initial focal point of conflict over micro-management arose over the decision by the Board to shift funding away from the national support centers in favor of the direct provision of legal services, utilizing where necessary its statutory authority, subject to judicial review, to defund unsatisfactory programs. Spokesman for the organized bar were vehemently opposed to this initiative which was favored by the White House; the Congress doggedly imposed line item controls over budget appropriations to ensure that the Board initiative would fail. This crisis of authority came to a head in an illuminating exchange between Warren Rudman and Philip Gramm on the Senate Floor on December 11, 1987 in the debate over the fiscal year 1988 budget appropriation to the LSC.

Senator Gramm had introduced an amendment to the bill designed, not to cut back the budget appropriation, but to require that 97 per cent of the appropriated funds be directed to providing legal services for the poor, thereby shifting resources from the national support and training centers that were not engaged in this activity. Such a shift would not deny staff attorneys access to consulting services in connection with litigation on behalf of the poor. It would ensure that such services were client orientated and not designed to promote law reform. Most particularly, the amendment was designed to prevent the diversion of legal services monies into special interest lobbying activities by organizations that skilfully exploited the fungibility of public with private funding to hide the ultimate illegality of their behavior. Senator Gramm explicitly referred to NLADA as one example of such an organization, noting that it had lobbied extensively against President Reagan's nomination of Judge Bork as Justice of the Supreme Court. Some 81 per cent of NLADA's fees and dues emanated from the LSC. Gramm responded to Rudman's defence of NLADA:

> In fact my dear colleague from New Hampshire in his defense reminds me of a fellow who might be running a Baptist fellowship hall near the college and the deacons come and find out there has been a brothel run in the back corner of this Baptist student center. So the guy running the center says: 'Well now, you have to realize, brothers that the money coming into this student center in part comes from private donations and it just happens that those private donations are funding that area where the brothel is.' (Senator Philip Gramm, Congressional Record Senate, December 11, 1987)

Senator Gramm did not propose his amendment without powerful outside support. He came armed with the backing of the US Chamber of Commerce, the American Farm Bureau Federation, Concerned Women of America, the Neighborhood Network, the National Right to Work Committee, the National Council of Agricultural Employers, and the National Federation of Independent Business. These interests were no match, however, for the American Bar Association and its associated attorney interests dedicated to the maintenance of legal services as a law reform mechanism. The national centers as Senator Leahy stated in defending the status quo were viewed as 'the glue that holds the Legal Services network together', and as such were strongly supported by some 90 per cent of all local Legal Services Program directors:

> These are intelligent, committed lawyers. They earn salaries that don't begin to compete with the private sector. Their case loads are staggering. Every dollar matters. If the national support centers weren't doing extremely valuable work these local Legal Services lawyers would support this amendment too. Instead, they overwhelmingly oppose it. (Senator Leahy, Congressional Record Senate, December 11, 1987)

Senator Rudman defended his position in favor of line item funding of the support centers on the ground that the LSC Board majority could not be trusted with discretionary authority:

> I want to be very careful in what I say. I have absolutely no trust at all in 6 of the 11 members. They know who they are, including the Chairman. I have nothing

but admiration for the other five who seem to believe that poor people deserve equal justice. (Senator Warren Rudman, Congressional Record Senate, December 11, 1987)

Senator Gramm's amendment went down to its inevitable defeat in a negative Senate floor vote of 70 to 28. With it went much of the authority and the credibility of the LSC Board majority as a governance body. Although the rhetoric of Senator Rudman was carefully tailored to the right to access issue, it is quite clear from a reading of the floor debate that the substantive issue was the maintenance of a legal services program favorable to the litigation appetites of activist elements within the American Bar Association.

The ire of the American Bar Association and of its spokesmen in the Congress was increasingly directed at the Chairman of the LSC Board, W. Clark Durant III, who had been confirmed into Board membership by the Senate in June 1985 and who was appointed and reappointed to its chairmanship continuously thereafter, until his resignation in January 1989 to make way for a Bush appointment.

Prior to his confirmation, Durant had served as acting chairman of the LSC's recess Board. Durant was an experienced Detroit lawyer, active in Republican Party politics, who had devoted the first six years of his professional career mainly to the representation of indigent clients. Committed to the notion of equal access to justice and opposed to the use of legal services monies for law reform, Durant was determined to end the corruption and mismanagement evident within the Corporation during the transition from the Carter to the Reagan presidency. In February 1987, following a period of internal investigation which provoked congressional disapproval, Durant directed his criticisms directly at the American Bar Association, and at the legal cartel that, in his view, was primarily responsible for depriving the poor of their right to justice. In his address to the American Bar Association at its New Orleans meeting, Durant spoke out in support of President Reagan's recommendation that the Legal Services Corporation should be abolished and suggested that the Corporation should be replaced by a truly independent body. He further charged that the legal profession was a monopoly that should be deregulated like the trucking and airline industries. He argued that the Corporation deserved to be replaced because it had strayed too far from its mission of serving the poor. He recommended that entrepreneurs, paraprofessionals and lay people be allowed to do much of the work currently reserved exclusively for the lawyer cartel, albeit within the framework of a publicly funded program.

Durant argued that the law profession had become a cartel that inflated prices, diminished the quality of service and reduced competition by restricting the supply of lawyers. He urged that bar examinations and statutes against the unauthorized practice of law should be abolished. Durant's remarks stimulated a sharply hostile reaction from those whose privileges were challenged:

> 'I gave the speech right in the belly of the beast, and that's why there was such a burp,' he said with a chuckle. (Nancy Belane, *Associated Press*, March 8, 1987)

Eugene Thomas, President of the American Bar Association, incorrectly suggesting that Durant had called for the *abolition* rather than for the replacement of the LSC, called for Durant's resignation, questioning how he could fairly administer a corporation that he had said should cease to exist. Thomas claimed that Durant was manipulating legitimate concerns about access to justice in America, and that, under his proposals, legal services would be provided by a cadre of commercial venders akin to auto mechanics:

> To have the Chairman of this Board charged with this responsibility by the people of America under duly enacted legislation – to have that Chairman stand up and propose again at this hour zero funding and to applaud it as an heroic, courageous position is startling and disturbing to me. I want to say here that every effort that I can bring to bear will be made to defeat that position, and every effort that the American Bar Association can bring to bear will be brought to protect the program of legal services for the poor ... to make America work for all its people. (Eugene Thomas, February 23, 1987)

Thomas characterized the arguments made by Durant as dangerous and misleading persuasive bits of sophistry designed to suggest that the solution for poor people is to send them into the market place of America to compete for legal services on the basis that one would compete for any offered service or commodity in this land. The idea that these poor people should go out in a world where they would have to provide funds for services that they need desperately is absurd and illogical.

Other special interests were quick to lend their support to the ABA President in his defense of lawyers' privileges. Clinton Lyons, executive director of the National Legal Aid and Defender Association, accused Durant of using his attack on the legal profession as an excuse to sabotage the Legal Services Corporation and suggested that Durant's chief priority was the advancement of his philosophical and political agenda rather than service to the needy:

> Really, Clark Durant is an ideologue. Where that takes him is to some absurd position that the unimpeded exercise of entrepreneur ventures and capitalism ... is able to solve all of our problems. This is an articulate fellow with plenty of I.Q. ... I think he's a very dangerous man. (Clinton Lyons, *Associated Press*, March 8, 1987)

The New England Caucus of the ABA acted swiftly and firmly to express its support for and add its voice to President Thomas' call for Durant's resignation in a unanimous resolution reprinted by 'Bar Leaders for the Preservation of Legal Services for the Poor' on February 23, 1987. This resignation request was strongly endorsed by two cofounders of Bar Leaders: Michael S. Greco, the past president of the Massachusetts Bar Association and president of the New England Bar Association, and L. Jonathan Ross, immediate past president of the New Hampshire Bar Association.

In an open letter to Durant, dated February 18, 1987, Senator Rudman reiterated the criticisms of Durant that had been made by the American Bar Association, though he was careful to acknowledge Durant's emphasis on the replacement of rather than the abolition of the Legal Services Corporation. The open hostility of Rudman to the Board Chairman is evident in the conclusion to his letter which is here quoted at length, since it underlines the serious nature of the principal–agent problem that dogged the entire term of office of the Reagan-appointed Board of the LSC:

How anyone in your position can state that LSC 'must be replaced' and needed federal provisions for legal services should be 'provided through an independent body' is beyond me. It is like saying that LSC should be replaced with LSC. Your comments regarding Congress and the lack of bipartisan support for legal services are silly. There is in fact tremendous bipartisan consensus in opposition to eliminating funding from LSC and in support of something resembling the status quo. This may come as a surprise, but the fact that you support radical surgery on LSC does not mean the two-thirds to three-fourths of Congress that feels differently is outside the mainstream. The sad thing about your speech is its demonstration that, despite more than two years as LSC Board Chairman and the admonitions of many, you have failed to grasp one elementary point about our political system. A reform or change occurs when its proponents marshal their facts, develop detailed alternatives, show how their alternative is an improvement over the status quo, and persuade a majority of the policy makers to accept that view. Achieving reform is hard work. Reform does not come about from fanciful theories, breezy comments, and unsupported statements ... I suspect you look forward to the day when we can really help the consumers of this country by abolishing money as a universal currency and advancing to a system of bartering for goods and services. (Warren Rudman, Letter to Clark Durant, February 18, 1987, Published in B.L.P.L.S.P., Legal Services Crises and Concerns, August 1, 1987)

The Board of Directors of the Legal Services, itself deeply divided, supported a motion presented by Thomas Smegal on March 21, 1987 that the Board 'go on record that it does not support the abolishment or replacement of the Legal Services Corporation'. The initial vote on this motion was seven in favor, none against and one abstention. In May 1987, however, the motion barely survived a second hearing with a vote of five in favor, five against and one abstention. In the interim, Durant had narrowly headed off a resolution by his own State of Michigan Bar Association calling for his resignation from the Bar. Henceforth, he was to be a marked man by the organized bar and its representatives in Congress.

In May 1987, without presenting evidence or naming the individuals involved, Senator Rudman accused employees of the Legal Services Corporation of working against his re-election to the Senate in 1986. He advised the LSC Board and its President that the Corporation's staff members should 'keep their cotton-picking hands out of politics'. 'If anyone has those tendencies, they're going to run into a buzzsaw', he added (*Associated Press*, May 20, 1987; *Legal Times*, May 25, 1987). Durant had already completed an inconclusive investigation into this allegation at the request of Board member Thomas Smegal (*Legal Times*, December 22, 1986). Senator Rudman was dissatisfied with this action and threatened (though he did not pursue) a further investigation either by the Department of Justice or by the General Accounting Office.

Early in 1988, the personal attack on Durant switched from the Senate to the House of Representatives as Robert W. Kastenmeier and Bruce A. Morrison charged him with significant improprieties in the financial management of the Corporation, including unauthorized travel expenses and phone calls. 'It's very unlikely that Durant could explain these matters satisfactorily' said Kastenmeier in an unseemly rush to judgment. Morrison (who once headed a Legal Services program in New Haven) promptly demanded Durant's resignation. Hearings on the charge were carried out by the House Judiciary subcommittee on courts, civil liberties and the administration of justice, clearing Durant of any impropriety (*Barron's*, September 26, 1988).

Over the period of 18 months relevant for the inquiry, Durant, by his own admission, had inadvertently billed the Corporation inappropriately for 16 telephone calls (out of a total of 2360 made on LSC business) at an aggregated cost of $27.58. Over the same time period, Durant had failed to bill the Corporation for telephone calls chargeable to its account at an aggregated cost of $96.05. Furthermore, a review of Durant's travel expenses, conducted by the Comptroller of the Corporation determined that he had failed to submit claims for chargeable fees and expenses at an aggregated cost of $8874. Durant evidently was subsidizing the LSC from private sources (*Wall Street Journal*, September 28, 1988).

The charges levelled against Durant were baseless, a waste of federal tax dollars in their diversion of Durant and his LSC staff from productive activity, and, indeed, a thinly disguised form of political harassment designed to weaken the sharpening governance initiatives of the LSC Board. For, on the basis of the slim six to five majority of Board members enjoyed on most issues by Durant, he had launched, during 1987 and 1988, a powerful agenda to eliminate political lobbying, to force the field offices into accountability, and to introduce competitive bidding into the disbursement of monies through the federal program. The highly politicized environment of the LSC, however, was not conducive to this kind of firm and farsighted management.

The weakening of the LSC presidency
The president of the Legal Services Corporation is appointed by and serves at the pleasure of the LSC Board. He must be a member of the bar of the highest court of a State. He is a non-voting ex-officio member of the Board. He may not receive any salary or other compensation for services from any source other than the Corporation, except as authorized by the Board. As an officer of the Corporation, the president is remunerated at rates determined by the Board, but not in excess of the rate of level V of the Executive Schedule specialized in section 5316 of title 5, United States Code. The maximum rate of pay is low by comparison with the remuneration available to moderately successful attorneys in private practice.

The President of the Corporation, subject to general policies established by the Board, may appoint and remove such employees of the Corporation as he determines necessary to effect the purposes of the Corporation. No political test or political qualification may be employed in selecting, appointing, promoting, or taking any other personal action with respect to any officer, agent or employee, or in selecting or monitoring any grantee, contractor, or person or entity receiving financial assistance under the 1974 Act as amended. Otherwise, the President of the Corporation is endowed with considerable managerial discretion, subject to the approval of the Board. In particular, the President is authorized to make grants and enter into contracts, to monitor and to evaluate supported programs, to initiate and to respond to independent audits of such programs, and to initiate defunding procedures against non-compliant programs.

In practice, the authority of the LSC President to supervise the legal services program was never fully realized during the two terms of Reagan's presidency. This failure had its roots in the battle for survival during the period 1981 to 1982 during which President Dan Bradley abused his authority to insulate the legal services program from reform initiatives. Almost inevitably, Bradley's excesses in favor of legal law reform stimulated a conservative reaction. Late in 1982, this reaction sharpened as Clinton Lyons announced his resignation and with Donald P. Bogard appointed president of the Corporation.

Bogard's appointment was controversial among poverty lawyers, in part because his background, first as a staff member of the Indiana attorney general, and subsequently as a corporate attorney, had provided him with no exposure to assisting the poor with their legal problems. Fundamentally, however, many legal services staff attorneys and program directors were angered by the fact that Bogard, as head of litigation for Stokley Van Camp Inc., had defended that company against litigation by LSC lawyers on behalf of migrant farm workers. Bogard's appointment was ratified by eight votes to three at a raucous meeting of the LSC Board, delayed for 30 minutes by a hostile female LSC client who blocked the entrance to the meeting, and provoked the walkout of one Board member, Howard H. Dana, who objected both to the closed nature of the meeting, and to the nature of Bogard's contract.

The congressional attack on Bogard's appointment was launched by Harold Sawyer and Robert Kastenmeier, members of the House Judiciary subcommittee, with a demand that Bogard's contract should be nullified 'because it is excessive and was negotiated in violation of the corporate board directions' (*United Press International*, December 17, 1982). The $57 500 a year contract included a one-year severance pay clause, transportation, lodging and food for six months, and the cost of membership in a private club. The General Accounting Office reviewed the terms of the contract and, in September 1983, reported that it was generally consistent with the hiring practices of the Corporation. In the meantime, however, the Congress had attached restrictions to an emergency appropriations bill barring board members and officers of the Corporation from fringe benefits superior to those available to other federal workers.

Bogard's first initiative as president was to clamp down on political lobbying. In July 1983, he despatched LSC officials to eight of the nine regional offices of the Corporation with instructions to impound documents relating to the period 1980 to 1982 and to forward them to headquarters for a detailed review. The allegations of illegal lobbying that stemmed from these services were eventually corroborated by the General Accounting Office and the Department of Justice.

In September 1983, Bogard moved again, prohibiting staff members of the regional offices from involving themselves in programs, activities, training sessions or meetings with government institutions, bar associations, the National Legal Aid and Defender Association, the Project Advisory Group or other special interest groups. The prohibition also encompassed all contact with elected officials and the media, and was clearly designed to constrain the regional staff from obstructing the policy agenda of the LSC Board. Thirty-seven directors of legal aid programs financed through the Corporation publicly expressed their outrage at this prohibition.

Bogard provoked hostility within the field program by proposing a set of regulations (subsequently endorsed by the Board) enabling local programs to disqualify from legal assistance potential clients with more than $15 000 equity in a home or $4500 in a car. With more than 46.5 million people allegedly eligible for legal services, this action was designed to concentrate scarce resources upon the neediest clients. Many critics, however, viewed the intervention as an attempt to run down the legal services program. Such critics were already outraged by Bogard's presentations before congressional committees supporting a total ban on legislative advocacy, the expediting of program defunding with diminished due process rights, the elimination of attorney's fees and the removal of congressional restrictions on LSC Board discretionary authority. Bogard's requests were denied by the Congress notwithstanding the fact that the Senate was Republican controlled and that his proposals carried White House support.

In late 1983, Bogard attempted to force the closure of the branch offices established by the 17 national support centers in Washington DC, and to restrict to 10 per cent the amount of federal monies that those centers could spend in representing poor clients directly in lawsuits, lobbying and administrative proceedings. This move provoked a hostile reaction from lawyers of the support centers who claimed that 'his real purpose is carrying out the Administration's deathless wish to destroy the program' (Florence Roisman, the National Housing Project, *New York Times*, December 24, 1983). The real fear of activists within the legal services movement was aptly summarized by Stuart Taylor Jr:

> Such offices are, in effect, the eyes, ears and voices of the legal aid movement in the capital, lobbying in Congress, and keeping a sharp watch for cases that can be used to test rules and regulations affecting the poor. (*New York Times*, December 24, 1983)

By summer 1984, the tension between Bogard and the Congress was running high as the LSC president continued to press for policy autonomy to enable him to return legal services to its statutory role and as the Congress responded to bar pressures to preserve legal activism. Senator Warren Rudman and Bogard clashed repeatedly over this policy divide, as the Senate Appropriations Committee refused to end restrictions imposed on LSC officials, and denied them the right to enforce regulations restricting lobbying by LSC staff attorneys. These restrictions precluded the use of 1985 funds to enforce LSC regulations, specified the amount that each LSC grant recipient was to receive, placed a limit on LSC funds expendable on a private bar involvement project and mandated an increase in funding for LSC national and state support centers.

The Senate vote on these issues prompted a strongly worded letter from Bogard to Rudman on July 23 noting that the action was 'a clearly unwarranted and inappropriate intrusion on the management of this politically independent, private, nonprofit corporation' (*National Law Journal*, August 13, 1984). The senator fired off a harsh reply, signalling the effective breakdown of any effective relationship with the existing officers of the LSC.

Beset by internal staff divisions and overt congressional hostility towards his governance initiatives, Bogard tendered his resignation as President in January 1985. In April 1985, he was criticized by the General Accounting Office for improperly awarding three grants to law centers one day before the end of the 1984 fiscal year. Representatives Bruce A. Morrison and Barney Frank had called for the investigation of the grant awards, which they claimed to be illegal. The GAO report confirmed that Bogard should have notified the House and the Senate Appropriations Committees of the reprogramming of funds.

In June 1985 James H. Wentzel was appointed to the LSC presidency following a six-month nationwide search. Wentzel had been assistant director for litigation at the Federal Trade Commission's Bureau of Competition since 1982 and vice chairman of Fairfax County's Redevelopment Housing Authority. He was a graduate of the University of Denver College of Law who had worked for the Denver district attorney after graduation and for the Justice Departments' legislative office from 1973 to 1979. He was a former associate of the National Legal Center for the Public Interest, a conservative foundation that advocated government deregulation. His appointment was not well received by legal services advocates who noted that he had no prior experience of legal aid. With the LSC Board of Directors now confirmed by the Senate, and with a new president in position, the relationship between the Congress and the Corporation might have been expected to improve and with it the governance of the legal services program. This, however, was not to be.

As early as October 1985, three Democratic members of the House subcommittee, Howard Berman, Bruce A. Morrison and Barney Frank, attacked Wentzel over a $335 000 grant to the Constitutional Law Center in Cumberland, Virginia that had been made the previous year by Bogard, even though Wentzel had withheld a portion of the grant. Berman further accused Wentzel and the Corporation of taking sides against migrant farm workers in California by naming Jack F. Anzell, a long-time foe of the United Farm Workers, to a team monitoring a program of legal help for the migrants. The California program had been criticized for funding a lobbying organization and for its union organizing efforts – scarcely the kind of legal service to the poor envisioned in the 1974 Act.

In November 1986, Wentzel suddenly resigned the LSC presidency to return to legal practice following a bizarre shoplifting incident. Following a shopping visit to the Annandale branch of Magruders Stores on November 18, he was allegedly apprehended and searched by a security official of the store, George J. Pearce. Merchandise valued at $5.66 was allegedly found in his possession. The police were not notified of the incident, nor were any charges brought against him. Nevertheless, the *Washington Post* was alerted and offered front page coverage to the alleged incident, thus provoking media harassment of the LSC president. The employee who allegedly apprehended Wentzell was a student of Antioch Law School which had recently been defunded by the LSC. Although Antioch Dean, Isaac Hunt, denied any role by the Law School in the affair, Clark Durant, Chairman to the LSC Board, refused to dismiss the conspiracy theory out of hand.

In January 1987, John Bayly, Jr was appointed to succeed Wentzel, raising hopes among the staff attorneys that the Corporation was on the road to repairing relations with Congress and with the legal services community. Bayly had served for 11 years in the US attorney's office in Washington, DC, had worked at the Corporation for Public Broadcasting and the Federal Communications Commission and had served through 1975–76 as Republican counsel to the Senate Select Committee on Intelligence. Bayly, who was serving as LSC's general counsel at the time of his appointment, was welcomed by a wide cross-section of LSC associates. 'Unlike other candidates, he has not demonstrated any overt hostility to the program' said Anh Tu, director of the Project Advisory Group. 'It's good to see they've chosen a competent, honest lawyer', added a congressional aide. 'He's reputedly "straight forward" … not an ideologue' interjected another (*National Law Journal*, January 26, 1987; *Legal Times*, January 19, 1987).

Within a few months, however, Bayly was to be subjected to vigorous criticism from the field and to congressional harassment as he tightened the monitoring process, hiring consultants, requesting records and threatening to defund deviant programs. In July 1987, the National Legal Aid and Defender Association despatched to Senator Warren Rudman a lengthy report detailing program directors' complaints about alleged abuses in LSC's monitoring activities and requesting his intercession. Rudman in the Senate and Kastenmeier in the House strongly opposed an ultimately unsuccessful request by Bayly to shift $4.5 million of the $305 million budget of the LSC from field operations to administrative programs as a means of strengthening his monitoring arm. The American Bar Association was also hostile to this initiative.

Bayly's brief honeymoon with the legal services program ended with Clark Durant's provocative address to the American Bar Association in February 1987 calling for deregulation of the US bar. Thereafter, Bayly was beset by field resistance to his governance initiatives. In 1988, controversy sharpened further as President Reagan shifted his support for zero budgeting of the LSC to recommending a budget of $250 million in return for significant program reforms, including strict accountability, closure of the national support centers and mandated competitive bidding for the right to deliver federally financed legal services.

In April 1988, Bayly, acting for the LSC, hired three law firms to lobby Congress in favor of the Reagan budget reduction proposal. Congress reacted adversely, claiming that the expenditure of LSC funds to lobby Congress on this issue was 'illegal and an outrage' (Bar Leaders for the Preservation of Legal Services for the Poor, Summer 1988 Update). The Corporation immediately cancelled the contracts. Within a week, however, ten Senators called for Durant to be reprimanded and requested his resignation. Eight weeks later, at a house Judiciary Committee oversight hearing, John Bayly assumed full responsibility for the lobbying initiative.

His position weakened both outside and inside the Corporation, and, his relationship with the Board majority deteriorating, Bayly resigned the presidency on June 26, 1988. Once again the continuity essential to effective governance had been disrupted. On this occasion, neither the Congress nor the LSC Board could escape responsibility.

The LSC Board moved quickly to fill the vacancy, appointing, by a six to five majority, Terrance Wear to the presidency of the Corporation. Wear's appointment angered the legal services attorney interests because of his prior service 1981–1986 as counsel to Senator Jesse Helms' Agricultural Committee. Helms was viewed as hostile to legal services in general and to migrant legal representation in particular. Representative Kastenmeier was moved to term Bayly's resignation and the late night hiring of Wear as 'LSC's own version of the Saturday Night Massacre' (Bar Leaders for the Preservation of Legal Services for the Poor, Summer 1988, Update).

Wear pressed forward with the $5 million program of monitoring LSC grant and contract recipients, of defunding aberrant programs and of generally imposing central governance on the legal services program. He introduced changes in the legal services refunding process, requiring additional documentation despite complaints that this increased bureaucracy. Regulations were issued to reduce the funding made available to programs that were in receipt of attorneys' fees as a consequence of successful litigation. None of these actions endeared Wear to legal services activists or to their congressional representatives.

In Spring 1989, the outgoing LSC Board and its president once again came into direct conflict with Warren Rudman. In part, the bone of contention was the issue of attorneys' fees, in part an attempt to expedite the process of competitive bidding promised by Congress once a new Board had been confirmed. The political turmoil that completely engulfed legal services is perhaps best reflected in the following commentary:

An angry Senator Warren B. Rudman (R. New Hampshire) charged that the hearing (on competitive bidding) flouted Congress' intent. 'As a conservative senator, I'm sick and tired of the bad faith being displayed by the Legal Services Corp,' Rudman said as Wallace and Wear sat in stunned silence. Told by Wear that the attorneys' fees rule would be implemented even if the congressional panels object, Rudman exploded, 'I'm disgusted with you, I'm disgusted with the way this is being run. We're going to have to straighten this whole mess out after this group is gone.' (Bar Leaders for Preservation of Legal Services for the Poor, Summer 1988)

9 Conclusions

Throughout the 1980s, Congress kept the Legal Services Corporation alive, despite the relentless efforts of the Reagan administration to abolish it. The Board of the Corporation itself was torn with dissension about the mission of the organization. Funding had been held down to its 1980 level in nominal terms as a consequence of the deep cuts imposed in 1982, and its buying power had been eroded by inflation. The discretionary power of the Board had been curtailed by restrictions attached to appropriations bills, notably to protect the national support and training centers from budget cuts and defunding attacks.

The legal services attorneys themselves, however, have not emerged unscathed from congressional interventions. The 1989 appropriation bill for example barred LSC funded lawyers from bringing class action suits against any local, state or federal government (with certain exceptions); political activities such as boycotts and strikes; abortion litigation; and most lobbying. The LSC Board has moved further to prohibit legal services programs from handling cases involving redistricting, anticipating a rash of such activity following the 1990 Census. The Board has also moved to seize any attorneys' fees received by any program through court judgments or other settlements, despite congressional hostility. Clearly the controversy has not ended with the closure of the Reagan presidency.

This chapter has chronicled the serious and continuing problems of governance that have plagued the Legal Services Corporation from its creation in 1974 and has suggested that these problems are not the particular consequences of specific individuals' behavior but rather are endemic in the Corporation's statutory position in the no-man's land between the legislative and the executive branches of government. The chapter has provided a framework for understanding reported opportunistic behavior of legal services attorneys and program officials in an area of endeavor characterized by bounded rationality and asset specificity.

It should now be clear that the objectives of the 1974 Act as providing poor Americans with an adequate access to justice have not been achieved, be it from the perspective of the utilitarian, the classical liberal, the contractarian or even of the liberal democrats and the Marxist New Left. The program is riddled with internal inconsistencies, with overt ideology, with technical inefficiencies and with possible, though minor, outright illegalities. Disappointment crosses party lines, is a source of significant inter-party dissension, and has left a residue of distrust and hostility corrosive to program efficiency. In few areas of public policy is a thorough-going review and reassessment more warranted or more important.

In all the confusion that now surrounds the legal services program, however, one important fact stands out. Somehow and somewhere the original idea behind the 1974 Act that it was to help the individual poor Americans has been lost or discarded in the rhetorical debate among rich and middle-class Americans over goals and constraints. The notion that the individual poor should be helped – and the individual poor alone – by federal dollars to support access to justice has become submerged in a special interest pursuit of *group* goals, which only partly, peripherally and intermittently are issues of substantive concern to the poor themselves.

Legal services is not the first program involving the redistribution of income and wealth through the federal budget to be manipulated and subverted to the advantage of the already well endowed. Nor will it be the last. That clearly is one of the most important contributions of public choice scholarship. It is, however, a program that is especially vulnerable because of the absence of any market nexus between those who supply and those who consume the services made available by the taxpayer-voters who endorse the transfers. It is most especially vulnerable because such taxpayer-voters, imbued as they often commendably are by the Kantian imperative that the act of charity itself is good, fail to inquire too closely whether or not that which is given actually finds its way to the deserving poor.

13 The nemesis of poverty

Give me your tired, your poor,
Your huddled masses yearning to breathe free.
The wretched refuse of your teaming shore
Send these homeless, tempest tossed, to me,
I lift my lamp beside the golden shore.

Emma Lazaras, The New Colossus

1 Introduction

The original intent of legal aid in early twentieth-century America was to provide the poor with an adequate, though certainly not an unlimited, access to justice. With the winding down of President Johnson's mostly discredited 'Great Society' program, the 1974 Legal Services Corporation Act re-invoked this original intent with respect to non-criminal and non-fee generating legal advice and litigation by offering a public conduit to ensure the right to justice for the poor within the financial constraint imposed annually by Congress in its budget appropriation.

It is very important to note that the right to justice does not necessarily imply any right to wealth or wealth transfers, though it may in some cases result in such an outcome. It is the right of reasonable access to a process of law and not to an end-state defined in terms of a socially engineered change in the distribution of national income and/or wealth. It is a right which may or may not be exercised by those to whom it is made available with consequences which may not even be capable of anticipation at the time of its exercise. In this elemental form, it is endorsable almost, though not quite, as a fundamental constitutional right, or 'basis' principle, necessary to support equality of opportunity as categorized by Rawls as justice as fairness and as immortalized by President Abraham Lincoln in his address at Gettysburg in the words:

> Four score and seven years ago our fathers brought forth on this continent, a new nation, conceived in liberty, and dedicated to the proposition that all men are created equal.

Of course, there is often a great gap between expressed intent and outcome in the provision of public policy, a gap which is sometimes the consequence of accident or unforeseen disturbance, but which not infrequently is the consequence of deliberate human intervention (Lee and McKenzie, 1988).

Such indeed has been the history of legal services as bureaucrats within the anti-poverty program and as special interests in search of rents and privileges systematically have subverted the right to justice initiative into conformity with their own alternative and competing implicit agendas.

Furthermore, by its existence, the 1974 Act significantly adjusted the margins of cost and reward available to those for whom access to justice was intended, thus shifting the behavior of those as well as other citizens in ways that public choice can predict but which are not always those which the charitable impulse might have anticipated. The old saw 'the poor are always with us' has a meaning more uncomfortable and more fundamental than the altruists who enunciate it are usually willing to accept. Yet, by ignoring the volume of evidence that a market exists in poverty, with demands that emanate from the already well-endowed as well as from the poor and with supplies that respond to the net benefits perceived from various states of poverty, the naive anti-poverty enthusiast has helped to heap unintended costs not only upon those coerced into giving by the tax authority of the state but also upon those who experience the high costs of behavioral dependency that anti-poverty programs always impose (Tullock, 1971, 1983a and b, 1986).

The right to justice has strategic advantages when compared with traditional instruments of taxes and subsidies and, even regulations as an instrument for the redistribution of income and wealth. Foremost among such advantages is its relative non-transparency among voters relative to these other instruments (Crew and Rowley, 1988, 1989). As the margins of redistribution extend and narrow, so voter resistance increases and the political market at some point forecloses against additional transfers of income and wealth. The right to justice then becomes an indispensable instrument in extending the effective margins of the rent-seeking society. By invading the judicial branch of government to exploit vulnerabilities in the common law and to challenge statutes designed to defend property rights, the anti-poverty lobby may be able to extract wealth and income transfers that otherwise are denied to special interests as a result of voter resistance in the legislature.

Section 2 of this chapter outlines complexities and ambiguities in the definition and measurement of income inequality and poverty in the US as a means of assessing the real magnitude of the problem. Section 3 evaluates the underlying costs of the anti-poverty program and the serious problem of behavioral dependency to which it gives rise. Section 4 explores the varying motives that support the poverty program and identifies the principal actors in the anti-poverty market. Section 5 examines the right to justice objective both as a constitutional imperative and as an instrument in the anti-poverty program. Section 6 concludes with an examination of the implications for both the poor individual and the legal process of extending the right to justice through a legal services program.

2   Complexities and ambiguities in the definition and measurement of poverty

Most people concerned about poverty base their perceptions on the degree of income inequality revealed by the Census Bureau's data on the distribution of money income. For example, when the noted social critic, Sam Donaldson, remarked on David Brinkley's television show that the distribution of income 'is obscene', he was referring to the Census figures. Similarly, when the Catholic Bishops, in their Pastoral Letter, concluded that 'the degree of inequality is quite large' the only evidence offered was the Census figures (Browning, 1989, pp. 819–820).

On this basis, the facts concerning income inequality are quite simple and have changed relatively little over the postwar period (Wagner, 1989, p. 21). As Table 13.1 indicates, the lowest 20 per cent of families by income rank earns about 5 per cent of total family income. The second lowest quintile earns about 12 per cent, the third quintile earns a little less than 20 per cent, and the fourth earns about 25 per cent. In contrast, the highest 20 per cent of families earn a little more than 40 per cent of family income. Donaldson's anger, no doubt, was based upon a perceived earnings differential between the highest and the lowest quintile of some eight or nine times. Much of the argument in favor of anti-poverty programs revolves around the judgment that this degree of inequality is unwarranted and unacceptable.

Table 13.1   Percentage income shares for families, various years income quintile

Year	Lowest	Second	Third	Fourth	Highest	Top Five Per cent
1952	4.9	12.2	17.8	24.0	41.3	15.9
1965	5.2	12.2	17.8	23.9	40.9	15.5
1970	5.4	12.2	17.6	23.8	40.9	15.6
1975	5.4	11.8	17.6	24.1	41.4	15.5
1979	5.3	11.6	17.5	24.1	41.6	15.7
1983	4.7	11.1	17.1	24.4	42.7	15.8

(R.E. Wagner, *To Promote the General Welfare*, Pacific Research Institute 1989).

As Browning (1989) has demonstrated, however, the Census data do not measure effectively the degree of economic inequality in the US. Their shortcomings are by now well known. The figures refer only to before-tax incomes; they exclude income earned in kind; they make no adjustment for differences in family size (the top quintile is 30 per cent larger than the bottom quintile); they make no adjustment for differences in labor supply (the top quintile works four times the number of weeks as the bottom quintile); there is no adjustment for the benefits of government spending on public goods or on public schools; there is no adjustment for earnings made in the underground economy and not reported to the IRS; and there is no adjustment for income variation over the life cycle of a family unit.

The crude figures are biased significantly in favor of inequality and provide an unjustifiably pessimistic view of the extent of poverty within the US. For example, after correcting only for taxes, differences in family size, and some in-kind transfers, Levy (1987) determined that, in 1984, the bottom quintile shared 7.3 per cent and the top quintile 36.8 per cent of total family income, suggesting a differential of only five to one, which is much smaller than that of the Census figures.

An important defect of the Census statistics is the fact that they measure incomes only for a single year. Yet, the relative well-being of an individual or a family is more realistically measured in terms of a longer-term horizon, perhaps encompassing an entire lifetime. Lifetime incomes are substantially more equally distributed than are annual incomes, reflecting the high rate of mobility of families within the income distribution even over relatively short periods of time. For example, more than half of those in the highest income quintile in 1971 were in lower income quintiles by 1976; nearly half of those in the lowest income quintile in 1971 were in higher income quintiles by 1976 (Duncan, 1984). Without adjusting for other defects, Hoffman and Podder (1976) found that the income share of the highest quintile based on seven-year income averaging was 39.8 per cent, down from 42.3 per cent for the median year 1973 alone. The income share of the bottom quintile, similarly averaged, was 5.5 per cent, up from the 4.6 per cent for 1973 alone. By this correction, the income differential fell from nine to one to seven to one.

Of course, seven-year averaging is much too short to measure lifetime effects, failing to capture systematic life cycle changes, such as the persistent evidence that middle-aged families on the average earn twice the income of young or old families. In the absence of consistent lifetime earnings data, Browning (1989) cites indirect evidence from consumption statistics which are much more smoothed than income over the life cycle. Consumption expenditures of the top quintile are less than four times larger than those of the bottom quintile and the top quintile of consumer units contains 60 per cent more individuals than the bottom. Of particular note is the tendency for consumer expenditures by the bottom quintile to run at rates three times higher than their before-tax incomes. The relationship between poverty and family income is more complex and ambiguous than many poverty analysts are prepared to acknowledge. The statistics most commonly used to evaluate income inequality in the US certainly exaggerate its significance.

This exaggeration is important, in determining policy towards income redistribution, for three principal reasons (Browning, 1989). First, it implies that inferences based on crude annual income data when determining the distributional consequences of social policies may frequently be wrong. For example, it is possible for annual data to show net transfers to the lowest income quintile each year, and yet for all low income families to be harmed by the policy because of families' mobility over time through the quintile categories. If this extreme error is unlikely, a modified mistake involving a sizeable proportion of apparently low income families is entirely feasible.

Second, if income inequality is less, the benefits to reducing income differences will also be less whatever the ethical motive for narrowing income equality, be it utilitarian, classical, liberal, contractarian, liberal democrat or Marxist, be it for reasons of self-interest or of altruism. The impulse to redistribute, whatever its source, must weaken as perceived inequalities diminish.

Third, as the degree of inequality becomes less, the efficiency cost per dollar of income redistribution – the marginal cost of redistribution – inexorably increases. As is well known, all redistribution policies carry deadweight costs, which reflect the distortion of economic decisions not least concerning labor supply, and which are reflected in a level of benefit to the recipients which is lower than the level of cost to those who bear the burden. The magnitude of this cost relative to achieved redistribution is important in the redistribution calculus. Browning (1989) illustrates the relationship between perceived inequality and the marginal cost of redistribution as follows (Browning and Johnson, 1984, 1986).

Suppose that income is to be redistributed from those with above to those with below average incomes through the mechanism of a 10 per cent linear income tax (positive for those above and negative for those below the average). Now consider a community of three persons, with incomes of $10 000, $30 000 and $50 000. Ignoring deadweight losses, the policy will transfer $2000 from the high-income person to the low-income person. The deadweight loss of this redistribution is the marginal cost of redistributing the $2000. Suppose that a mean-preserving reduction in income inequality occurs independently from redistribution policy in this small community, leaving incomes of $20 000, $30 000 and $40 000. The same transfer policy, at a linear income tax of 10 per cent, will now redistribute only $1000. Yet, the efficiency cost of the transfer will be the same as in the prior case, since the source of this inefficiency is the rate of income tax applied. In such circumstances, the marginal cost of redistribution doubles, as a consequence of reduced inequality.

The policy relevance of this insight depends upon the actual magnitude of the marginal cost of redistribution in the economy under review. Browning

(1989) demonstrates that, for parameter values that are plausible for the US, the efficiency cost of equalizing incomes among the bulk of the population is extremely (prohibitively) high, especially when lifetime effects are included – and this without accounting for other welfare costs, in the form of administrative and compliance costs, resources devoted to loophole searches and rent-seeking that are inevitably associated with redistribution programs. It is quite possible, in such circumstances, that the poor as a whole may become poorer in absolute terms as a consequence of income redistribution, though their relative positions may improve. Almost inevitably, some poor persons will suffer this fate even when their own labor supplies are not affected adversely by the transfer program.

The impact on economic efficiency, of course, will not always be a crucial factor in judgments on a transfer program, though this is usually decisive for adherents of strict utilitarianism. Classical liberals will reject even efficiency-enhancing transfer programs unless natural rights are effectively protected. Others, however, will be well-disposed to redistribution even when it is destructive of wealth, if it satisfies fairness conditions in sufficient degree. Such favorable judgments may not be restricted to liberal democrats and Marxists, but may also reach out to contractarians, certainly to Rawls (1971), should they be viewed as achieving universal consent behind a suitably designed veil of ignorance (Rowley, 1988).

Nevertheless, policies that are designed to equalize incomes almost invariably violate commonly accepted norms of horizontal and vertical equity (Browning, 1989). Even on the equity side of the ledger there are losses as well as gains, as a consequence of differing preferences among the poor concerning work and leisure and concerning saving and consumption. Because of these factors, any redistribution of income will produce real income differentials among those who otherwise might be viewed as being equally deserving.

This is true even when the transfer base is widely defined. For example, a linear income tax falls harder on those who evidence a stronger preference for market income than for leisure and the linear consumption tax falls more heavily on the person with the stronger preference for consumption than for saving, even when they are otherwise identical. It is much more pronounced when the transfer base is narrow. For example, agricultural subsidies more frequently than not benefit the very rich. Nearly half of the US workers employed at the minimum wage belong to families in the upper half of the income distribution (Browning, 1989). Any transfer program should be vigilantly scrutinized for such weaknesses if the real objective is to locate the deserving poor.

A program which is directed effectively at the deserving poor must be more attractive than one which is designed to equalize incomes, for reasons both of efficiency and of equity, irrespective of the ethical impulse that underpins it. For the marginal benefits will be higher and the marginal costs will be lower for anti-poverty programs. It is entirely consistent, therefore, for someone to support anti-poverty policy but to reject egalitarian policy even when they place no positive value on constraining the size of government.

Poverty was first defined officially in the US in 1965 at the outset of the Great Society program. In 1966, the official rate of poverty was calculated at 14.7 per cent of the total population. In 1987, following two decades of massive income redistribution, the official rate had fallen only to 13.5 per cent. There are reasons to suppose, however, that these statistics understate the favorable impact of the anti-poverty program.

Among the factors that support a more favorable scenario must be listed the slowing rate of growth of the US economy over the 1970s and 1980s and demographic changes of several kinds (Browning, 1989). During the 1960s, rising per capita real incomes had been a powerful agent in the reduction of poverty, but average real hourly earnings were approximately the same in 1987 as they had been in 1969, offering no autonomous help to the alleviation of poverty. The share of the population that was either young or old increased over this period by approximately 20 per cent, and immigration of unskilled persons with English language deficiencies significantly increased. Most important, the share of female-headed households nearly tripled, partly in response to welfare policies (Murray, 1984, 1986, 1987). Given these changes, the reported poverty rate might have been expected to increase over the period 1967 to 1987 in the absence of any poverty program.

Furthermore, the official poverty rate has increasingly come to overstate the number of persons living in poverty over the period under review. There are two main reasons for this overstatement. First, in-kind transfers, by providing work disincentives, may increase poverty as it is officially measured by reducing the level of cash earnings of the poor. Second, the consumer price index used to adjust the poverty lines upward systematically overstated the inflation rate throughout the 1970s and early 1980s as a result of a faulty housing cost adjustment factor. Although the fault was corrected in 1983, the poverty line was already 10 per cent higher than its 1960s equivalent, with damaging implications for the reported rate of poverty.

In combination, these factors exert a significant influence on the overstatement of the rate of poverty in the US. The Census Bureau itself has calculated that the inclusion of in-kind benefits would lower the rate by 33 per cent. This itself is an underestimate since some $41 billion of relevant annual in-kind benefits were omitted from the recalculation (O'Neill, 1986). Weicher (1987) has calculated that the poverty rate would now be lower by 12.5 per cent if the real poverty lines had not been allowed to drift upwards accidentally. Browning (1989) has conjectured that by combining these factors the poverty rate in 1987 would be reduced from the 13.5 per cent officially reported to approximately 7 per cent.

Given the mobility of persons who fall within the poverty definition, many of this 7 per cent may be poor but not destitute (Murray, 1987). As Browning (1989) reports 41 per cent of those officially listed as poor own their own homes, and the average net worth of poor families in 1983 was $30 000, approximately three times the average poverty line and five times the average annual income of the poor.

3   The cost of the anti-poverty program and the problem of behavioral dependency

Anti-poverty programs are comparatively recent phenomena in the US, for the most part creations of post-Second World War politics. As recently as 1950, as Charles Murray (1984) has outlined, most surveys of the US economy were content to dwell on the benefits of growing postwar affluence and to warn against the dangers of 'mindless materialism' (*Life*, April 24, 1950). Philanthropists concerned themselves to find useful things to do with their money 'now that most of the crushing burden of relieving destitution has been removed from the shoulders of the individual giver to those of society, where it belongs' (F. Emerson Andrews, December 1950). Yet poverty undoubtedly was widespread as the *New Republic* concluded in its 'State of the Union' editorial and as Robert L. Heibroner confirmed in *Harper* magazine, with some ten million American families estimated to be earning less than $2000 per annum.

By applying retrospectively the definition of poverty now employed by the federal government, there were in 1950 approximately 45 million American poor, or 30 per cent of the total population – a percentage that would now be viewed as constituting a crisis. Yet, in 1950, the federal response was restrained, with total spending on social welfare, excluding programs for veterans and for railroad and government personnel, costing a little over three billion dollars (11 billion dollars at 1980 prices). This figure, which included Social Security, Aid to Families with Dependent Children and Unemployment Insurance, represented less than $250 per annum of expenditures on the individual poor. At least, however, it seems to have found its way to the poor and not to the middle classes who for the most part relied upon savings and private insurance to protect themselves against unforeseen contingencies. In 1950, there was little or no organized anti-poverty lobby in the US as is evident from the fact that only in 1965 was poverty granted the political accolade of an official definition.

The period 1950 to 1980 was one of unprecedented advance by the anti-poverty industry, especially after 1965 with the introduction of the Great

Society program. The transfer statistics themselves show extraordinary increases in federal social welfare expenditures using a constant, official definition and constant dollars as the basis for comparison (Murray, 1984):

> Health and medical costs in 1980 were six times their 1950 levels; Public assistance costs in 1980 were thirteen times their 1950 levels; Education costs in 1980 were twenty-four times their 1950 levels; Housing costs in 1980 were one hundred and twenty nine times their 1950 levels.

An important factor in this explosion in federal social welfare expenditures was the effective political pressure to include non-poor as well as poor recipients. This pressure was exerted not only by potential non-poor recipients but also by the principal suppliers of the transfer programs themselves, including both bureaucrats and private suppliers. The farm lobby was aggressive and politically effective in pressing for the expansion of the food stamp program. The American Medical Association lobbied extensively for expansions in Medicaid and Medicare. Construction industry associations exerted political influence to raise the provision of low-income housing. The American Bar Association was a major lobbyist for the expansion of legal aid.

Most of this lobbying was not concerned with helping the poor. Anti-poverty slogans became instruments of rhetoric to reward the special interests. The political effectiveness of such supplier groups in structuring poverty programs in ways that served their own specific interest is evidenced by the act that, between 1965 and 1981, of those transfers that were means-tested, in-kind transfers increased 13 times faster than cash transfers, despite the relative inefficiency of the in-kind mechanism (Lee and McKenzie, 1988). Moreover, in 1983, only 16 per cent of direct government transfers (both in money and in kind) were means-tested or specifically aimed at the poor (Goodman, 1984). Between 1965 and 1984, means-tested expenditure programs grew from 1–3 per cent of gross national product, but much even of these expenditures was diverted from the poor or wasted in the transfer process (Tullock, 1983a and b, 1986). For, had these resources alone effectively reached the poorest 10 per cent of the population, they would by themselves have supported a consumption standard equal to 45 per cent of the national average (Browning, 1989). In addition, there should have accumulated the benefits of the larger social insurance policies designated in part for the poor together with the private resources of the low-income population.

Viewed from this perspective the modest impact of the anti-poverty program in reducing the incidence of poverty in the US between 1965 and 1987 is seen to have been purchased at high cost. That so great a commitment of resources, in combination with a 70 per cent real gross national product could leave poverty all but unchanged is suggestive of a significant misallocation and/or dissipation of resources. This interpretation is reinforced once the concept of poverty is extended to reflect not just a lack of income but the extent to which individuals are dependent and unproductive citizens. For illegitimacy, school dropouts, drug use, crime and illiteracy continue at levels that are as high and in some cases dramatically higher in 1987 than in 1965, or even in 1950. A serious and growing problem of behavioral dependency appears to have been a principal consequence of the anti-poverty program, as is evidenced by the fact in 1987, that almost 50 per cent of AFDC households consisted of families headed by unwed or divorced mothers (Murray, 1984, 1986). An economic underclass may well have been established by the poverty program.

Those who argue that welfare programs in the US are losing ground – indeed that such is the predictable and inevitable outcome – tend to place a greater emphasis upon the problem of behavioral dependence even than upon problems of theft and rent-seeking (Murray, 1984; Lee and McKenzie, 1988). If anti-poverty programs create behavioral dependency they contribute to a long-term poverty problem that will respond, if at all, only to policy adjustments away from the enabling environment that has been established.

The problem of behavioral dependence is not exclusively a consequence of the responses of the poor to available transfer programs. The behavior of the initially non-poor also merits attention. For poverty programs, even when they are designed to transfer resources exclusively to the poor, are seldom allowed to do so. Once the rules of eligibility become known, those who are ineligible not infrequently adjust their economic conditions to qualify for the transfers that are available even when such behavior threatens long-term dependency upon the welfare state. Thus, it is, for example, that the middle classes became dependent on Medicare, once Medicaid had been established, and that wealthy farmers became dependent on farm subsidies initially intended only for marginal farms. This rush into dependency is certainly not restrained by the special interests who thrive on the provision of services that the transfer state supports (Tullock, 1989).

Furthermore, when government actually transfers wealth to the poor, or even when vote-hungry politicians exaggerate the magnitude of such transfers, such gains, whether real or imaginary, are offset, in part at least, by a decline in the private charitable impulses of the non-poor. In this sense, public sector transfers crowd out private transfers (Lee and McKenzie, 1988). Abrams and Schmitz (1978) have calculated that the direct offset was 28 per cent for the period 1948 to 1972. Roberts (1984) claims that this is an understatement, in view of the composition changes in private charity away from donations to the poor towards donations to evidently non-poor recipients such as religious, educational and artistic organizations.

What really matters, however, is the response of the poor to the anti-poverty program; the extent to which state transfers reduce the incentives for the poor to provide for themselves. Perverse incentive effects are predictable in any transfer program, even if it should take the form of a negative income tax, but especially in the more usual in-kind, pork-barrelled packages that are funnelled through political markets.

During the 1970s and 1980s America experienced increasing unemployment among the young, increased dropout rates from the labor force, higher rates of illegitimacy, rising rates of welfare dependency and escalating rates of crime. All of these are entirely predictable and rational responses to the anti-poverty program. The AFDC program provides a helpful insight into the nature of the problem.

In 1960, this program was narrowly defined to ensure that it was unattractive by comparison with full-time, minimum wage employment. For example, a mother with one child received $63 per week (in 1980 dollars) to cover accommodation, living and medical costs. This remittance was reduced on a dollar-for-dollar basis against any outside income, and was completely withdrawn if the woman cohabited with any male. Attempts to evade these restrictions, if detected, were punished by indefinite ineligibility for any welfare support.

This scheme provided no incentive for any couple or single person to procreate in order to obtain access to the welfare program. It offered no incentives for unmarried parents to remain unmarried as long as one of them could obtain minimum wage employment. It offered no incentive for anyone to remain on welfare if full-time employment should become a viable option. On all counts, therefore, the 1960 ADFC program had built-in safeguards against the reinforcement of behavioral dependency (Murray, 1984).

By 1970, all the above-mentioned safeguards had been eliminated and the ADFC program had become a major enabler of voluntary unemployment and of family disintegration. First, the ADFC payment available to a mother with one child, at $106 per week (in 1980 prices), had risen to a level more comparable to earnings from full-time minimum wage employment. Second, the package was now augmentable by food stamps worth an additional $23 per week (in 1980 prices), by housing subsidies variously valued from a wide range of federal sources, and by access to Medicaid, valued according to the cost of doctors' bills and medication. Furthermore, this welfare package could be supplemented from outside earnings without penalty for the initial $30 per week of earnings and with welfare reduced by two dollars for every three dollars of weekly income once that threshold was passed.

Moreover, as long as the male cohabitor was not legally responsible for the child the cohabitor's income did not count against the mother's welfare eligibility. By a ruling of the Supreme Court, the presence of a man in the house of a single woman could not be used as a reason to deny a woman her welfare benefits. In such circumstances, the marriage solution to an unanticipated pregnancy, coupled with full-time employment for the male, was frequently less attractive than a live-in relationship supported by welfare. Not surprisingly, rational individuals confronted with unplanned pregnancies have shifted, at the margin, from marriage to single-parent choices in response to welfare incentives. It is even possible that some couples, or single women, may have planned illegitimate births as a means of accessing the welfare roles, without prejudice to the earning capacity of the father (Murray, 1984). Certainly, the 'thirty-and-one third' rule, in offering a positive incentive to women already on welfare to enter into gainful employment, nevertheless provided a much stronger (if perverse) incentive for women not on welfare to access its roles. As Murray (1984, p. 164) has noted 'it is the total effect of well-intentioned changes in the incentive structure, not any one specific change, that is the key to comprehending what happened'.

One reason that economic growth in the 1970s failed to reduce poverty was that many of the poor were unemployed. In particular, the job market behavior and experience of young black and Hispanic males changed radically from the mid-1960s onwards, arguably in response to the incentives of the anti-poverty program. From this time onwards many of this group became only intermittent members of the recorded workforce, though in some cases this may have been interfaced with membership of the growing underground economy (Bennett and DiLorenzo, 1984). During the early 1960s, the rate of unemployment for black and Hispanic youths had stabilized at the then unacceptable rate of 25 per cent. This was an important target of the Great Society program. Yet, through the late 1960s and throughout the 1970s this unemployment rate rose steeply for this group (Murray, 1984, p. 73), whereas older black males fared relatively well. This discrepancy between the young and the less young does not appear to be a generation gap phenomenon since young blacks lost ground to young whites in terms of unemployment experience throughout the period under consideration despite affirmative action legislation.

Large numbers of young black males simply ceased to engage in the process of seeking and holding jobs in the above-ground economy. For the most part, they were neither welfare loafers nor steadfast job seekers but rather intermittently employed following the incentives of the welfare program. By such behavior, they forfeited any future as economically independent adults, in marked contrast to the large majority of their white peers. Most especially however, this forfeiture was made against the major advance of older blacks relative to white, both in occupations and real wages (Murray, 1984, p. 85).

Many of those only intermittently engaged in the above-ground labor market were functionally illiterate and poorly endowed with marketable labor skills. They survived economically in part by periodic employment, in part by accessing the underground economy, in part by accessing the welfare roles and in part by engaging in criminal activity. Throughout the 1950s, violent crime in the US had remained low and relatively stable, though property crime had increased slightly during the latter half of that decade. Rates for both types of crime remained stable during the early 1960s. From 1964, however, the rates climbed rapidly both for violent crimes and for property crimes, almost tripling in the case of the former and doubling in the case of the latter by 1973. Thereafter, the rates appear to have stabilized at the dramatically high levels achieved in 1973.

For the most part, the criminals are male, especially in the case of crimes of violence, where male responsibility is 90 per cent. They are also young, with 60 per cent of all arrests for violent crimes involving persons under 25 years of age. They are also disproportionately black, with some 50 per cent of all arrests for violent crimes involving black persons. As crime rates soared during the period 1964 to 1973, the augmented risks of daily life fell disproportionately upon the poor, and especially upon the poor black populations of the US inner cities. In 1979, poor whites were 169 per cent more likely to be raped, 382 per cent more likely to be robbed and 768 per cent more likely to be subject to aggravated assault than the average American. Poor blacks were 211 per cent more likely to be raped, 1143 per cent more likely to be robbed and 660 per cent more likely to be subjected to aggravated assault than the average American (Murray, 1984, p. 122).

There can be no doubt that the dramatic fall in the expected cost of crime to the potential criminal – measured as the product of the probability of arrest and conviction and the penalty applied – has been a major stimulant to criminal activity (Bidinotto, 1989). The criminal justice system's failure to provide justice coincided with a growth in government programs intended to eradicate alleged causes of crime and with sweeping changes in the criminal justice and corrections systems, intended to supplant punishment with rehabilitation. These supposed reforms increased incentives for individuals to engage in criminal activity (Murray, 1984; Bidinotto, 1989).

Just as the changed incentives of the anti-poverty program induced a major increase in the rate of crime, so they encouraged the disintegration of family structures especially among the urban poor where they wrought havoc in terms of the rate of illegitimate births and the number of families headed by a single female. The two events are interrelated and are especially marked in the case of teenage black and Hispanics, in many respects the most vulnerable segments of the US population. Once the changed pattern of incentives is recognized the statistics effectively speak for themselves.

In 1960, 22 out of every 1000 single women gave birth to a live baby. In 1980, this figure had risen to 29, a significant but not a dramatic increase. The birth rate among single black women was much higher, at 77 per 1000 women. The crisis in illegitimacy exists in part because it has taken place against a general pattern of falling birth rates down from 118 per 1000 for women aged 15–44 in 1960, to 68 in 1980; in part because it has been centered upon the black (and Hispanic) populations (Murray, 1984, p. 126).

In 1963, black illegitimate births accounted for 23 per cent of all black births, a rate which represented a slow but steady increase from 17 per cent in 1950. By 1980, this rate had more than doubled to 48 per cent of all live births among blacks. Over the same period white illegitimate birth rates increased from less than 2 per cent in 1950 to 11 per cent in 1980. Most dramatic, however, was the rate of illegitimate births among black teenagers aged 15 to 19 years, which climbed to 82 per cent in 1980, accounting in that single year for 562 000 illegitimate births. For all other groups, except for whites aged 15 to 19 years, the illegitimacy rates were falling under the combined influence of improving birth control technology and easing access to legitimate abortion facilities. Inevitably, these teenage families constituted an important, intractable proportion of America's poor population, and a dangerous portent for the future. For as Murray (1986) has emphasized, 'poor, uneducated, single teenaged mothers are in a bad position to raise children, however much they may love them'.

In 1950, 88 per cent of white families consisted of husband and wife households, compared with 78 per cent of black families. In 1967, the white percentage remained at 88 per cent, whereas the black percentage had fallen to 72 per cent. By 1980, however, the proportion of black husband and wife households had collapsed to 59 per cent, whereas that for whites had dropped only to 85 per cent. In 1980, 65 per cent of all poor blacks who were living in families were living in families headed by a single female. The corresponding statistic for whites was 34 per cent. Indeed by 1980, the number of one-parent, low-income black families actually exceeded those of low-income whites, despite the overall population difference.

The increasing prevalence of the one-parent family is an important factor in the persistence of poverty in the US despite substantial anti-poverty transfer programs. Such families, historically, have shown high rates of poverty, in part because of lack of work skills and in part because of the need to stay at home to care for the children. When it becomes concentrated in the teenage population it is especially tragic and particularly intractable to conventional welfare programs.

Apparently, the public transfers create perverse responses on the part of the recipient poor and reduce the poor's ability to extricate themselves from poverty and to become productive members of society. The perverse incentives extend and possibly intensify over future generations, creating a self-sustaining category of the poor even in an increasingly affluent and fully employed economy. Even those, like Sawhill (1988), who are most determined to find some good in the anti-poverty program cannot deny the statistical evidence. They can and do question the direction of causation-welfare spending to behavioral dependency-posited by Murray (1984, 1986).

Yet, they rightly refrain from alternative explanations, such as genetic or cultural inheritance, which carry with them distasteful implications. Even if Murray is correct only at the margin, this is an important criticism of a transfer program which dissipates wealth and encourages fraud, with only some one-third or less of the tax transfers ever reaching those for whom initially they were designated. It is especially interesting to note that a critical stepping stone on the way to poverty entrapment was the Supreme Court decision rejecting the 'man-in-the-house' justification for denying ADFC benefits. Legal Services lawyers were responsible for that test case.

4 The poor and the right to justice

Given the apparent failure of the anti-poverty program to eliminate poverty in the US – indeed the strong probability that it may have induced a particularly intractable brand of behaviorally dependent poverty – it is important to review the relationship between the poor and the right to justice, not least to determine whether such access is helpful or damaging to the poor. For such a review, the right to justice concept must be carefully defined to distinguish between civil justice and social justice. The concept of poverty also must be distinguished from that of racial discrimination with which it is frequently related but not exclusively identified.

In the absence of a legal assistance program, the poor can exercise only a limited access to the process of civil justice, since they cannot usually purchase legal advice or pay court costs. In such circumstances, they are significantly dependent upon self-help, which usually requires an unattainable knowledge of the relevant laws, upon pro bono contributions by private attorneys (which tend to be strictly limited in a profession as wealth-motivated as the US bar) or upon contingency fee contracts with private attorneys (which are feasible only in cases where damages awards are achievable). At best, this combination of opportunities does not match up to the wealth of legal support available to a fee-paying client.

Of course, the poor are disadvantaged, by reason of their poverty, in all their potential contacts with a non-subsidized market economy, and there is no evident presumption that their particular disadvantage is the more serious with respect to the civil legal process. Indeed, the presumption is strong that their relevant disadvantage is typically less in this than in other markets since the legal wrongs of discrimination, fraud, breach of contract and of warranty mostly are associated with the market place from which the poor are relatively absent. The beneficiaries of the Ralph Nader lobby are not the destitute who cannot afford to purchase products whose prices reflect the high costs imposed by consumer protection legislation. Yet, there remain other dimensions in which the relative disadvantage of the poor with respect to civil justice raises an important policy question.

There are four alternative viewpoints concerning the rights to justice of poor Americans. The first, conservative viewpoint argues for the abolition of legal assistance to the poor and for a policy of encouraging the individual poor to resolve their own legal problems by self-help, to explore the opportunities provided by the charitable, pro bono offerings of the legal profession, and to engage in contingent fee contracting where the opportunity for an award of damages presents itself. This alternative, harsh though it may appear to some, in effect is an extension of the willingness-to-pay principle to the market in justice and a commitment to the notion that civil justice is not a commodity worthy of any especial public subsidy. More, it reflects a view that the subsidization of access to the civil justice market in itself may be a determinant rather than a palliative of poverty, yet another enabling mechanism leading the poor into behavioral dependency.

There are good reasons why many citizens (and a majority of their political representatives) are reluctant to accept the conservative solution. The substantive rules of the law in certain respects do affect the poor adversely not least because they do not take into account (perhaps cannot do so) the fact that the poor often lack the cognitive ability and the resources to enforce the rights that such laws theoretically provide. The procedure of almost all courts and of many agencies is based upon the adversary system which offers to the parties in dispute the opportunity and responsibility for developing and presenting the relevant facts and legal contentions. In such a process, ineffective parties are simply allowed to suffer their fate. Similar problems arise in administrative agencies that do not employ the adversary system whenever they exercise discrimination among equally eligible applicants. In both cases, procedural injustice may result, and reinforce pre-existing disadvantages, in the absence of an effective program of legal assistance.

Recognition of this potential threat to procedural injustice, and concern for its amelioration, informs the classical liberal approach to legal assistance. The legal aid program endorsed by this ethic should be orientated to individual clients, concerned with individual cases, and focused on the routine disorders of daily life – domestic discord, trouble with creditors and landlords, involvements with the police, welfare agencies and other organs of government. If the instrument of such a program must be the publicly funded law office – and that is an issue of dispute – then that office essentially should be a replica of its fee-earning private counterpart (Hazard, 1969).

The characteristic problem-solving technique associated with this approach to legal assistance is accommodation-reduction of acrimony, extension of time limits, compromise of differences – and procedural advice. Litigation, though an appropriate instrument, is a measure of last resort. The classical liberal program must be diffuse in nature, reflecting the disparate concerns and preferences of the individual poor. In many respects, the important work involved is nevertheless microcosmic and dull, and, as such, unlikely to command the attention let alone the vocation, of ambitious, politically charged, reformist attorneys. Yet, it does serve the expressed individual needs of the poor, leaving issues of wider social justice where, arguably, they ought to rest: on the conscience of the electorate and its sense of prudence, as expressed in the legislation of its political representatives (Hazard, 1969, p. 712).

Effectively implemented, this approach would clearly assist the poor to assert individual rights, both civic and economic, and, to that extent, to protect their freedoms. To the extent that the advice and support thus provided directs property and income settlements that are favorable to the poor, the economic well-being of the poor may also improve.

Unfortunately, however, negative effects may also occur from such an apparently beneficent process, not for reasons of caprice or of abuse, but by the very nature of a non-entitlement, publicly subsidized legal assistance program. Following Tullock (1980), the problems will be reviewed within the context of a disputed case in civil litigation concerning requested legal aid for a contested suit for divorce.

First, suppose that the divorce case under consideration concerns one party who is poor, and who requests legal assistance and another who fails the eligibility test for access to the program, but, who, nevertheless, is far from well endowed in terms either of wealth of income. Success or failure in this petition for divorce will be determined in part at least by the resources made available by the law office to the plaintiff, on the one hand, and by those supplied by the defendant on the other. The plaintiff, whose principal resource contribution is time (the opportunity cost of which is likely to be low), will press the staff attorney to allocate resources heavily to the case. The attorney, aware of the budget constraint imposed upon his office, will weigh resource commitments against his expected return from pressing the case. It is by no means clear that resources will always be directed to the most deserving of the poor. A major factor in the movement of resources will be the ability of the attorney to establish a legal precedent and, thereby, to advance his post-legal services career.

If such a slippage from high ideals should occur, not only are there costs for the plaintiffs whose cases are managed for attorney benefits, but also for the defendants of publicly-litigated suits who find themselves investing resources not so much to defend themselves alone as to defend a category of people – people in their same situation – from the establishment of an unfavorable precedent (Tullock, 1980, p. 153). Thus, the ambitious staff attorney, in deciding to take a contested divorce case, is not only deciding how government resources are to be allocated, but also, before any court proceedings have begun, is inflicting heavy costs on other possibly equally poor individuals.

Now suppose that the divorce petition under consideration pits poor person against poor person and that both parties to the case approach the legal services program in search of public assistance. How should the legal services office proceed? If a decision is made to support only one of the litigants in the case, effectively the office itself becomes the judge in a case that surely would be forfeited by the unsupported party. Yet, if a decision is made to support both parties, will the office coordinate its activities to minimize the total outlay, thereby denying each litigant the benefit of independent support, or will it engage in an expensive competition with the one staff attorney driving up the resources committed by the other in some perverse strategic interaction? Neither solution at first sight appears to be welfare maximizing. Indeed, there is no self-evident way to determine the optimal amount and the optimal distribution of public resources to such a case.

It might be argued (Tullock, 1980) that the adversary procedure itself is at fault as an essentially costly and inherently unfair mechanism for resolving legal disputes in a system dominated by the willingness to pay criterion. However, as Goetz (1987) has indicated, it is by no means clear that an administrative procedure would fare better given the many problems of bureaucracy (see Chapters 6 and 7). In a world of less than perfect institutions, the more able and the better endowed will typically dominate the lesser able poor even in the classical liberal political environment.

The third approach breaks with adherence to the civil justice objective and envisions legal assistance as a bridge between social (rather than individual) grievances (bad housing, racial discrimination, expensive credit, chronic unemployment) and social reform. The model approach and outcome, for its advocates, is the school segregation litigation which culminated in *Brown* v. *Board of Education* and which helped to curtail racial segregation in the US public school system. The crucial shift of emphasis (the cause of most of the conflict and tension in the US legal services program) is away from individual to group concerns, away from methodological individualism to constructivist rationalism in the goals and the means of legal assistance to the poor.

This approach, which attacks the apparent causes of poverty from a social engineering perspective, concentrates upon changing the civil laws themselves – reform of welfare, school administration, landlord–tenant relationships, creditor–debtor relationships and the like – albeit from within the endorsed legal and political structures. The characteristic problem-solving techniques of this approach are aggressive lobbying, protesting and complaining on behalf of group poor interests, the stimulation and formation of special interests to this end, and aggressive litigation, frequently through class action suits, targeted on law reforms through an assault on established legal precedents, whether or not such reforms are relevant to the litigation interests of the individual poor.

This approach, perhaps unfortunately, has tended to merge and confuse the separate issues of poverty and discrimination, not infrequently diverting monies designated for the poor to the pursuit of the group objectives of specific minorities, the members of which are far from universally poor, in a bid to achieve reforms through litigation that have been denied by the democratic political process. The resulting confusion of objectives has tended to weaken legal services as a coherent program of assistance to the poor. For example, there are many more poor whites, in absolute numbers, than there are poor blacks, poor Hispanics and poor orientals and poor native Americans combined. There are many well-paid members of each of these minority races. There are many more well-paid than there are poor women, many more well-paid than poor members of the gay community.

The confusion of objectives which has denied the social engineering approach logical consistency, is viewed as a blessing by adherents to the fourth approach, the Marxist critical legal studies scholars who seek root-and-branch removal of the existing institutions of US society and their replacement by socialism. For, by confusing quite separate social engineering goals, this approach widens and magnifies the extent of the alienation and anger that fuels its impact, submerging internal policy differences in an attempt to radicalize the law and legal institutions.

This most radical of all approaches to the right to justice visualizes the legal services program offices essentially as nuclei for the community action program. Such offices are envisioned as activist neighborhood center locations, staffed with politico-legal sophisticates, to develop and energize community actions and to provide a pervasive program of organization, training and funding for radical reaction to the established legal and political systems. Initially, this approach was implemented only in a few communities and even there it led a tenuous existence because of the suspicion if not outright hostility of the organized bar and of most major city governments. During the 1970s, however, as critical legal studies begin to penetrate the American Bar Association and as American legal opinion radicalized under the influences of Vietnam, civil rights and Watergate, this approach secured for itself a militant toehold in the legal services program.

It is interesting to speculate on how these four approaches to resolving the problem of the right to justice for poor Americans relate to the alternative goals of policy outlined in Chapter 2. The first approach conceivably

approximates the Paretian outcome in a society which has satisfied its altruistic instinct through private charity and which rejects public good arguments
for welfare transfers on the grounds of absence or inadequacy of outstanding
gains-from-trade. Some might view this approach as an implication of Vir-
ginia-blend conservatism (Rowley and Peacock, 1972) consistent with the
early, Paretian-based, scholarship of Buchanan (1959).

The second approach clearly approximates the classical liberal's vision of
a society in which the rule of law plays a central role and in which individuals are not deprived of their legal rights simply because of inadequate
wealth endowments. Of course, legal advice and litigation, as scarce commodities, must be economized and the classical liberal's fear of the Leviathan
state ensures that levels of legal aid to the poor will be limited, and will not
be directed to the expansion of state empowerment. The importance attached
by classical liberals to individual freedom of choice guarantees a methodological individualistic approach to legal assistance which emphasizes a client
rather than a staff attorney model of delivery. Finally, the classical liberal's
emphasis upon individuals bearing full responsibility for their actions suggests that legal assistance should be channelled on a self-help basis to
achieve individual empowerment and not state dependency.

The third approach approximates the liberal democrat's social engineering ethic. Depending on ones' views as to what might occur were individuals
able to confer behind a Rawlsian veil of ignorance, this approach could
conceivably approximate to the contractarian ethic of Rawls, though much
depends, for this to happen, upon the prevalence of extreme risk-aversion
among all actors in the original position (Rowley and Peacock, 1975). Even
if the Rawlsian view should hold, contractarians would part company on the
level of legal assistance that would be endorsed, with Buchanan for example
sharply constraining such transfers for fear of the Leviathan state (Brennan
and Buchanan, 1980). Furthermore, whereas Rawls clearly envisages individuals as engaging in protracted social engineering in their negotiations
behind the veil, it would be a betrayal of Buchanan's scholarship to suggest
any deviation from methodological individualism. For this reason, the staff
attorney model of legal services delivery, which arguably might be advanced
by Rawls, would be rejected outright by Buchanan in favor of client control,
perhaps through a voucher scheme.

Finally, the fourth, most radical, approach to legal aid, enunciated by the
critical legal studies adherents, embraces the ethic of Marxism and seeks the
socialist Utopia. The emphasis placed in this approach upon destroying
capitalism is compatible with both old and new versions of Marxism. However, the emphasis placed upon statist solutions to the poverty problem
places the fourth approach more comfortably in the old Marxist tradition.
The New Left, with its disdain both for markets and for bureaucracy, in the

apocalytic vision of 'Jerusalem', is really hard-pressed to find any acceptable reform solution compatible with modern industrial or post-industrial society (Rowley and Peacock, 1975). The New Left, especially since late 1989, typically dissociates itself from the behavior of all real-world Marxist-based autocracies, and claims that an American, Marxist-based reform would be different, even perhaps a bucolic agrarian paradise?

5   Legal services and the poor: The pre-1974 philosophy

The particular objectives of the federal legal services program with respect to these four right to justice alternatives have never been articulated. In view of the tension that exists between the advocates of each approach, and the uneasy political compromise on which the federal program has always rested, ambivalence in stated political objectives is the predictable public choice outcome (Tullock, 1967a). Indeed, such ambivalence is essential to maintaining non-transparency in wealth transfers through which the margins of redistribution can be extended (Crew and Rowley, 1988). In such circumstances, the particular equilibrium achieved, together with changes in that equilibrium over time, can be ascertained only by reference to the program itself.

The concept of a federal legal services program was launched in 1964 with the influential article by Edgar and Jean Cahn (Cahn and Cahn, 1964). The political launching pad for the venture was President Johnson's Great Society program into which legal services was incorporated as part of the Organization for Economic Opportunity. From such initial mainsprings, legal services philosophy inevitably started out within the social engineering perspective of liberal democracy, categorized as approach three above. Left-leaning as this approach undoubtedly was, it retained traces of the self-help perspective of classical liberalism and little or nothing of the radical reformism of the Marxists who had yet to recover from McCarthyism, and to achieve the toehold grip on American politics that civil rights, Vietnam and Watergate was later to provide.

The philosophy of the movement originated where the movement itself started, in 1919 with Reginald Heber Smith and his book, *Justice and the Poor*. This philosophy was that of classical liberalism, emphasizing access to the existing law and not social reform:

> We can end the existing denial of justice to the poor if we can secure an administration of justice which shall be accessible to every person no matter how humble... (Heber Smith, 1916, p. 257)

The constitutional implications of this philosophy were emphasized in 1926 by Chief Justice Taft:

The real blessing of our Bill of Rights is in its provision for fixed procedure securing a fair hearing by independent courts to each individual ... but if the individual in seeking to protect himself is without money to avail himself of such procedure, the Constitution and the procedure made inviolable by it do not practically work for the equal benefit of all. Something must be devised by which everyone, however lowly and however poor, however unable by his means to employ a lawyer and to pay court costs, shall be furnished the opportunity to set fixed machinery of justice going.

This theme continued to dominate the legal aid movement from its initial recognition in 1920 by the American Bar Association through the 1950s, throughout which period Reginald Heber Smith continued to play an influential role. As Johnson (1978) has noted (p. 12), 'it is difficult to detect much sympathy for the social and economic deprivation of the poor in the writings of the leaders of legal aid, but their sensibilities as lawyers clearly were shocked by the deprivation of due process caused by poverty'. There was no hint of any necessity for law reform to secure for the poor their right to justice, as the following passages from Heber Smith (1919) demonstrates:

The body of the substantive law, as a whole, is remarkably free from any taint of partiality. It is democratic to the core. Its rights are conferred and its liabilities imposed without respect of persons ... (I)t is instantly apparent that the legal disabilities of the poor in nearly every instance result from defects in the machinery of the law and are not created by any discriminations of the substantive law against them

and

On examination and on authority, the statement is warranted that the substantive law, with minor exceptions, is eminently fair and impartial. In other words, the existing denial of justice to the poor is not attributable to any injustice in the heart of the law itself. The necessary foundation for freedom and equality of justice exists. The inimical struggle is half won.

This philosophy was reflected in the policies of legal aid organizations. For example, the 'Standards' of the National Legal Aid and Defender Association played down the taking of appeals to establish useful principles stating that, unlike other appeals, they should be undertaken only when costs were available. Actions to create legal machinery for the social betterment of the poor were not even accorded the status of 'required standards' by the NLADA, but were characterized merely as 'recommended policies' to be implemented by local legal aid societies only insofar as local conditions permit. In fact, no civil legal aid lawyer ever brought a case to the US Supreme Court in the 89 years of the legal aid movement up to 1965 (Johnson, 1978, p. 14).

In 1941 the American Bar Association, through its President Jacob Ashley, explicitly committed itself to a legal aid movement planned and organized through a nationwide network of offices, to be as well known publicly as the courthouse, to which poor persons in need of advice and assistance could apply. Even at this stage, however, the American Bar Association and other bodies that advocated an extension of legal aid to the poor, were reluctant to petition Congress for the federal funding of such a program, largely because of fears that a federal program might invade the traditional territories of the private bar and become a vehicle for 'creeping socialism' within the United States economy. It was against this essentially moderate conservative or classical liberal background that the federal program for legal services was conceived and initiated during the early 1960s. Already, however, a more radical philosophy was attaching itself to the movement, emerging from certain neighborhood lawyer experiments, notably in New Haven, New York and Washington, DC, and stimulated by Ford Foundation funding.

The 1964 article by Edgar and Jean Cahn notably assumed as its central theme for legal services the concept of a war on poverty and not a war on unequal access to justice. The neighborhood law office was envisioned as providing a voice for the poor, conceived as a group rather than as individuals, in the design and implementation of anti-poverty programs (Johnson, 1978, pp. 32–33). Attorneys, with their own monopoly status over access to the courts, were to provide the requisite influence over the decisions of local anti-poverty agencies, and thus to bring a civilian perspective to the war on poverty.

Unlike most supporters of legal aid, leaders of the neighborhood lawyer experiment were concerned with something more palpable than procedural due process. They were committed to the reduction of poverty and dedicated to this goal in their support for a legal services program. In 1964, this reformist group joined forces with two quite distinctive reformist entities, namely the social rescue group based in New Haven and the law reform group pioneered by Wickenden and Sparer, to lobby for a federal legal services program. The New Haven approach was that of treating the social, psychological and educational deficiencies of persons who were poor in order to enable them to compete economically. Lawyers were to work on the legal problems of poor families in close coordination with other members of the rescue operation. Wickenden and Sparer wanted to modify rules and practices to divert wealth and income to the impoverished class. Their primary method of attack was test litigation. All three groups shared a joint commitment to reduce poverty through a federal legal services program. Variously, but decisively in pursuit of this commitment, all three diverted from the ethic of classical liberalism to embrace legal activism from the political perspective of the liberal democrats.

The reformist coalition entered the political market place fortuitously, at a time (1965) when the United States government had just discovered poverty, when constructivist rationalism was newly re-emergent as a dominant political tide, and when President Johnson was seizing the political advantage offered to him by the assassination of President Kennedy to launch the Great Society program. The success of the coalition in riding such good fortune to legislative success is charted in Chapter 1. The active support for the coalition provided by the American Bar Association was essential to carry the reform program through political obstacles mounted by advocates both of conservative and of classical liberal ethics. Most important was the impact of the organized bar in ensuring that staff attorneys and not community action agencies controlled the levers of the federal program and in quelling a backlash of resistance among the more conservative attorneys and local bar associations.

The reform coalition gained dominance over the legal services program as it emerged as an important arm of the Great Society program. From the outset, law reform – test cases, legislative advocacy and other techniques directed toward changing the laws and practices which formed the social and economic structure of poverty – was the top priority of the program. The leading components for this approach – social rescue, economic development and community organization – did not even include access to justice (Johnson, 1978, p. 128). The dominance of supplier rather than of client preferences, of constructivist rationalism rather than of methodological individualism in this priority ordering is evident in the following passage:

> Law reform possessed several advantages. To begin with, it offered the possibility of benefiting many of the poor who could not possibly be served directly at Legal Services offices. A single test case or legislative change or modified administrative regulation can benefit thousands of individuals. Moreover, law reform is a function that fully employs the lawyer's skills and training. Nobody else is in a position to prepare and file test cases and only a very experienced, knowledgeable and probably well educated individual is serious competition to the lawyer in legislative advocacy. (Johnson, 1974, p. 131)

Given this priority, the behavior of the OEO legal services program officers was entirely predictable. Commitment to social reform led many lawyers and most administrators to take only those cases which promised a major quantum of social change. Over the period 1965 to 1971, there was ten-fold expansion in financial outlays on legal services and a five-fold enlargement of the lawyer force. Yet, the number of clients processed for legal assistance increased less than three-fold, from 426 000 to 1 237 000. Moreover, a much higher percentage of the cases handled in 1971, by comparison with 1964, involved welfare problems. There was a sharp reduction in the proportion of domestic relations cases (Johnson, 1978, p. 188).

The rate of litigation rose significantly, with legal services lawyers taking 17 per cent of their cases to court in 1971 as compared with only 6 per cent in 1964. In 1964, appeals were rare or non-existent. By 1971, legal services lawyers were averaging well over 1000 appeals every year. The most revealing statistic, however, was that concerning the rate of access to the Supreme Court. From 1895 to 1965 not a single legal aid attorney had taken a case to the United States Supreme Court. Yet in five years – 1967 to 1972 – 219 cases involving the rights of the poor were brought to the high court, 196 were decided on the merits, and 73 of these were won.

If litigation was to be an effective instrument in the war on poverty, then it must be directed at a small number of strategically selected targets. Such targets should be group and not individual in nature and should be pursued irrespective of the concerns of the individual clients whose cases provided the federal funding for law reform activity.

One plank in the group strategy was targeted litigation to increase the earnings of specified categories of the poor. For example, one campaign of litigation was dedicated to the protection of agricultural workers in California and other border states from competition by controlling the influx of temporary workers from Mexico during the harvest season. The war on poverty evidently stopped at national boundaries. In 1967, legal services attorneys filed suit successfully to stop the importation of foreign workers. The movement claimed that this action added in excess of $2 million per annum to the income of domestic farm laborers. It ignored losses as a handicapped US agricultural industry experienced domestic market penetration by and a loss of export markets to less regulated foreign competition. Litigation was targeted at laws that denied farm workers and employees in service industries coverage under the National Labor Relations Act as well as at the expansion and enforcement of minimum wage laws.

California once again was the major battleground. The most notable legal services success was the raising of wage levels for 200 000 California farm workers by 25 cents an hour, thus increasing annual earnings for that group by almost $100 million. Overall, these actions were effective in wealth redistribution, but at a significant cost in terms of efficiency.

The second plank, in the group strategy of the OEO legal services lawyers, was that of exploring the political market place in search of wealth transfers. In the late 1960s, transfer payments of various kinds accounted for approximately 50 per cent of the income received by those below the poverty line, with approximately 30 per cent of the poor in receipt of some form of public assistance (which represented over 20 per cent of total income to the poor), with some 30 per cent in receipt of social security transfers (18.7 per cent of total income to the poor) and with 9 per cent in receipt of unemployment compensation. The remaining one-third of the poor received no direct government assistance. The laws governing these transfers were a compendium of federal and state statutes, federal and state regulations, local ordinances, regulations and practices, and determined both eligibility and the value of aid remitted to the poor.

Prior to legal services intervention, the eligibility criteria for transfer payments was constrained by two important rules, namely the substitute parent rule and the residency requirement rule. Approximately 400 000 poor individuals failed to satisfy one or other of these requirements. Following legal services lawsuits filed during 1968 and 1969, the Supreme Court overturned these limitations, thereby increasing public assistance transfers estimated at $400 million per annum. At the time of the Court decisions, this increase translated into a 5 per cent increase in the welfare dollars distributed to the poor and into a 1 per cent increment in the total income received by the bottom quintile of the US population. Much more significantly, however, these court decisions triggered an increase in behavioral dependency now evident in the single-parent poverty syndrome.

The second strand of the transfer augmenting strategy was directed at the benefit levels established in existing transfer programs. In most welfare programs, the amount of such payments was established by state or local authorities, with the federal government agreeing to supply a given per cent of the total cost of the program. In a series of Supreme Court tests, legal services lawyers sought to outlaw certain common devices used by state and local governments to hold down benefit levels for certain classes of poor people. These practices included 'maximum grant' provisions limiting the total sum that would be awarded to one family units, irrespective of the size of that unit, smaller grants for the children of dependent mothers than for the blind and the totally disabled, and percentage reductions from the minimum standards of need required by the federal government.

For the most part, these challenges were unsuccessful, with the courts showing a fairly consistent unwillingness to revise or to cast down well-drafted statutes, regulations and ordinances. Nevertheless, legal services lawyers were successful in invoking existing laws to constrain state governors from exceeding their authority, for example, in reducing medical payments to the poor. By this mechanism, legal services attorneys restored over $200 million in benefits to low-income residents of the State of California, and thus registered an indelible entry into the memory bank of then Governor Ronald Reagan.

Many federal welfare benefits were administered through state or local governments. Some of these programs, most notably those involving food stamps, failed to reach all of the eligible poor because the relevant authorities elected not to participate. In the late 1960s over one-third of the poorest jurisdictions had refused to join these programs. In 1969, legal services attorneys filed lawsuits in 26 states, claiming that countries were legally bound to administer the federal food program and that the Agricultural Department was required to furnish the food itself to non-compliant jurisdictions. Within two years, all but eight counties had joined the programs and the food stamp programs had been augmented by several hundred millions of dollars per annum. Similar actions on school lunch programs encountered substantial, though less universal success.

Nor was this all. Many so-called public goods, such as education, police protection, garbage collection, street maintenance and other similar services, are provided to the general public supposedly on an equal basis, roughly approximating per capita distribution. In a number of states and communities, legal services attorneys filed suit, claiming that the poor were not provided with their rightful share. In other jurisdictions, they filed suit claiming that low-income groups were required to pay above average rates for the same level of services. Some of these actions were successful, and were reflected in millions of dollars of wealth transfers to the poor.

As a result of legal services pressure, several million dollars of federally financed housing and some economic development funds were channelled to the low-income community, though much of this was undoubtedly dissipated in the bureaucracy. Further assaults were targeted on the alleged bargaining disadvantages of the poor in those markets in which they could participate, for example, higher mark-ups in the shops, higher interest charges in the usury markets, and inefficiencies in housing code enforcements. The fact that such interventions systematically tended to eliminate, or at least to erode, markets in which differential charges or rates of code enforcement reflected differential rates of default, or of property maintenance as between poor and non-poor communities, escaped the calculus of the social engineering enthusiasts within the legal services program (Johnson, 1974, pp. 206–210).

The third plank in the OEO legal services strategy was pursuit of equality of opportunity for poor Americans. In principle, this objective would be widely endorsed. In practice, the routes chosen to pursue equality of opportunity by OEO legal services attorneys were in some instances counterproductive, serving indeed to widen the differential upward mobility between the poor and the non-poor.

Most especially, those interventions that weakened competition in the product and in the labor markets systematically weakened equality of opportunity. For, as Friedman (1962) and Williams (1984) have emphasized, competitive capitalism is the most powerful human artifact ever designed for protection against prejudice and discrimination in a society in which discriminatory preferences are manifest. Those who discriminate in competitive markets sacrifice profit opportunities and even jeopardize the viability of their enterprises. In sharp contrast, regulated private markets and the entire political market place are breeding grounds for discrimination precisely because of the existence of discretionary powers unconstrained by direct competitive impulses.

The unqualified success of OEO legal services attorneys in this field was the ending of de facto segregation of public schools in several communities, and thus the enforcing of the Supreme Court judgment in *Brown* v. *Board of Education* across resistant schooling districts. For, although this action was an exercise in social engineering, and was targeted as much on racial discrimination as on the poverty problem, it was supportive of a constitutional imperative and undeniably benefited poor individuals, even indirectly, with respect to the right to justice, since lack of a good education is a major handicap in accessing the legal process.

Other interventions, however, were more dubious, certainly with respect to equality of opportunity, and even as a component of the overall anti-poverty program. For example, litigation promoting bilingual education for Hispanic children encourages long-term English language inadequacies which limit the labor market opportunities of those who are so handicapped. Actions that compel employers to adopt affirmative action in their employment policies are categorically incompatible with equality of opportunity goals, encourage behavioral dependency on the part of those who gain employment and/or promotion on the basis of sex, race or physical handicap rather than of productive contribution, and jeopardize the competitive position of enterprises thus handicapped by litigation in markets frequented by less regulated foreign rivals.

Most of the legal services anti-discrimination cases were brought not by attorneys in neighborhood law offices, responding to the complaints of individual clients, but by staff attorneys in the national support (back-up) centers, such as the Western Center on Law and Poverty and California Rural Assistance, utilizing class-action suits to maximize the impact of their litigation. In many cases, staff attorneys went well beyond the ensuring of due process and its underlying notion of fair play, and engaged in a process of law reform through the channels of participatory politics. By 1972, over 50 legislative advocates were employed by legal services agencies to appear before committees, to lobby the legislatures, to analyse and even draft proposed bills, all as a part of a sustained anti-poverty campaign.

All of these developments, however, laudable their aims, were far removed from the concept of right to justice, at least in its utilitarian or classical liberal connotation. Indeed, they tended to run counter to that concept by downgrading the importance of access to the civil law for poor Americans in favor of a group-orientated attack on the existing distribution of wealth and income. As the momentum of this attack increased, and as policy activists began to wrest control of the political process from the voter majority, so the voters reacted with ballot-box signals that spelled out the end of the Great Society program and which culminated in the termination of the Office of Economic Opportunity. This foreclosure did not embrace the legal services program itself, not least because of the unswerving and powerful support of the American Bar Association.

6   The Legal Services Corporation and the poor: 1974 to 1988

The transition period between the War on Poverty and the 1974 legislation on legal services was rocky as Chapter 1 outlines. However, the legal services program, with its established national and local structure, survived remarkably intact. Although many of the radical lawyers who had joined the program during the 1960s to use it as a lever for societal change became exhausted with the survival battle and departed into more lucrative private practice or moved on to other public interest vocations, enough of them remained to insure effective continuity and an ongoing commitment to the reform objectives (Dooley and Houseman, 1984).

The five elements which differentiated legal services from legal aid, and which were the distinctive contribution of the War on Poverty, were preserved in the post-1974 program and indeed remain in place even following the reform attempt by the Reagan administration. The first was the notion of collective responsibility to all poor people as a 'client community', the organic vision of the right to justice. The second was the recognition of an organized client role in ordering the priorities of the federal programs of legal services. The third was the commitment to redressing historical inadequacies in the enforcement of legal rights of poor people, the affirmative action imperative. The fourth was the responsiveness of the legal services program to 'legal needs' rather than to 'client demands', the social engineering perception of the anti-poverty activists. The fifth, and final element was the provision of a comprehensive range of service and advocacy facilities that encompassed not only litigation and appeals in federal and state courts and administrative representation before agencies, but also legislative advocacy, rule drafting and the delineation of far-ranging strategies to implement policies advantageous to the 'underclass' of the US economy.

The 1974 Act was designed to rein in the legal services program and to transform it from social activism to a more conservative role of offering legal representation to poor individuals. Law reform and social change were no longer to be the goals of the federal program. However, this shift of vision was not endorsed by major players in the field, notably the Project Advisory Group, the National Legal Aid and Defender Association, the National Clients' Council, the staff attorneys and (most significantly) the American Bar Association. Given the pattern of LSC Board appointments, especially during the Carter presidency, social activism was unavoidable, with individual client representation playing a subsidiary if important role.

The initial phase of the Corporation's authorization, 1974 to 1977, was one of steady budgetary expansion, consolidated political independence and program stability. The transition from the Office of Economic Opportunity to the Legal Services Corporation was accomplished smoothly and the basic program structure emerged unscathed. The staff attorney base, local program independence, national training and clearinghouse capabilities and the national support centers were retained and reinforced despite ongoing conservative objections and a reduction in congressional support following the failure and demise of the Great Society Program. By 1977, the Corporation was well on its way to achieving its funding goal of nationwide geographic coverage for all poor Americans at minimum access levels. 'Minimum access' was defined as residing in an area covered by a local program that supported two lawyers per 10 000 poor persons. This level of coverage was attained in 1981 and, despite subsequent budget reductions, was maintained throughout the Reagan presidency.

From 1977 onwards, and until 1982, the Corporation became increasingly activist in its approach to law reform, more concerned with advancing minority rights and with a 'second war on poverty'. As earlier chapters indicate, these initiatives cost the Corporation support within the Congress, led to the failure to re-authorize the Corporation from 1980 onwards, and triggered a reform agenda toward legal services from the Reagan White House throughout two presidential terms. Despite the eventual confirmation in 1985 of an anti-law-reform majority of LSC Board members, grass-roots activism continued at regional and local levels and was especially powerful in the national support and training centers. The American Bar Association, speaking for the professional attorney elite, has been steadfast in its support for legal services activism, even though the large minority of the legal profession is cool or hostile even to the nuts-and-bolts of the legal services program.

Within the legal services movement, the minimum access strategy, successful as it was in raising the budget of the Corporation, did not meet with unqualified approval (Bellow, 1980). The policy was criticized on the ground that the quality of client service was jeopardized by low salaries and heavy case loads resulting in the employment of poorly trained and inexperienced lawyers in frustrating and tension-laden situations:

> Such a work situation is, at best, a difficult one. For most recently graduated lawyers – totally untrained in law school to do most of the basic tasks of practice and often unskilled at learning from experience in such situations – it is nearly impossible. The pressures on these attorneys, who make up the bulk of the program's staff, to take the path of least resistance – to convince clients and themselves that nothing much can be done for them, that additional research or investigation on the

case is unnecessary, that the result they obtained was all that was possible – is very great indeed. The net result of these pressures is to induce patterns of practice throughout the legal aid system which depart substantially from norms of care and competence which I believe most program people would agree are reasonable to expect in legal services work. (Bellow, 1980, pp. 341–343)

In part, however, the minimum access plan was criticized for diverting legal services efforts away from the political issues of the anti-poverty program, and, in particular, from the establishment of meaningful and coherent priorities that would drive a reform strategy:

Choosing among clients and cases requires a relatively sophisticated political view about what legal assistance can or should be attempting. Not only has there been too little discussion of such political questions ... there has not been any experience with or legitimation of such an analysis. Programs are being asked to make essentially political decisions within the framework of an apolitical ideology. (Bellow, 1980, p. 343)

Despite Bellow's lament for law reform, the evidence of legal services, certainly over the period 1974 to 1982 does not support his pessimism. The regional and local programs throughout that period pursued a culture of significance which required legal services attorneys to litigate significant cases that would advance the anti-poverty cause. This strategy attracted a sequence of talented young lawyers from the more prestigious Eastern-establishment law schools into the legal services program with the intent of building reputations by winning controversial cases in the appellate courts before moving on to private practice. Although the flow of such talent declined after Reagan's election victory, it did not peter out completely. Thus, Legal Services was able to retain a reformist edge even throughout the uncongenial climate of the Reagan presidency (Chapter 15).

7   The case load characteristics of the local programs
Eligibility for legal services is determined in terms of maximum permissible income levels determined by the Legal Services Corporation in consultation with the Director of the Office of Management and Budget and with the state Governors. These income levels take account of family size, urbanized rural differences and regional cost-of-living. The LSC grantees set their own maximum income levels, in some cases below those established by the Corporation. LSC regulations set the maximum generally at no more than 125 per cent of the current official Federal Poverty Income Guidelines. In addition, preference is to be accorded to those least able to obtain legal assistance save by legal services provisions. The local programs are expected to verify client income statements, in a manner consistent with maintaining an attorney–client relationship.

The types of legal problems addressed by the local programs fall into nine principal categories, namely family, housing, income maintenance, consumer/ finance, individual rights, employment, health, juvenile and education. A range of other problems are also addressed. The only reported available quantitative measure of the relative importance of these categories is the 'closed case', which is defined as 'one in which there is a resolution of the client's problem, or an instance in which the client's problem is not resolved but it is determined that no further action will be taken' (Besharov and Tramontozzi, 1990).

Of the 1.2 million cases closed by legal services attorneys in 1984, over 29 per cent involved family issues, including adoption, child support, custody and visitation, divorce, separation and annulment, guardianship and conservatorship, name change, parental rights termination, paternity, spouse abuse and other family problems. Approximately 50 per cent of all family cases concerned divorce, separation and annulment.

Approximately 19 per cent of all cases closed involved housing, including federal and public housing problems, home and property ownership, and landlord and tenant disputes. Almost two-thirds of housing cases involved landlord and tenant disputes. A further 18 per cent of all cases involved disputes with government agencies regarding claims for benefits. About 27 per cent of these involved AFDC and other welfare, about 20 per cent social security and about 20 per cent supplemental security income.

Approximately 12 per cent of all cases closed concerned consumer and finance problems, which included bankruptcy collection, contracts and warranties, credit access, energy, loans and instalment purchases, public utilities and unfair sales practice. Collection accounted for 39 per cent of this case load.

The remaining categories each accounted for a relatively small per cent of all cases closed with employment at 3 per cent, individual rights at 2 per cent, health at 2 per cent, juvenile at 2 per cent and education at 1 per cent. The remaining 11 per cent of all cases included incorporation and dissolution, Indian and tribal law, licenses, torts, wills and estates, and other miscellaneous problems.

The governing bodies of the local programs, who set the case priorities, are controlled by a majority of lawyers appointed by the local bar associations. These attorneys tend to work in close association with the program managers (Besharov, 1990). In essence, the approach adopted is paternalistic, reflecting the Corporation's formal policy that lawyers know best; clients are simply not trusted to make rational choices with respect to their individual rights to justice, as is evident from the following statement by Alan Houseman:

> The assertions made by ... conservative critics [concerning client choice] are simple-minded and abstract ... They assume that clients will identify their legal

problems accurately ... But not all legal problems are of equal importance or of equal magnitude ... Clients, whether poor or not, may not be able to identify the legal problem accurately and often cannot outline the appropriate solution. (Besharov, 1990, p. 5)

However, according to Besharov (1990), the available statistics indicate that the lawyer-dominated system, far from creating a flexible planning mechanism capable of responding to changing legal priorities, has acted simply to preserve a status quo. Table 13.2 indicates that, over the ten-year period 1975 to 1984, field programs hardly changed their priorities, despite major changes in funding and the nature of poverty in the United States.

Table 13.2   Legal services cases closed by type 1975–1984[a]

Case Type	1975	1976	1977	1978[b]	1979	1980	1981	1982	1983	1984
Family (%)	35.0	35.0	31.0	32.4	33.7	29.7	29.1	27.5	28.4	29.2
Housing	15.0	15.0	18.0	18.2	18.3	17.2	18.3	19.3	18.4	19.1
Income Maintenance	15.0	15.0	19.0	16.2	13.4	17.3	18.3	19.3	19.4	18.2
Consumer/ Finance	15.0	15.0	14.0	13.1	12.1	13.2	13.6	14.0	13.2	12.4
Other	20.0	20.0	18.0	20.1	22.5	22.6	20.7	19.9	20.6	21.1
Total (%)	100.0	100.0	100.0	100.0	100.0	100.0	100.0	100.0	100.0	100.0

[a] Data from Legal Services Corporation, *Facts Concerning Legal Services Programs Funded by the Legal Services Corporation* (April 1978), p. 6; *The Legal Services Corporation and the Activities of Its Grantees. A Fact Book* (Spring 1979), p. 22; *Legal Services Corporation Annual Report 1980* (No date), p. 11; *1984 Fact Book* (May 1984), p. 12; and *1985 Field Program Data* (No date), pp. 38 and 40.
[b] Actual data for 1978 are not available. These figures are the mean of the figures for 1977 and 1979.
Besharov, 1990.

The categories listed in Table 13.2 accounted in 1984 for over three-quarters of all cases closed. With the important exception of family cases, these problem areas remained in approximately constant proportions between 1975 and 1984. This consistency actually reached down to the principal subcategories of each of the four problem areas (Besharov and Tramontozzi, 1990), and is evidence of a quite remarkable program inflexibility. In 1981, the National Organization of Legal Services Programs explicitly acknowledged the existence of inflexible priorities:

We have to admit that priority-setting has produced mixed results in the past. Many programs have been bogged down in the process without any results that clearly determine program operations. Conflict among participants and inadequate participation have often plagued priority-setting processes. Many programs have failed to make a serious effort in this area because of fear of the results. (LSC, 1981, pp. 47–48)

A significant exception to this consistency is in the area of family problems, where the proportion of the total case load fell from 35 per cent in 1975 to 29.2 per cent in 1984, a decline of 17 per cent. This decline occurred over a period in which family problems escalated among the poor community, and dramatically changed in nature. In particular, the poverty that energized the 1960s, caused by real economic deprivation and racial discrimination, was much diminished in the 1980s, indeed became transformed into a poverty increasingly marked by family breakdown and dysfunctional behavior (Murray, 1984). Poverty is increasingly a problem of family breakdown, of divorce and illegitimacy, appropriately encapsulated as the 'feminization of poverty', as the following statistics indicate (Besharov and Tramontozzi, 1990).

In 1984, the median income for female-headed families was about 26 per cent of that of intact families ($7608 as compared with $29 739). Female-headed families with children under 18 years of age were almost three times as likely to be poor as other families with children. For all families with children, the poverty rate was 16.6 per cent; for female-headed families with children it was 45.5 per cent. Female-headed families accounted for 21 per cent of all families with children in 1985; yet, they accounted for 56 per cent of all such families characterized as poor.

In 1984, approximately 60 per cent of female-headed families were in receipt of AFDC or other means-tested benefits, and 84 per cent of all children on AFDC were eligible because their mothers were unwed, divorced or separated.

Over the period 1969 to 1984, the proportion of non-elderly female-headed families climbed from 24.1 to 33.2 per cent of all families, adding some one million persons to the poverty category. A special analysis of the Census Bureau determined that the poverty rate for black families would have been 20 per cent in 1980, rather than the 29 per cent recorded if black family composition had remained as it was in 1970 (Working Seminar on the Family and American Welfare Policy, 1987).

Family cases are the largest single category of cases handled by the local legal services programs. In view of the upheaval in US family structure evident over the period 1975 to 1984, and the rising incidence of female-headed family poverty, a public interest theory of legal services would predict that case loads would have adjusted in favor of family law cases designed to facilitate the right to justice of this growing category of impoverished individuals. Instead, the reverse response is evident for reasons far-removed from any notion of public interest, but deriving instead from public choice notions. Laura Woods, Director of the National Center on Women and Family Law, precisely defined the nature of the problem:

> Family law has traditionally been the area of legal work with the lowest status. Many attorneys in local offices where there is no specialization among the attorneys refused to handle family law cases. I was in such an office. In fact, I was initially able to handle family cases only because I agreed to do so while still handling a 'regular case load' and sitting on 'regular intake'. (Woods, 1985)

Family breakdown, important though it is to those involved, and tragic though its implications undoubtedly are for those thus impoverished, is not a classic target for the legal services attorney. It offers only limited opportunities for new law reform and is not at the center of the anti-discrimination movement. Family cases often require lengthy consultations with emotionally distressed clients, usually women, and involve hunting out for child support, elusive low-income fathers, often themselves in and out of the poverty pool. The legal services programs show little appetite for such pursuits:

> LSC has historically been an organization run by men. The leadership (project directors, managing attorneys, litigation directors, etc.) has traditionally been white and male or, to a much lesser extent, minority and male. Ironically, it is only recently, during the Reagan Administrations' attempt to eliminate legal service, that women have advanced significantly into these positions. (Woods, 1985)

In consequence, poor women with children by absent fathers are simply not well served by the child support system. In 1985, only 40 per cent of poor women had child support awards, and of those only 42 per cent received all that they were due. Some 24 per cent received partial payments, and 34 per cent received nothing. In contrast, non-poor women, who could afford their own attorneys, fared significantly better. In 1985, 71 per cent had court orders to receive child support payments, and 53 per cent of these received all that they were due. This differential is in no small part an indicator of legal services' indifference to the non-political poor.

With some $30 billion of unpaid child support in 1985, as against only $7.2 billion paid, legal services ignored a significant opportunity both to provide access to justice and to lower the cost on AFDC support. Such neglect is entirely predictable in terms of a legal services staff attorney bureaucracy which provides a 'market' in which suppliers do not sell, clients do not buy, and owners do not control.

8   Conclusions

In reviewing the particular circumstances of the clients of legal services in the US – the poor individuals concerned to gain access to advice and/or litigation on matters of civil law – this chapter presents a pessimistic story. Of the five perspectives on the right to justice identified – the utilitarian, the classical liberal, the contractarian, the liberal democratic and the Marxist – it is clear that the battle within legal services has centred on the classical liberal and the liberal democratic alternatives, engaging the conflicting visions of methodological individualism and constructivist rationalism. It is equally clear that the forces of constructivist rationalism have proved to be almost everywhere victorious and that the concerns of the individual poor have been subjugated to the special interests in a program dedicated not to ensuring the right to justice but to the pursuit of law reform (see Chapter 15).

The program of law reform thus pursued, in large part, has been envisioned as an anti-poverty campaign, tinged with affirmative action, anti-discrimination designs. As such it is to be viewed as an active residual of the Great Society Program which faltered and for the most part failed during the mid-1970s amidst growing evidence of incompetence misdirection and malfeasance.

Law reform of this kind does not help the individual poor but rather creates an enabling environment which entraps the non-poor into long-term, inter-generational poverty. Such has been the law reform experience in the US over the period 1960 to 1989, which has left its particular consequences of inner-city poverty, violence and drug addiction, which are now increasingly recognized as being intractable problems, invulnerable to the impulses of the transfer society. Legal services itself bears a significant responsibility for the human tragedy that has ensued.

14 The triumph of the special interests

Cade: Be brave, then, for your captain is brave, and vows reformation. There shall be in England seven halfpenny loaves sold for a penny: the three-hooped pot shall have ten hoops; and I will make it a felony to drink small beer: all the realm shall be in common; and in Cheapside shall my palfry go to grass: and when I am king, as king I will be, –

All. God save your majesty!

Cade: I thank you, good people: there shall be no money; all shall eat and drink on my score; and I will apparel them all in one livery that they may agree like brothers, and worship me their lord.

Dick: The first thing we do, let's kill all the lawyers.

Cade: Nay that I mean to do.

Shakespeare, *King Henry VI, Part 2*

1 Introduction
Of the various ethical approaches to policy outlined and reviewed in Chapter 2 as a basis for evaluating the legal services program, classical liberalism is unique in endorsing the doctrine of the minimal state in which government is small and heavily constrained and acts as night watchman for an otherwise unconstrained market economy. In reaching this judgment, classical liberals are not condemning the vote motive itself – indeed they were always among the vanguard of those who have sought franchise extensions to encompass excluded adult citizens – but rather evidence their fear of the excessive powers accorded to special interests by unconstrained political markets. Indeed, the recognition that individual freedoms can be protected only at the price of eternal vigilance itself is a reflection on the insidious, coercive activities fostered by untrammelled special interests once the minimal state gives way to the concept of the productive and the transfer state.

Recognizing that in the republican form of government the legislative branch will inevitably tend to dominate, James Madison and Alexander Hamilton in *The Federalist* agonized over the nature of checks and balances that would weaken the impact of the more powerful special interests. Thus, in *Federalist* No. 51 the following concern is expressed:

It is of great importance in a republic not only to guard the society against the oppression of its rulers, but to guard one part of the society against the injustice of the other part. Different interests necessarily exist in different classes of citizens. If a majority be united by a common interest, the rights of the minority will be insecure.

Writing in the late eighteenth century, before the insights drawn from public choice had become available, and before the inadequacies of their constitutional safeguards had been exposed (Rowley, 1991b), Madison and Hamilton failed to recognize that interests need not constitute an electoral majority in order to control the legislature. In particular, those special interests that are able to overcome the free-rider problem (Olson, 1965) either because they are relatively small and/or because they can coerce their members to pay subscriptions, and/or because they can extract clearly private benefits for their members, and/or because they can attach public objectives as byproducts of private policies, can exert a disproportionate impact on the legislature. By taking advantage of the rational ignorance of individual voters (Tullock, 1967a), such special interests may exercise dictatorial control over policies pertinent to their membership. By spreading the costs of their self-seeking across a wide population they avoid alerting the majority to the yet significant costs that they impose (Gwartney and Wagner, 1988).

The situation is even more insidious than this. For the special interests, if they are established primarily for non-political purposes, may themselves be controlled for the purposes of politics by a minority of the membership who suborn the members' subscriptions to activities that have little or no majority appeal – even that may be detested by the majority – relying upon rational ignorance to protect them from internal retribution. In such circumstances, a minute vote minority can impose its coercive will upon a vast majority in areas of legislation that significantly erode individual freedoms and even reduce the wealth of a nation. Such, it will be suggested in this chapter, is the particular situation of the minority of activist US attorneys who control SCLAID, a powerful political wing of the American Bar Association, specialized in legal aid and indigent defendants' issues, which, in turn, exerts its powerful lobbying influence on the giant jigsaw puzzle of Congress (Shepsle, 1978).

The impact of special interest activities is not restricted to the distortion of legislative outcomes away from the preferences of the median voter, serious though that is for the democratic vision. The invasion of politics – rent-seeking in the sense outlined in Chapter 5 – and the rent-protective counter-actions that rent-seeking provokes, is a wasteful process diverting resources from wealth-enhancing to wealth-dissipative transfers (Tullock, 1967b). Democracies in which such special interests have become particularly entrenched, notably Britain and the USA, experience relatively low rates of economic growth which reflect sclerosis of the wealth-producing arteries (Olson, 1982).

In this perspective, politicians are modelled as providing a brokering function in the political market for wealth transfers. Special interest groups capable of effective economic organization 'demand' such transfers. Other, more general, groups incapable of such effective organization, 'supply' such transfers. Politicians effect political market equilibrium, balancing benefits against costs at the margin, in order to maximize utilities weighted variously in terms of expected wealth and expected votes (Rowley, Shughart and Tollison, 1987).

The concepts of 'demand' and 'supply' in this model require a special interpretation. 'Demand' consists of the willingness to pay, either in the form of money transfers or of votes, by well-organized special interests, in return for wealth transfers carrying a positive net present value to the groups concerned. Such positive returns induce rent-seeking behavior not only from the immediate beneficiaries but also from those departments and branches of government and those government-dependent private contractors whose budgets and/or profits can be enhanced by accelerations in the transfer of private wealth.

Supply consists of the unwillingness or inability of those from whom wealth transfers are sought to protect themselves at the relevant margin by offering countervailing votes and/or money transfers to the politician-brokers. The existence of such supply does not imply an absence of rent protection expenditures since political market equilibrium need not imply political market domination (Crew and Rowley, 1988). Supply, in this sense, is a marginal concept which, in political markets, is not untainted with connotations of coercion. Although government bureaus act as the agents of the politicians in the delivery of transfer commitments, they do not constitute supply in the sense of this model. The bureaucrats themselves often play an active role on the demand side of the market with the objective of enlarging the size of their bureaus' budgets. Politicians may also exert a demand influence if their motives extend beyond those of wealth and votes to encompass ideology (Kalt and Zupan, 1984).

Section 2 of this chapter identifies the nature of rent-seeking and of anti-poverty rhetoric in the market for legal services and explains why interests groups rather than the individual poor exert a powerful influence on the political market. Section 3 outlines the involvement of the organized bar in legal services politics from the late nineteenth century to the present time, notes the relationships that have been forged between the American Bar Association and the legislature and reflects upon the behavior of attorney splinter groups that have emerged to manipulate ABA policies by exploiting the rational ignorance of the legal profession. Section 4 outlines the involvement of the organized field in legal services politics and reviews the nature of its rent-seeking into federal appropriations provided for the poor. Section

5 outlines the involvement of the legal services bureaucracy in legal services politics, despite statutory prohibitions. Sections 6 and 7 outline the separate rent-seeking and ideological roles of the regional and local offices and of the national support centers.

2 Rent-seeking and anti-poverty rhetoric

The most striking feature of the US market in legal services is the relative absence of the deserving poor as an effective interest group rent-seeking for wealth transfers. Evidence indeed suggests that the deserving poor fail to muster their relative vote strength at national and state elections recording a significantly higher rate of vote abstentions than the overall electorate (Enelow and Hinich, 1984).

In part, this lacuna must reflect lower intelligence, education and drive, disadvantages which manifest themselves in lower organizational skills, as well as in lower income-earning potentials. Yet, these disadvantages would be overcome through the emergence of skilled social entrepreneurs seeking returns from the forging of a collective action program if the logic of such action was favorable (Breton, 1974). The fact that the poor have not been mobilized in this way as a force to achieve effective wealth transfers suggests that the logic of collective action, in their case, is relatively weak.

There are several reasons underlying this apparent weakness. First, the poor, unlike more effective groups who rent-seek through political markets, do not constitute a stable group. Individuals coalesce into poverty for many reasons, including low intelligence, poor education and sloth, but also as a consequence of ill-health, family break-up, financial misfortune or theft. In consequence, poverty is a dynamic and not a static condition, with a continuously changing membership. Those who find themselves only temporarily in its clutches do not welcome wealth transfers that will entrap them into longer-term membership. To be poor temporarily bears no connotation of shame or guilt. To contemplate remaining in poverty in order to live off the productivity of others, when that condition is escapable, however, brings with it humiliation and self-degradation.

Secondly, the poor constitutes a relatively large and heterogeneous group within society and as such is vulnerable to free-riding incentives which erode its group energies. Such rights or wealth transfers as might be achieved through collective action cannot easily be denied to those who fail to participate and attempts to energize individuals' support by offering private benefits are likely to fail since the poor cannot pay for selective benefits.

Thirdly, the poor cannot easily be coerced into active participation since, typically, they do not belong to organizations – professions, trade unions or their clubs – which can threaten them with job deprivation or wealth losses should they refuse to participate. The fact of poverty safeguards them from the coercive power of threatened wealth deprivation exerted by interest group activists within the professions.

The absence of the poor as an organized special interest from the market in legal services does not imply that market equilibrium rests upon the vote motive alone. Many interest groups predate upon this potentially fruitful market, utilizing the rhetoric of anti-poverty and of the right to justice as a masquerade for their own rent-seeking ends (Crew and Rowley, 1988). Rent-seeking of this kind is especially prevalent with respect to poverty programs given the Kantian nature of the poverty gift relationship as it impacts upon the median voter.

If those who care casually about the poor gain satisfaction from the act of giving and not from the impact of the gift upon the poor, and if they carry over this Kantian regard from private charity to the government transfer program, sizeable sums of relatively unrestricted money will float about in the political market place attracting the scavengers of the system. With the relatively transparent margins of the social security system saturated by rent-seeking, those in search of other margins have focused attention upon less transparent rents, created through such programs as federal legal services.

It is important to note that rent-seeking behavior is not costless, but requires a significant diversion of potentially productive resources to the process of achieving wealth transfers (Tullock, 1967b). Indeed, rational rent-seekers, competing over the distribution of such available wealth, may dissipate the full value of the wealth transfer. Indeed, one reason why the poor do not appear to benefit from anti-poverty programs is the fact that much wealth is dissipated in the transfer process (Tullock, 1981b, 1986, 1989).

3   The organized bar

Many of those who criticize labor because of the coercion entailed in labor unions are themselves members of organizations that depend upon compulsion (Olson, 1965, p. 137). Pre-eminent among such organizations in the US are the American Bar Association, the state and local Bar associations which preside over a prosperous and prestigious profession like a professional guild with purposes that differ little from those of guilds in the Middle Ages. Compulsory membership has always been the first rule of the guild system.

In the judgment of Mancur Olson (1965, p. 138) the self-regulating guild with compulsory membership 'has reached its furthest degree of development in many state bar associations'. Many state legislatures have been induced to require by law that every practicing lawyer must be a member of the state bar association. Since the bar associations control membership, they have imposed closed shops enforced by government. Moreover, such bar associations exercise powers normally exercised by government. They have wrested from governments the authority to govern themselves (and to a degree their clients) and to discipline any members of the profession that do not satisfy the ethical standards that the profession finds it expedient or appropriate to maintain. Whatever his views on the guild system, the individual attorney in private practice has a clear interest in maintaining good standing with those who run it.

The American Bar Association is a large member interest group that takes advantage of compulsory membership at state and local levels to resolve the potential free-rider problem and, on this basis, lobbies to control the behavior of the US Congress on matters of direct concern to the legal profession. As the most significant players in the legal services market, the agencies of the organized bar deserve detailed consideration.

Approximately 1000 occupations are regulated by some or by all of the 50 states in the US. The three most important categories of regulation, in ascending order of restrictivity, are registration, certification and licensing. Licensing requires each individual to obtain a license prior to practicing in a particular profession. The license granting body can thus establish professional standards, dictate the rate of entry into the profession and enforce standards of conduct for those who remain in good standing. The license granting body can also extract membership fees, acting essentially as a closed professional shop. A licensed profession ranks among the most effective of all interest groups, since it possesses statutory authority to punish free-riders by expelling them from their occupations.

The licensed professions justify their monopoly privileges on the ground that they protect consumers from incompetent practitioners; that they substitute 'credat emptor' for the more usual 'caveat emptor' presumptions that dominate the unlicensed professions. The fact that the less stringent restriction of 'registration' offers an almost identical degree of protection, while allowing consumers to choose lower levels of protection should they so desire, is ignored as is the importance of regular re-examinations of those with licenses to safeguard clients from knowledge attrition. In reality, occupational licensing serves to insulate incumbents from competition and thus secures a higher average remuneration for the cartel.

Lawyers have practiced in America since early colonial times with the early settlers enjoying a period of free entry into legal markets. Dispute resolution services were made available by a wide range of 'scriveners', from such diverse occupations as the clergy and the taverns (Brough and Kimenyi, 1989). This informal bar provided little by way of special training in the law, emphasizing instead skills in penmanship and dispute resolution. As the colonies became more established and populated with new immigrants trained in the English law, pressures for regulation mounted with claims that the law had been overrun by 'untrained pettifoggers' who posed a nuisance to society. In essence, the main goal of the colonial bar was to restrict entry into the profession through a licensed barrier to entry.

In the battle to establish exclusivity in the legal profession, the colonial bar established three important tiers of regulation. The first was the establishment of training standards and educational requirements for all individuals seeking to practice law. This is now a major barrier to entry, with the accreditation requirement serving not only to restrict entry but also to enable the American Bar Association and the state bar associations to police the curricula of the law schools.

The second tier of regulation, the bar examination, is designed to restrict the number of attorneys who are permitted to appear before the courts. Maurizi (1974) has estimated that between 1940 and 1950 in the US a 10 per cent increase in excess supply generated a decrease in the pass rate in bar examinations ranging from 1 to 10 per cent. Rayack (1976) determined in the case of ten out of twelve licensing systems under review, that bar failure rates increased as general unemployment increased over a 58-year period. Brough and Kimenyi (1987) found a positive, statistically significant relationship between pass rates in the bar examination and increases in attorney incomes. They also detected an inverse statistical relationship between excess demand for entry and pass rates in the bar examination and an inverse statistical relationship between the numbers admitted to the bar in any one year and the pass rates recorded in the following year. Such results are consistent with the hypothesis that the bar examination is used as an entry barrier and not as a protector of legal standards.

The third tier of regulation, licensure, established the bar as the exclusive enforcer of standards and as the exclusive authority over the number of lawyers who can practice. This is characteristic of the present legal system. All state bars police the profession through the use of 'unauthorized practice of law' statutes, which make it illegal for unlicensed individuals to practice law. External competition is suppressed by the state bars through the application and enforcement of those statutes, which themselves are products of the state bars' lobbying influence over the state legislatures.

The contemporary American bar bears the full legacy of these early efforts to regulate the legal profession. The three tiers of entry regulation are now firmly entrenched throughout the US legal system. Thirty-four states require attendance in an ABA-accredited law school for admittance to the bar. Fourteen states require attendance in a law school accredited either by the state or by the ABA. Only Georgia and California are exempt from these requirements. All states have legislated to impose mandatory bar examinations, one section of which is uniform nationwide and the other section of which is written by the state bar association. These examinations are graded by licensed members of the legal profession, who are exempt from antitrust regulations following the 4–3 ruling by the US Supreme Court in *Hoover* v. *Ronwin* (1984).

The American Bar Association was founded in August 1878, in Saratoga Springs, New York, by 100 lawyers from 21 states. The original constitution defined the purpose of the ABA as being for 'the advancement of the science of jurisprudence, the promotion of the administration of justice and a uniformity of legislation through the country'. With more than 356 000 members, it now represents approximately 50 per cent of all lawyers in the United States and an estimated 80 per cent of all lawyers practicing in firms of two or more members. In addition, the Law Student Division of the ABA has more than 38 000 members. The ABA describes itself as 'the world's largest voluntary professional association' (ABA, 1990, p. 1). Membership is open to lawyers admitted to practice and in good standing before the bar of any state or territory of the United States.

The ABA governing structure is composed for the most part of members 'who have actively served the public and the profession for many years' (ABA, 1990, p. 4). Many of the governing bodies are leaders active with their state and local bars, with only a limited interest in day-to-day client matters through their law practices. The policy-making body of the Association is the House of Delegates, which was established in 1936 and which meets twice a year, at ABA annual and mid-year meetings. At the mid-year meeting the House Nominating Committee nominates officers and members of the Board of Governors. The full House votes on these nominees, together with any nominations made by petition, at its annual meeting. Action taken by the House of Delegates on specific issues becomes official ABA policy.

The 460 member House of Delegates is composed of 52 state delegates, 191 state bar delegates, 52 local association delegates, one Virgin Islands bar association delegate, 15 assembly delegates, 81 present and former officers and board members, 44 section, division and conference delegates, two ex-officio members and 22 affiliated organization delegates. The 36 member Board of Governors, which acts and speaks for the ABA when the House is not in session, is composed of 18 members elected from the 18 geographical districts, and nine members-at-large, two of whom must be aged less than 36 years, one of whom must be an active member of the judiciary and six of whom represent the sections of the Association. In addition, the Board has nine ex-officio members, each of whom holds executive office within the ABA.

The ABA is composed of 2200 sub-groups. Its membership structure includes 21 sections, four divisions and 63 standing, special, forum and other committees. These units monitor legislation, conduct studies and make policy recommendations to the House of Delegates. The standing committees – of which SCLAID, the Standing Committee on Legal Aid and Indigent Defendants is the most relevant for this study – have small memberships and focus on specific assignments or narrower issues. Committee members are appointed by the ABA president. There is considerable opportunity for activists to seek committee office in order to press upon the ABA policies that would not find favor within the rationally ignorant profession.

Inevitably, the American Bar Association through SCLAID and other relevant committees, is a major player in the federal legal services program. Such has been the case since the legal aid movement began in 1920 following the publication in 1919 by Reginald Heber Smith of his book, *Justice and the Poor*:

> the essentially conservative bench and bar will vehemently deny any suggestion that there is no law for the poor, but, as the legal aid societies know, such in the belief today of a multitude of humble, entirely honest people, and in the light of their experience it appears as the simple truth. (Smith, 1919, pp.11–12)

The keystone of Smith's proposed strategy was the formation of a national association of legal aid offices authorized to represent and to speak for the organized legal aid movement in the councils of the bar, at the meetings of charities, and in the law school conference. He requested the support of the bar in the implementation of his proposal, initially without success. His book was received negatively by the legal profession, and the American Bar Association refused to turn over the membership list when Smith said he wanted to send a copy of his book to every member of the profession (Johnson, 1978, p. 7).

Nevertheless, at the 1920 meeting of the ABA a special committee on legal aid was created and, in 1921, was converted into a Standing Committee on Legal Aid (now SCLAID) with Heber Smith named as chairman. In 1923, Heber Smith's proposal became a reality when the National Association of Legal Aid Organizations (later to become the National Legal Aid and Defender Association, NLADA) was formed. Shortly thereafter, a number of state and local bar associations formed committees to promote legal assistance to poor people in their jurisdictions. The 1920s appears to have been a decade of promise for bar support of legal aid, with the total financial resources available for legal aid more than doubling. This promise quickly faded with the onset of depression.

As corporations collapsed or began to trim expenses, and as private wealth collapsed, so the market for private attorneys experienced a sharp setback. Only the legal aid societies experienced increasing custom, with their total caseload more than doubling, over the period 1929 to 1932. As their client rolls expanded, however, financial support declined, and client dissatisfaction increased. In consequence, from 1934 to 1939, the legal services caseload declined. This decline was accentuated by hostility of bar leaders to the development of legal aid facilities. As the NLADA President, Harrison Tweed complained in 1955:

Anyone who has had anything to do with legal aid knows that local bar associations do not always rally to a man in the fight to the finish for the establishment of adequate service to the poor. (Johnson, 1978)

Emery Brownell, a long time staff leader of the NLADA, was more critical:

Whether due to unfounded fear of competition, inherent lethargy, or mere lack of interest, the failure of local bar associations to give leadership, and in many cases the hostility of lawyers to the idea, have been formidable stumbling blocks in the efforts to establish needed facilities. (Johnson, 1978)

With pleas to private attorney altruism falling largely on stony ground, the advocates of legal aid redirected their arguments to appeal to self-interest:

What sold lawyers were documents that stressed practical advantages of the legal aid office: a legal aid society will keep undesirable, non paying clients out of the private practitioner's office; a legal aid society will secure back wages for a discharged employee or support funds for a deserted wife, thus keeping people off the relief rolls; a legal aid society will educate people who have not used a lawyer before about the value and necessity of lawyers, which will increase the business of private attorneys; a legal aid society offers an opportunity for younger members of the profession to gain valuable experience; and a legal aid society builds relations image of the bar with the general public. (Johnson, 1978)

Expressions of concern for the poor made little headway in influencing legal opinion. Fear of government intervention, however, was more effective, especially following the institution by the British Government in 1950 of its Legal Aid and Advice Scheme. During the 1950s, many formerly apathetic or even hostile state and local bar associations established private legal aid societies, albeit with a strictly limited financial provision. In 1962, the combined budgets of all legal aid societies totalled less than $4 million, less than one-fifth of one per cent of the nation's total expenditure for lawyers' services. Yet, the poor at that time officially accounted for approximately 25 per cent of the total US population.

The legal aid movement throughout the 1950s and early 1960s was largely privately financed with bar associations contributing some 15 per cent of the limited total financial support. The bar itself was firmly committed to this system and hostile to the 1950 proposal from the left-leaning National Lawyers' Guild, for a system of federal government support for legal aid. Robert G. Storey, former president of the American Bar Association summarized the fears of the organized bar:

It is obvious that certain members of the bar and particularly the National Lawyers' Guild are spearheading the organized effort to obtain a federal legal assistance act. It is true that they represent a minority of the bar; yet the previous illustrations [the methods by which Hitler and Lenin secured their revolutions by taking over the legal professions in their respective countries] emphasize that an organized minority with ruthless methods has been responsible for the downfall of many governments. (Johnson, 1978)

Through the early 1960s, the organized bar remained committed to a privately financed and controlled program of legal aid and, indeed, failed to testify when Congress conducted its hearings on the war on poverty. The initiative for federal involvement in legal aid did not arise either from within the American Bar Association or from the National Legal Aid and Defender Association. Rather it arose from a sequence of neighborhood lawyer experiments in New York, Boston and New Haven funded by the Ford Foundation and by intermittent and small federal grants.

The bar was stirred from complacency by a speech on November 17, 1974 given by the OEO head, Sargent Shriver, in Chicago at the Eleanor Roosevelt Memorial Dinner, in which he announced the inauguration of a new network of 'supermarkets of social services', including legal assistance for the poor, for the nation's cities. Within days, ABA headquarters was inundated with letters from lawyers urging Association President, Lewis Powell, to counter the government threat to the profession (Johnson, 1978, p. 50).

Instead, Powell took stock of a situation in which continued ABA indifference might result in the Association forfeiting influence over a major initiative by the federal government. In particular, Powell was sensitive to the damage inflicted on the reputation of the American Medical Association as a consequence of its unsuccessful decade-long battle against Medicare. The bitter struggle had damaged the reputation of the AMA within Congress and had destroyed its public image as the guardian of the nation's health (Johnson, 1978, p. 57). At risk for the ABA, in Powell's view, was its monopoly privilege as the sole provider of legal counsel. Although the war on poverty was very unpopular among the legal profession, Powell took a proposal of ABA support for legal services to the latter's House of Delegates and won a unanimous vote. Self-interest was the driving factor:

> The majority of the delegates favored the resolution because they knew legal aid required more money for much-needed expansion. The rest of them knew that if the Federal government was set on starting a legal services program, the ABA had better be involved in the formulation and administration of the program. It was a bit of the carrot and the stick. In effect, they had no alternative. (Johnson, 1978, p. 64)

Sargent Shriver promised that no appointment would be made to the directorship of legal services without the concurrence of the American Bar

Association. In September 1965, following the endorsement of the ABA, Clinton Bamberger, a Baltimore attorney, was appointed to the directorship. Bamberger was not a long-time supporter of legal aid, steeped in the goals and methods of that program; nor was he a radical reformist antagonistic to the legal access orientation of that program; nor was he a bar politician or a tool of the legal establishment. He epitomized the compromise struck between the reformist OEO and the conservative bar, essential for legal services to expand; and he preserved for the ABA a guaranteed central role in the formulation of legal services policy.

The ABA, by its own wish, would not administer the legal services program in the way of the Law Society in England. Rather, its members would engage in 'meaningful participation' in the determination of policy, together with the OEO bureaucracy and members of the NLADA administration while lobbying for organized bar support through conferences and pamphlets and through its regular publications, namely the *ABA Journal*, the *ABA News* and the *ABA Washington Letter*. Bamberger's and the bar leaders' persuasions fell upon relatively fertile soil:

> Lawyers are, fortunately, and at the same time, ironically, generally not only among the most persuasive, but among the most easily persuaded people there are around. (Johnson, 1978, p. 81)

The conflicts were many during this first phase of the legal services program and, almost always, were related to the rent-seeking and rent-protection agendas of the various constituencies of the legal profession. By far the most important of such conflicts, and the most long-lived, was that between the establishment bar leaders and the rank and file lawyers, pitting the bar association leaders against their local memberships. The bar association leaders for the most part were members of the larger, relatively prosperous law firms which tended to counsel to major financial and industrial interests, and were concerned to maintain close relationships with government. The rank and file, for the most part, were individual practitioners and small partnerships, which tended to represent small commercial interests and middle-income individuals. The rank and file rebelled against legal services because they feared that the Agency would take away some of their clientele and harm others, notably landlords, credit companies and collection agencies. The President and the Executive Secretary of the Tennessee Bar Association summed up this rent-protecting viewpoint:

> In other words, the program is one which provides competition for the independent practicing lawyer, the competition acting in flagrant violation of the Code of Ethics of the legal profession, providing few, if any, of the proven and time-honored safeguards needed by the individual client, and all supported by the

taxpayers. Ironic it is indeed for the lawyer of today to find himself contributing, in the form of taxes, to a government that's program is dedicated toward his own destruction. This is truly pulling one's self down by one's own bootstraps. (Johnson, 1978)

One outcome of such local opposition was an attempt by the rank and file to seek OEO funding for a judicare system – a delivery system in which private attorneys would be reimbursed for handling the cases of poor persons. Such systems were occasionally introduced, notably in Landerman County, California and in Wisconsin. Local bar battles over such issues were acrimonious, frequently involving verbal abuse and, occasionally, physical violence. The OEO itself eventually refused outright to fund judicare, fearing a major loss of political power in such a client-orientated system. There would be little opportunity for law reform advocacy in such a decentralized arrangement.

A second area of conflict especially evident in Miami, New York, and New Orleans, concerned issues of program design and control. Community action agencies were hostile to the bar-sponsored legal aid societies. At issue was ideology as well as rents, since the typical CAA board was dominated by middle-income liberal democrats and the local bars by upper-income conservatives. The OEO sided strongly with the local bar associations in the resolution of this unequal contest. Systematically, the CAAs lost control to the bar associations in already established legal services programs. New programs developed under the undisputed leadership of the bar associations, which not only resisted the specific demands of the community action agencies, but also objected to the direct participation of the poor in agency administration, and to any interventions into agency policy formulation by local and city governments. From the viewpoint of effective bar association rent-seeking, the securing of all routes to agency control was essential.

Given the domination of local outlets by the bar associations, the OEO had no opportunity to countenance other interests in its assertion of national policy. In particular, many of the interest groups that later would react against the law suits brought by poverty lawyers had no voice in the establishment of the legal services program. Landlords, credit merchants and welfare administrators 'seldom knew of the plans for local legal services agencies and, if they did, scarcely imagined the consequences for their own practices' (Johnson, 1978, p. 86). In this sense, regulatory equilibrium reflected the total domination of the bar and not the balancing of competing forces.

By April 1966, internal conflicts, for the most part, had been resolved. The judicare option had been crushed by the OEO and the bar establishment and the local bar associations had adjusted their positions into line with that of the American Bar Association. In April and May 1966, the OEO issued legal services grants in excess of $12 million and, by June, further grants in excess of $11 million. With financial support for legal assistance to the poor elevated from $5 million to more than $25 million per annum, Bamberger vacated his position as Director of the OEO Legal Services Program and was succeeded as acting director by Earl Johnson who set about quelling remaining dissidence within the legal profession.

The Tennessee State Bar Association in December 1965 and the Florida Bar in early 1966 had passed resolutions condemning the Legal Services Program and instructing its local associations not to participate. In summer 1966, the North Carolina bar threatened to disbar any attorney who became associated with the Program. Most threatening, however, was the campaign mounted by Al Cohn, President elect of the American Trial Lawyers' Association, warning that the Program was a harbinger of socialization of the legal profession, lower income for lawyers and a federal dictatorship over legal assistance. At that time, the ATL, with a membership of 25 000 lawyers, was approximately one-fifth the size of the ABA.

Cohn's campaign, which was associated with growing state bar opposition in the south, represented a serious rank-and-file attorney backlash, motivated by fears of income reduction, and levelled against the leadership of the American Bar, the OEO, and the legal services program. Earl Johnson played a high profile leadership role on behalf of the Program, successfully negotiating the cessation of ATL hostility in return for a seat on the National Advisory Council, and placating southern attorneys. In consequence – and despite his own known predilections in favor of neighborhood lawyer experiments – the ABA supported Johnson for the directorship of the legal services program.

The law reform thrust of the local programs was reinforced by the composition of their boards of directors. Approximately one-third of such directors comprised representatives of the poor, approximately 55 per cent comprised lawyers and the remainder comprised a mix of middle-income laymen representing the Community Action Agency, various ethic organizations, local governments and liberal democratic volunteer groups. Not all of the lawyers were selected by the organized bar. Some were chosen by law schools and some by such organizations as the ACLU.

With lawyer domination of the local programs assured, the national leadership of the organized bar openly embraced the objectives of law reform. By November 1967, the ABA President, William Gossett, was justifying law reform in public speeches to local bar associations. For example, in his address to the Chicago Bar Association he demanded that 'the whole nation must face up to the need for social and economic innovation in our cities, and do it now!' (Johnson, 1978, p. 169). By May 1969, the conservative Chairman of the ABA Standing Committee on Legal Aid and Indigent Defendants (SCLAID), John Robb, was motivated to testify before Congress that:

> I would say that in discussing legal services without a law reform program, what you are doing here, it is much like an eight cylinder car that is running on two cylinders. You are chugging along, making a lot of noise, but not going anywhere. (Johnson, 1978, p. 169)

By July 1969, having sensed the economic rents available to lawyers from root-and-branch law reform, Robb urged such a program upon president elect of the ABA, Edward Wright:

> Legal Aid Agencies can achieve only limited although gratifying results on a case-by-case basis. Band-aids can't do much to attack deeply rooted infections. The real challenge for Legal Aid and for the bar is in achieving basic changes in the law so as to attack the underlying conditions which contribute to poverty, crime and the problems of our ghetto areas. (Johnson, 1978, p. 170)

The bar leaders, in embracing law reform, ignored the protests of their rank-and-file members. For the most part, such leaders practised law in major law firms, in which the techniques required for law reform – test cases, legislative lobbying, advocacy before administrative agencies, class-action litigation and the like – were commonplace. For the most part, also, such leaders were out of touch with individual clients and with day-to-day litigation, and immersed in the politics of the ABA. Fearful of riots, even of revolution, many leaders shared with Earl Johnson the view that there was no alternative to law reform if the basic structure of property rights was to be protected:

> I submit that every member of the bar, conservative and liberal alike, has reason to embrace this program and that every citizen of this nation, conservative as well as liberal, has reason to pray for its success. It is our last, best hope to achieve essential change within a framework of law and order and to preserve law and order amid the turmoil of a tide of rising expectations. (Johnson, 1978, p.172)

In pursuit of law reform objectives, and in a bid to weaken any backlash from the local bars, the ABA leadership established a network of national incentives. A National newspaper – *Law in Action* – was founded in March 1967 and published monthly through July 1969 to feature law reform successes and to publicize the attorneys responsible for such successes. This newspaper was mailed to 40 000 subscribers, thus offering neighborhood activists a prospect of national recognition. A national clearing house of legal memoranda and pleadings in law reform cases was introduced. A

Clearinghouse Review published summary accounts of recent litigation successes and named the lawyers responsible for specific law reforms. A loose leaf reporter, *Poverty Law Report*, was introduced to network the national program and to create a new field of poverty law.

A national training program was instituted to orientate and motivate staff attorneys toward the reform of laws and practices considered to be harmful to the poor. A Project Advisory Group (PAG) was founded, comprising legal services agency directors and staff attorneys, to advise the OEO Legal Services Program and to nominate members to the National Advisory Committee. National law reform centers were established to motivate attorneys to pursue law reform and to advise on techniques of test cases litigation and legislative advocacy.

To facilitate the recruitment of highly qualified law reform activists to the local programs the Legal Services Program funded the University of Pennsylvania to establish the Reginald Heber Smith Community Lawyer Fellowship Program. This program assigned lawyers to the legal services offices as interns and encouraged their longer-term commitment to the Program. By 1971, almost 25 per cent of all Legal Services attorneys then employed had been recruited through this program. Prior to internment their orientation had exposed them to poverty lawyers, community agencies and ghetto residents in an explicit strategy of indoctrination into law reform. Earl Johnson (1978, p. 180) recorded that 'the Fellows achieved more improvement in law reform performance than in the overall quality of local agencies'.

In September 1967 only 12 per cent of the Fellows rated the local agencies in which they were assigned as 'very active' in law reform; one year later they reported more than 60 per cent of these agencies as 'very active'. Over this period some 16 000 cases were reported each 'with significance beyond the client served'. Three times – in 1967, 1969 and 1971 – bills were introduced in Congress following lobbying by landlords, merchants, welfare administrators and government officials to inhibit legal services law reforms. These Murphy Amendments failed primarily because of lobbying intervention by the American Bar Association which, in 1967, had launched its own sustained policy of anti-poverty law reform.

By 1971 the excess of OEO Legal Services radicalism, the aggressive pursuit of law reform, the lobbying of legislatures, test case and class-action litigations induced a voter backlash that threatened the federal legal aid program in its entirety. With the Great Society Program in ruins, The American Bar Association moved to head off a total shut down of a lucrative source of rents for those of its membership now specialized in the emergent field of poverty law. A great deal of ABA expertise was devoted to writing into the 1974 Act safeguards against executive branch review designed to insulate the Legal Services Corporation from presidential or executive branch supervision.

To this end, the bar manoeuvred its lobbying of Congress through an organization called Action for Legal Rights (ALR) composed of project directors of legal services programs, but supported by a large advisory board of bar leaders. By 1971, the American Bar Association was aware of the rent-seeking opportunity that a legal services program offered to attorneys in a court structure as complex as the US with its overlap of local and federal systems. Even in a program which, in 1971, employed directly only 2200 lawyers, litigation to effect social change offered a tempting opportunity for a much larger number of lawyers to do well while apparently doing good, while excluding the poor from smart private offices and relieving attorneys of any guilt over the failure of the pro bono ethic.

The Legal Services Corporation Act became law in 1974 establishing the Legal Services Corporation as a private, non-profit organization, independent of the executive branch of government with responsibility for supporting legal assistance to the poor in civil matters. In sharp contrast to the development of legal services programs in Europe, where the public sector accounts for only a small part of legal services provisions to the poor, the ABA supported a monopoly socialist model of legal aid. There remains at present no effective alternative to the neighborhood law office in the United States for the poor person who has a civil legal problem other than the public interest law firm catering for class action cases, private attorneys prepared to take on personal injury cases on a contingency fee basis, the rare pro bono contributions of private attorneys and the new legal clinics specializing in routine, low cost case work.

As a creation of the legal services community and the organized bar, the Legal Services Corporation was to provide stable and increased funding, to support and provide aggressive advocacy, and to act as a buffer between political pressures and legal services representation. In the words of its chief architect, Alan Houseman, 'LSC was not to regulate or enforce, not to lead, but to assist the field and follow their leadership on most issues' (Dooley and Houseman, November 1984, p. 3). In this vision, the national leadership role expected of the Corporation was that of an agent responding to local program principals and not that of a principal controlling local program outlets.

To safeguard the Corporation from political pressure, the 1974 Act was written to ensure that there could be no federal government redress against violations of the regulations circumscribing the legal aid program. Only the Corporation itself has the power to ensure that it and its grantees are complying with the Act. No third party has standing to sue to force compliance. If the Corporation itself should behave unlawfully within wide areas of discretion the Congress and the Executive have no right of intervention, unless they write new legislation into the statute books.

Few federal programs provide a comparable degree of immunity for their senior officials, immunity which amounts to 'rex non potest peccare' and which is conducive to bureaucratic license. The General Accounting Office, in 1984, stated before the Senate Human and Labor Relations Committee the potential danger inherent in such privilege:

> In our May 1 opinion of 1981 we indicated that we didn't have authority to settle the accounts of the Corporation, and it is possible for the Corporation to willfully violate the law and any restriction of the law wouldn't prevent them from doing so if there is not significant enforcement authority there to make someone pecuniarily liable for the funds. (Hatch, 1985, p. 13)

Legal services remained vulnerable to one form of outside interference. The Congress can curtail its appropriations or legislate for its demise. However, the Congress, given the grip exerted by the ABA over its judicial committees, is unlikely to take such disciplinary action. Many senators and congressmen remain rationally ignorant of the continued disregard by the Corporation of congressional prohibitions. Others, with knowledge and insight, are pressured into acquiescence. The cognoscenti, for the most part lawyers, are bought and sold by the ABA with one eye on lucrative post-congressional careers in the private bar and with the other on a possible future federal judgeship. Their sympathy for the ABA's agenda is consolidated by the sizeable political action campaign funding that emanates from the larger legal practices.

In essence, the 1974 Act placed legal services above the law, immune to the constraints that the federal government elsewhere has placed upon its agencies, and free to exceed the remit of civil justice defined by the 1974 Act and to enjoin a social justice law reform agenda. This opportunity was not lost upon ideologically-motivated attorneys who swelled the ranks of the local legal services programs and whose professional code of practice, as defined by the ABA, requested that they should actively pursue reforms of any law, whether procedural or substantive, which in their judgment contributed to an unjust result.

Although the Corporation was the immediate recipient of federal legal services appropriations, the American Bar Association strongly endorsed the decision to allow local programs to establish their own expenditure priorities, a decision which, with ABA support, was formally required by legislation in 1977. This decision was to become especially important through the decade of the 1980s when the priorities of the Corporation and many of its local programs began to diverge and when relations between the Corporation's Conservative board majority and the left-leaning political wing of the

ABA became acrimonious. At this stage, the political insulation provided to the local programs by the 1974 Act became particularly valuable. Whereas during the early 1970s some 40 per cent of the nation's legal services programs had been forced to close during the 1980s relatively few would suffer such a fate:

> If the legislation creating statutory legal services is sufficiently carefully designed to ensure that there are widely based vested interests in its survival, and considerable safeguards against its removal, the political task of removing it becomes very great indeed. (Cooper, 1983, p. 285)

Throughout the period 1974 to 1980, the ABA played a significant role in the consolidation and expansion of legal services and in tilting the priorities of the program away from the right to justice in favor of law reform. To be sure, the ABA endorsed the 'minimum access' goal of the Corporation despite criticisms from its radical fringes which viewed this as competitive with law reform. But, in the absence of comprehensive coverage and nationwide funding, the Association's leaders recognized that the Corporation would be politically vulnerable in the more conservative mood of the mid-1970s. Moreover, program expansion was not without financial benefits to the sizeable intellectual tail of the profession which found difficulty in meeting the requirements of the private market, and which sought shelter in the socialist sector.

Simultaneously, however, the ABA helped to consolidate the independence of the Corporation from Executive control by protecting the Corporation from the Impoundment Control Act of 1974, by extracting from the Office of Management and Budget an acknowledgement of the LSC's authority to present its own budget to Congress, without OMB approval, and by supporting the national training, clearhousing capabilities and the national support centers on which the reforming strategies of the LSC would come to rest. In particular, the repeal of the Green Amendment to the 1974 Act in 1977 reaffirmed the reformist role of the support centers and paved the way for five successful years of radical law reform in which the ABA pursued an entirely sympathetic approach.

To this end, the ABA helped to shift oversight responsibility for the Corporation away from the House Education and Labor Committee to the Judiciary Committee. This move secured the support of many moderate congressmen for a radical program. Oversight in the more liberal Senate was left with the Labor and Human Resources Committee, a decision that was to cost the Corporation re-authorization in 1980. For the most part, however, the ABA inculcated for the LSC a false image of conservatism.

'The Corporation was perceived to be controlled by 'responsible professional' lawyers and law professors and local programs by conservative locally-appointed boards'. (Dooley and Houseman, 1984, p. 7)

Despite this image, the expansion of legal services over the period 1977 to 1980 and its aggressive pursuit of minority law reform programs rendered the program politically controversial. In particular, the emphasis placed by the Corporation on lobbying, despite restrictions imposed in 1978 by the Moorhead Amendment, and its bid to represent aliens, despite similar statutory restrictions, provoked resistance within the Congress as did the growing practice of local programs in pocketing fees generated by publicly-funded litigation. Concern mounted within the Congress over the rash of class-action-based environmental litigation and over abortion-rights litigation directed by legal services attorneys despite statutory prohibitions.

The bid to re-authorize the Corporation in 1980, for these reasons, and despite ABA support, ran into unanticipated resistance. Political reaction was measured in some 20 proposed amendments in the Senate and the House to the 'clean bill' re-authorization attempt. These amendments, if enacted, would have transferred attorney's fees, increased the use of private attorneys, further restricted abortion litigation, reduced the re-authorization period to one year, lowered the federal appropriation, severely restricted legislative advocacy and denied legal assistance to aliens. Other amendments would have provided a sunset provision on the program, provided for state and local government veto power over grants, and would have required mandatory negotiation before filing suit and would have restricted litigation against migrant workers.

To protect legal services from such restrictions, the ABA pressed for removal of the bill. On November 19, 1980, with the outcome of the presidential election determined, the House Judiciary Committee removed the bill from the House calendar. Legal services thus limped into the Reagan era unauthorized, with five of its Corporation directorships vacant but with its agenda still protected from executive branch scrutiny.

It is an indictment of the American Bar Association that the leadership of an organization in principle dedicated to upholding the law remained silent throughout the period 1981–1982, offering no criticism of the illegal survival program activated by members of the Legal Services Corporation in conspiracy with the national support and training centers, the regional centers and many of its local program offices. As evidence of illegalities mounted, following investigations by the General Accounting Office, this silence continued, in growing testament to the rent-seeking predilections of the organized bar towards the federal monies appropriated to legal services and to its malleable vision of the rule of law.

The organized bar had supported legal services from its 1964 beginnings throughout the ensuing 16 years. In 1981, however, it engaged in an unprecedented effort to lobby Congress and to provide support on a local level (Dooley and Houseman, 1984, p. 23). This effort was spearheaded by Reece Smith, then president of the ABA, and commenced with a press conference on March 10, 1981, the day on which the Reagan budget was delivered to Congress with a recommendation that the LSC should be eliminated. On April 1, 1981, the ABA brought 120 lawyers to Washington, representative of some 60 bar associations to meet with over half of all members of Congress. A CBS TV crew was detailed to follow this lobby and provide nationwide publicity for its campaign. This effort was followed up by local rallies throughout the US designed to shore up a moderate, conservative basis of support for legal services against the Reagan initiative:

> The efforts of the ABA and the strong support of the organized bar in communities across the country was a major factor, if not a deciding factor, in the survival of LSC and the federally-funded legal services program. (Dooley and Houseman, 1984, p. 24)

The ABA support for the continuation of legal services came at a significant price. The ABA House of Delegates voted to seek a statutory requirement that LSC should provide increased support for the delivery of legal services through the offices of private attorneys. The House adopted a resolution which would have required the LSC to ensure a private bar component with open participation rights. Before Congress could act, however, the LSC promulgated an instruction requiring legal services programs to allocate ten per cent of their appropriations to the private sector. This instruction, which was widely though not universally honored, confirmed that private bar involvement included such activities as training, fund raising, counselling and community legal education as well as private bar delivery of legal services.

By encouraging a limited private attorney role in legal services, the ABA sought to extend the rent margins available to its members and to placate local bar hostility to the federal program. The organized bar was well aware of the limits of such a strategy which must stop well short of arousing within the private bar any significant desire for a judicare solution. Jeremy Cooper summed up the importance of the ABA's contributions:

> The support of the ABA, hard won in the very early stages of policy formulation in the history of the United States legal services movement, is now proving of critical importance in the struggle for survival. (Cooper, 1983, p. 297)

From 1983 onwards, with the battle for survival won and with legal services confirmed as an ongoing federal program, the American Bar Association shifted its focus back to law reform, offering unwavering support for the right of legal services attorneys to utilize class action suits even in the absence of clear standing among the listed litigants. It resisted all attempts by the Corporation to place itself under the Hatch Act as a mechanism to discourage local legal services officers from using tax dollars to lobby against federal government policies. It denounced proposals, notably by LSC Chairman Clark Durant, to deregulate the legal profession in order to allow non-lawyers to offer routine legal services to the poor. It consistently used its influence to prevent the emergence of grant and contract competitions designed to expose local legal services programs to the market test, to contain legal services costs, and to limit bureaucratic discretion.

Central to the organized bar's orchestration of legal services support was a fear that some variant of judicare or of a voucher system would replace the staff attorney delivery system, and, with it, that power within the legal services market would pass from the organized bar to the individual poor client of legal services. In a client-based system, law reform would be replaced by access to civil justice as the focal point of the subsidy program. Without law reform, the litigation multiplier, from which the private bar clearly benefits, would be much diminished. Predictably, therefore, studies of the delivery system have always been closely monitored by the ABA, as the example of the 1988 Cox Report most clearly illustrates.

In 1985, the Legal Services Corporation and the American Bar Association entered into a Memorandum of Understanding concerning the implementation and evaluation of a Voucher Project in San Antonio, Texas which would effect a comparative evaluation of three service delivery models – voucher, private law firm contract and staff attorney – in the provision of legal services to poor individuals in the San Antonio area. The study was restricted to uncontested divorces, contested divorces not involving domestic violence or child custody issues and contested divorces including domestic violence but excluding child custody issues.

The ABA agreed to fund all research costs up to a maximum of $64 000. The LSC agreed to fund all service delivery costs to a maximum of $152 000. In addition, LSC agreed to fund the San Antonio Bar Association up to a maximum of $25 000 for the salary and fringe benefits of the Project Supervisor, who was to be appointed by the ABA. The ABA hired an economist, Professor Steven Cox of Arizona State University, to supervise this three-year project.

The study proved to be favorable both to vouchers and to private contracts by comparison with staff attorney delivery. Divorce cases were delivered in 35 per cent less time, with a 27 per cent higher level of quality, with 40–50 per cent fewer errors and deficiencies, at from 10 to as much as 60 per cent lower cost by the voucher method. The ABA unilaterally rewrote Cox's conclusions to omit important details of his research and to water down his most cogent and telling observations. The censored report was published by the ABA despite the protests of its author who claimed that the laundered version 'now contains inaccuracies, contradictions and sheer speculation' and who insisted that his name be removed as its author (Letter from Steven Cox to Mr James Podges, ABA, dated March 31, 1989). The LSC offered to publish Professor Cox's own version of the report but was threatened by the ABA with court action should it attempt to do so (Letter from Darryl L. Priest, General Counsel to ABA to Timothy B. Shea, Vice President and General Counsel, Legal Services Corporation, dated April 4, 1989). Warren Brookes commented cryptically upon this behavior:

> 'It is not surprising that the ABA, which has shaped the courts to kill the nation's competitive spirit, cannot tolerate the free market for ideas of a competitive market for legal services for the poor. Shakespeare's King John had it right when he said "First we must kill all the lawyers." That is, if we really want to be competitive'. (*Washington Times*, June 14, 1989, F1)

The American Bar Association has also lobbied to protect its rent base within the federal legal services program by exaggerating the extent of unrequited demand for legal services. The technique adopted is that of ignoring for purposes of enumeration the well-established fact that demand schedules slope downwards from left to right in price-quantity space and that the quantity demanded of any service at zero price tends to infinity. Sample statistics ignoring this law are augmented by assuming that the number of US households earning less than 125 per cent of the official poverty income is 17 569 000, a figure that exceeds by a factor of approximately two the actual number of poor households (see Chapter 13). On this basis, the ABA concluded that there are 19 million problems for which low-income households annually obtain no legal assistance as compared with the 1.6 million cases handled annually by the federal legal services program and the 3.3 million problems resolved by low-income households through private or pro bono channels.

This argument, essentially for a quintupling of federal support to the legal services program from its 1989 level of $308.5 million to $1.5 billion per annum was projected from telephone conversations with 500 US households with incomes of 125 per cent at the poverty line or below, selected randomly from telephone directories. These interviews identified a total number of 682 legal problems, 142 of which involved legal assistance of some kind. Ignoring the well-known problems of bias and of questionnaire integrity associated with telephone balloting of the kind conducted in this 1989 study by the Spandenberg Group, and sponsored by the American Bar Association Consortium on Legal Services and the Public (ABACLSP), the ABACLSP presented these findings to the June 1989 Conference on Access to Justice in the 1990s as an authoritative assertion of the degree of inadequacy of the existing federal program:

> Based upon data published in March 1988 by the United States Bureau of the Census, we have determined that there were 17.569 million households below 125% of poverty. Applying the above rates of 0.28 and 1.08 there would be in 1987 approximately 4.9 million civil legal problems for which low income households had legal assistance and approximately 19 million civil legal problems for which there was no legal help – a ratio of about 80% to 90%. (American Bar Association, May 1989)

The President of the American Bar Association, Robert D. Raven, utilized these dubious statistics in statements before the relevant appropriations sub-committees both of the Senate and the House in May and July 1989. Claiming the strong support of the ABA and its 350 000 members for his testimony, President Raven requested that $383.5 million be appropriated to legal services for fiscal year 1990 as compared with $308.5 million actually appropriated in fiscal year 1989 – an increase of almost 25 per cent. This 'inadequate' request, he claimed, would not even restore the local programs to the minimum access funding (two attorneys per 10 000) achieved in fiscal year 1981. To restore the program to such a funding level would require an appropriation of well over $500 million. At that higher level, only about 20 per cent of the legal needs of the poor would be met. By inference, the ABA was looking for a federal appropriation for fiscal year 1990 of $2.5 billion. No reference was made by President Raven of the tax base from which such a sum would be raised. Perhaps a poll tax on each ABA member of $7000 per annum was envisaged?

President Raven noted that even such an augmented federal program should not be viewed as the entirety of the legal services commitment to the poor. The ABA was making tremendous efforts to identify and tap into other sources of funding and support. In 1981 there had been fewer than 50 formal pro bono programs, of rather modest proportions, in operation throughout the country. By 1988, there were 625 such programs, with over 120 000 attorneys contributing some service. The *Washington Post* (October 1, 1990) illustrated the failure of the pro bono program in Washington, DC, where four out of ten lawyers do not even perform 20 hours of pro bono work per annum, which is only half the minimal guidelines of 50 hours per annum established by conferences of local lawyers and judges. Washington, DC, is viewed as a model for the legal profession with respect to pro bono contributions!

The average US attorney deals approximately with 600 'matters' per annum. If each attorney were to contribute only five pro bono 'matters' per annum from this total, or less than 1 per cent of his annual case load, the present legal services program would be fulfilled without federal involvement. If each attorney would offer the biblical 'tithe' as a pro bono contribution, President Raven's civil justice dream would be resolved at no cost to the US taxpayer.

As part of the private fund-raising exercise for legal services, President Raven drew the attention of the Congress to the IOLTA program of interest on lawyer trust accounts. These state and local bar-inspired programs seek to have banks generate and pay interest on trust funds held in escrow by attorneys for their clients. By 1989, such programs existed in 48 states and in the District of Columbia, and generated $54.3 million, of which $44.8 million was allocated for civil legal services for the poor. President Raven failed to discuss the dubious ethics, if not outright illegality, involved in diverting the property of clients, without informed consent.

Unswerving though the dedication of the American Bar Association has been to extending federal funding for legal services since the advent of the Great Society Program, it pales into insignificance by comparison with its dedication both to the preservation of its bar monopoly, which generally serves to raise prices and to restrict supply, and to the preservation of a legal services supply monopoly which 'rivals the patents of monopoly handed out by the English kings in the 18th century' (Durant, December 1988). A challenge to both forms of privilege was mounted by W. Clark Durant III, Chairman of the Board of the Legal Services Corporation, at the ABAs mid-year meeting in New Orleans in February 1984.

The monopoly power of the bar in all 50 states emanates from statutes extracted by attorney special interests from each state legislature, which prohibit the unauthorized practice of the law and thus provide members of the bar with a closed-shop privilege. As Durant correctly observed, these statutes are used by the bar to deny paralegals and other trained individuals the opportunity to supply the poor with a low cost legal service even in routine matters of the law. In consequence a cartelized legal profession excludes access to justice by elevating the price of legal services from the competitive to the monopolistic level, by limiting and distorting supply and by creating dislocations in the market place:

> They have built a dam across the rivers of justice and then they complain of the drought in the field below. This has never been a debate about second class justice nor a debate about whether there should be a Cadillac in every garage. It is a debate about whether some people will have access to Chevrolets and other forms of transportation rather than none at all. Many Legal Services clients just need an effective advocate, someone who can help them file a divorce, obtain child support, deal with the Social Security Administration, or to do battle with a dishonest landlord. These problems don't always require lawyers.

Durant's solution was the proposed repeal of statutes that make it a crime for lay people to practice law and the elimination of bar examinations as a licensing entry barrier into the legal profession. The poor would be better served, in Durant's judgment, if unregulated entrepreneurs were free to enter the market place to handle the legal matters of the poor.

Durant's speech was not well received at the New Orleans meeting. ABA President, Eugene C. Thomas, demanded Durant's resignation or ouster from the Legal Services Corporation and characterized Durant's arguments as 'dangerous and misleading persuasive bits of sophistry designed to suggest that the solution for poor people is to send them into the market place of America to compete for legal services on the basis that one would compete for any offered service or commodity in this land'.

Among the many voices raised against Durant's proposal was that of Senator Warren Rudman, the leading Republican supporter of the existing legal services program and the ranking member of the Sub-committee on Commerce, Justice State, the Judiciary and Related Agencies which exercises appropriations authority for the federal legal services program. Although Rudman claimed to be sympathetic to competition within the legal profession, he derided Durant's proposals as taking a sound proposition to an absurd extreme:

> In the abstract, all regulation hinders economic efficiency. There surely are regulations which serve mainly to limit economic competition, but there are also needed consumer safety and protection regulations. There can be legitimate debate over when a regulation falls in the latter category, but only fools and zealots fail to recognize the existence of and need for such. In proposing to get rid of all standards for the legal profession, you have ignored this entire issue. Your own statement acknowledges that the profession is opening up. Advertising by lawyers is now legal, price-fixing in the profession is not, and the use of low-cost legal clinics, alternative dispute resolution centers, and the like have greatly expanded in recent years. These changes have helped reduce the price of legal assistance for common legal problems, and that is good for the consuming public. Maybe more should be done in this area, but how you connect that to the existence of the Legal Services Corporation escapes me entirely. It is like suggesting that total deregulation of the medical profession would permit the elimination of Medicare and Medicaid. (W. Rudman, February 18, 1987)

Rudman failed to qualify his judgment with references to the systematic suits for unauthorized practice of law entered by state and local bar associations against those who attempt to offer cut-price legal packages for do-it-yourself divorces, wills, name changes, bankruptcies and the like. Such bar resistance to opening up the profession is widespread and has drawn criticism from leading consumer groups. For example, Alan Morrison, director of the Public Citizen Litigation Group, claims that 'some of that's protectionism; some of it is paternalism; most of it is bad' (*Washington Times*, July

18, 1988, p. A3). HALT, a Washington-based legal reform group that claims unauthorized practice of law statutes are too stringent has charged that 'the legal profession is primarily interested not in public protection, but in perpetuating its own monopoly over legal services' (*Washington Times*, July 19, 1988, p. A3).

The bar's outrage notwithstanding, Durant's strictures did not go entirely unheeded. In 1989, the Public Protection Committee of the State Bar of California recommended unanimously that the state should eliminate unauthorized practice of law statutes and allow qualified legal technicians to offer specialized services. The hierarchy of the California bar categorically opposed such a change.

Durant's speech was not restricted to an attack on the guild-monopoly privileges of the organized bar, but also reached out to attack the existing supply monopoly through which federal appropriations to legal services were disbursed to poor Americans. Evidently, his vision of unregulated legal entrepreneurs, paralegals and the like, offering an efficient, low cost service to the poor in the less complicated reaches of the law, was not compatible with the existing network of local programs dispensing legal services under the tight control of attorney dominated boards of directors.

The Legal Services Corporation, in its existing statutory form, subject to oversight by an attorney dominated Congress, is incapable of exposing legal services to competition impulses which would extend the margins of access to civil justice. Therefore, Durant proposed reforms which would require the replacement of the Legal Services Corporation by a new, more independent agency, more flexible to client demands, more cost effective, and competitively constrained. In such a system, Durant suggested that consumer preferences might be prioritized by requiring a modest co-payment from those who utilized the program. In this way, client rather than supplier preferences would dominate the allocation of resources to civil justice for the poor.

This proposal was not well received by an organized bar, that had become accustomed to engrossing rents from the legal services program. The ABA President, Eugene C. Thomas, castigated Durants' address as an 'incredible and dangerous proposal, of all things in the Bicentennial year of our Constitution' and urged Durant to resign immediately from the chairmanship of the LSC board:

> If he wishes to commit himself to a zero budget, to a removal of the footings and foundations from beneath the Legal Services Corporation, that's his privilege. It's a free country and we're all entitled to espouse our ideas. But he should not do that and at the same time hold the responsible position of Chairman of the Board, or even of a director of the Corporation where his obligation is to accomplish the purposes of the entity, and the purposes are to serve the poor and to make the system work. (Thomas, 1987)

President Thomas made it clear that the resources of the organized bar would be moved against Durant to head off such reforms in the US legal services program:

> I want to say here that every effort that I can bring to bear will be made to defeat that position, and every effort that the American Bar Association can bring to bear will be brought to protect the program of legal services for the poor ... to make America work for all its people. (Thomas, 1987)

This reaction was mirrored in the response of Bar Leaders for the Preservation of Legal Services for the Poor, whose representatives also demanded that Durant should resign his chairmanship. Michael S. Greco, a co-founder of the organization, and president of the New England Bar Association commented that:

> Mr Durant's speech is both extraordinary and irresponsible. It is now quite evident to bar leaders across the country that Mr Durant should step aside as chairman and as a member of the LSC Board. Mr Durant has now made his personal views public, and they clearly conflict with his statutory responsibilities as Chairman of the LSC Board. (February 23, 1987)

Greco was joined by fellow co-founder of Bar Leaders, L. Jonathan Ross, director of the New England Bar Association, who added:

> Mr Durant clearly can no longer execute his fiduciary responsibility as Chairman of the Legal Services Corporation Board. He should resign immediately, and any other LSC Board members who were a party to his remarks before the ABA or who subscribe to this statement should follow him out the door. (February 23, 1987)

Durant's challenge was not without result. In 1988, with the help of key leaders in the Congress, language was incorporated into the 1989 Appropriations Act encouraging the introduction in fiscal year 1990 of a system of competitive bidding for legal services contract. The language was less than categorical, and the reform was to be delayed until President Bush had removed President Reagan's reformers from the LSC board and had replaced them with members more sensitive to the interests of the organized bar. Yet the notion of competition in the provision of legal services had found its way into the legal services policy debate.

The ad hoc group, *Bar Leaders for the Preservation of Legal Services for the Poor*, came together early in 1980 with the primary objective of fighting President Reagan's bid to close down the federal program of legal services and to replace it with block grants that might be utilized by the states at their own discretion to support legal services at state, regional or local levels. In essence, Bar Leaders recognized the logic of collective action. A small, highly specific interest group would exercise significant political influence in support of the staff attorney model of legal services supply. Its publication, *Legal Services Crises and Concerns*, consists of regular articles in support of the existing program together with propaganda directed against conservative legal services reforms.

Bar Leaders also acts as an important fulcrum for law reform within the legal services network, publishing lists of cases or client services, nationwide, which are thought to have important policy implications and featuring articles on issues of apparent law reform potential. Members of Bar Leaders, notably Michael S. Greco of the New England Bar, have been a driving force behind 'legal needs' studies which have promulgated a call for massive increases in federal funding.

Bar Leaders have also worked assiduously among the state and local bar associations to identify support for the existing program listing over 100 bar associations considered to be in the forefront of the campaign to expand the program. To this end, they have developed a Sample Resolution in support of legal services for the poor which has been widely circulated to local bar associations for their consideration and 'unanimous approval' (Legal Services Crises and Concerns, August 1, 1988). Bar Leaders have mounted hostile campaigns against attempts by the Legal Services Corporation to monitor field programs and to defund offices found to be unacceptably deficient.

4   The organized field

The organized field comprised until 1986 the National Legal Aid and Defender Association (NLADA), the Project Advisory Group (PAG) and the National Clients' Council (NCC). In 1986, the NCC was defunded by LSC and is now defunct. The field is supported in its legal services objectives by the deans of some 143 of the nation's 168 accredited schools of law and by the left-leaning National Lawyers' Guild (NLG). The organized field has continuously acted as an ideological special interest pressure group throughout the period of existence of the Legal Services Corporation, exerting influence on the demand side of the legal services market. From the outset, the organized field viewed the Corporation as a creation of the organized legal services community and the organized bar. It was to be utilized as an instrument for aggressive advocacy for law reform, indeed as an effective medium for translating the law reform agenda of the group into litigated policy at a time when the legislature had narrowed the margins for such behavior in response to voters' rejections of the Great Society program.

NLADA was established in 1911 by members of the private bar who had become concerned that the American Bar Association was insufficiently involved with the provision of legal services to poor people. Since 1911, NLADA has matured into a coalition with two types of members. The primary membership comprises groups that provide civil and criminal representation to the poor. The vast majority of LSC funded programs, probably in excess of 90 per cent, are members. In addition, almost all non-LSC funded civil programs are members. A majority of organized public defender offices are affiliated, although the percentage is lower than that for civil representation. NLADA also has individual attorneys among its membership.

In 1982, NLADA received $330 000 in civil program dues of which approximately $250 000 was derived from LSC funds paid to grantees. The dues structure at that time was 0.005 per cent of the total program budget, with a minimum payment of $50 and a maximum payment of $2000 per annum for civil programs. Individual membership dues were $40 per annum for each attorney. NLADA attracts membership support for its special interest activities by offering a malpractice insurance program, on the basis of a special relationship with Lloyd's of London, which cannot be obtained elsewhere. NLADA is governed by a Board of Directors which consists of five civil legal services and legal attorneys, five public defenders, five persons representing clients, and six representing the public, together with the President-elect, the President and the immediate to Past President.

NLADA remained dormant over the period 1911 to 1922, its meetings having been discontinued at the onset of war. It regrouped in 1923 following a meeting in Cleveland stimulated by Heber Smith's book (1919). The early work of NLADA centered on the promotion among state and local bar associations of committees to promote legal assistance to the poor. This role was pursued over the period 1923 to 1964 despite lukewarm general support, indifference or outright hostility to its approach to the problem of civil justice. As late as 1964, however, NLADA was concerned with the development of a private, state supported program and showed little interest in federal financial support. Indeed, in late 1964, NLADA eliminated itself as a potential supporter of OEO legal services:

> The creation of separate, duplicating agencies to offer legal services under Economic Opportunity programs will be more costly and less effective than will the proper use of existing facilities, and serious ethical questions will be raised where non lawyers attempt to practice law. (NLADA, 1964)

By late 1965, however, NLADA was tempted by the prospect of federal funding and the NLADA leadership, including President Theodore Voorhees, became committed supporters of a federal legal services program, though many of the members remained sceptical. Clint Bamberger, the first director of the OEO Legal Services Program, was primarily responsible for obtaining active NLADA support in return for representation by the NLADA President, on the National Advisory Committee.

NLADA provided continuous support for the OEO program throughout the latter's decade long existence and lobbied in support of the creation of a Legal Services Corporation following the collapse of the OEO and the elimination of the Great Society program. In 1974, NLADA joined forces with the Project Advisory Group (PAG), which comprised the agency directors and staff lawyers of the local programs, and the National Clients' Council (NCC) to support the staff attorney model of legal services provision.

In this vision, the LSC was the agent of the organized field, and expected to follow rather than lead the field in the implementation of the legal services program. Early on, the organized field successfully challenged a proposed bylaw which would have provided substantial leeway for the LSC board in the holding of executive sessions. This challenge culminated in an amendment to the LSC Act in 1977 incorporating the Government in Sunshine Act. Thereafter, the open meetings were to offer opportunities for the organized field to pressure the LSC board into an activist program of law reform. Ultimately, many of the law reform issues were to be farmed out to a new national support project, Access to Justice, sponsored by NLADA and firmly under organized field control.

The policies of the Corporation were developed through a series of regulations aggressively shaped by the organized field partnered by the ABA Standing Committee on Legal Aid and Indigent Defenders (SCLAID). Representatives of the umbrella group participated virtually as co-equals with members of the LSC board and the LSC staff in this exercise.

Following the 1980 election of Ronald Reagan as President, the LSC and the legal services community set into place a lobbying effort designed to secure program survival against an anticipated attack from the White House. Beginning in December 1980, a series of regional meetings were held to inform project directors and legal services staff about the survival plans, to develop media support for legal services, and to organize support from the egregious coalition of minority interests, including the Minority Caucus, the Rural Advocacy Group, Women in Legal Service, Farm Workers Caucus and the National Association of Indian Legal Services Programs, which looked to the LSC for litigated law reforms denied to them by elected legislatures.

In 1981, the Coalition for Legal Services was formed as a 501 (c) (4), lobbying, organization to coordinate the efforts of all such legal services supporters other than the LSC and the organized bar. After 1981, and the demise of the Carter Board of Directors at the LSC this Coalition assumed central control over legal services policy development and was active in the program of opposition mounted against regulations that would have restricted LSC legislative representation and class action suits against government agencies. It was also active in the survival campaign for legal services:

> The coalition members will be forming an outside entity to lobby and coordinate survival activities on behalf of the legal services community. (Houseman, December 29, 1980)

The organized field was represented in this coalition and motivated by its dependence on LSC funding. The PAG represented by Melvin D. Miller, was in receipt of some $180 000 per annum of taxpayers' funds through voluntary contributions from LSC program affiliates. The NCC, represented by Bernard A. Veney, was in receipt of a 1981 LSC grant of almost $750 000. NLADA, represented by Howard Eisenberg, was a major LSC grant recipient, and was in receipt of a grant of $2 195 000 from the Corporation in 1981 as part of the Phoenix project. Despite the fact that the NLADA was a 501 (c) (3), non-lobbying, organization, the letterhead on the Coalition stationary was the NLADA business address, and some of the 1981 NLADA grant was used to hire a full-time experienced lobbyist to work on legal services (Coalition letter, February 20, 1981). The LSC itself was protected from Hatch Act infringements by the non-federal nature of its corporate status, though its funding of lobbyists was in clear violation of the specific wording of the Moorhead Amendment.

> No part of this appropriation shall be used for publicity or propaganda purposes designed to support or defeat legislation pending before Congress or any state legislature.

NLADA was designated by the LSC staff to play a key role in segregating and protecting the large accumulated technical assistance balances from possible appropriation by President Reagan. Traditionally, these balances had been a source of loosely controlled funding within the LSC, a contingency fund available to help field programs meet unexpected problems. In 1981, it was viewed by LSC President Dan Bradley as the most important of the rubies to be saved from a White House that had threatened to shut down the federal legal services program.

During Fall 1981, in a sequence of grant contracts, the technical assistance function, together with all accumulated balances, was transferred from the LSC to NLADA without even the tacit knowledge or consent of the LSC Board of Directors, but with the consent of Dan Bradley, the LSC President, Clinton Lyons, director of LSC's Office of Field Services and Bucky Askew, his deputy. NLADA went from holding $72 900 in LSC-granted public funds at the beginning of 1981 to being the repository of some $2.2 million in rubied tax dollars by December 1981. In addition, NLADA's Access to

Justice project, which had received only $53 000 in LSC funding by early 1981, by the end of the year had become a major grant recipient. In June 1983, only six months after leaving LSC, Clinton Lyons was to become executive director at NLADA responsible for the oversight of technical assistance funding. Bucky Askew also joined the NLADA payroll as a consultant.

In order further to protect the rubies, the LSC altered its contract with NLADA to include a waiver of LSC's standard rights and of NLADA's obligations with respect to the Access to Justice project. This waiver removed all provisions that NLADA comply with LSC guidelines and instructions or other directives, loosened required audit procedures for the grants, waived LSC's legal remedies to enforce the contract, granted NLADA termination funding for six months and provided NLADA with extensive defunding hearing rights. In essence, NLADA was to be free to utilize federal tax dollars without any effective scrutiny by the LSC.

Senator Denton (1985, pp. 82–84) chronicles the dubious nature of NLADA's fund disbursements, for example, the charge of 43 per cent applied to overhead expenses in its 1982 expenditures of $429 278 and the $159 000 expended merely in deciding how the $500 000 Leadership Development Grant should be utilized – despite the prohibition in the LSC Act ruling out funding by grant or contract of broad legal or policy research unrelated to eligible clients (Sec. 1006 (a) (3) (A)).

In September 1987, the Legal Services Corporation published the final report of its Office of Monitoring, Audit and Compliance evaluating the five projects funded by NLADA from the 1981 LSC grants awards. This LSC report was based on investigations conducted by the Office in May 1984, despite resistance from the executive director of NLADA, Clinton Lyons, which had involved the cancellation by NLADA of five separately scheduled visits.

Although eventually acquiescing to the LSC visitation, NLADA systematically obstructed the investigation, refusing to provide copies of participant lists for training programs, denying access to its general ledgers, denying access to IRS Form 1099s concerning consultant contracts and refusing to allow the investigation to take away copies of documents reviewed at NLADA's offices. Clinton Lyons refused to answer any questions regarding his decisions as an LSC staff employee. The Justice Department subsequently refused to introduce criminal proceedings with respect to the 1981 NLADA episode. The inquiry predictably was inconclusive concerning alleged wrong-doings at the NLADA.

Although NLADA was the most significant of the three major agencies of the organized field, the PAG and the NCC were by no means ciphers. Both agencies were members of the Coalition for Legal Services, an organization with the primary function of lobbying against proposed reforms in legal services. Both agencies allocated federal tax dollars to the Coalition relying on the non-federal status of the Legal Services Corporation and the empathy of the Corporation's President Dan Bradley towards their goals to protect them from Hatch Act violations and from LSC defunding initiatives.

The National Clients' Council, which was dependent almost exclusively upon LSC support, and which received $750 000 from the LSC in 1981 alone, eventually over-stepped its mandate and, in 1986, was defunded. Unable to support its ventures from private sources, the NCC ceased business and is now defunct. PAG, which is dependent substantially, though not exclusively, on the voluntary contributions of some 70 per cent of LSC program affiliates, has benefited from agency discretion which enables such affiliates to fund organizations hostile to current LSC policy, and has retained a significant lobbying presence. In the words of De Miller, an influential PAG leader, PAG activities are run 'essentially by a few aggressive radicals who are anxious to act as the movement's conscience and the overseer of corporate bureaucracy as manifest in the Legal Services Corporation'. NLADA and PAG, 501 (c) (3) both non-lobbying organizations, helped to orchestrate the successful lobby against the appointment of Judge Robert Bork, as Justice of the US Supreme Court.

5   Legislative advocacy within the Legal Services Corporation bureaucracy

The legal services regional and local offices and the support centers are an integral part of the federal program of legal services, with well-defined supply-side responsibilities. Their role as lobbyists on the demand side of the political market should not be under-estimated, despite carefully worded statutory limitations.

The text of the Act, read in accordance with traditional rules of statutory interpretation, indicates that the Corporation should not allow a broad exception for lobbying and other political activities (Price, 1986, p. 212). Congress placed numerous restrictions in the Act specifically to prevent such activities (1982 Sections 2996 e (d) (3) (4) and (5)). Corporation funds must not be used to influence elections for office; to influence ballot measures; to lobby legislatures or administrative agencies; to finance voter registration or other election activity. Taken as an aggregate, as well as individually, these expressions of congressional intent to avoid financing political activities carry considerable authority.

Where the prohibitions in the statute allow for exceptions, these exceptions are narrowly drawn to permit only the provision of legal advice (Price, 1986, p. 212). For example, the prohibition against participation in ballot measures provides that an attorney may provide legal advice and representation as an attorney to any eligible client with respect to such clients' legal rights (1982, Section 2996 e (d) (4)). This exception does not allow legal services attorneys to advocate or to oppose a ballot measure with LSC funds; they may only provide legal advice, such as information about voting and campaigning rules to their clients. Similarly, attorneys are prohibited from providing assistance in an election or in voter registration other than legal advice and representation (Section 2996 f (a) (6)). Other provisions containing similar stipulations also make it clear that legal services attorneys may only provide legal advice.

As Price (1986) has emphasized, the term legal advice in these various provisions of the Act, is not to be construed in a broad and open-ended way. Just because private attorneys engage in legislative and administrative lobbying does not imply that Congress intended legal services attorneys to perform the same functions at a client's request. For, if this were the case, it would create an exception that emasculated the general anti-lobbying prohibition (Price, 1986, p. 213). The rules of statutory construction hold that a statute should not be construed in a way that renders some of its provisions superfluous. Indeed, if the exceptions were construed to permit attorneys to do anything at all on a client's behalf then the repeated references to legal advice in the Act would be pointless (Price, 1986, p. 213).

The legislative history of the 1974 Act further confirms the stringent limits on lobbying and other political activities expressly stated by the Act itself (Price, 1986, pp. 213–217). Congress has repeatedly stated that it did not intend Corporation funds to be so expended except under strictly limited conditions. For example, a report by the House Committee on the Judiciary, explaining the 1977 amendments to the Act, stated that 'the committee expressed its concern that the language directly affecting eligible clients ... [should] not be a *carte blanche* for legal services employed to lobby on any issue which may affect the poor' (H.R. Rep. No. 310, 95th Congress, 1st Sess., 12). A House report on the 1981 appropriations bill similarly emphasized the restrictive nature of the tolerated legislative activity:

> This language is intended to specifically prohibit representation on matters of general concern to a broad class of persons as distinguished from acting on behalf of any particular eligible client. (H.R. Rep. No. 97, 97th Cong. last Sess. 1981)

This view was reaffirmed in a Senate report:

> The Committee recognizes that there may be occasions when legal assistance to an eligible client requires representation of the client before an agency to resolve a specific claim directly involving the client's legal rights and responsibilities. (S. Rep. No. 265, 97th Cong. 1st Sess. 59 (1981))

The General Accounting Office has consistently read the Act to permit only a narrow exception to the rules governing political activity. For example, in 1981, the GAO states that:

> The exception in 42 U.S.C. 5.2996 f (a) (5) (13) (ii) ... should be construed so as to preclude expenditures of appropriated funds by recipients for grass roots lobbying. Here again, the Corporation has erroneously construed this exception broadly to permit recipients to expend appropriated funds to solicit others to contact their congressmen in connection with legislation affecting the recipient or the Corporation. (GAO Report B-202116, May 1, 1981)

In 1983, the GAO was even more specific:

> The legislative history makes it plain that grantees and contractors may not use the funds provided by the Corporation to initiate the formation or act as organizer, of any organization, network, or coalition. However, providers of legal services may give advice to eligible clients and assist them with matters that would enable them to plan, establish and operate an organization that the clients believe is in their best interest. (GAO Report B-210338/B-202116, Sept. 19, 1983)

The 1974 Act is by no means the only instance in which Congress expressly has declined to subsidize lobbying and other political activity. For example, Section 501 (c) (3) of the Internal Revenue Code prohibits tax-exempt organizations from attempting to influence legislation or political campaigns. In one court opinion, Section 501 (c) (3) is based on a policy that 'the United States Treasury should be neutral in political efforts and that substantial activities directed to attempts to influence legislation or affect a political campaign should not be subsidized'. (*Christian Echoes National Ministry* v. *United States* 470 F. 2d 849,854 10th Cir. 1972). This policy against the funding of political activity is stated yet more directly in 18 J.S.C. Section 1913 which prohibits the use of congressionally authorized funds for legislative lobbying. The policy is reaffirmed in 31 U.S.C. Section 6715 which prohibits states and localities from using federal revenue sharing funds for lobbying purposes.

As Price (1986) concludes, the 1974 Act, as amended, together with the outlined history of legislative intent, imposes an unequivocal prohibition on lobbying, with very tightly drawn exceptions. In such circumstances, it is doubtful if the Legal Services Corporation has any discretion save to penalize, if necessary by defunding, any of its grantees or contractees who stray beyond the limits so clearly demarcated. Certainly, there is a clear enough signal from Congress to allow the Corporation to impose very strict limits on lobbying to advance the interests of legal services clients and of tax payers. The Supreme Court itself has emphasized that the level of judicial review of an agency's construction of its statute is extremely limited:

When a court reviews an agency's construction of the statute which it administers, it is confronted with two questions. First, always, is the question whether Congress has directly spoken to the precise question at issue. If the intent of Congress is clear, that is the end of the matter ... If, however, the court determines Congress has not directly addressed the precise question at issue, the court does not simply impose its own construction on the statute, as would be necessary in the absence of an administrative interpretation. Rather, if the statute is silent or ambiguous with respect to the specific issue, the question for the court is whether the agency's answer is based on a permissible construction of the statute (*Chevran v. Natural Resources Defense Council* – U.S. 104 S. Ct. 2781–82 (1984)).

The court proceeded to explain that a court must employ a reasonableness standard in determining whether an agency's construction is permissible, and emphasized that the administration of a federal agency necessarily requires the foundation of policy and the making of rules to fill any gap left, implicitly or explicitly, by Congress. The Corporation has therefore considerable authority to use its rule making and enforcement powers to limit political activities. Private enforcement suits are not permitted by the 1974 Act.

The prohibition on lobbying in the LSC Act, if enforced, promotes three separate categories of interest none of which appear to be important to those who would evade the restrictions and use tax payer dollars to support their legislative activities. The first such category is the potential poor client who is concerned not with a law reform agenda but to gain access to civil justice to uphold his/her individual rights under the existing law. Monies diverted from the basic outreach programs to support legislative activities are monies diverted from the eligible poor in furtherance of the self-serving goals of the non poor.

The second category comprises tax payers who do not choose to subsidize political views with which they disagree or which they do not deem to be sufficiently important. In the absence of lobbying restrictions, they too may see their tax dollars expropriated for purposes that they do not endorse. As Thomas Jefferson pointed out two centuries ago, 'to compel a man to furnish contributions of money for the propagation of opinions with which he disbelieves, is sinful and tyrannical' (Price, 1986, p. 204). The Supreme Court has recognized that such diversions constitute an infringement of political liberties, and indeed violate the First Amendment to the US Constitution (*Wooley* v. *Maynard* 430 U.S. 705 (1977)).

As Price (1986) has noted, the advocacy funded by the Legal Services Corporation is almost uniquely offensive in this respect. The choice of political position to be advocated in one sense is delegated to a third party, the grant recipient, but in another sense is made by the Corporation, which selects those who are to receive its grants. The Corporation thus hides behind a facade of grantee independence, supporting particular legal reforms without exposing itself to charges of bias. Furthermore, since program defunding is extremely expensive – in contested cases at least $1 million per program – the pre-1982 indulgence of the Corporation has posed severe monitoring problems for the past-1982 Board of Directors of the Corporation.

The third category comprises the actual clients of staff attorneys in the legal service program. Prohibitions on political activity are particularly important for protecting clients because they offer the client protection from staff attorney abuses. Politically motivated attorneys working in a poorly remunerated legal services environment have incentives to pursue far-reaching law reforms at the expense of the immediate litigation interests of a client. In 1970, the Cahns had outlined the nature of this potential conflict of interest:

> We have seen this take place in the legal services programs – where lawyers 'for' the poor decide what in their professional collective wisdom is in the best interests of the poor. Consequently, they draft legislation; they handle test cases, and for the most part studiously avoid all contact with those insights which came from neighborhood offices, from contact with live clients, from group representation or from any structural mechanism of accountability to the constituency they ostensibly serve. (Cahn and Cahn, 1970, p. 1040)

Legislative advocacy often takes the form of class action litigation dedicated to law reform objectives. The goals that drive such suits were clearly identified by Derrick Bell, a one-time staff attorney of the NAACP and professor at the Harvard School of Law:

> the class action provides the vehicle for bringing about a major advance toward an idealistic goal. At the same time, prosecuting and winning the big case provides strong reinforcement of the attorney's sense of his or her abilities and professionalism ... The psychological motivations which influence a lawyer in taking on 'a fiercer dragon' through the class action may also underlie the tendency to direct the suit toward the goals of the lawyer rather than the client. (Bell, 1976)

In theory, constitutional standing requirements and the common interests requirement of Fed. R Civ. P. 23 serve to protect dissenting class members in litigation. However, the individual plaintiff in public interest class action litigation is usually an insignificant player and many courts ignore the position of dissenting class members on the ground that paternalism is often offensive in principle but desirable in practice. The Code of Professional Responsibility directs that clients should generally have control in deciding what rights and remedies to pursue (EC 7-7, 1981). In practice, this Code is ignored by many staff attorneys in the legal services offices.

6   The regional and local offices

Although the Legal Services Corporation has a central office in Washington, until 1983 it delegated many of its administrative responsibilities to nine regional offices. However, a serious principal–agent problem, which manifested itself in a failure of governance throughout the period 1981 to 1982, eventually led the Corporation to centralize its administrative responsibilities and to scale down the regional offices.

The regional office staff, many of whom were appointed from the local field programs, tended to share the social engineering values of those organizations and offered support for law reform initiatives. The regional offices played an active role in the 1981–82 survival campaign. The Regional Directors of the Chicago, New York, Philadelphia and San Francisco offices were listed in the 'Core Group' organized by Alan Houseman to mastermind the LSC survival effort. This group organized eight large scale grass roots training for survival meetings through the regional offices, one session each for Boston, New York, Chicago, Northern Virginia and Atlanta, and a combined session for the San Francisco and Seattle Regions. These 'training events' funded through legal services appropriations included workshops on such topics as coalition building, media relations, public relations, private bar relations and staff involvement and utilization. Thousands of individuals from the local programs attended these essentially political meetings (Denton, 1985, p. 35).

In 1983, the congressional investigation of the LSC regional offices unearthed detailed information concerning the radical survival campaign role of the regional offices funded through monies appropriated by the Congress to the Legal Services Corporation. In the Atlanta Region, for example, a full-time survival coordinator was hired to direct the various survival campaigns in 13 southern states. The coordinator, Larry Hamblen, had an office in the LSC Atlanta Regional Office and was on the LSC payroll. Similarly, Colin Bull, Hamblen's counterpart in the New York Regional Office, was engaged in orchestrating a grass roots campaign not only to protect legal services, but also to protect a range of other threatened programs from budget reductions. In the view of Senator Denton (1985), there was no doubt that the regional offices orchestrated a major lobbying campaign against President Reagan's legal services policies.

Not surprisingly, the new LSC President, Bogard, hired by the Reagan LSC recess Board, began, early in 1983, to rein in such activities. He replaced most of the experienced career policy staff in the Washington headquarters of the LSC, and forced a number of regional directors to resign. For example, Bucky Askew, acting director of the Office of Field Services and a long-standing LSC official, was relieved of his position in February 1983. Colin Bull, the regional director in Atlanta, was relieved of his duties in March and transferred to New York. Martie Thompson, the regional director in Philadelphia, resigned under pressure in May 1984. Two regional directors, Salvadore Tio in New York and Judy Raphael in Chicago, took other jobs. On August 10, 1984, Paul Newman, regional director in Boston and David Gilbert, regional director in Denver, summarily were fired for failure to enforce the LSC Act and the appropriation riders. The regional offices were scaled down in size, restaffed, and stimulated into exerting greater control over local program operations. They were also encouraged to increase the involvement of the private bar in the legal services program.

The Corporation centralized training and support activities that had been diverted for local lobbying purposes, and shifted many of the functions of the regional offices to Washington, including authority over compliance deadlines, choice of program monitors, final approval of monitoring reports, the handling of complaints concerning grantee's behavior, approval of re-quests for fund balance waivers, subgrants and the like. Regional office personnel were also instructed to disenfranchise themselves from contracts with elected officials and with media organizations.

The Legal Services Corporation also experienced serious principal–agent problems in its relationships with the local programs responsible for dis-pensing legal services to indigent clients. From the outset, the field partici-pated aggressively to limit the regulatory rule of the Corporation and to ensure that the restrictions imposed by the 1974 Act would be narrowly interpreted. From 1977 onwards, increasing evidence accumulated that aber-rant local programs were abusing their discretionary powers by representing ineligible clients, filing class action suits indiscriminately against govern-ment entities, failing to negotiate with opposing parties prior to filing suit, representing such controversial parties as farm workers, aliens and children, and engaging in prohibited activities (Dooley and Houseman, 1984, p. 12). Prior to the Reagan Board readjustment, a complaisant LSC Board encouraged such illegal behavior, and, for this reason, encountered problems with Con-gress culminating in its refusal to re-authorize legal services in 1980.

The budget cut imposed by the Congress upon legal services in 1982 came in the middle of a major insurrection by the organized field against the 1974 Act and its restrictions. In this struggle, the local field programs played an active role. A major thrust of the survival strategy, developed by the 'Core Group' in December 1980, was the improvisation of a strong local political basis to survive possible efforts to regulate the program by the introduction of decentralized block grants and the empowerment of local bars. Regional meetings were funded by the Corporation to train program personnel to lobby for LSC's survival.

The local programs were encouraged by the Core Group to saturate both the media and the Congress with pro-legal services mail and to draft letters

of support for the use of such sympathetic organizations as the League of
Women Voters, the NAACP, the elderly groups and the coalitions of human
services organizations (Denton, 1985, p. 36). In consequence, by May 1981,
the survival campaign was well advanced and the Congress was overwhelmed
by pro-LSC press editorials, inundated with calls from bar association leaders and swamped with LSC client mail. The local programs were actively
turning away eligible clients to make way for networking and coalition
building while exhorting the public to support legal services. In 1981 alone,
360 000 eligible clients were denied legal services as a consequence of
politicization of the local program offices, and the diversion of grant support
to lobbying activities.

As part of this politicization program, many local field programs participated in the Client Advocacy Project, which came to be known as Law in
Neighborhoods and Communities Survey (LINCS/CAP). This project provided training manuals to be shared with other community groups as a basis
for effective pro-legal services lobbying. According to Denton (1985, p. 60):

> Virtually everything that was spelled out in either the grant application narratives,
> or in the filings as to what was to be done with the funds, was in violation of the
> LSC Act or Moorhead Amendment restrictions. Under no stretch of the imagina-
> tion can 'Accountability Day' meetings, where votes are sought on a wide range
> of budget issues, be passed off as 'legal services' activity. It was grass roots
> lobbying.

and

> Thus, the hard record again confirms that LSC funds were being used to finance
> the most radical anti-Reagan political groups in the nation.

The training program and manuals funded by the Legal Services Corporation in 1981 and 1982 were focused particularly upon the use of targeted
litigation by local field programs as a technique designed to force conces-
sions from unwilling adversaries. The Law and Direct Citizen Action manual,
for example, recommended a sequence of small suits since 'the opposition's
costs may be significantly higher if it has to defend itself against a lot of
small suits which are factually distinct ... and this can enlarge the organization's bargaining power' (p. 11). Gary Bellow, in 'You Bet Your Job' emphasized that '(a) lot of small suits humming away, where each time they
have to file a response, each time they have to answer interrogations increases the pressure', and, 'the way to cause pressure on in-house counsel is
to bring actions in out-of-the-way places (make them travel) or generate a
lot of action (make them work hard to keep up) ... Always work with the
group to find handles to increase the costs.'

However, the programs were warned not to allow excessive litigation to interfere with organizing and grass roots political activism. According to Denton (1985, p. 102):

> the true goal, trainees are reminded, is not the achievement of the limited goals which are the stated purpose of the organization's actions (e.g. raising the wages of the minority women to conform to minimum wage laws), but the achievement of political power by a community organization.

In this perspective, the proper role of the legal services attorney is to function as an arm of community action groups. Service to individual clients is denigrated, is described as a 'revolving door' and as an interference in the attorney's effort to engage in effective community advocacy:

> The lawyer who wants to serve poor people must put his skills to the task of helping poor people organize themselves. This is not the traditional use of a lawyer's skills; in many ways it violates some of the basic tenets of the profession. (Isaac, 1985)

Endemic in the training materials sent out to the local programs is hatred of capitalism and of the US corporation as the root cause of poverty. Government is viewed as a hand maiden of the corporation and is targeted for this reason. It is worth quoting the speech by Steve Max at a March 1982 LSC-funded training conference on 'Strategies and Substances for the Eighties' as an indication of some of the attitudes which still prevail in the local programs of legal services:

> Capitalism is starting to become a foreign power in this, the very country which was its leading exponent. A foreign power which bankrupts cities, which destroys jobs, which creates poverty and economic chaos ... Now that the corporate program is creating ruin in the economy, the corporations have joined the attack, leaving government holding the bag ... the most important thing which we can do in the coming years is to keep up the anti-corporate campaign, in the knowledge that the right cannot for long conceal the fact that it is the organizational expression of the corporate program and that the corporate program is nothing less than the recolonization of America. (Isaac, 1985)

7   The National Support Centers

The principal impact of these centers is to be found on the demand side of the legal services market where they have been extremely active in promoting law reform through legislative activities and impact litigation, notably through the class action suit. Indeed, these demand side activities were a major factor in the demise of OEO legal services in 1974 and its replacement by the Legal Services Corporation, initially with a remit to close down the support centers (the Green Amendment).

The national law reform offices – or back-up centers as they became known – were first funded by the OEO in 1966 as vehicles to bring national test cases and to advocate legislative changes. These centers were to ignore local priorities – they were not governed by local boards – and were to make law reform activities their principal priority. They were modelled on the Center for Social Welfare Policy located at Columbia University and initiated in 1965 with a grant from the Ford Foundation. Located in urban areas and affiliated usually with universities, some 12 such centers received OEO financial support during the late 1960s and early 1970s, concentrating each in a special area of substantive law.

By 1971, most of the current centers were functioning and their activities were generating intense controversy. They were involved heavily in policy advocacy and in disseminating policy concepts and legal reform agendas among legal services programs through services, training groups, publications, conferences and research. They offered house counsel services to advocacy groups such as the National Welfare Rights Organization, the National Tenants Association, the NAACP, the American Indian Movement and similar groups. They engaged in lobbying, drafting model legislation and in the provision of staff assistance to legislators who shared their reform agendas (120 Cong. Rec. X-967-968 (1974)).

In response to mounting criticism, the OEO undertook a study of the back-up centers in 1973 which recommended that they should be transferred into research or clearing house units, consolidated geographically and administratively and brought in-house. Before any such initiative could be mounted, however, the OEO was defunct and the legal services program had been moved to the jurisdiction of the 1974 Act, with a serious legislative threat to the future of the centers. In 1973, Congresswoman Edith Green had proposed an amendment to the Bill creating LSC with the intent of eliminating the back-up centers, once the Corporation was chartered. Under this amendment, research, training, technical assistance and clearing house functions were to be performed only by the LSC itself, and not by grant or contract (Section 1006 (a) (3) of the 1974 Act). In May 1974, the Green Amendment, which had been dropped in conference, was restored by the Senate when President Nixon threatened to veto the bill unless the centers were abolished.

In 1975, the Board of Directors of the newly formed Legal Services Corporation commissioned a review of the 17 functioning centers in light of the Green Amendment. The review members were drawn largely from the local programs and concluded, in the Polikoff Report, that with few exceptions the centers should be maintained. The LSC Board resolved to continue funding 14 of the centers, terminating only two training centers and the NLADA Management Assistance Project and reclassifying Clearinghouse as part of the corporation itself. This decision was made despite evidence that the centers had expended a large majority of their budgets – from 50 to 80 per cent – on direct litigation and legislative activity.

The Board took advantage of loose drafting in the 1974 Act to obviate the intent of the Green Amendment, concluding that Section 1006 (a) (1) (A) authorized funding of national support centers for the purpose of furnishing legal assistance to eligible clients, but that Section 1006 (a) (3) precluded funding for support centers for activities relating to the delivery of legal assistance, namely research, training, technical assistance and information clearinghouse. By this artifact, the Corporation neutralized the very amendment on which its existence earlier had depended.

In 1977, the Corporation successfully requested the repeal of the Green Amendment as a means of eliminating an ambiguity in its operations, while preventing unnecessary growth of an in-house bureaucracy. The Congress emphasized that the repeal did not signal a return to the unrestricted remit of OEO's Legal Services Program. The conferees accepted the Senate provision which prohibited the undertaking by grant or contract of broad general legal or policy research unrelated to representation of eligible clients. The Corporation was restricted to expending no more than 10 per cent of its total appropriations on such activities in any fiscal year. Furthermore, by emphasizing Section 1006 (a) (3) as the justification for support center funding, the Congress made it clear that the support centers, unlike the local programs, had no presumptive right to refunding. Responsibility for oversight and evaluation was to be concentrated in the LSC Research Institute on Legal Assistance, headed by Alan Houseman.

The response of the national support centers was not one of curtailing political activities, but rather of augmenting their lobbying capabilities. Most of them opened branch lobbying offices in the District of Columbia in response to a memorandum by the Ad Hoc Committee of the Legal Services Community which advocated an increased federal advocacy presence in Washington. Alan Houseman and Judy Riggs in a report entitled 'Support Needs and Options' (1977) urged the centers to develop strategies, communication networks and coalitions essential to effective representation, as well as engaging in law reform litigation and legislative advocacy. The support function which, in theory, had been the fundamental justification of the centers' existence, received only a passing reference in this document. The report also stressed the role of the centers in organizing outside groups for law reform activism.

Throughout the late 1970s, the national support centers continued to expand. In 1976, 14 such centers were funded. In 1979, the Corporation initiated three new centers. By 1981, the number of centers had increased to 20 and total LSC funding had more than doubled from $5.2 million in 1976 to $10.9 million. In February 1980, Senator Ernest Hollings, chairman of the Senate appropriations subcommittee, queried a 'stay-even' LSC budget request which accommodated a 65 per cent increase in national support center funding. In October 1981, a national support center self-study of the 17 functionally operative centers showed that more centers were engaged in national policy representation than in litigation. Furthermore, the centers orchestrated active networks of national policy representation through a coalition policy.

The election of Reagan as President in November 1980 foreshadowed serious problems for the national support workers, most especially with respect to their questionable activities in legislative advocacy, coalition building, networking and law reform. LSC President Dan Bradley, designated Alan Houseman to spearhead a survival campaign within the Corporation, which would pay particular regard to the threatened support centers. A particular objective of the survival program was to establish a 'corporation in exile' capable of preserving the law reform concept of legal services through the Reagan 'inter-regnum'. The national support centers became one of the four components of the legal services community considered to be fundamental to carrying through the law reform agenda, and designated as 'the rubies'.

Early in the survival campaign, Houseman identified the national support centers as vulnerable. The Corporation moved quickly to fund them with special grants that would enable them to pursue a law reform agenda through 1983 irrespective of the budgetary policy of a new LSC board. At the March 6, 1981 meeting of the Corporation's board, it was determined that $1.7 million would be allocated to national and state support programs. In return, the centers were expected to participate actively in grass roots lobbying, to generate regular letter writing to members of Congress and to arrange meetings with key legislators as well as to engineer passage of local bar association resolutions praising the LSC. In May 1981, the Comptroller General of the United States rendered an opinion (60 Comp. Gen. 423) that the Corporation had allowed its grant recipients to engage in lobbying activities prohibited by Federal law.

By the end of 1982, the national support centers had developed a formidable investment to protect their law reform agenda from LSC retrenchment and to ensure that their activities would not be exposed to outside scrutiny. The reformist LSC board confronted services obstacles to effective monitoring, not least from the US Congress.

Nevertheless, in 1986, the Corporation exercised its powers under Section 1007 (d) of the Act to monitor the national support centers. One of the first centers to be monitored, the National Social Science and Law Center was found to have ignored its responsibilities in complying both with the

1975 Act as amended and with the LSC's Regulations. Many of the actions taken by the well-funded Center were found to be trivial. Within six months of the visit, the Corporation initiated action to deny refunding to this center. Following a lengthy appeal process, which cost the Corporation approximately $1.5 million, the center was defunded.

The next monitoring visit was scheduled for the Migrant Legal Action Program (MLAP). Prior to the visit, the Corporation received documents detailing the misappropriation of tens of thousands of dollars by the former MLAP executive director. Once again, monitoring resulted in a report which led the Corporation to initiate defunding procedures.

Thereafter, the Corporation encountered delays and obstructions in its monitoring efforts which appeared to be part of a coordinated effort to obstruct the Corporations' execution of its statutory responsibilities (LSC, September 1986, p. 41). The NLADA appears to have played a role in this obstruction of the monitoring process. A particular feature of this non-cooperation was withholding of information without which the Corporation could not ensure compliance with the Act. A serious obstacle to monitoring was the lack of record keeping and time keeping at the national support centers which prevented the Corporation from executing sections 1007 (d) and 1008 (b) of the Act. In the two instances where such records were available the Corporation determined that federal funds had been wasted and misused.

Section 1006 (a) (1) (A) of the Act, as amended, authorizes the Corporation to provide funds to qualified programs furnishing legal assistance to eligible clients. Section 1006 (a) (3) further authorizes the Corporation to undertake directly, or by grant or contract, research, training, technical assistance and clearinghouse functions relating to the delivery of legal services. In the 1986 Refunding Application, the Corporation requested that the National Support Centers distinguish their activities according to these two separate funding components. The centers refused to respond to this request. In consequence, the extent of the centers' compliance with the Act is unknown except in the few cases where violations could be documented.

Immediate oversight of the National Support Centers is the responsibility of a properly constituted board of directors. Section 1007 (c) of the Act requires that the Corporation insure that recipients of grants or contracts are governed by a body consisting of at least 60 per cent attorneys who are members of the bar of a state in which legal assistance is provided and at least one-third of individuals who are eligible for legal services. Prior to 1983, LSC permitted the centers to retain control of board appointments. In 1983, however, with the implementation of 45 C.F.R. Port 1697.3, the centers were required to vest appointment power for a majority of the board members with the bar association whose membership includes a majority of attorneys practising in the centers' service area. In practice, most appointments are made in the name of the state bar associations.

A review by the Corporation of the bylaws and board minutes of the support centers demonstrated that the centers attempted to control the appointment of attorney board members. To this end, the centers rather than the bar associations typically interviewed, screened and nominated prospective attorney board members. With the bar associations playing only a subsidiary role, there was a significant prospect that independent candidates might be screened out of consideration as centers ensured that they would be governed by self-perpetuating boards. The majority of attorney board members, at the time of the inquiry, had served on their center's board in excess of seven years.

Client board members usually are selected by the centers' boards of directors in conjunction with their staff. Client organizations typically are not solicited even for nominations. In most instances, recommendations emanate from LSC field programs or from other centers. Once again, the national support centers control the appointment process, drawing assistance from such outside bodies as The Farm Worker Labor Organizing Committee, the Gray Panthers and the National Coalition of Title One Parents.

The Corporation discovered that conflicts of interest, proscribed by statute, nevertheless were not uncommon among board members of the national support centers. Section 1007 (c) of the Act states that no attorney board member, while serving on a recipient's board of directors, shall receive compensation from a recipient. This prohibition evidently is intended to preserve independence and to avoid conflicts of interest. Yet, in 1986, the centers' boards of directors included at least 30 staff attorneys currently employed by, and in receipt of compensation from, an LSC recipient. Field programs employing these staff attorneys received a disproportionately high allocation of legal services funding.

Section 1007 (a) (5) of the LSC Act and 45 E.F.R. Part 1612 prohibit the use of LSC funds for lobbying and certain other activities unless certain applicable exceptions are met. All of the national support centers nevertheless, engage to differing degrees in legislative and administrative advocacy and/or in the monitoring of legislation and regulations. The centers claim that such activities are supported with non-LSC funds or with unrestricted LSC monies. The centers argue that most private funds are not donated for legal assistance and thus fall outside the restrictions of the Act. Some 22 per cent of their total funding is from such sources. They further assert that such activities are often undertaken on behalf of eligible clients, or at the request of government officials in accordance with the LSC Act. The centers also provide support to field programs which themselves engage in legislative and administrative advocacy.

Thirteen of the national support centers admitted to conducting legislative advocacy. Of these, five actually registered employees as lobbyists with the US Congress. Eight centers maintained branch offices in Washington for the purpose of monitoring legislation developments and for conducting legislative as well as administrative advocacy. In such circumstances, it is predictable that a Congress, bought out in part by taxpayers' monies, will refuse the LSC an adequate monitoring and defunding budget to contain the illegal behavior of the national support centers and, if necessary, to defund them. In this way, the Congress contributes to those forces which threaten to destroy democracy and to erode the rule of law (Bennett and DiLorenzo 1985b).

8   Conclusions

For those concerned to provide the poor with access to justice rather than to promote law reform the contents of this chapter make disturbing reading. The interactive and complementary powers of the organized bar, the organized field and the legal services networks are immense and the countervailing consumer interests are relatively weak. In such circumstances, the logic of collective action predicts a political equilibrium in which activist law reform predominates at a serious cost in terms of diminished access to civil justice for eligible poor Americans.

15 Inky blots and rotten parchment bonds

The 'common good' of a collective – a race, a class, a state – was the claim and justification of every tyranny ever established over men. Every major horror of history was committed in the name of an altruistic motive. Has any act of selfishness ever equated the carnage perpetrated by disciples of altruism? Does the fault lie in men's hypocrisy or in the nature of the principle? The most dreadful butchers were the most sincere. They believed in the perfect society reached through the guillotine and the firing squad. Nobody questioned their right to murder since they were murdering for an altruistic purpose. It was accepted that man must be sacrificed for other men. Actors change, but the curse of the tragedy remains the same. A humanitarian who starts with declarations of love for mankind and ends with a sea of blood. It goes on and will go on so long as men believe that an action is good if it is unselfish. That permits the altruist to act and forces his victims to bear it. The leaders of collectivist movements ask nothing for themselves. But observe the results.

Ayn Rand, *The Fountainhead*, 1943

1 Introduction

The market in legal services – its principal actors and its central institutions – has been evaluated in depth in this book, its behavior refracted through the powerful lens of public choice and its existence assessed in terms of several competing ideologies which have been condensed into the ultimate philosophic divides of the late twentieth century: methodological individualism versus constructivist rationalism. A central thesis of the book is the judgment that the individual's right to justice has been subverted into collectivist law reform and that the legitimate concerns of the poor individual have been frustrated by the non-poor who have invaded the market in legal services both to seize its tax dollars and to perpetrate their preferences on the near-helpless victims of their altruism. This chapter draws upon the accumulated wisdom of the book to assess the predominantly adverse consequences of the legal services program over the period 1964 to 1988 in the United States.

Section 2 is devoted to an assessment of the degree of technical inefficiency with which general tax dollars have been utilized in the supply of legal services. Section 3 presents the results of an original, computer-based statistical evaluation of differences in litigation patterns between the staff attorney legal services program and a control panel of private litigation. This study does not reject the hypothesis that legal services attorneys are significantly more concerned than their private counterparts to reform the law through class action suits directed at government agencies. Section 4 sur-

315

veys the nature of the attack on the family mounted through legal services litigation. Section 5 surveys the nature of the attack on the institutions of capitalism mounted through legal services litigation. Section 6 surveys the nature of the attack on the republican principle mounted through legal services litigation. Section 7 concludes with an overall assessment of the consequences of legal services in a market where suppliers do not sell, customers do not buy and tax payers exert only minimal control.

2   Technical inefficiencies in the provision of legal services

Treatises on economic policy often proceed on the assumption that suppliers – be they private firms, public enterprises or government bureaus – obtain the maximum output from given resource inputs or, to put it technically, that they operate on an outer-bound production possibility surface consistent with their resources. With technical (or X-) efficiency thus assumed to hold, attention is centred exclusively upon the issue of allocative efficiency, that is whether the correct volume of resources has been allocated to each sector of the economy in accordance with the Pareto principal (Rowley and Peacock, 1975).

The essence of the X-efficiency hypothesis (Leibenstein, 1966) is that such economic treatises are misguided, especially with respect to public sector provisions, and that many enterprises typically operate well within the outer-bound of their production possibility surfaces. The explanation of such divergences between maximum and attained efficiency rests upon a distinction between human and physical factor inputs and an interpretation of the pressures that are placed upon human factor inputs in various market and non-market environments (de Alessi, 1983).

Specifically, it is assumed that all individuals involved in economic decision making pursue objectives of their own, which may well be inconsistent with X-efficiency, and that they maximize these objectives subject to the institutional constraints that confront them. If the constraints are loose, significant inefficiencies may occur in work effort as it manifests itself in terms of the pace of activity, the quality, time pattern and length of the work commitment. Contracts of employment alone cannot eliminate this potential for X-inefficiency since human capital cannot be bought outright. What is purchased, for the most part, are units of labor time which are not the critical units from a production perspective. Incompleteness of contracts thus leaves considerable scope for inefficiencies, even when those who purchase the labor inputs are motivated to achieve X-efficiency. Such scope is markedly greater in the case of monopoly supplier government bureaus than in any other enterprise form, since both external and internal constraints typically are extremely weak (Peacock, 1979, a, b).

Following Niskanen, Chapter 6 notes that senior bureaucrats, responsible for separate, identifiable budgets, typically though not always seek to maximize their discretionary budget as a proxy for such underlying personal objectives as salary, perquisites of office, public reputation, power, patronage and ease of management. To the extent that they are demand and not budget constrained, such bureaucrats have little direct incentive to insist upon X-efficiency but indeed will be tempted to purchase ease of management at some price in X-efficiency. Because such bureaus are publicly financed they are protected from capital market depression of stock valuations which would signal distress in the case of inefficient private enterprise and ultimately would trigger a takeover bid (Fama, 1980; Fama and Jensen, 1983). Because they are monopolistic, potential clients must either use their services or sacrifice legal aid. The competitive constraint on X-inefficiency is absent.

Even should the government itself be concerned to achieve X-efficiency – and public choice casts doubts upon such a supposition – problems exist in defining output for a commodity as complex as legal services. Such measurement problems leave scope for X-inefficiency to be hidden by the bureau and its staff, especially in view of monopoly supply. Given regional differences, each bureau can claim a uniqueness of service which explains any apparent deficiency in the output–budget relationship by comparison with other legal services bureaus. The government or its oversight committees are unlikely to be well-informed on such matters, given the multi-dimensioned nature of output and the limited insight offered to the production function of the bureau.

Staff employees of legal services bureaus themselves have low incentives to police out technical inefficiencies tolerated by their senior bureaucrats. The pay and working environment of legal services staff attorneys is poor by comparison with the private sector, and internal promotion prospects negligible. Predictably, those who join such programs do so because they are relatively poorly qualified, and/or have a predisposition to the easy life, or because they want to indulge ideological preferences by trail blazing law reforms as a prelude to moving to the private sector. None of these attributes augurs well for X-efficiency in the basic civil justice programs of legal services offices. Since such attorneys are salaried there is no market incentive for them to do other than indulge their personal preferences. In such a generalized environment of X-inefficiency, even those who initially are motivated by the work ethic encounter substantial peer pressure not to signal the inefficiencies of others by a markedly superior individual performance. Few will survive such pressures and remain long in the legal services program.

Such evidence as exists – and inevitably it is sparse and difficult to interpret – does not refute the hypothesis that legal services offices suffer from X-inefficiency. Two studies in particular offer useful insights, namely the 1990 study by Besharov for the American Enterprise Institute and the 1988 study by Cox for the American Bar Association. Although each study is limited in scope, interactively they suggest that legal services offices typically do not operate on the outer-bound of their production possibility surfaces.

The Besharov study is restricted exclusively to the legal services offices and makes no comparison between the staff attorney and the private attorney offices. Inferences are drawn from a study of management accountability and from a time series productivity evaluation which, though not conclusive, certainly is not flattering to the legal services program. Despite the responsibility vested by Congress in the Legal Services Corporation to manage a $300 million program with over 300 grantees, employing 5000 lawyers and 7000 other staff, Besharov claims that the federal legal services program has not adopted the kinds of management tools necessary to ensure the efficient use of tax payer funds.

Although a number of local programs appear to make use of modern technology, of paralegals and of private bar law school clinics – Metropolitan Denver is an outstanding example – many others operate little differently than law offices did 20 years ago, significantly under-automated and improperly staffed by comparison with state-of-the-art private law firms. Moreover, the limited data available within the Corporation suggests a substantial decline in productivity over the period 1980 to 1984 save for cases closed by settlement without litigation. Across all categories involving litigation, cases closed declined by almost 42 per cent. The 1982 budget cut reduced allocations to the local programs by 25 per cent, allowing for an associated fall in productivity of approximately 17 per cent over the period under review. This decline in negotiated settlements began prior to the Reagan cuts and failed to improve even after funding rose again. Besharov suggests that there has been a significant long-term decline in the productivity of legal services attorneys, perhaps by as much as 20 per cent. Cases of settlement without litigation do not present opportunities for law reform and for demonstrating litigation skills that might be attractive later to private attorney offices.

Using the same data, Besharov found that, in 1984, 71 per cent of local workloads involved work that he classified as non-extensive. Considerable time was expended in giving advice but otherwise in deciding not to serve potential clients. Furthermore, the average extensive case appeared to take about 2.5 days of staff time despite the routine character of the cases involved. Besharov concludes that 'it appears that many LSC attorneys lack the skills, experience or supervision to handle cases as expeditiously as they should' (Besharov, 1990, p. 55). He notes policy recommendations by the National Organization of Legal Services Programs directed in 1988 to the resolution of this low productivity problem:

Legal services programs must develop ways to improve their productivity, with particular attention to private attorney involvement in service delivery, and staffing issues such as specialization, compensation, recruitment and training.

To these recommendations, Besharov adds his own judgment that the Legal Services Corporation itself should engage in regular program monitoring, not merely to ensure financial accountability and statutory compliance but also to raise the quality of service. To this end, the Corporation should collect on a regular basis sufficient information to understand grantee caseloads, clients and operations, and should upgrade its own date processing capacity. It should also upgrade its own ability to provide management-orientated technical assistance and to stimulate innovation in the local program offices. Whether or not the political incentives exist for the Corporation to pursue these objectives is not discussed.

The 1988 Cox Report on the San Antonio Voucher Project provided a less extensive but potentially more valuable insight into the productivity of the staff attorney supply mechanism for legal services. The purpose of this study was to test the relative cost efficiency and quality effectiveness of three different legal service delivery systems: a competitive bid contract system, a voucher system and the traditional staff attorney model. To permit valid inter-mode comparisons, all three modes had to deliver the same legal services in each geographic site. Divorce cases met the service criterion well since both private and staff attorneys had experience in handling them. Three types of divorce cases were included in the study, namely, (1) uncontested, (2) contested involving some dispute other than child custody, but with no domestic violence, and (3) cases involving some dispute other than child custody, with some domestic violence. San Antonio, Texas was selected as the geographic site because Bexar County Legal Aid (BCLA) was the only legal services program that expressed a willingness to cooperate with an experimentally designed comparative study and because handling divorce cases was a local program priority.

Details of the study itself are clearly set out in the Cox Report and are too detailed to be reviewed in this section. Suffice it to say that care was exercised to maintain study integrity by random distribution of clients to the different supply modes and by a well-defined case fractionalization system which identified the status of each case at closure and the estimated time spent on the case. For cases closed by judicial resolution, additional case-related information was gathered from the study attorney and court records to assist a peer review panel in judging the quality of service rendered.

During the one year of study case intake and referral (November 1985 to October 1986) 3000 client intake interviews were scheduled of which 1400 were not kept (a no-show rate of 45 per cent). Of those who attended the intake interview, varying percentages across the three modes were closed at zero (failure to show up for the initial attorney interview or, in the case of the voucher mode, failure to pick up the voucher). The number of zero cases as a percentage of total case referrals ranged from 6 per cent for the staff model, 13 per cent for the contract model to 33 per cent for the voucher model. There was no recorded explanation for these differences, though the process of choosing an attorney may have deflected some clients in the case of the voucher mode.

Equally sharp inter-mode differences were found with regard to case completion rates. The number of cases closed by judicial resolution as a percentage of all cases closed at some fraction greater than zero was 89 per cent for the voucher model, 80 per cent for the contract model and 51 per cent for the staff model. In addition, 75 per cent of all the fractionalized staff cases were closed at one-quarter (that is, following an initial attorney interview, but prior to filing a divorce petition).

Significant differences were evident also in the promptness of case closures across the delivery modes. The number of cases still open in June 1987, some 20 months after the study began, and 8 months after it ceased case referrals, was substantially greater for the staff mode than for either of the private attorney modes. Expressed as a percentage of net case referrals (that is, gross case referrals minus the number of cases closed at zero), this number was 25 per cent for the staff mode, 10 per cent for the voucher mode and 7 per cent for the contract mode.

Consistent with this result was the significantly greater amount of time taken by staff attorneys in completing judicially resolved cases. The average time for processing a case was in excess of 200 days from initial attorney interview to final divorce decree for each of the three staff mode case types as compared with 120 to 160 days, depending on case type for each of the private attorney modes.

The study's review suggests that quality of service, while generally low for legal services divorce cases, was a particularly severe problem for the staff mode. The bases for this conclusion were (1) the unexpected low level and high variation of service quality grades across all case types and delivery modes, and (2) the significantly lower average grades received by staff mode cases compared with those received either by contract or by voucher modes. The peer review panel consisted of three private practice attorneys in the San Antonio area, each board certified in family law by the Texas Board of Legal Specialization. Gradings were based on a points scale and on a peer professional review rating.

Staff mode cases on average earned 60 per cent of all possible points, whereas voucher and contract modes separately averaged 78 per cent of all possible points. The mean professional review rating for staff mode cases, on a scale from one to five, was 2.40, compared with 2.80 for contract mode cases and 3.07 for voucher mode cases. All inter-mode differences were statistically significant.

Because of the lack of full comparability in cost data across the three modes, the cost efficiency results were less robust than those for quality review. Service costs per case closed for each of the private attorney modes were calculated on the basis of the paid attorney fee. For the staff attorney mode, per case service costs had to be estimated indirectly. The reporting of time data crucial for such an estimate proved to be of questionable validity. Therefore, an alternative estimate was made based on BCLA budget expenditure and case closure statistics for BCLA's divorce section. The budget estimates were three to four times greater than the time-based estimates. On balance the study concluded that 'it is very difficult to conclude that the staff mode is any bargain cost-wise, at least so far as the delivery of the kinds of legal services examined in this study is concerned' (Cox, 1988, p. 46).

The study was restricted to one area of legal services, divorce, albeit one accounting for 16 per cent of legal services cases during the period under review. It was restricted to one geographic region only and to one staff attorney program. Nevertheless, the evidence unequivocally and overwhelmingly points to a judgment that the staff attorney mode is technically inefficient by comparison with available private alternatives. Economic theory unequivocally predicts such an outcome (Leibenstein, 1966; Faith, Higgins and Tollison, 1984).

On the basis of economic theory and institutional analysis it is difficult to avoid a judgment that the legal services staff attorney program is inflicted with X-inefficiencies which would be reduced if a shift were made to some form of private provision. Given the importance attached to the right to justice policy objective by the advocates of legal services federal funding and given the budget constraints that will always apply to such a program, such X-inefficiency, and the resource waste that it implies, establishes a strong case for reconsideration of the mode of legal services delivery.

3 The class action suit and other legal tactics

Much has been made in this book of the distinction between the right to justice and law reform, though of course an absolute divide cannot exist between the two. Even those who claim to be strict construction constitutionalists and who defend stare decisis as a cornerstone of the common law cannot reasonably advance the case for an immutable system of laws. There are a number of reasons why the law must evolve in any society, most notable of which are (1) the filling of gaps not addressed by the existing laws, (2) changes in the underlying preferences of individuals within a society, and (3) the correction of widely recognized errors in the existing structure of stare decisis. To deny any process of legal adjustment where such grounds exist, simply because such a process opens up opportunities for social engineering litigation aimed at root-and-branch law reform, is also to reject an opportunity for spontaneous legal adjustment. In itself, such a denial must be construed as social engineering – an attempt to lock individuals into a legal strait jacket. It is relevant, however, to review the legal tactics, including class action suit litigation, that many legal services attorneys utilize, not as a means of accessing civil justice on behalf of indigent individual clients, but as an instrument of federally-funded social engineering.

The class action suit, utilized as an instrument of litigation against government agencies by many legal services attorneys, has become a focal point of criticism by those opposed to the use of legal services as an agent of law reform. Yet, class action suits are not unknown within the private sector and can play an efficiency-enhancing role (Posner, 1986). It is important, therefore, to review the economic function of this legal instrument, together with its implications for the legal concepts of standing and justiciability, prior to evaluating this aspect of the legal services program.

In principle, the class action suit is a legal response to the problem of large numbers of individually small claims or cases which are jeopardized by the high fixed cost of litigation if each must be brought separately to the courts. If, however, the fixed costs can be spread over many claims, it may be possible to vindicate more claims, with a resulting reduction in the error costs of the legal system and without incurring prohibitive direct costs. The modern class action suit generalizes this technique and is authorized by Rule 23 of the Federal Rules of Civil Procedure, and/or by the individual states.

In the private sector, the class action device is of least value where it is most needed, namely where the individual claim is very small. In this case, the defendant can be compelled to pay a judgment equal to the total cost of his violation – but to whom? The cost of identifying the members of the class and giving each his individual damages may exceed the value of the judgment. Of course, the most important point from the economics perspective, is that the violator should be confronted with the costs of his violation, and not that he should recompense his victims. A problem remains that the cost of actually effecting compensation to the members of numerous class may be extremely high; and in some cases may exceed the benefits in deterrence yielded by the action. This problem is compounded by the fact that the absence of a real client impairs the incentive of the lawyer for the class to process the suit to a successful conclusion.

At first sight, these problems appear to be of little significance for class action suits initiated through the legal services program. For the most part, such suits are dedicated not to any judgment for damages but to the safeguarding of individual rights, the prohibition or the mandating of government or administrative behavior. The cost of distributing compensation, in such circumstances, is zero. Moreover, since the attorneys are salaried, their performance is independent of case-specific fees, thus avoiding any temptation for attorney conspiracy to settle for a small judgment and a high negotiated fee.

Furthermore, the rules that regulate class action litigation also at first sight appear to be well designed to prevent excessive and inappropriate uses of that instrument. If a party wants to move the court for an order certifying a class action, that party must show the court that all the following factors are present:

1. the class is so large that it is not practical for them to sue or defend as individual parties in a consolidation of cases or joinder of parties in a single action;
2. there are common questions of law or fact affecting the right or obligations of all members of the class the same;
3. the party or parties applying for class certification are truly representative of the proposed class;
4. separate suits by or against individual members of the proposed class might result in varying or inconsistent determinations for the members;
5. a class action can effectively dispose of all the legal and fact issues that exist between members of the proposed class and the adverse party;
6. the individual members of the proposed class do not have a superior interest in controlling the handling of the litigation;
7. there is no other pending litigation which would be adversely affected by certifying the class action; and
8. commencement of a class action would not unduly burden the court and would not cause prejudice to persons who might choose to have their case presented in another form.

Crucial to these controls, in principle, exercised by the courts, is the notion of necessary 'standing' or 'justiciability' which is central to the Anglo-American adversary system. Not everyone qualifies as an adversary entitled to set the court machinery in motion. Not every kind of alleged injury to an alleged interest will suffice. The court must be satisfied that the plaintiff has suffered the necessary kind of injury to the necessary kind of interest. To this end, certain criteria have been established.

The courts have required that the dispute be a live one, rather than one laid to rest by subsequent event; involve plaintiff's own injury and not someone elses'; be concrete and immediate, rather than a hypothetical dispute or one presenting a premature question for a mere advisory opinion; be not feigned or collusive; and not involve a question that is 'non-justiciable' as are deemed certain kinds of political questions. In discussing these requirements, the Supreme Court has often invoked a constitutional source in Article III, Section 2, which extends the judicial power of the United States to specified categories of cases and controversies. The states, by state constitutional provision or otherwise, have adopted a similar view of the judicial function.

Although the terms 'standing' and 'justiciability' have been used interchangeably by the courts, more recently the Supreme Court has been careful to distinguish between them. As the Court explained in *Flast* v. *Cohen* (392 U.S. 83 (1968)), 'no justiciable controversy is presented when the parties seek adjudication of only a political question, when the parties are asking for an advisory opinion, when the question sought to be adjudicated has been mooted by subsequent developments, and when there is no standing to maintain the action'. Standing has been called one of the most amorphous concepts in the entire domain of public law (Mermin, 1973, p. 186). As such, it is predictable that its limits will be explored by ambitious legal services attorneys anxious to impact on the law through class action suits encompassing plaintiffs who are unaware of their involvement in the suits.

There can be no question that legal services attorneys are trained to use litigation as a means of harassing an economic system that is viewed as alien and corrupt (Isaac, 1985). To this end, training was one of the rubies protected from Reagan's expected budget cuts throughout the first term of his presidency. In a video training program issued at that time, entitled 'You Bet Your Job', subsidized by the LSC, Gary Bellow noted that new lawyers in Legal Services must practise 'way beyond their level of training and preparation'. The need for such effort was reflective not of flaws in the attorneys themselves, but 'rather the way they get screwed like everyone else in this country'.

The LSC manuals and training materials reflected this ambivalent attitude toward litigation, arguing that it 'must be conceived of as a means to the goal of building organization, and not an independent goal' (ACORN, 1981). In the Law and Direct Citizen Action, prepared for the LSC by ACORN's Institute for social justice, litigation is recommended primarily as a form of intimidation, 'as an important bargaining technique that inspires a fear in the target that it stands to lose something if it won't negotiate'. The manual recommends the harassment of defendants by a series of small suits since 'the opposition's costs may be significantly higher if it has to defend itself against a lot of small suits which are factually distinct'. The cost of such lawsuits is not to be measured in terms of financial outlays:

> Lawsuits are expensive only if they are taken seriously ... Win or lose you start to escalate the cost of resistance to the group's demands. (Bellow, 1981)

Bellow advised legal services attorneys to utilize other techniques of harassment in their litigation programs, directed at the defendants' in-house counsels:

> The way to cause pressure on in-house counsel is to bring actions in out-of-the-way places (make them travel) or generate a lot of action (make them work hard to keep up) ... Always work with the group to find handles to increase the costs. (1981)

According to the LSC manuals, the right to pre-trial discovery in court cases comprises an especially effective means of intelligence gathering. Indeed, 'the Law and Direct Citizen Action' identifies discovery as the key to victory over a target, for example, by extracting 'information about a person's financial resources and ability to withstand certain sorts of losses, corporate and professional links with other individuals and entities, existence of insurance coverage and so on'. So important is discovery, says the manual, that it 'may be one of the most important reasons you want to go to court.'

The LSC training materials emphasize the central role of the legal services attorney as an arm of community action groups. From this perspective, service to individual clients is denigrated as a revolving door and as an interference in the attorney's effort to engage in effective community advocacy (Isaac, 1985, p. 102). From this perspective, whether an action is legal or illegal, ethical or unethical, is less important than whether it will be effective in achieving an organization's goals. 'Power analysis' (1981), one of the training documents developed for the 1981 upstate New York conference, quotes the following passage from Mao Tse-Tung:

> Deception is not enough – the enemy's leaders must be confused: if possible driven insane.

The same training document, with complete disdain for the legal ethics established by the American Bar Association, urges the legal services attorney to harass defendants into total confusion: 'Drive him crazy and bewilder him so that he disperses his forces in confusion'.

The training materials acknowledge that this role of the attorney differs sharply from the traditional model. In essence, his role is less one of representing individuals than one as organizing groups. His reward is an excitement not usually offered to the private attorney:

> Life is to be exciting. The organizer's stock in trade is change. Change of the existing power structure of a precinct, ward, city, state. Change of the financial community. Change of the existing roles of oppressor and oppressed ... Such

change does not happen without excitement ... In the movie 'A Thousand Clowns,' Jason Robards, in talking about his adopted nephew says, 'I want him to give the world a goosing before he dies. A goosing is a very exciting experience, either negatively or positively for all involved'. (California Legal Services, Inc., 1981)

The very existence of training materials of this kind, funded by legal services monies, raises serious questions of legality. For advice is given on picketing, demonstrations, boycotts, referenda, criminal procedures, bail, and citizens arrests – activities in which Legal Services attorneys may not encourage clients to participate. The training materials also encourage legal services attorneys to provide extensive in-kind services to community action organizations, once again without any authorizing legislation that supports such disbursements. In effect, the manuals recommend the use of federal dollars to foster disobedience to the law (Isaac, 1985, p. 109). Mindful that the LSC itself, in 1981, was under activist control, 'You Bet Your Job' reminded attorneys that: 'Congress has given the Corporation alone the responsibility to enforce the provisions of the LSC Act and regulations'.

It is against this background that the use made by legal services attorneys of the class action suit must be reviewed and evaluated. For, the class action suit is a potent instrument for defendant harassment as well as for attempted law reform, given the vulnerability of the law to targeted litigation. It is a low cost instrument for legal services attorneys, since plaintiffs can be added to the suit in the absence of evidenced concern or interest on their part, without any significant risk of a standing challenge being upheld by the courts. Since the legal redress required of a successful suit is not normally damages, but rather a write of mandamus, certiorari or prohibition, the legal services offices need not anticipate the high costs of disbursing benefits that tend to deter private attorney class action suits where the list of plaintiffs is extensive. With law reform benefits projected to be high and the cost of litigation very low, it is not surprising that legal services programs have been criticized for the use of excessive class action litigation as an instrument of defendant harassment and for the wilful disregard of the legal needs of poor individuals.

In order to clarify the magnitude of class action litigation by legal attorneys lawyers by comparison with private attorney experience, an independent research investigation was conducted in Fall 1987. The results of that investigation are recorded in this section. The hypotheses that were subjected to empirical investigation were as follows:

1. The class action suit is an instrument directed more at government agencies and the constitution than at private organizations.
2. The class action suit is employed more frequently against government agencies by legal services than by private attorney offices.

3. Class action litigation is employed less frequently in the field of family
    law, where law reform is now less relevant, than in other areas of the
    civil law.

The researchers made use of Lexis Nexis to conduct a computer-based
investigation of a sample of legal services court cases and to compare these
cases with a random sample of private attorney court cases utilized as a
control panel. To this end, a comprehensive, up-to-date list of all staff
attorneys employed by legal services programs, together with the specific
offices with which they were associated, was provided by the Legal Services
Corporation. In searching for legal services cases, the names of these attorneys
were randomly sampled. The attorneys chosen were searched through Lexis
in conjunction with the names of their offices to ensure that only LSC
funded cases were located in the Lexis retrieval system. The cases thus
retrieved were subdivided by subject matter to determine the areas most
frequently litigated within the total sample. The cases most frequently retrieved were education, family, migrant workers, housing and social security.

Once the major areas of legal services litigation were established, a
control panel of privately litigated court cases was retrieved for each such
area. Cases were retrieved by the application of general phrases for each
category. From these retrievals, the central panel was compiled by a process
of random sampling.

The total sample of legal services cases was 390. The total control panel
consisted of 105 cases. Results are summarized in Table 15.1.

From Table 15.1 it is evident that the percentage of class action suits is
much higher for legal services than for the control panel of cases. The

Table 15.1   The overall results

	Legal Services Cases	Control Panel
Number	390	105
Number class action suits	113	19
Percentage class action (%)	28.9	18.0
Number class actions against govt/constitution	93	18
Percentage class action against govt/constitution	82.3	94.7

difference is statistically significant. This result does not contradict hypothesis 1. Furthermore, the large majority of legal services class action suits and almost all private class action suits are directed at government agencies, government officials and the Constitution. This result does not contradict hypothesis 2.

Tables 15.1–15.6 categorize these results by a reference to each of the major subject areas identified by the investigation: Table 15.2 outlines the results in the area of Education.

Table 15.2   Education

	Legal Services Cases	Control Panel
Number	39	23
Number of class action suits	7	8
% of class action suits	17.9%	34.8%
Number of class actions v. govt/constitution	7	8
% class actions against govt/constitutions	100%	100%

In the area of Education, Table 15.2 indicates a level of legal services class action suit activity significantly below the overall average, and indeed well below that for the private sector. All such class action suits concerned the Board of Education of the Supervisors of Education, i.e. government appointees. Since the education of poor families overwhelmingly takes place in the public sector, it is to be expected that legal services litigation will be directed at government and its agencies.

Table 15.3 outlines the results in the area of Migrant Workers.

In the area of Migrant Workers, Table 15.3 indicates a rate of class action litigation much closer to the overall legal services average, and significantly in excess of that for the private market. In view of the small numbers concerned the apparently high rate of legal services litigation against government may be due to chance.

Table 15.4 outlines the results in the area of Housing.

In the area of Housing, Table 15.4 indicates a significant rate of legal services class action litigation, though somewhat below the overall average reported in this study. No private class action litigation was revealed. Almost all legal services class action litigation was directed at government agencies, much of it in the field of rent control.

Table 15.3   *Migrant workers*

	Legal Services Cases	Control Panel
Number	19	19
Number class action suits	5	2
% class action suits	26.3%	10.5%
Number class actions actions v. govt/ constitutions	2	1
% class actions v. govt/ constitutions	40.0%	50.0%

Table 15.4   *Housing*

	Legal Services Cases	Control Panel
Number	58	19
Number class action action suits	11	0
% class action suits	19.1%	0%
Number class action v. govt/constitution	10	na
% class actions v. govt/constitution	10.1%	na

Table 15.5   *Social security*

	Legal Services Cases	Control Panel
Number	181	23
Number class action suits	64	7
% class actions suits	35.4%	30.4%
Number class action v. govt/constitution	55	7
% class actions v. govt/constitution	90.0%	100%

Table 15.5 outlines the results in the area of Social Security.

In the area of Social Security, Table 15.5 indicates a high rate of class action suit activity both by legal services and by private attorneys. Given the nature of the area, it is unsurprising to discover that almost all such litigation is directed against government agencies.

Table 15.6 outlines the results in the area of Family Law.

Table 15.6   Family law

	Legal Services Cases	Control Panel
Number	14	21
Number class action suits	1	1
% class action suits	7.1%	4.8%
Number class actions v. govt/constitutions	1	1
% class actions v. govt/constitutions	100%	100%

In the area of Family Law, Table 15.6 indicates a relatively low rate of class action litigation by legal services attorneys but a yet lower rate by private attorneys. This evidence supports the view that family law is now a relatively unproductive area of activity for the reformist legal activist, although it is the most important area of civil law from the viewpoint of the indigent client. Table 15.6 does not refute hypothesis 3.

It has been suggested that local legal services programs may act in concert to initiate class action suits simultaneously on identical issues of law. A search of the sample discovered two such examples. Two class action suits challenging the application of the so-called 'lump sum' rule contained in the 1981 amendments to the AFDC program were retrieved. The first, directed by Rhode Island Legal Services Inc., and directed against the Department of Health and Human Services, dated February 4, 1983, resulted in an injunction in favor of the plaintiffs. The second, directed by the Virginia Poverty Center, also against the Department of Health and Human Services, an appeal dated May 6, 1985, also resulted in the upholding of an injunction in favor of the original plaintiffs. Two class action appeal cases concerning the denial of Medicaid to clients who owned real estate were also retrieved. Both appeals were upheld in favor of the original clients by the United States Court of Appeals for the Fourth Circuit. One case was brought by the Virginia Poverty Center; the other by the North Carolina Legal Services

Resource Center, Inc. The fact that four class action suits out of a total sample of 113 were so interrelated is worthy of note.

4 The attack on the family

The family is the basic institution in society, the most important safeguard of American liberty because it furnishes the independent and self-reliant citizens upon which a limited form of government is dependent (de Bettencourt, 1988). For this reason, when President Kennedy proposed a series of welfare programs to Congress in 1962, he stated that the first principle of a sound welfare policy was to 'stress the integrity and preservation of the family unit'. Chapter 13 indicates the failure of a welfare policy which has served to destroy and not to strengthen US families and which has helped to create a current situation in which 21 per cent of all live births are out of wedlock, 59 per cent among blacks, and in which 80 per cent of single-parent households are headed by women. With family disintegration has come poverty. In 1985, 48 per cent of families headed by women without a husband were categorized as poor. Of those where the woman was under the age of 25 years, 74 per cent of such families were categorized as poor. Welfare reforms initiated through the legal services program have contributed significantly to family disintegration and to single-parent household poverty (Murray, 1984, 1986).

The first series of test cases brought by legal services attorneys, following the establishment of the OEO Legal Services Program, involved the Aid to Families with Dependent Children (AFDC) program. The first Supreme Court case dealing with AFDC, *King* v. *Smith* (1968), was brought by the Center for Social Welfare Policy and Law, supported by *amicus curiae* briefs on the part of Bexar County Legal Aid and Legal Aid Society of Alameda County. In King v. Smith, the legal services attorneys challenged an Alabama regulation that denied AFDC benefits to a woman who cohabited with a man – a rule that was operative in 19 states in 1967. The state argued that the regulation discouraged illegitimacy and fostered familial values. The Court invalidated the regulation because the substitute father 'did not have a state-imposed legal duty to support the children in his house'.

In 1969, legal services attorneys consolidated this attack, once again in a case argued before the Supreme Court. In *Shapiro* v. *Thompson*, the one-year residency rule imposed by the states for welfare applicants was successfully challenged as constituting an unconstitutional restriction on the right to travel. The Court overruled the state's objection that tax payers' funds should be reserved for the state's own citizens. In 1973, in *New Jersey Welfare Rights Organization* v. *Cahill*, legal services attorneys successfully argued before the Supreme Court that the AFDC statute violated the equal protection clause of the Fourteenth Amendment by excluding illegitimate children from benefits. The precedent established by these cases pre-empted attempts by the states to develop programs that favored traditional families.

Since the 1970s, the number of legal services challenges to AFDC regulations provision has increased sharply, both in the federal and in the state courts. Through such test case litigation, a program that was designed initially to support the family has been forged into a welfare support program which encourages the dissolution of families (Murray, 1984). During the early 1980s Congress made several changes in the AFDC program explicitly to reinforce the family as a cooperative, self-supporting group (de Bettencourt, 1988, p. 7). One major change required the states to include the income of all members of a family unit when determining eligibility for AFDC. The income of a spouse and of siblings is deemed to be available to the entire household, except in certain cases. Since these laws were passed and the corresponding regulations promulgated, more than 30 cases have been filed by legal services attorneys, challenging these deeming regulations.

In *Bowen* v. *Guillard* (1987), legal services attorneys from North Carolina, with assistance from the Women's Law Project of Colorado Rural Legal Services, challenged the constitutionality of these regulations, claiming that reduction of AFDC benefits represented in impermissible taking of property without due process. The Supreme Court rejected the argument, and overturned a lower court opinion that would have resulted in $5.2 million additional benefits to welfare mothers in North Carolina alone. The Court held that legislative decisions, even where they may result in inequities, are not unconstitutional.

A second series of cases, challenging another deeming regulation, has also impacted adversely on the family. In order to receive AFDC benefits, minor children who are themselves parents must reside with their parents or guardians. This policy complies with the American tradition that parents are responsible for their children. The Tax Reform Act of 1986 amended the Social Security Act to consolidate this tradition by requiring that when an unmarried mother under the age of 18 years is living with her parents the income of her parents is considered available to the minor and her child. Legal services attorneys have challenged this provision successfully through several federal courts.

In *Jiminez* v. *Cohen*, brought by Community Legal Services of Pennsylvania, a federal court declared that the Secretary of Health and Human Services had misconstrued congressional intent in applying the grandparent deeming provision to 18-year-old minor parents living at home. The court required that the entire class of 18-year-old minor parents be considered eligible for separate AFDC benefits. Similar judgments were handed down in *Cash* v. *Kirk* (North Carolina), and in *Malloy* v. *Eicher* (Delaware).

Legal services attorneys have also challenged state policies that require minor parents who seek welfare benefits to live with their parents or guardians. The Legal Aid Society of Oneida County has filed a class action suit representing minor children who want AFDC benefits without having to live at home (*Nafzinger* v. *Blum*). Legal services attorneys have also successfully challenged a California requirement that minors under the age of 18 must live with their parents to be eligible for AFDC payments (*Hypolite* v. *Carleson*). By rewarding illegitimate childbirth with benefits that carry no corresponding obligations there is little incentive offered for teenage unwed mothers to behave responsibly. A cycle of dependency and deprivation is thus induced which manifests its sad consequences in the statistics reviewed in Chapter 13.

A similar, successful attack on the family was launched by legal services attorneys against food stamp policy. When Congress wrote the Food Stamp Act in 1964, and amended it in 1971, it stipulated that households consist of related individuals – that is, members of a family. This intent has been challenged in a sequence of class action suits claiming that since the food stamp program provided benefits only for family households, it discriminated against households of unrelated individuals, thus violating the equal protection component of the due process clause of the Fifth Amendment.

In *US Department of Agriculture* v. *Moreno*, brought by the Food Research and Action Center, the Supreme Court held that there was no rational basis for legislative discrimination against the class of 'unrelated individuals'. On this ground, the Court invalidated the provision that favored families over non-familial groups. The Court also rejected the stated intention of Congress to eliminate fraud and abuse by preventing such groups as college students and communes from banding together into a household as a means of accessing the food stamp program.

In 1986, the Supreme Court denied another challenge to the household provision in the food stamp program, In *Lyng* v. *Castillo*, legal services attorneys from Texas Rural Legal Aid brought a class action suit to invalidate an amendment to the Food Stamp Act that distinguished between family households and households composed of unrelated individuals, refusing to treat the latter as a single household unless they shared in food preparation and purchasing. Once again, the class action suit alleged violation of the equal protection clause of the US Constitution.

The Supreme Court, in rejecting this argument, overturned a District Court decision. Justice Stevens, for the majority, rejected the lower court's holding that the family was a suspect classification and held that a congressional assumption that families who live together will share expenses is not constitutional discrimination. In other court cases, legal services attorneys have challenged the same provision.

Chapter 13 has demonstrated that the disintegration of families is a major cause of poverty and that the best means of escaping poverty is through family support. Yet, in terms of numbers of cases and resources spent, many legal services grantees give highest priority to divorce proceedings (de Bettencourt, 1988, p. 15). One LSC-funded national support center, the National Center on Women and Family Law, has ventured to argue that mediation – an important means of resolving domestic disputes – should be avoided because the woman is always at a disadvantage (Woods, 1985). Yet single-parent families are five times as likely to be poor as are two-parent families, and much less likely to escape from the poverty situation. Studies indicate that only 47 per cent of women entitled to receive child support actually receive the full amount (Roberts, 1984).

To alleviate some of the problems faced by children after their parents divorce – sexual promiscuity, pregnancy, abortions as well as poverty – family specialists advise that the best arrangement is often joint custody (Miller, 1979). Legal services advocates, however, typically counsel against joint custody, or even arrangements which include frequent visits by the father, so that the mother can receive AFDC (Roberts, 1986). In so doing, such attorneys contribute to the feminization of poverty.

Historically, American courts have insisted on the dependent status of children. Laws supporting parental authority traditionally have recognized that a child needs the care of a responsible adult, ideally of parents, who will transmit high values to their children and raise them to be responsible citizens. In the past, moreover, it has been argued almost universally that the relationship between parent and child transcends state interference. In recent years, however, under the stimulus of legal services attorneys, courts have advanced the privacy of the rights of the individual and have discarded the traditional deference to family privacy (de Bettencourt, 1988. p. 17).

A pivotal component of the legal recognition of the special relationship between parent and child is the parental consent requirement. Parent consent laws are written largely for the protection of the minor, prohibiting or re-stricting their actions with respect to marriage, contracts, and medicare and requiring parental consent. Legal services attorneys have attacked such con-sent laws, and have mounted litigation in pursuit of minors' rights, notably with respect to reproductive rights.

The National Center for Youth Law challenged Utah's parental notifica-tion law for abortions performed for minors, filing a brief in *H.L.* v. *Matheson* (1981) for a 15-year-old pregnant girl, living at home and dependent upon her parents for support, who wanted an abortion without her parents' knowl-edge. The physician, in recognition of the Utah statute, had refused to perform the abortion. The National Center argued that mandatory parental notification violated a pregnant minor's right to privacy. The Supreme Court rejected this plea with Justice Burger, writing for the majority, stating: 'There is no logical relationship between the capacity to become pregnant and the capacity for mature judgment concerning the wisdom of an abortion.' The parental notification statute was legitimate for it 'plainly serves the important considerations of family integrity and protecting adolescents'.

Legal services attorneys have experienced more success in overturning parental consent and notification status in the lower courts. For example, in *Lady Jane* v. *Maher*, attorneys from the Legal Aid Society in Connecticut, successfully challenged a statute that required consent of a legal guardian as a precondition for abortions performed for minors. In *Doe* v. *Zimmerman*, the Central Pennsylvania Legal Services attorneys successfully challenged a Pennsylvania parental consent provision, as well as spousal consent provision.

In yet another attempt to further minors' rights, in *Parham* v. *J. R.* (1979), legal services attorneys from Georgia Legal Services, with the assistance of the National Center of Youth Law, filed a class action suit on behalf of minors who were voluntarily committed to mental health institutions by their parents or guardians. They argued that the children's loss of liberty – their inability to have full adversarial hearings to contest their parents' decision – violated their rights to due process of law. They claimed that minor children have a right to privacy which allows them to make autonomous decisions on important matters, regardless of their parents' wishes. The Supreme Court denied the suit, holding that parents were responsible for the health of their children, and concluding that putting child and parent in an adversarial hearings would be 'at odds with the presumption that parents act in the best interests of their child.'

In another set of suits, legal services attorneys have litigated to attempt to absolve parents from responsibility for their minor children, so far without notable success. In *Payless Drug Stores Northwest Inc.* v. *Brown*, Oregon Legal Services challenged the constitutionality of Oregon's shoplifting statute, which allows stores to sue parents for damages and civil penalties when their children steal. Parental rights, according to this plea, included the right not to take care of one's children. The Oregon court denied the plea. In *Davidson* v. *Duval County School Board*, Jacksonville Area Legal Aid attorneys defended parents of two minors who vandalized state school property on 22 separate occasions, claiming unconstitutional discrimination because parents of children who committed torts in Florida could not be held liable for damages. In *Woe* v. *Perales*, Greater Upstate Law Project filed a class action suit against the New York Medicaid program, claiming as unconstitutional the taking into consideration of the income of parents of pregnant minors in determining eligibility for Medicaid payments. So far, the courts have confirmed parental responsibilities in these matters.

Legal services attorneys have been particularly active in defending the sexual activity of minors, despite the fact that such activity is illegal, and is conducive to all the problems of the unwed teenage mother. The National Center for Youth Law, through its publication, *Youth News*, for example, advocates increasing the number of school clinics that offer contraceptives without parental notification. In *Planned Parenthood Affiliates of California* v. *Van De Kamp* (1986), the National Center filed suit in a challenge to an opinion of the California attorney general which required health professionals to report incidents of adolescents seeking health care for sexual activities as potential cases of child abuse. The Center argued that minors have a constitutional right to privacy – to engage in voluntary sex. The California court upheld this plea, confirming federal and state constitutional protection for voluntary sexual activity even among minors under the age of 14 years. In *Wort* v. *Vierling*, attorneys from Land of Lincoln Legal Assistance Foundation in Illinois represented a pregnant under-age student who had been dismissed from the National Honor Society because of deficiencies in moral character. The district court held that the school had violated the equal protection clause of the Constitution by discriminating against pregnant students.

The most radical separation of the parent from the child occurs with the act of abortion (de Bettencourt, 1988, p. 23). Despite a clear prohibition in the Legal Services Corporation Act, as amended in 1977, against providing legal assistance in litigation concerning abortion, legal services attorneys have been actively involved in most of the major abortion cases filed both in state and in federal courts, filing a large number of challenges to state and federal abortion regulations. In *Planned Parenthood Association Inc.* v. *Department of Human Resources*, Oregon Legal Services represented Planned Parenthood, which is not an eligible client, in a suit challenging the constitutionality of the Department of Human Resources rule that limited the number of elective abortions for which the state medical assistance program would pay. The legal services attorneys argued unsuccessfully that indigent women should have access to an unlimited number of abortions at public expense.

A number of support centers and legal services grantees participated in *Committee to Defend Reproductive Rights* v. *Myers* (1981) seeking unlimited public funds for abortions. Yet others intervened in *Williams* v. *Zbarez* (1980) in a suit to enjoin the enforcement of an Illinois law prohibiting the funding of all abortions except those necessary to save the life of the mother. They argued that Medicaid required states to pay for medically necessary abortions and that since Medicaid paid for other medically necessary services, the Illinois law violated the equal protection clause of the Fourteenth Amendment by not paying for all medically necessary abortions. In *Doe* v. *Zimmerman* (1975), Central Pennsylvania Legal Services filed a class action suit to void a provision for spousal consent and for parental consent for minors with respect to abortions. In *Roe* v. *Casey* (1980), Community Legal Services in Philadelphia contested a Pennsylvania statute that limited the number of abortions for which the state would pay as an unconstitutional infringement of a woman's right to have an unlimited number of abortions.

Parents have a legal as well as a moral obligation to support their children. Yet, a third of all American children live in poverty mostly because they receive no support from their fathers. In 1981, only 35 per cent of single mothers received any child support. By contrast, only 6.7 per cent of families with two parents live in poverty (de Bettencourt, 1988, p. 25). Many legal services attorneys do devote efforts to the collection and enforcement of child support. Others have represented clients who wished to avoid supporting their children; yet others have consulted clients who preferred the security of welfare to parental assistance (Roberts, 1986). For the most part, such behavior is designed to ensure maximum access to the AFDC program, at whatever cost in terms of diminished familial responsibilities.

In one Clearinghouse Review article, the author advised legal services attorneys representing low-income clients seeking divorce to ensure that agreements were signed absolving the absent parent from paying support (Roberts, 1986). This would save such clients from reimbursing AFDC welfare payments received in lieu of child support. Training materials provided by the National Center on Women and Family Law in June 1986 advised legal services attorneys, when formulating divorce agreements, to reduce the amount of visitation time allowed the father and to avoid cash settlements to ensure that the mother would be eligible for welfare.

In *Curtis* v. *Commissioner of Human Services* (1986), Pine Tree Legal Assistance attorneys in Maine filed a class action suit for parents on welfare to enjoin the Commissioner from filing liens on the plaintiff's property or from withholding federal income tax refunds to secure child support debts. In *Thompson* v. *Smith* (1981), San Francisco Neighborhood Legal Assistance Foundation attempted to enjoin the District Attorney's office from seeking reimbursement of AFDC benefits paid for a child on the ground that child support had not been awarded. In *Johnson* v. *Mattison* (1987), legal services from the Volunteer Lawyers Project in Massachusetts represented a client who had been ordered by three different courts to pay child support for four children he had fathered by three different mothers. The court determined that the cumulative amount of court ordered support was too high and limited the client's obligation to a total of $88 per week.

Legal services attorneys have also represented several mothers who refused to identify the fathers of their children, thus barring the state from collecting child support. In *Isaac* v. *Outgamie County* (1983) attorneys from

Legal Services of Northeastern Wisconsin challenged the constitutionality of a paternity questionnaire required for AFDC applicants. The women represented by the class action suit objected to supplying detailed information about their sexual activity sought by the state so that it could identify the fathers of their children. In *Patterson* v. *Michigan Department of Social Services*, Legal Services of Eastern Michigan attempted unsuccessfully to overturn a Michigan Department of Social Services decision finding its client ineligible for AFDC because of failure to cooperate in identifying the father of her child.

In order to expand welfare payments and other benefits to individuals, legal services attorneys systematically have litigated to challenge the constitutionality of the family which is the foundation of welfare policy in America. To this end, they have used the equal protection clause of the Constitution to contest statutes and regulations, with scant regard or total hostility towards the concept of the family central to such legislation. In *Curry* v. *Dempsey* (1983), Berrien County Legal Services attorneys attempted unsuccessfully to expand the AFDC program to non-familial groups by arguing that unrelated legal guardians of minors should be eligible for AFDC benefits. The court denied the suit, holding that Congress had created the program to confront one particular issue of poverty – the disintegration of the family. In *Two Associates* v. *Brown* (1986), the Legal Aid Society challenged a provision of the New York rent control laws on behalf of a client who had been evicted from a rent controlled apartment after his roommate, the holder of the lease, had died from AIDS. The New York Supreme Court held that equal protection required that a gay life-partner be treated as a family member, and called into question any laws that discriminated in favor of 'traditional families' at the expense of other groups.

Because of litigation strategies of test cases and class action suits often filed simultaneously in several states, the legal services programs have exercised a disproportionate impact on family policy relative to budget (de Bettencourt, 1988, p. 29). Their actions have inexorably eroded the family concept in America despite legislation designed explicitly to reinforce that culture. By making individuals rather than the family the basic unit of welfare policy, legal services attorneys have contributed measurably to the problem of feminized poverty.

The harm to poor families that has been inflicted by legal services litigation in part has been intentional, in part accidental. Many legal services attorneys clearly do support a policy agenda that is dedicated to the advancement of alternative life styles, to women's rights or even to child rights and which is pursued at the direct cost of family stability. Others merely respond to the case priorities of their local programs, seeking effective advancements to more lucrative private sector careers. They are also the victims of adverse institutions just as their clients are. The unintended consequences of altruistic preferences in an adverse institutional environment are rarely more clearly evident than in the destruction of families and the feminization of poverty that has resulted from legal services litigation.

5 The attack on the institutions of capitalism

If the attack on the family by legal services attorneys in part has been the unintended consequence of short-sighted altruism, the same cannot be claimed for the unremitting attack on capitalist enterprise that has become a central focus of legal services since 1974. This attack has been partly motivated by the intent of crippling capitalism itself as a precondition for the advancement of socialism. The attack has also been launched for rent extraction purposes (McChesney, 1987, 1989) utilizing extortion techniques to extract side payments for legal services offices and/or for their associates from organizations prepared to buy off the adverse consequences of hostile litigation. In no case has such extortionate behavior acknowledged the economic harm to the poor imposed by actions that slow the pace and distort the direction of capitalist development (DiLorenzo, 1988).

A complete evaluation of the anti-business thrust of legal services litigation is beyond the scope of this book. A partial review centers attention on specific aspects of the attack, notably on agriculture, public utilities, and (particularly) the financial institutions. Legal services lawyers have collaborated with ACORN – an anti-capitalist lobbying organization – in their litigation against these organizations.

The relationship between LSC grantees and ACORN (Association of Community Organizations for Reform Now) was cemented during 1981–82 as part of the LSC's survival campaign whereby the Corporation formed 'networks and coalitions of organizations so as to effectively operate a nationwide grass roots campaign to lobby Congress in support of the policies advocated by the Corporation' (ACORN, 1983). ACORN claims to have affiliated in 25 states. Its 'principal activity is organizing, and all other functions are designed to enhance this capability' (ACORN, 1983). The Washington representative of ACORN recently declared: 'I am a socialist. It's because society is based on collectivity and interpersonal relationships that capitalism will fail' (Hall, January 1984, p. C-3).

The types of policies advocated by ACORN activists are outlined in its 'peoples' platform' which calls for overhauling the economic system. The 'energy plank' (put people before profits at the utilities) indicates that government-owned utilities are preferable to privately operated firms. Utility rates should not be based on the cost of providing service or consumption, but on social considerations. Discontinued service for non payment of bills should be prohibited. Political activists should control state and regulatory commissions. Gasoline, heating oil and propane should be subjected to price controls.

The 'health care' plank calls for a national health care system controlled by community-based committees with fixed salaries for doctors and zero-priced health clinics. The 'housing plank' calls for at least one million new units of federally-subsidized housing each year, rent controls, limitation on eviction of non-paying tenants and myriad housing subsidies. The 'jobs and income' plank proposes augmented government employment, a guaranteed annual income for everyone and various workers' rights, all financed by taxation. Other planks propose more progressive income taxation and compulsory worker representation on corporate boards of directors. The justification for these efforts according to the ACORN Organizing Manual is that people are 'getting nailed' because 'a bunch of corporate directors and New York bankers have the power to unilaterally make decisions that affect the lives of ACORN members' (ACORN, 1983).

To these ends, ACORN has established a political action committee, has participated in state and local initiative campaigns, and claims to have 'shared experiences since 1972 with legal services programs ... through a variety of training programs, consultations and publications' (ACORN, 1983). LSC grantees typically provide legal and financial assistance for political activists employed by ACORN. For example, Community Legal Services of Philadelphia provided legal representation for ACORN on a variety of issues including 'challenging [bus] fare increases ... electric company increases ..., water and sewer rate increases, negotiating with the state Insurance Commissioner regarding "redlining" practices of insurance companies and challenging automobile insurance rate increases' (DiLorenzo, 1988, p. 12).

Legal services attorney, Will Collette, explained in ACORN's journal, *The Organizer*, how legal research might be an important tool for ACORN activists. (Collette, 1982, p. 27). He outlined the importance of LSC training described as 'action research ... which can serve two strategic purposes: identifying a constituency for your campaign and, second, getting the goods on your target' (Collette, 1982, p. 23). The targets are usually businessmen. Political agencies are taught that county courthouses contain a goldmine in damaging information about such individuals. For example, divorce proceedings with 'messy property settlements' are 'an especially useful weapon'. Such personal information about a target can provide activists with leverage.

Legal services attorneys have directed a significant litigation attack against farmers and the mechanization of US agriculture. In 1979, as part of this anti-farmer campaign, the LSC established a special budget line earmarking funds for migrant farm worker advocacy. LSC attorneys have been extremely active throughout the 1980s in organizing farm labor, agitating strikes and imposing restrictions on farmers which both reduce the number of agricultural jobs and increase the prices of agricultural produce. A few examples illustrate the nature of the attack.

An attorney from Texas Rural Legal Aid encouraged farm laborers harvesting perishable goods to strike, despite attempts by their employer to negotiate, according to an affidavit by a farm labor contractor (Legal Services Corporation, 1988e). In consequence, the farmer lost 47 800 cartons of lettuce. The farm labor contractor stated that 'the farmers ... lost over a half a million dollars because I could not get the men back. I personally lost income and lost income for my men of over $75 000'. According to the contractor's statement, Jesus Moya of the International Union of Agriculture and Industrial Workers accompanied the TRLA lawyer and promised each farm laborer $5000–$15 000 if they would allow TRLA attorneys to file suit.

In another case, dismissed by the judge as a frivolous action (Legal Services Corporation, 1988e), Farm Workers Legal Services of North Carolina brought suit on behalf of clients, Sherman and Debra Paulk, against the Department of Labor and the Virginia Agricultural Growers Association for refusing to provide transportation advances to US migrants. The judge's opinion stated: 'I believe ... that the Paulks were no more than pawns in the hands of the FLS and that many of the counter-claims and cross claims promulgated on their behalf were frivolous.'

The Legal Services Corporation and its grantees are prohibited by statute from inciting workers to strike. However, a comic book distributed by Texas Rural Legal Aid and by California Rural Legal Aid depicts the American farmer as a greedy, overweight pig. Farmers are portrayed as refusing to listen to their worker's demands. The CRLA version of the comic ends with the declaration: 'STRIKE' (Legal Services Corporation, 1988e). No disciplinary action has been taken by the LSC for this statutory infringement by a significant grantee.

Lopez-Rivas v. *Donovan* (1986) illustrates how legal services attorneys pursue activities that harm their clients. The Migrant Legal Action Program, a national support center funded by LSC, represented a class of migrant Puerto Rican workers, claiming that, under the Wagner-Peyser Act, the defendant apple growers were obligated to hire them because the growers had advertised positions. The plaintiffs claimed, in effect, that the job offer constituted a unilateral contract requiring the growers to hire them. They claimed damages for mental anguish, loss of income and expenses incurred in preparation for their trip to the United States. The judge found this allegation to be absurd holding that the purpose of the Wagner-Peyser Act was to match job offers and applicants throughout the nation. It was not a contract of employment. In dismissing the case, the judge stated: 'Stretching our limited jurisdiction on such frail grounds may work to the detriment of precisely this distressed group ... in view of the likelihood of reduced job offers due to the growers' possible abandonment of the system that would expose them to the onerous effects the plaintiffs propose.'

The most significant and potentially the most damaging attack on US agricultural productivity launched by legal services attorneys involves a suit over agricultural mechanization research. The suit was brought by the LSC-funded California Rural Legal Assistance on behalf of 19 migrant farm workers and a coalition (now defunct) of labor and agricultural reform groups calling itself the California Agrarian Action Project. The target of the law suit is the agricultural mechanization research program of the University of California at Davis.

The CRLA alleges that the mechanization program is designed to replace workers with machines, that such mechanization would eliminate small farms, will concentrate production and raise prices to consumers, that it will 'have a severe detrimental effect on the quality of life in rural California and that it will assist California agri-businesses in attempting to thwart the effects of farm workers to act and bargain collectively'. This Luddite suit first went to court in 1979 and still has not been resolved, since the plaintiffs appealed the 1987 judgment for the defendant. CRLA has expended more than $1 million on the case, to the detriment of other potential clients of legal services. It is difficult not to view this suit as a case of legal services running amok.

The representation of poor clients in utility cases has always been a concern of local legal aid offices. Power cutoffs and rate increases are issues which commonly confront potential clients on low or fixed incomes. Some legal services attorneys, however, have pursued issues well beyond this remit, often with end results which increase the cost of utility provisions, as part of elaborate social engineering programs.

In *Northern States Power Company* v. *Hagen* (1982) the National Consumer Law Center represented a client in a suit designed to force a power company to average natural gas rates across two geographic regions. The Supreme Court of North Dakota overturned a lower court judgment for the plaintiff holding that no benefits accrued to users in one of the groups. The net effect of the lower court decision, and the intent of the legal services lawsuit, was pure redistribution: lower prices for one group, higher prices for another, and no change in service.

In 1987, Palmetto Legal Services went before the Public Service Commission in South Carolina to protest a proposed rate increase in bus fares in Columbia and Charleston. The then current fare was 25 cents. The company had received its last increase in 1982 and was losing $7.9 million annually before taxes at the 25 cent fare. Legal services attorneys exercised no foresight that their protest might lead to service withdrawal with serious consequences for low-income residents of Columbia and Charleston.

In a New York administrative law case, the judge recommended that the Public Service Commission mandate a $14.5 million rate increase for the year starting February 15, 1988. The power company had earlier requested a rate increase of $14.1 million. The court determined that $11.2 million should be 'flowed back' to the rate payers. The Public Utility Law Project, a legal services support center, pressed the court to enforce short-term 'flow backs' despite carefully argued warnings by the utility that such an order would affect its finances adversely and result in an increased cost of capital, raising utility prices in the longer term to the disadvantage of low-income consumers. The judge found in favor of the utility and endorsed its proposed flowback plan.

The Legal Services Corporation is an important component of a political coalition that has been labelled the anti-energy industry (DiLorenzo, 1988, p. 15), and which uses tax funds to promote an anti-energy agenda. The strategy of this coalition was clearly exposed in *Simer* v. *Olivarez*, a class action suit brought by legal services attorneys against the federal Community Services Administration alleging the mis-appropriation of funds earmarked for energy assistance to the poor. Some $18 million had not been expended by a deadline set by Congress and was to be returned to the US Treasury. Legal services attorneys rounded up eight plaintiffs in a class action suit enjoining such a return of funding (three of the plaintiffs later stated that they had no knowledge of the suit and the others claimed that they had been steered into it). The suit was settled out of court, with each of the plaintiffs receiving $250. The remaining $17 998 000 was to be divided between the National Consumer Law Center, the Citizen/Labor Energy Coalition and other activist groups for further energy advocacy programs.

The court subsequently determined, however, that the bargaining between legal service attorneys and CSA was a conspiracy to expropriate taxpayers' money and to fund an anti-energy campaign. The strategy was for CSA to leave congressionally ear-marked funds unspent, then have the legal services attorneys sue to retrieve the funds for themselves and other activists. The judge revealed the conspiracy and foreclosed on the redistribution.

Another display of disregard for the poor is a statement made by a representative of the LSC-funded National Consumer Law Center regarding the proposal to spend some of the revenues from the federal Windfall Profits Tax imposed on the oil industry for low-income energy assistance:

> It would be a real crime if, after ten years and $50 billion or so [from the tax] that poor people ... had absolutely nothing to show for all that money spent other than the fact that it passed through their hands into the oil companies. (DiLorenzo, 1988, p. 16)

The legal services activist suggested that, instead of giving the money to the poor, as Congress intended, it should be spent on energy advocacy, which, for the most part, must be read as 'anti-energy industry' advocacy. Legal services activists favor alternative energy, i.e. solar power to oil, natural gas or electricity, but not if provided by capitalist enterprises. They have complained that private companies 'are investing in solar technology that is too durable, that is excessively efficient in converting sunlight to usable energy and that requires ... little maintenance' (DiLorenzo, 1988, p. 17).

Perhaps the most effective attack launched by legal services attorneys against the institutions of capitalism is that targeted on financial institutions – banks, mortgage companies, insurance companies and the like – exploiting leverage offered by legislation. These institutions comprise an important segment of the US capital market, which plays a crucial role in the relative success or failure of the US economy in an increasingly competitive world market.

An efficient capital market exercises ultimate control over capitalist enterprise, ensuring that resources flow to the most efficient suppliers of commodities in volumes that correspond to the prevailing configuration of consumer preferences as reflected in the willingness-to-pay principle. Any intervention that impedes capital market efficiency, including the raising of the cost of financial services, threatens capitalism, encourages technical inefficiency in production and overall inefficiency in the allocation of scarce resources. Legal services attorneys have played and continue to play a pivotal role in this distortive exercise. Their role is not an unintended consequence of altruism, but rather an important plank in an explicit anti-capitalist agenda:

> You can bankrupt the capitalist system through legal action ... (James D. Lorenz, Jr, founder of California Rural Legal Assistance)

Of course, legal services attorneys have long represented clients in disputes involving personal financial matters, including problems with landlords and creditors. Such representation constitutes an important element of the right to civil justice and of any effective rule of law. In recent years, however, legal services attorneys, funded in whole or in part by the Legal Services Corporation, have invaded a wholly new arena, challenging major financial institutions, in a compact with community activists, by threatening the use of legislation to raise their costs of business should they refuse to make specific side-payments to named groups and organizations. Examples of such behavior are here restricted to the Community Reinvestment Act 1977. Similar behavior is associated also with the Home Mortgage Disclosure Act 1975 (Bradford and Schersten, 1985) and the Equal Credit Opportunity Act 1976 (Hally, 1988).

The Community Reinvestment Act (CRA) came into effect in 1978 and imposed on regulated financial institutions an affirmative obligation to help meet the credit needs of the local communities in which they are chartered, including low- and moderate income neighborhoods, as long as such obligations are consistent with the safe and sound operations of such institutions. As a Barron's editorial commentary, entitled 'Shades of Willie Sutton'! intimated this Act was 'a triumph of the unlamented era in which government was widely viewed as the solution, not the problem' (Bleiburg, 1987). The Act was not much utilized in the 1970s since it was drafted to meet either a non-existent need or a largely fictitious threat, ... the threat of redlining, the allegedly systematic, discriminating refusal by commercial banks to make mortgage loans to borrowers in low-income or blighted neighborhoods. However, the law stayed on the books, quietly ticking away like a time bomb. In 1985, that bomb was activated and exploded on the US banking system.

In 1985, a Supreme Court ruling made it possible for the states to authorize some form of regional banking, opening up opportunities for the acquisition or merger of commercial and savings banks across state lines. All 50 states legislated to take advantage of this judgment, unwittingly offering a rent-seeking opportunity to legal services programs and to community activists who moved to exploit the CRA provisions in a newly destabilized banking environment.

Under the CRA, groups or individuals are afforded the opportunity to lodge protests regarding a financial institution's reinvestment record whenever that institution files for a merger, acquisition, relocation, expansion, or to receive federal deposit insurance. Depending on the nature of the institution, such protests are reviewed by the Federal Reserve Board, the Comptroller of the Currency, the Federal Home Bank Board, the Federal Insurance Corporation or the Federal Savings and Loan Insurance Corporation. When a protest is filed, the organization with oversight authority investigates its merits. If merit is found, hearings may be required before approval of an application is granted. Even though hearings have been rarely required in the history of CRA protests, any protest automatically results in a delay of application approval, sometimes of several weeks, but frequently of several months. This potential delay is the lever that is exploited by legal services attorneys.

Delayed mergers may cost banks millions of dollars in legal fees and in foregone business, costs which must eventually be paid for through higher fees charged to the bank's customers. Legal services attorneys and associated community organizations threaten to stall bank mergers by lodging protests unless the banks give them money or earmark low interest loans or grants for projects proposed by the organizations. Many banks accede to this extortion rather than risk high cost delays under CRA procedures. According to DiLorenzo (1988, p. 11) some $5 billion of CRA concessions were made by US banks to avoid CRA protests over the decade 1978 to 1988. The large majority of these concessions were extracted after the 1985 Supreme Court ruling on inter-state banking.

The number of cases handled by the Federal Reserve Board alone rose from two in 1978 to more than 30 in 1987. Thirteen of the 25 holding banks were challenged on CRA grounds during this short period. One LSC group has announced publicly that, as a matter of course, it will protest every bank merger application filed in its region (DiLorenzo, 1988, p. 11). Legal services attorneys have held meetings with Federal Reserve officials in Atlanta in 1987 to learn more about CRA protest opportunities. This information has been relayed to CRA activists in training sessions that have been organized on a nationwide basis. A May 1986 document circulated by the North Carolina Legal Services Reserve Center and Central Florida Legal Services, entitled 'Some Notes on Negotiating CRA Agreements', discloses the intent of the protests:

> You are playing a game of chicken. The bank does not want you to file and pursue your protest, you don't particularly want to file it either. What you both want is to reach an agreement which will assure that your clients improve their ability to obtain banking services. Pursuing the protest only helps your clients if by doing so you can obtain better promises from the bank regarding those services. The protest itself doesn't accomplish this. What the protest does do is cost the bank money. You know these facts, and the bank knows you know these facts. You need to convince the bank that you will really go over the edge – and pursue the protest – unless the bank agrees to needed terms ... The most powerful way you can use these tools are as threats – as once they are used, they lose their potency.

This bank extortion strategy has been perfected by ACORN, advised and supported by legal services attorneys. ACORN participated in 30 bank merger challenges nationwide in 1986 alone. Indeed, ACORN has furnished a pictorial image to celebrate its CRA triumphs. The cartoon depicts a tree thickly covered with leaves of dollar bills. The branches of this tree hang beyond the grasp of those reaching for its greenery. A second caption features a character sporting an ACORN cap and holding a hatchet labelled CRA. The Money Tree then is cut at the trunk and is ready to fall to the ground, its dollar-decorated branches in easy access to those anxious to seize its fruits. ACORN shows no awareness in this cartoon of the truth that money does not grow on trees.

Following the ACORN-LSC lead, community groups have negotiated charitable contributions from banks as a common feature of CRA agreements. For example, Landmark Bank of St Louis agreed to lend $6.5 million in specified business and housing loans, including $500 000 at rates 4 per cent below market. In addition it provided $10 000 to ACORN and other groups as an outright gift to assist the publication of their programs (American Banker, 1986). In 1987, when Riggs National Bank of Washington, DC acquired First Fidelity Bank of Rockville, Maryland, Riggs committed a minimum of $50 000 per annum of its charitable contributions to community organizations. As part of its agreement to branch into Arizona, Chase Manhattan was obliged to place $100 000 on five-year deposit in an ACORN credit union and to make a gift of $100 000 to Arizona non-profit groups in 1987. In the same year, First National Bank of Chicago committed more than $500 000 in grants for community activities. Among these grants was a stipend of $30 000 to enable a leading organizer of CRA protests, the National Training and Information Center (NTIC), to rehabilitate an abandoned Chicago beauty school as its main office (Schmitt, 1987).

The NTIC claims to be a center for training, information, consultation, technical assistance and research. It subdivides its activities into various categories, notably, state and local activities, corporate negotiations, demonstrations, conferences and seminars on special issues, providing training and technical assistance, publishing books and pamphlets, testifying before congressional committees and lobbying. NTIC concentrates on supporting community organizations, coordinating many of its activities with those of the National People's Action. In 1986, in Chicago alone, the NTIC negotiated over $200 million in lending agreements with four major Chicago banks.

Over the period 1985 to 1987, more than 25 legal services grantees and at least one national support center were involved in organizing and/or representing community activist groups (not individual poor clients) in protesting financial mergers and acquisitions through the CRA. Two legal services employees, Margot Roten (North Carolina Legal Services Resource Center) and Carl Webster (Central Florida Legal Services) produced a 13 point guide for legal services attorneys in negotiating CRA agreements. Legal services attorneys have compiled a Community Reinvestment Act Manual, a legal consortium containing important CRA information for potential CRA protesters.

In September 1985, legal services attorneys protested the proposed merger between the First Union Corporation of North Carolina and Atlantic Bank Corporation of Florida under the CRA, claiming that the Florida bank discriminated against the poor and minority groups in its distribution of loans. The Federal Reserve Board was asked to block the merger unless the banks set aside $50 million for low interest mortgage and business loans to poor and black neighborhoods. The program must also utilize minority-owned advertising corporations and must require the appointment of minority members to local boards of directors.

Jay Rose of Greater Orlando Legal Services Inc., one of the protesting attorneys, stated 'we intend to use the CRA to ensure that regional banking opens the doors of the banks to poor people and minorities in the state of Florida'. The protest further required the banks to donate at least $500 000 per annum to community development programs. Mr Crutchfield of FUC condemned these requests as a form of blackmail. An agreement was negotiated, nevertheless, whereby FUC guaranteed that minority firms would receive a 10 per cent share of its general advertising assignments and that needy neighborhoods would receive a series of special loans.

Legal services attorneys have been especially active in threatening CRA protests in Florida and in the Carolinas, usually filing protests on behalf of community development organizations, minority business interests or ad hoc groups. Eligible individual clients are rarely represented by legal services attorneys in CRA protests. Prominent among legal services protests have been the mergers between Citizens of Southern Corporation of Atlanta and Landmark Bank Corporation of Fort Lauderdale (1985), Suntrust Banks Inc. of Florida and a Tennessee bank holding company (1986), Barnett Banks of Florida and the Home Federal Bank of Florida and United First Federal Saving and Loan (1986), and South Carolina National Bank and the Bank of Fairfield (1987). In each case, the protests were withdrawn upon the payment of protection. The National Economic Development and Law Center exercised a pivotal coordinating role for legal services attorneys in Georgia, South Carolina, Tennessee, Alabama, Mississippi, Louisiana, Texas, Missouri, Washington and California as the CRA protest strategy expanded.

The CRA is a further example of the unintended consequences of well-motivated legislation. No doubt many of the government bank regulations were intended to ensure that depository institutions would serve the convenience and needs of their communities while protecting the safety and soundness of their investments. Contrary to this intent, the CRA has become a tool used to reallocate credit. This reallocation carries with it adverse implications for economic efficiency, retarding the process of wealth creation and deepening the incidence of localized poverty in the US.

A 1981 study by the Federal Home Loan Bank Board concluded that, while CRA shifts housing-related credit into low-income areas, the increase is only temporary. If banks determine that operating in a community is too costly, they find ways to leave that community, or curtail their service provisions. Those who fail to do so raise doubts concerning soundness and safety that not infrequently result in liquidation. Banks are now failing at the highest rate since the Great Depression. In 1986, the US commercial banks charged off $17 billion in bad debts, as compared with only $28 billion for the entire 30-year period, 1951 to 1980. From 1979 to 1986, the annual loan losses provisions of the banks tripled from 0.24 per cent to 0.76 per cent; ignoring Third World debt. The CRA pressures a banking industry already in serious trouble with bad loans to worsen its competitiveness by ignoring prudent banking practice and forcing them to finance high risk clients (Barker, 1985).

Financial markets are no longer localized in the wake of the information technology revolution. In a competitive world market banks will survive only if they optimize investment portfolios, specialize and regroup. If market process is impeded by inappropriate legislation and by redistributive legal services interventions, capitalism will be damaged and the problem of long-term poverty will be significantly accentuated. Only those who pursue a rent-seeking agenda and who do not care about the poor benefit from the CRA protest strategy.

6 The attack on Republicanism

Legal services in America has been subverted from its original purpose of providing poor clients with a right to justice into a major program of activist law reform. To this end, litigation has been utilized to attack the principle of Madisonian republicanism. Reformist legal services attorneys, dissatisfied by the relatively slow pace of law reform, have turned their attentions to the vote mechanism in an attempt to strengthen the representation of redistributionist groups within the federal, state and local legislatures. Redistricting and reapportionment activities form a major focus of this essentially self-serving strategy.

The principal national goal of the Legal Services Corporation is the provision of basic legal services to eligible poor individuals. To this end legal services grantees are precluded by statute from engaging in political activities. Yet, legal services grantees have expended legal services appropriations on redistricting and reapportionment matters to a degree that stimulated the LSC in Fall 1989 into the promulgation of a final rule prohibiting such behavior:

> 'Involvement' means the use or contribution of LSC or private funds, personnel, or equipment in redistricting activities and 'redistricting' means any direct or indirect effort to participate in the revision or reapportionment of a legislative, judicial, or elective district at any level of government, including the timing or manner of the taking of a census. (Legal Services Corporation 45 CFR 1632, August 1989)

Substantial policy considerations underpinned this ruling by the Board of Directors of the Legal Services Corporation. First, redistricting cases are not peculiar to the interests of the poor, since the relief sought typically affects entire communities composed of non-poor as well as of poor individuals. Since the poor represent a minority (7 to 14 per cent) of the United States population, the group of eligible poor in most communities is relatively small. Thus, since most redistricting cases are class actions, and certainly affect large blocks of residents, the putative plaintiff class often consists of a majority of ineligible individuals.

Similarly, the relief sought in redistricting cases often would not go to the poor. This is so even in cases involving discrimination issues, since only a small part of the protected minority typically is eligible. Consequently, the expenditure of recipients' funds on redistricting commonly results in an allocation of resources for the benefit of non-eligible persons.

Second, redistricting cases generally have not been identified as a priority by LSC recipients. A 1987 survey of the types of cases handled by LSC recipients revealed that approximately 27 per cent of the cases involved family matters, 21 per cent involved housing, 16 per cent involved income maintenance and 12 per cent were consumer-related. Yet, LSC programs have committed considerable resources to redistricting litigation. The Corporation estimated that at least 28 000 hours were devoted to handling redistricting cases from 1978 to 1984, years surrounding the 1980 Census. Three recipients, Legal Aid Society of Central Texas, California Rural Legal Assistance and Mississippi Legal Services Coalition, claimed that voting rights or redistricting cases were priorities for their programs.

Third, LSC determined that recipient funds could be better used elsewhere. Alternative organizations and private attorneys are available to handle redistricting matters. Such cases usually provide incentives to members to the private bar since, under the Voting Rights Act, 42 U.S.C. 1973, and the Civil Rights Attorneys' Fees Award Act of 1978, 43 U.S.C. 1981 and 1988, the right to recover attorneys' fees is specifically given to prevailing parties. Redistricting matters are also undertaken by such organizations as the Mexican American Legal Defense Fund, the Southwest Voters Registration Project, Common Cause, the American Civil Liberties Union, the Native American Rights Fund, the NAACP, the Lawyers Committee for Civil Rights, the League of Women Voters, the Democratic National Committee and the Republican National Committee. In such circumstances, it is not economical to channel legal services funds into a massive effort that does not primarily affect the poor.

Fourth, the past involvement in redistricting activities by legal services recipients has been subject to abuse. Legal services attorneys have linked their redistricting activities to obtaining favorable support from Congress for their own parochial objectives. One LSC recipient openly addressed this issue in its grant proposal (Federal Register, August 3, 1989) arguing that it must involve itself in State and local redistricting matters in order to develop powerful political allies in the battle over the direction of legal services programs. By influencing redistricting, the recipient clearly hoped to affect the political character of the legislatures in the United States.

In 1984, the Senate Committee on Labor and Human Resources requested that the LSC should conduct a study of its grantees to determine the extent and nature of their involvement in legislative redistricting activities relating to the 1980 Census. As a result of two separate monitorings and 34 responses to an LSC questionnaire mailed to all LSC grant recipients, LSC estimated that at least 28 182 hours had been spent on the handling of legislative redistricting cases. These resources had been diverted from eligible poor clients seeking legal services in legitimate areas.

The LSC study determined that clients only rarely visited legal services offices to complain that they had been malapportioned. Yet, LSC recipients had sought resources for specialized computer equipment and for computer specialists to draw new election district boundaries. In addition, recipients had hired lobbyists to work on reapportionment issues in the absence of any documented requests from eligible clients or elected officials that they should undertake such activities. This behavior was in evident contravention of section 1007 (a) (5) of the LSC Act. Further, recipients had sought to orchestrate a state-wide effort of legal services programs to ensure the election of specific individuals who would be relied upon in turn as powerful allies in anticipated battles over funding for legal services programs.

The LSC study revealed that certain LSC recipients had requested and had received federal funds from the LSC to establish a Voting Rights Project Center for the purpose of strengthening Mexican–American political power via the 1980 Census. There had been no request from eligible clients for such an initiative. The grant recipients had prepared a voting rights litigation manual outlining how to locate and to solicit clients for a redistricting battle.

Finally, the LSC determined that redistricting risks entanglement with political activities. In this judgment they cited *Gaffney* v. *Cummings* (1973) to the effect that politics and political considerations are inseparable from redistricting and apportionment. The LSC Act explicitly declares that, to preserve its strength, the legal services program must be protected from political pressures. The LSC Act specifically prohibits legal services involvement in any political activity.

Yet, LSC recipients have been actively involved in reapportionment cases on behalf of both the Democratic and Republican parties (*Upham* v. *Seaman*, 1982; *Thornberger* v. *Cingles*, 1986). Such activities risk an impermissible political alignment under the Act and may well distort the processes of republicanism (Crain, Davis and Tollison, 1990).

7   Conclusions

The conclusions drawn from this survey of the consequences of legal services are bleak for those who view the program as an important foundation of the right to justice for poor Americans. The staff attorney model of legal services delivery appears to be technically inefficient by comparison with other delivery modes and to be excessively prone to class action forms of litigation. Legal services attorneys appear to have abused their organizations' discretionary power by litigating for law reform rather than to resolve the legal problems of individual clients. Their litigation, by outcome if not always by intent, has been damaging for the central pillars of the United States economy, namely the family and the institutions of capitalism. Further, they have attacked the electoral foundations on which the calculus of constitutional consent must ultimately rest. The evidence reviewed supports overwhelmingly the hypothesis outlined at the outset of this book that constructivist rationalism has defeated methodological individualism in the provision of legal services and that law reform has defeated the right to justice as the central focus of the political market in civil justice.

This outcome is not to be viewed as the accidental consequence of specific individuals or as the temporary impact of an organization that has yet to locate its equilibrium. The existing political equilibrium is strong, as the Reagan White House found to its chagrin, and as the Bush White House has been quick to acknowledge. Yet, it is an equilibrium that depends upon the rational ignorance of the electorate and upon the persuasive authority of powerful special interests who also control the press and the television media. Ultimately, it cannot be an equilibrium that satisfies the legitimate expectations of the many poor individuals who are turned away from legal services offices or who are provided with inadequate legal support by attorneys anxious to pursue career and political agendas that offer no place for routine legal service.

A market in which suppliers do not sell, in which customers do not buy and in which those who fund the service cannot influence its direction ultimately is no market at all. There must be – and indeed there is – a better way to furnish the poor with access to civil justice, a method of supporting the right to justice which is less vulnerable to rent-seeking and less susceptible to political manipulation. Chapter 16 charts such a route to reform in legal services which appears to be feasible from the perspective of public choice.

Part VII

TOWARDS TOMORROW

16 The route to institutional reform

Then out spake brave Horatius,
The Captain of the Gate:
'To every man upon this earth
Death cometh soon or late.
And how can man die better
Than facing fearful odds,
For the ashes of his fathers,
And the temples of his gods?'

Thomas Babington Macauley, *Lays of Ancient Rome*

1 Introduction

The political market in legal services has been scrutinized in detail in this book, its principal actors clearly identified and their behavior evaluated, through the lens of Virginia political economy. Only by refracting seemingly inconsistent, even random, behavior through this lens has it proved possible to assemble the complex jig-saw puzzle of legal services and convincingly to make sense of past events. As the true image of this Dorian Gray emerges to displace the artifact inculcated by special interests on a rationally ignorant electorate an opportunity emerges for significant institutional reform which yet may offer indigent US citizens a reasonable access to civil justice.

The task remains for this chapter to define a superior and yet feasible organization structure sufficiently attractive to a decisive potential political coalition as to offer a realistic prospect for root-and-branch reform. The approach adopted is thus not that of social engineering but rather that of locating a Schelling point (Schelling, 1963, 1984) and offering it to a better informed political market as a testable proposition that it is to be preferred to the status quo (Buchanan, 1959).

Section 2 of this chapter reviews the US legal services market from the perspective of Chicago political economy, outlining the questionable assumptions that are necessary to endorse as efficient the staff attorney model of legal services provision. The bizarre nature of Chicago's tight prior equilibrium approach becomes obvious in this evaluation. Section 3 replaces the Chicago public interest mirage with a cold dash of public choice reality and demonstrates the superiority of Virginia's diffuse prior equilibrium approach in the analysis of political markets. Section 4 reviews in depth the nature and consequences of a class action test case litigated by legal services lawyers against the State of Florida to highlight the strength of the Virginia case for institutional reform.

Once institutional defects have been identified, and a case for institutional reform established, judgment can be entered on the respective merits of piecemeal and root-and-branch organizational reform. Section 5 outlines the public choice route on which any program of institutional reform must hinge. Section 6 outlines the minimal requirements for a half-way house program of piecemeal reform that would yet retain the staff attorney model of legal services provision. The vulnerability of this piecemeal reform to ongoing special interest group pressures and its likely long-term non-viability is established. Section 7 concludes the book with a proposed voucher solution to the problem of legal services provision which holds out some prospect of frustrating the existing wealth transfer special interests by shifting market power in favor of individual clients and which appears to be feasible and durable given the identified constraints of the US political market.

2 The mirage that what is is efficient

An outline of the tight prior equilibrium approach of Chicago political economy, and of its implications for political market analysis, is presented in Chapter 3. The salient features of this research program are revisited in this section with specific regard to the staff attorney model of legal services provision.

More than most economists, Chicagoans view competition as endemic in society, especially in private markets (Mitchell, 1989). Markets are characterized by low information costs and high resource mobility. In consequence, wealth is maximized by the unregulated market interactions of resource constrained utility maximizers. Market failure is rare, even by comparison with ideal standards and is absent within a comparative institutions framework.

This predilection presents a potentially serious problem for a research program grounded on the axioms of rational behavior and dedicated to the empirical testing of its theories: how is the rapid growth of government in the twentieth-century democracies to be reconciled with the wealth-enhancing power of private markets? The answer, supplied by Stigler (1971) and by Peltzman (1976, 1984) and by Becker (1983, 1985), is that redistributive motives have come to dominate those of wealth creation, and that government is the efficient vehicle for such redistribution. Ultimately, for Chicago, the cost of transfers is merely the ordinary cost of doing business and political markets act as efficiently as private markets in satisfying the redistributionist predilections of the late twentieth-century democracies.

Chicagoans share with Virginians a recognition that political markets are characterized by peculiarly attenuated property rights – rights that can be shaped by rational political actors. In the absence of institutional adjustments certain consequences mostly harmful for efficiency follow from that fact. Voters cannot sell and buy votes on an open market, bureaucrats cannot capture for themselves the wealth that they might create from efficient choices and politicians cannot openly appropriate for themselves the wealth that might ensue from an efficient legislature. Left unresolved the consequences are potentially harmful for the economic performance of the political market place.

Nor is this all. These same property right alternatives define whose wealth is spent by whom on whom, a consideration of great significance in distinguishing private from political markets (Mitchell, 1989, p. 285). Those who are decisive in political markets may spend their own wealth or that of others and they may expend it on behalf either of themselves or of others, or they may allow still others to do the same. In contrast, private markets are dominated by the spending of one's own wealth upon oneself, with a price mechanism, largely absent in political markets, channelling individual choices into efficient resource allocations.

Chicagoans rely upon assumptions of low information costs and high resource mobility to safeguard political markets from these apparent public choice dilemmas. If voters individually are rationally ignorant, then returns exist for informed political entrepreneurs to provide information as a vehicle for gaining political office. The development of party brand names and candidate reputations reduces yet further the cost of information acquisition by rational voters (Wittman, 1989). Efficiency does not require informed voters, any more than efficient private markets require all stock holders to know the intimate workings of the firms in which they hold stock or all principals perfectly to monitor their agents.

Chicago recognizes the potential threat to efficiency in the form of divergences between private and social cost classically manifest in the majority's ability to shift the costs of its policies onto an unwilling minority. They claim following Coase (1960) that such a divergence will exist only if transaction costs are high. They argue that democratic political markets are structured to reduce such costs. For example, majority rule, instead of a unanimity requirement, prevents monopoly hold outs, thereby lowering negotiation costs. Representative rather than direct democracy and a federal rather than a unitary system of government are other democratic designs to lower decision-making costs. The small number of members in the House and in the Senate is designed to lower negotiation costs and to create the conditions for efficient logrolling and vote trading (Wittman, 1989).

Efficient exchanges are further facilitated by the committee system of Congress which allocates assignments to committees according to those most interested in the issues at hand. The committees are designed with strictly limited range so that the negative externalities that they can impose on others are likely to be slight. The committee structure also creates property rights which allow committees to logroll among themselves at relatively low cost (Wittman, 1989).

To the extent that some committees may be viewed as representing special interests, the latter's influence is weakened by the existence of other committees, such as Budget and Appropriations, that take a more global view. Furthermore, national political parties exist to take credit for national policies and to internalize the negative externalities that might arise from local interests trying to shift costs onto other districts. In this perspective, the political party is an efficiency enhancing coalition that facilitates Pareto-improving trades, restrains opportunism and is ultimately responsible for assigning its members to committees in a welfare enhancing manner (Wittman, 1989). In this view, the party majority would not make assignments that would result in wealth destructive legislation. Even the existence of cycles and the opportunity thus provided for agenda manipulation does not imply inefficient outcomes. It provides the agenda setter and his constituents with greater political wealth, since agenda setting rights will be traded for the most highly valued output (Wittman, 1989).

Although Olson (1965) and Niskanen (1971) have warned of the governance problems that permeate political markets as a consequence of principal–agent problems between voters and their representatives (exploited by special interests) and as a consequence of principal–agent problems between representative government and its bureaucracies, (exploited by the senior bureaucrats), these potential inefficiencies are played down in the Chicago research program. In this respect, Chicagoans rely upon Becker's notion that interest groups minimize the deadweight loss of public policies as an unintended consequence of inter-group competition (Becker, 1983, 1985; Stigler, 1988) and upon Fama's notion (1980) that the internal and external labor markets monitor shirking behavior out of bureaucracy. In this perspective, competition, low transaction costs and low information costs combine to avert to disperse prisoners' dilemma situations and to ensure organizational efficiency.

Every operative public policy has deadweight losses – costs that have no corresponding benefit to any party directly involved in the policy. Tax payers end up with larger reductions in income than the treasury receives because of collection costs, because of constraints imposed by law upon the tax payers and because of the cost of actions taken by tax payers in response to taxes. Similarly, the beneficiaries of a public policy receive less than the amount disbursed by the treasury, again because of administrative costs, because of the regulatory restraints imposed upon the recipients and because of their behavioral adjustments. Becker (1983, 1985) has utilized this calculus of deadweight losses to model interest groups as welfare maximizing institutions essential to the efficiency of political markets. For political success competing coalitions of such interests must so organize themselves and behave as to select policies, including the size of policies, that minimize deadweight losses.

In developing this theory of pressure groups, Becker parts company sharply with old Chicago nostrums (Friedman, 1962) as well as with Virginia political economy, and rejects the notion that voters can be fooled systematically in any way. It is the comparative size of deadweight losses and not the rational ignorance of voters that determines the forms and amounts of political transfers. The fact of survival of various in-kind transfers indicate they have proven to be relatively efficient means of income redistribution given certain elasticities of political market demand and supply, and given relevant information and transaction costs. There is no publicness problem in collective action, and no asymmetry in special interests accessing the political market.

Within this new Chicago political economic vision to say that something exists is to say that efficiency prevails; for that which does not prevail cannot be efficient. In such a vision, if yesterday does not unfold, itself into tomorrow, change is not to be viewed as the reaction to perceived past errors or indeed as the consequence of errors newly committed. For error cannot or will not be accommodated in Chicago theory. Rather perceived change must be the consequence either of exogenous adjustments in individual preferences and/or of exogenous changes in technology. Throughout unfolding history, scholars are mere spectators and scholarship a means of understanding and interpreting but never of effectively impacting on the evolution of political markets. Ideas do not matter and economists who preach simply waste their time (Stigler, 1988b). 'Jerusalem' is feasible, indeed will be achieved by rational, utility maximizing individuals moving across economic and political markets in response to economic stimuli.

In this section, the staff attorney model of federal legal services is reviewed, within the framework of Chicago political economy, as if it represents such an efficient political market equilibrium. It is important to emphasize that this rationalization represents no more than a testable hypothesis, dependent entirely upon the political market assumptions that underpin it, and falsifiable in terms of the available evidence as outlined in this book.

In the interpretation of Chicago, the domination of the US Congress by attorneys must reflect the preferences of well-informed and rational voters in favor of the legislative and brokering skills of individuals trained in the law. Similarly, the preponderance of attorney representation on the committees and subcommittees of the House and the Senate charged with oversight and appropriations responsibilities for the Legal Services Corporation must reflect transaction cost advantages in legal specialization. The decentralized nature of the subcommittee structure also must reflect gains-from-trade obtainable through logrolling and vote trading, and the greater responsiveness of small and specialized decision-making bodies to the preferences of the median voter. In its institutional complexity, the giant jigsaw puzzle of the Congress must convert the preferences of rational voters into efficient legal services provisions, given environmental constraints.

To this end, the significant interest groups in the legal services market – the American Bar Association, the NLADA, the PAG, the national support centers, the state and the local legal services programs as well as the coalition of specific minority groups – must reflect the preferences over legal services of the median US voter and must be viewed as supporting methods of legal services provision which minimize deadweight losses for society as a whole. By comparison, the weak or non-existent interest groups in the legal services market – the individual poor, the farmers, business groups, bankers, and merchants, as well as the tax payers – must be viewed as unrepresentative of median voter preferences, or as passively acquiescent in the policies of the dominant interest groups. The 1974 Legal Services Act, as amended, must be interpreted as the efficient outcome of a deadweight cost minimizing legislative process in which a well informed electorate imposes its majority will through a low cost network of interest group coalitions.

The Act itself must be endorsed as being carefully devised to allow the special interests responsible for its passage to breach the specific wording of the statute without fear of legal retribution. The voters must have been fully aware of such drafting, its intent and its probable consequences, and indeed must have endorsed the legislation in full recognition of its nature. The Congress must be viewed as efficiently protecting the bureaucrats who divert the legal services program from access to justice to law reform by techniques explicitly prohibited by the statute. The wording of the statute itself must be viewed as rhetoric, a charade in which all actors recognize as being intentionally barren of meaning. If a US President should mistake rhetoric for reality and attempt to move the Corporation into compliance with the Act, Congress must be viewed as efficiently aborting his interventions and upholding the original intent, and the gains from trade that are dependent on it. If attempts are made by what must be a temporarily misguided Corporation to restrict grantees from lobbying Congress for self-serving purposes, then Congress must be viewed as intervening efficiently to protect the lobbyists whose behavior is a predictable component of the initial political compact. Lobbying is wealth-enhancing, indeed is an essential component of the perceived gains from trade that induced the initial legislation.

The consequences of legal services litigation as outlined in Chapter 15, for the family, for capitalism and for republicanism must also be interpreted as part of the rational expectations in the original political compact. As such, they constitute efficient end-states of an efficient political market process, and not the unintended consequences of flawed legislation. If class action suits are widely employed, then they must reflect voter preferences effectively transmitted at relatively low cost into the policy supply mechanism and pursued through an efficient court process. If the staff attorney model appears to be technically inefficient, this can only be because important output characteristics are not properly accounted for. For error is impossible in the choice of the instruments of supply. If wealth transfers are executed in kind rather than in cash any apparent excess burden must be a chimera, to be explained away as an efficient consequence of paternalistic concerns for the welfare of the poor rather than as the wasteful consequence of political market failure, of voter error or of interest group distortions.

The political equilibrium that currently exists in the US legal services market must reflect a Pareto-equilibrium despite the chronicled evidence of some voter and interest group dissent. The robustness of the equilibrium, even in the face of presidential attack, must indicate that it continues to pass the Kaldor–Hicks potential compensation test, that those who gain from legal services provisions can overcompensate those who lose. In the judgment of Chicagoans, therefore, there can exist no Pareto-preferred move from the partial equilibrium that is observed, given voters' preferences over legal services policies and given the alternative technologies of legal services provision.

3   The realities of political market failure

The world as envisaged by Chicago economists is almost unrecognizable to Virginia scholars grounded in the public choice research program pioneered during the early 1960s by Buchanan and Tullock (1962). Yet, the generating assumption of the public choice program, like that of Chicago, is homo economicus, even perhaps narrow wealth-seeking man. Indeed, if utility maximization assumptions were to be challenged, say by some public interest alternative, both Chicago and Virginia political economy would be no more. It is with respect to auxiliary hypotheses that the diffuse prior equilibrium approach of the Virginia program departs categorically from that of Chicago.

For Virginians, unlike contemporary Chicagoans, the future is a murky environment shrouded in a Knightian (1921) uncertainty which cannot be countered efficiently through portfolio diversification alone. The present is also characterized, at least with respect to political markets, by a pervading voter ignorance that is the rational individual response to political market indivisibilities. Access to political markets by interest groups is characterized by asymmetries that derive from a combination of rational ignorance and knowledge specialization driven by the logic of collective action logic outlined in Chapter 3 (Olson, 1965). Even where potential gains from trade are perceived, prisoners' dilemma situations may put them out of the reach of those who seek them out, in the absence of effective entrepreneurship in institutional design.

In such an environment, government is envisaged more often than not, as a problem rather than as the solution. Homo economicus is less sure footed and more error prone in political than in private markets, driven more by preferences and less by constraints and thus more prone to ideological diversions from a still predominantly wealth-seeking agenda (Rowley and Wagner, 1990). Vote paradoxes that manifest themselves in cycles and opportunities for agenda manipulation abound. In consequence, political equilibria are often not unique and do not reflect median voter preferences, which themselves in no sense necessarily reflect Pareto optimality (Rowley, 1984). Nor does the cost of government typically represent the ordinary minimal cost of doing business, but rather is reflective also of X-inefficiencies (Leibenstein, 1966) as well as of rent-seeking and rent-protective outlays (Tullock, 1967b) all of which dissipate the wealth of a nation (Tollison, 1989).

In the Virginian perspective, political markets are not necessarily always efficient and are not continuously reordered by competing interest groups to minimize social cost (Rowley and Vachris, 1990). Indeed, the presumption of the Virginia research program is that political markets are allocatively and technically inefficient, that they are grid-locked by entrenched interests and that there are often better and cheaper ways of going about business. In this sense, the approach is utilitarian or classical liberal and essentially reformist (Rowley and Wagner, 1990; Tollison, 1989), and not merely interpretative as is the case with Chicago. Ideas do matter, and what is is not always efficient (Rowley and Wagner, 1990).

In this section, as throughout this book, the staff attorney model of federal legal services is reviewed, within the framework of Virginia political economy, as a political equilibrium characterized by serious inefficiencies, both technical and allocative in nature. Chapters 6 to 15 chronicle the serious nature of this failure of the political market in legal services by reference to the right to justice intent of the 1974 Act and the harmful consequences of this failure both for poor Americans and for the wealth of the nation.

Chapter 6 outlines the opportunities that exist for senior executive discretion within the Legal Services Corporation and explains how such opportunities survive despite the legislative safeguards of congressional oversight, as a consequence of an inescapable principal–agent problem. The chapter employs the Niskanen model of bureaucracy to predict early tendencies within the LSC bureaucracy to maximize the size of their discretionary budgets, and to over-supply their products by reference to median voter preferences. Evidence strongly supports this model over the period 1974 to 1982 of rapid bureau expansion. By modifying Niskanen's theory through the application of ideological constraints, Chapter 6 also predicts the sharp reversal in legal services budgetary ambitions following the replacement of the Corporation Board of Directors by Reagan nominees in 1982.

Chapter 7 shifts attention from the Corporation itself to the wider jigsaw puzzle of the US Congress and to the executive branch of government in order to evaluate the nature of political market equilibrium and the dynamics of disequilibrium adjustment within the federal legal services program. The chapter identifies the intricate system of truncated property rights that has emerged within an increasingly specialized US Congress to enable vote- and wealth-seeking politicians to control the federal program of legal services and to direct that program on behalf of powerful constituency interests. Given the rational ignorance of individual voters concerning legal services, the constituencies served tend to be the powerful interest groups that demand legal services policies, notably the American Bar Association, the Rainbow Coalition, the organized legal services field, the state and local legal services programs and the national legal services support centers. Particularly notable for their absence as effective constituents of the US Congress are those poor Americans in whose name and on whose behalf the rhetoric of right to justice is promulgated.

The domination of the executive branch by the Congress with respect to legal services policy is chronicled in Chapters 11 and 12 which record the major budgetary battles, the battles over appointments to the LSC Board, and the battles between the Congress and the LSC Board, all of which were persistent features of the two Reagan presidential terms. The ultimate victory of the Congress over the President, which manifested itself in congressional budgetary dominance and in the weakening of LSC Board governance over the federal program, reflects the powerful grip of special interests over a Congress that in other policy areas proved to be supportive of a popular and strongly-mandidated President. The large majority of voters are seen to have been totally unaware of the existence of a federal program of legal services, and the poor themselves to have been the hapless victims of a program of law reform in which they played no significant role and which played itself out to their long-term detriment.

Chapters 13 and 14 demonstrate the way in which the special interests first crafted and then manipulated the federal program of legal services as a vehicle for their own self-serving agendas. These chapters bear witness to the entrapment of the politically helpless poor into a situation of long-term, inter-generational poverty as law reforms systematically eliminate self-help incentives, feminize poverty and foster racial discrimination. Chapter 15 identifies the damage wrought by the dominant minority-based interest group coalition upon the technical efficiency of legal services provision, upon the concept of justiciability in the litigation process and even upon the validity of the class action suit.

In this Virginian perspective, the federal program of legal services is dislocated almost entirely from the individual concerns of poor Americans. It becomes instead a powerful mechanism for social engineering controlled by a well-heeled minority coalition of elitist constructivist rationalists. As such, it represents a continuing threat to the central pillars on which a large majority of Americans mark out their Dream: the family, capitalism, and republicanism. As such, what is quite evidently is not efficient. Indeed, the case for root-and-branch institutional reform appears to be particularly attractive to a potential vote majority and even to be endorsable by a decisive interest group coalition if rational ignorance can be moderated and the logic of collective action ameliorated by skilled political entrepreneurs utilizing the evidence of this book. This indeed is the testable proposition developed in the closing sections of this chapter. First, however, the myth of the efficient class action suit must be identified and exposed.

4 The myth of the efficient class action suit

Test cases and class action suits are permitted by law. They are attractive litigation instruments for legal services activists because they can make a great deal of difference to a great many individuals very quickly. Because they play such a prominent role in the legal services program, perhaps accounting for one-third of the outlays of the national support centers and more than one-fifth of the outlays of the local programs, Chicago economists must endorse them as a cost-effective component of an efficient litigation system (Posner, 1986). Virginian political economists, however, will reach an altogether more circumspect judgment, noting significant potential inefficiencies in an unconstrained use of these powerful legal instruments.

Test cases, in which a single decision affects a large number of individuals, have been part of the US legal system since its early origins. The history of civil rights litigation leading up to *Brown* v. *Board of Education* is an outstanding example of how the law can be reformed and improved by the strategic use of a series of test cases. However, it is the class action suit which best exemplifies the logic of legal services law reform and which has become, apart from illegal political lobbying, the leading instrument of law reform utilized by legal services attorneys. Nor is this surprising. For the change in Rule 23 of the Federal Rules of Civil procedure governing class actions, introduced in 1966 coincidentally with the beginning of the OEO Legal Services Program, has proved to be pivotal in the use of the courts by attorneys to achieve law reform.

Under the old version of Rule 23, the members of the class who could be represented in an action were restricted to those individuals who knowingly acknowledged their membership. Under the revised version, the membership of the class includes every individual who falls within the definition set out by the attorney who files suit in a case, whether or not such individuals agree with the merits of the case, or are even aware of its existence. The only way that an individual who satisfies the attorney's definition would not be treated as a participant in the case is if that individual explicitly informed the court that he or she did not wish to be so considered. This presumptive membership concept has been a key factor in permitting a wide range of class action suits to be brought to the court under the rubric of helping the poor (Murray, 1986, p. 30).

Clearly, within the context of the Virginian concept of efficiency as based on contractual consent, there is a potential in such situations for damage as well as benefit even when the circumstances of eligible poor clients alone are under consideration. Several categories of class action suit can be distinguished from this perspective. In the first category, all members of the class would endorse the suit if asked, and there are no losers from the suit in the unrepresented poor population. This category would be endorsed both by Chicago and by Virginia as unambiguously efficiency-enhancing. In category two, all individuals represented in the suit would endorse it, if asked, but some members of the unrepresented poor population would not. The gainers potentially can over-compensate the losers; but compensation will not be paid. This category would be endorsed by Chicago, though not by Virginia (Buchanan, 1959). In category three, some members of the suit, as well as some of the unrepresented poor, would not endorse the suit. In both sub-groups, the potential compensation test is satisfied, but compensation is not paid. This category would also be endorsed by Chicago, though not by Virginia.

In category four, some within the suit would endorse it, but some would not, as with the unrepresented poor population. The gainers within the represented group cannot compensate the losers; overall, however, the potential compensation test is satisfied, but compensation is not paid. This category would also be endorsed by Chicago, though not by Virginia. In category five, all members of the class would endorse the suit, but some members of the unrepresented poor would not. The gainers cannot compensate the losers. This category would be rejected both by Chicago and by Virginia. In category six, the gainers cannot compensate the losers either within or without the represented group and the potential compensation test fails completely. This category would be rejected both by Chicago and by Virginia. In long-run equilibrium, Chicagoans would deny the continued viability of category five and of category six class action suits.

Two kinds of legal services attorney can be distinguished with respect to class action suit litigation, namely those (type one) who are concerned with the well-being of all members of the class (as each member subjectively perceives that well-being) and those (type two) who are concerned with their own paternalistic (or self-seeking) vision of the welfare of society. Type one attorneys would file suit under categories one, two, three and five, but would forego litigation with respect to categories four and six. Type two attorneys would file suit in all categories, one to six if the class action suits satisfied their own reform agendas. Table 16.1 outlines the various litigation outcomes:

Table 16.1   The class action suit judgment call

Type of Class Action	Chicago	Virginia	Type One Attorney	Type Two Attorney
Category One	File	File	File	File
Category Two	File	Do not file	File	File
Category Three	File	Do not file	File	File
Category Four	File	Do not file	Do not file	File
Category Five	Do not file	Do not file	File	File
Category Six	Do not file	Do not file	Do not file	File

In terms of this categorization, it is pertinent to evaluate the efficiency characteristics of a class action suit successfully filed against the State of Florida by *Bay Area Legal Services* involving a series of trials and appeals culminating in *Debra P.* v. *Turlington* (1983). This suit persuaded the federal district court to prevent the implementation of state-wide functional literacy tests as a prerequisite for high school graduation. The prohibition was granted because the high failure rate on these tests among black students was deemed to be attributable, in part, to past discrimination. At issue is the question of the efficiency or inefficiency both of the initial decision to file and of the ultimate judgment of the court.

In this class action suit, the target was a statute enacted in the State of Florida which imposed a literacy test as a prerequisite for obtaining a high school diploma. Students who failed this test, and who could not remedy the initial failure even following remedial assistance, could not receive a high school diploma. In consequence, they entered the labor market with two handicaps, namely a fundamental inability to read and write, and a missing credential, the absent diploma, which signalled this weakness to perspective employers. Since high school diplomas are widely recognized as effective incentives for academic achievement and as efficient filters of prospective labor market quality, the statute, prima facie, appears to be efficient. A public school system, especially, in the absence of such a constraint, otherwise might accede to parental pressure and weaken incentives to effective scholarship as well as diluting the value of the filter by allowing inadequate scholars to graduate.

By ruling against the statute, the court unambiguously lowered the value of the high school diploma to all who would pass the literacy test and graduate as effective scholars under the statutory constraint. The court simultaneously raised the cost to employers who henceforth must screen prospective employees by testing them for literacy even when they carry the diploma or who must assume the risk that illiterate employees may be hired into positions that demand the minimal ability to read and/or to write. The court simultaneously imposed long-term harm on those marginal high students who would have worked to achieve literacy under the lash of the statute, but now who will take their diploma and proceed to a lifetime of illiteracy. In so far as their incapacity for legitimate employment ultimately might lead such graduates onto the welfare rolls or into the criminal environment, the population at large also suffers.

Let us now review the initial decision to file suit by reference to Categories One to Six outlined above. The State of Florida, in 1982, had a population of 10.4 million individuals, the vast majority of which were harmed by the court's judgment. The public school system, in that year, contained 96 000 high school seniors, of whom only 3000 were denied diplomas because they had failed to pass the literacy test. Of those 93 000 who graduated, 48 000 all (presumably) functionally literate, proceeded to go to college and would not use their high school diplomas as their main academic credentials. Of the remainder, 45 000 were harmed as the value of their diploma plummeted both in Florida and elsewhere, given the publicity that the case received, while 3000 benefited, at least in the short term. Of those who would have failed, approximately 2720 were black and 280 were non-black, a ratio of almost ten to one. The number of black seniors in the Florida state school system was approximately 16 000.

In such circumstances, the utilitarian judgment, both against filing suit and against striking down the statute, is overwhelming. Categories one through four simply do not apply. Furthermore, the criterion embodied in category five also fails since the large majority of black students represented by the suit was seriously harmed by the removal of the test. Even ignoring non-blacks completely, the gainers even potentially could not compensate the losers given the nominal imbalance between those blacks who achieved functional literacy and those who did not (approximately 13 200 as compared with 2720). Category six, however, is the relevant perspective for the suit under consideration. Only the type two, law reform activist, would rationally file suits in such circumstances. Of course the suit was filed and was successful. No doubt any requests for counter-suits by poor but literate blacks were screened out as socially unacceptable by Bay Area Legal Services attorneys exercising their monopoly discretionary powers. Litigating against literacy thus becomes a sadly predictable consequence of the staff attorney model of legal services provision.

Consider now the alternative scenario, in the absence of a legal services program, of the failing black student whose parents might contemplate litigation to mitigate the misery of his plight, and who might approach an attorney, pro bono, to review the situation. How would the attorney proceed? In the circumstances outlined, there would be no test case filed against the State of Florida. The private attorney is unlikely to be a law reform activist. Even if he were, the high cost to his practice of such major pro bono litigation would dampen his appetite for social engineering given the preponderance of the utilitarian case against such action even within the subgroup of poor black students.

Instead, more limited and more practical help might be offered, perhaps by calling on the school system to use the threat of litigation as a means of negotiating extra schooling for the student, an extra year of high school eligibility or some other out-of-court arrangement whereby the student learns to read and write. If negotiations should fail and litigation follow the test case itself would arise as a by-product of individual client litigation and not as a preconceived component of a social agenda. Alternatively, the attorney might simply advise the parents to accept the literacy handicap of their child and have him specialize in some area of comparative advantage that does not require a minimal level of literacy.

Under current legal services arrangements clear incentives exist for Category six class actions suits to be filed and, periodically, to succeed, in some cases with staggering costs to the class that has been represented.

5   The public choice route to legal services reform

The evidence systematically compiled in this book, and filtered through the lens of public choice, provides an extremely unflattering perspective on the legal services program. A program that entraps the poor into long-term poverty and which seeks to replace individual freedom of choice by paternalistic social engineering has no place in classical liberalism. A program that pursues law reform in defiance of the utilitarian calculus, even when applied exclusively to the poor, and which offers those that it purports to represent virtually no opportunity to pass judgment on its agenda, has no place in any contractarian ethic. A program which fails to deliver any redistribution of wealth to the poor, which further impoverishes them by taking away their independence and which dissipates the federal appropriations to their program in rent-seeking waste and in corruption must be given short shrift by the liberal democrat. A program that purports to weaken property rights by attempting coercively to redistribute wealth through the political market place will find no favor among conservatives. Only those small yet politically influential groups that rent-seek into the program, together with those who fret at the absence of an effective political platform for Marxism in America, shall find favor with the legal services program in its present form. Inevitably, these last mentioned groups will be significantly over-represented in the federal program of legal services.

If this judgment is correct the case for institutional reform, whether in piecemeal form or in root and branch reorganization, is worth consideration even if it depends upon some significant dislocation in the current, apparently robust political equilibrium. In particular, should the contents of this book be directed by effective entrepreneurs at the state and local bar associations in a program designed to dispel rational ignorance concerning the damaging long-term political agenda of SCLAID within the American Bar Association and its coalition allies, there is a prospect that legal services can be redirected from supporting law reform towards accessing civil justice. For such a social movement to succeed bar members would need to coordinate their vote power to remove from office those bureaucrats who currently control the political agenda of the ABA, and who ultimately bear responsibility for almost everything that has been chronicled in this book.

Public choice clearly indicates that only by effecting a long-term policy change within the body of the dominant interest group in the legal services political market can institutional reform effectively be pursued. Such a sea change predictably will not occur in response to scholarship on legal services alone. Fortuitously, there is a much wider public unease concerning the hidden political agenda of the organized bar, triggered by recent experiences in the appointment of Supreme Court justices and by the intransigence of the ABA against outside requests both for deregulation of the law and for higher internal ethical standards. This unease, which has culminated in a pitched internal battle over the issue of abortion policy, provides a realistic reform platform for the alert entrepreneur.

The poor of America stand to benefit greatly should the vote motive of the bar overwhelm the autocracy of its parent body and return legal services in America to the tasks for which originally it was created. Among existing entrepreneurs who might move to help them, HALT, an Organization of Americans for Legal Reform, must be a prima prospect. Two routes to institutional reform will vie for consideration within such a reformist movement.

6   Testable hypothesis one: Piecemeal, halfway house reform

The preamble to the Legal Services Act 1974 sets out the mission statement for the program in terms that categorically emphasize the importance of facilitating access to civil justice for poor individual Americans. Section 1001 of the Act is exceptionally clear in this regard:

The Congress finds and declares that:

1. there is a need to provide equal access to the system of justice in our Nation for individuals who seek redress of grievances;
2. there is a need to provide high quality legal assistance to those who would be otherwise unable to afford adequate legal counsel and to continue the present vital legal services program;
3. providing legal assistance to those who face an economic barrier to adequate legal counsel will best serve the ends of justice and assist in improving opportunities for low-income persons consistent with the purposes of this Act;
4. for many of our citizens, the availability of legal services has reaffirmed faith in our government of laws;
5. to preserve its strength, the legal services program must be kept free from the influence of or use by it of political pressures; and
6. attorneys providing legal assistance must have full freedom to protect the best interests of their clients in keeping with the Code of Professional Responsibility, the Canons of Ethics, and the high standards of the legal profession.

This mission statement has not been honored by the Legal Services Corporation and its grantees at any time throughout the period 1974 to 1990. Initially, the Corporation encouraged its grantees to pursue law reform as part of a perceived anti-poverty program, though it refrained from openly supporting illegal behavior. During the struggle for survival, 1981 to 1982, the Corporation joined with its appendages in clearly illegal as well as extra statutory behavior relying upon the wording of the statute to secure it from the penalties that would apply to any federal bureau that so behaved. From 1983 onwards, the Congress has ensured that attempts at good governance by a reformist Corporation Board must fail and has thus secured the law reform propensities of the American Bar Association from White House pressures.

Suppose, however, that the state and local bar associations were to overcome free-rider problems, recognize the public goodwill that can be garnered from internal bar associations reforms and succeed in ousting the self-serving autocracy that currently controls the agenda of the American Bar Association. What are the minimal reforms that they might contemplate should they attempt to re-assert the primacy of the right to justice over law reform within the framework of a staff attorney legal services program?

First, and fundamentally, the reformist ABA is likely to recognize that the federal program of legal services, though likely always to be the dominant, is by no means likely to be the exclusive, component of the overall supply of legal services to the poor. Private funding for legal services field programs has risen consistently throughout the period 1974 to 1990, and accelerated sharply from 13 to 25 per cent of total funding during the two terms of the Reagan presidency. Such private funding could be expanded by persistent state and local bar association advocacy. In addition, a reformist ABA would place much more emphasis than its predecessor upon energizing the pro bono publico ethical responsibilities of bar members, not least by requiring financial contributions from those who refuse to honor their ethical vows by making an in-kind contribution. A feasible goal might be a matching program in which federal dollars were matched equally by private dollars supplemented by in-kind contributions. Such a balance would defuse the political charge surrounding the Legal Services Corporation, would widen the support services of the local programs and would deflect tax payer resistance. In such circumstances, a federal appropriation stabilized in the region of $250 million in real 1990 terms might prove to be a negotiable equilibrium. With 12.5 per cent of the federal funding also allocated to Private Attorney Involvement Programs, as required at present by Part 1614 of Chapter 16 of the Code of Federal Regulation, the private bar would gain access to a lucrative market and would do well while doing good (Tullock, 1984).

Second, a reformist ABA would acknowledge the serious problems of governance that arise when federal monies are expended through a private corporation which is itself exempt from legislation that constrains the behavior of the executive branch of government. In this respect, the anomalous status of the LSC, imposed by the ABA in 1974 upon a severely weakened President, with the help of a Congress then alienated from the executive branch, may be viewed as having outlived its purpose. The Legal Services Corporation has not escaped political pressures as a consequence of its status – but rather has succumbed to the wealth dissipating pressures of special interests who have taken advantage of its discretionary powers to invade the organization itself as a low cost means of achieving politically divisive law reform agendas.

By reconstituting the Legal Services Corporation as an agency within the Department of Justice, the ABA would reduce the discretionary powers of the Corporation by placing its employees under federal civil services rules and by exposing its political lobbying to Hatch Act constraints. Congress has shown interest in such a relocation. With ABA support, the necessary statutory adjustments would have bipartisan appeal within the legislature, provide the principals with increased authority over their agents and thus rein in the lobbying and law reform aberrations of the staff attorneys and their associates. As a federal agency, the LSC and its grantees would be subject to some 27 federal anti-fraud and anti-abuse statutory provisions, including the False Claims Act, the fiscal constraints of Title 31 and various provisions of the Federal criminal code. At present, the Department of Justice cannot prosecute under these statutes because of the non-federal status of the LSC.

Third, the reformist ABA would seek to establish and implement a system for the competitive award of all grants and contracts within the field program and eliminate the presumptive refunding characteristic of the current program that is perceived widely as a hindrance to innovation and cost effectiveness in legal services delivery. Once awarded, grants are currently protected from competition by law. In the absence of egregious violations of the law, recipient organizations are guaranteed funding renewals. This guarantee, combined with inadequate oversight by the Corporation of its outreach programs, denies both to the poor American and to the American tax payer the efficient utilization of resources dedicated to the legal services program.

The reformist ABA would anticipate vigorous lobbying against this proposal by existing grant recipients. For competition rarely, if ever, is welcomed by those who enjoy monopoly control over the supply of a service, with the discretion that such control provides. Yet competition is almost always welcomed by customers, and most particularly by customers who do not buy and who, therefore, cannot exercise the threat of exit as a financial sanction on unacceptable supply behavior. In areas such as legal services where the suppliers often have strong ideological preferences competition narrows the range of suppliers' discretion and allows customers some freedom of individual choice and some ability to avoid socially engineered solutions. Albeit, given the monopolistic nature of staff attorney supply, only at the moment of contract auction will customers be able to mark out their preferences (Rowley, 1989b).

The federal government itself recognizes the importance of competitive tendering when contracting out supply to private corporations. After four years of debate, the Congress included in the 1989 Appropriations Act a provision directing the LSC to develop and implement a system for the competitive award of all grants and contracts to take effect after September 30, 1989, and following the replacement of the Reagan-appointed LSC Board of Directors by appointees of President Bush. Opposition to this provision from the legal services field programs has been well coordinated. It will take a determined ABA initiative to move the jigsaw puzzle of Congress into activating this important reform, and to provide for sufficient flexibility in the legal services budget to allow the Corporation to audit its current grantees.

Fourth, the reformist ABA would harness its interest group strength to dispense with the national support centers and thus to shut down much of the social engineering impetus within the federal program of legal services. From the perspective of the logic of collective action (Olson, 1965), this will be a hard-fought battle since the support centers are allied closely with other groups active in law reform (Chapter 14). Ultimately, however, the bar will win this battle given its captive membership and its extensive penetration of the legislature. In reality, the justification for the support centers has disappeared since poverty law is well established and widely disseminated. Staff attorneys who must lean on such support centers for legal advice have little prospect of making any significant career in the law. Computer techniques widely available in private practice offer a much less costly access to legal research. The demise of the support centers is a good idea whose time has come.

Fifth, the reformist ABA would seek to reroute legal services into its statutory mission by circumscribing class action litigation. For Chapter 15 clearly identifies the social engineering that this category of law suit has facilitated and section 4 of this chapter defines the limited and shaky ethical basis on which the class action suit can be endorsed. In restricting class action suits, the criteria will focus on who should be represented and not on the social implications of that representation. Law reforms that occur as byproducts of individual client representation are inevitable in any system of justice that is not set in stone. Reforms that proscribe all attacks on stare decisis and all questioning of the public law would harm both efficiency and liberty.

Indiscriminate class action suits which reference unknown clients in a coordinated bid by staff attorneys to impose their own policy agendas on society fall into an altogether more dubious category, however, and one which a reformed ABA might choose to scrutinize much more circumspectly. Perhaps the single most important reform of legal services, indeed, one which would solve a large proportion of what is currently wrong with legal services, would be a regulation proscribing legal services attorneys from representing anyone who has not visited a program office and provided written confirmation of a wish to be represented. If every legal services case were associated with named clients who have requested assistance in resolving a particular dispute, the thrust to law reform would lose much of its current force and activist attorneys would no longer find the legal services office such an attractive place in which to practice law.

Because this reform would reach out to the heart of the activists' agenda, it would be fiercely opposed by the organized field and by the local programs as well as by the egregious coalition of minorities who pursue their own reform agendas through the legal services outreach. It is on this issue also that the resolve of the state and local bar associations is likely to be vulnerable since successful class action suits undoubtedly open up lucrative channels for private litigation. The counter case will be advanced with vigor that the class action suit is the litigation weapon for the poor best suited to counteract the political lobbying of the rich, and that the ends justify the means. The case study of the Florida anti-literacy class action suit was interwoven into this chapter as a categorical rejection of this line of reasoning.

There is nothing in the bona fide client requirement that would prevent any grantee from filing a suit on behalf of a group, or from trying to establish or to change a legal precedent if that is helpful to the clients' case. The requirement would restrain grantees from manufacturing groups with causes that would not have existed in the absence of legal services intervention and would limit the damage to the rule of law that legal services' license and the courts' carelessness with respect to notions of standing and of justiciability have unquestionably imposed.

Sixth, the reformist ABA might contemplate the introduction of a co-payment scheme into legal services designed to test out the intensity of client preferences and thus to ration legal services provisions in favor of those poor individuals who have much rather than little to gain from accessing civil justice. Chapter 9 outlines the possibility in any market where customers encounter a zero price of clients accessing the commodity although their marginal valuations for the product are well below the marginal cost of supply to the disadvantage of those who would benefit greatly from it. A small co-payment requirement, say, of between $4 and $10 per litigated suit, would choke off such wasteful ventures without seriously isolating the determined poor from access to civil justice. The large majority of individuals with reported incomes of less than 125 per cent of the poverty level make discretionary outlays of $10 or more on commodities high in their preference priorities.

In order to allow staff attorneys to cater for genuinely hard cases, legal services programs might be allowed to remit the co-payment charge in say 10 per cent of their cases without incurring the budget cut that otherwise might be mandated. Such limited discretion appears to work well in the British system of legal aid which requires co-payments both as a signal of services client intent and as a means of rationing an otherwise open-ended system of support. Local legal services programs would also be free to utilize their private resources to counter the federal co-payment requirement should they consider this to be a cost-effective policy, consistent with the preferences of their major donors.

The institutional reforms set about above will not come to pass unless a large number of individuals change their minds over legal services, acknowledge the errors of the past and conclude that there is a better way (Murray, 1984). Evidence compiled in this book and evaluated through the powerful lens of public choice may focus minds but cannot change ideologies. The persons who must change their minds to prevent the institutions of tomorrow from mapping out as replicas of those that exist today are not conservatives, nor are they classical liberals. The swing votes within the local bar associations and among the wider public will come from the ranks of those moderate liberal democrats who once may have flirted with the Great Society Program. For the most part, they will shift position, if at all, not through altruism but through enlightened self-interest.

They will change their minds only by coming to terms with three important fallacies that shape their adherence to the current legal services program, namely that the poor are a class of people with common interests, that the destitute client is pitted in legal battle against a rich adversary, and that the Legal Services Corporation is the omniscient and impartial servant of the public good. These false images do not survive the examination accorded to them by this book. The entrepreneurs of legal services institutional reform will need to draw these fallacies into the open and to argue against them aggressively not least within the state and the local bar associations.

If there are different kinds of poor people with differing and even conflicting interests, a legal decision that goes in favor of one may prove to be directly and tangibly harmful to another. An even-handed system of justice will refrain from using the resources of government to promote social and economic causes that benefit some kinds of poor people and hurt others. It will concentrate instead on reviewing the request of each individual client on its merits and on providing each poor client whose case has potential merit with his justified day in court. It is arrogant and it is foolish for lawyers to think that they know what is good for the poor. If there is one lesson to be learned from the Great Society Program, it is how easily good intentions can produce bad results. Legal services grantees for the most part have not chosen to learn that lesson. The swing voters may yet come to recognize that it is the business of a legal services lawyer not to champion causes, but, rather, to protect a client's interest as that client himself perceives that interest to be.

The typical legal services case does not pit a destitute client against a multi-millionaire not least because the paths of two such persons very rarely cross. More commonly, it pits individuals of limited resources against other individuals with limited resources, the difference being one of degree. The borderline between poverty and non-poverty may be no more than an income difference of 1 per cent and a successful legal services suit thus may force a marginal business venture into untimely bankruptcy. In such circumstances, the poor client still deserves his day in court. Yet, the less than wealthy defendant deserves some protection against the crusading class action suit launched against him by an agency which is far better endowed with the resources of prosecution that he is with the resources to defend himself. In the American system of civil justice, unlike the British, the losing plaintiff may not be required to meet the costs of the successful defendant.

Even when the defendant is a government agency, the legal services lawyer is not always pitted against a powerful adversary supported by the unlimited power of the right to tax. The typical local public bureau does not have a large legal office with no other business except to defend itself against legal services law suits. Nor is it endowed with limitless clerical resources to provide the detailed records that legal services lawyers can demand under the complex regulations surrounding government grants. Government agencies dedicated to the service of the poor can be severely hindered in their activities by legal services orchestrated attacks of the kind urged in training sessions by members of the national support centers as outlined in Chapter 14 of this book. The legal services lawyer who is absorbed with establishing a legal precedent simply does not want an out of court settlement, does not desire to obtain the best available deal at the least cost to his client. In the absence of suitable constraints, such an attorney can impose great cost upon others even at a non-trivial cost to his own client.

The Legal Services Corporation was viewed by many of its advocates at the outset of the 1974 program as the independent upholder of civil justice for the poor impervious to the political pressures suffered by its OEO predecessor and proof against the corrupting influences of the private market place. Post-1974 history as refracted through the lens of public choice gives the lie to this false vision. The Legal Services Corporation is made up of individuals no less venal than others in society. There is no public virtue in a world of private vice, but rather there is non-perfectible homo economicus who acts out his essentially selfish role upon each specific stage according to the constraints that restrict his discretion and the rewards that tempt his actions. The Legal Services Corporation is an unusually unfettered recipient of federal appropriations. As such, it is exceptionally vulnerable to self-serving behavior both within its own organization and among its outreach programs. It is to the institution and not to the individuals that reforms must be directed.

7   Testable proposition two: Root-and-branch institutional reform

The reforms outlined above are necessary conditions for returning the US legal services program to its original mission of easing access to civil justice for the poor individual. Yet, public choice warns that these reforms alone may not be sufficient, indeed they must provide inadequate protection against the forces of self-interest that would seek to edge the program back to its rent-seeking roots. A political equilibrium that is insufficiently robust will unravel as the logic of collective action takes its predictable toll.

The weak link in the piecemeal reform proposal outlined above is the staff attorney model of legal services provision, which empowers the bureaucratic supply side of the market in the accessing of civil justice, and which distorts the demand impulses of the indigent client. In such institutional conditions, and despite piecemeal reform, incentives remain for rent-seeking coalitions to regroup and to divert the legal services programs to their own advantage. A customer without purchasing power is defenseless against such program invasion. Nor can such a customer rely with any confidence upon the good governance of the Legal Services Corporation to balance his legitimate interests against those of the special interests. The staff attorney offices become focused magnets which attract rent-seekers and zealots, which threaten individual clients' rights to justice and which dissipate tax payer appropriations in social engineering adventures.

Only by dispersing the cartelized sources of legal services supply and by removing such sources from the public sector to private competitive law firms can the constellation of such coalitions be weakened and their ability to rent-seek and to agenda manipulate be countered. To this end, the legal services voucher is an indispensable instrument of institutional reform (Rowley, 1969; Seldon, 1986).

Under such a voucher system, the total legal services budget appropriated by the US Congress would be disbursed by a newly-constituted Legal Aid Board (located in the Department of Justice) to newly-constituted, private legal aid offices franchised under limited term (five year) by competitive auction. The disbursement of such federal dollars would reflect the numbers of eligible poor located within the jurisdiction of each legal aid office and would be reviewed on an annual basis.

Each legal aid office which would be manned by a small number of attorneys and by a paralegal staff, would provide basic legal advice at a zero price to all eligible clients within its jurisdiction to the limit determined by its own budget. Following an initial scrutiny and the provision of such basic legal advice, the legal aid office would allocate to selected clients legal services vouchers tailored to the estimated regional cost of the particular legal service that they require less any co-payment requirement that the Congress periodically may impose. Recipients would be free to use this non-transferable voucher to secure the legal services of the private attorney of their choice. Vouchers that remained unused beyond a pre-specified time period would automatically become invalid and the funding committed to it would revert to the legal aid office. Unexpended balances would be returnable at the year's end to the US Treasury.

The legal services voucher is anathema to the current suppliers of legal services because it constitutes a mortal challenge not merely to their discretionary power but even to their continued existence. Proposals for its introduction will be strongly opposed by coalitions now well versed in the strategies of political lobbying. The individual poor who would be empowered were the voucher system to be introduced cannot organize effectively in its absence to counter the lobbying of the special interests. Their only potential effective champions are the state and local bar associations who first must wrest control of their own national association which currently coordinates the special interest constellation. Will the white knights mount their chargers and prepare to win their spurs?

The optimistic note on which this book closes is that the state and local bar associations have much to gain from this radical reform of legal services, both in terms of ultimate public esteem and also pecuniary benefit. Here indeed is an excellent opportunity to follow Tullock's (1984) advice and to do well while doing good. By diverting poor clients from the public to the private sector, the state and local bars would demonstrate the advantages of competitive capitalism over bureaucratic socialism both with respect to cost and to the quality of service. By foreclosing on the rent-seekers they would augment the volume of legal services that can be provided from any given federal budget and thus would extend the provision of civil justice among poor Americans. By loosening the grip of the central legal services bureaucracy in the determination of legal services policy they would also increase state and local influence over an important policy instrument now controlled by community activists. Their return would be the federal dollars now dissipated by the staff attorney delivery system, the additional private funds that would flow to a popular program and the increased esteem of the public for their profession.

Should the courage of the private attorneys fail before the prospect of a battle that must be hard fought if victory is to ensue, there remains another consideration that might energize them into action. The current system of legal services has failed lamentably to achieve its original mission and yet its diversions into law reform have accentuated the problems of poverty. There is a growing public awareness of the nature of this debacle and of the role played by the American Bar Association in its enactment. If the debacle is allowed to continue and ultimately to worsen, as must be the case in the absence of reforms, public awareness will eventually transform itself into public rage, as ignorance becomes irrational, and will finally threaten the privileges of the state and local bar associations. As recent experience in Eastern Europe suggests, non-reforming autocracies are not endlessly immune from the popular will. Those who enjoy legal privileges, as far reaching as in the legal profession, but who fail to exhibit any willingness to contemplate much-needed institutional reforms, may end up by losing all of their privileges. Better by far to do well by doing good to assist the poor in achieving their right to civil justice and to rebuild a public goodwill that has been dissipated by those who now abuse the power vested in the standing committees at the American Bar Association and who coordinate the special interests in looting the market in legal services.

References

Abrams, B. and Schmitz, M. (1975), 'The Crowding-out Effect of Government Transfers on Private Charitable Contributions', *Public Choice*, **33**, 28–40.

ACORN (1981), *Community Organizer Handbook*, Washington, DC.

ACORN (1983), *Members Handbook*, Washington, DC.

ACORN (1985a), 'Bucks for Buildings', *USA – United States of Acorn*, **7** (1).

ACORN (1985b), 'Bank Challengers Strike It Rich', *USA – United States of Acorn*, **8** (1).

Alchian, A.A. (1968), 'The Economic and Social Impact of Free Tuition', *The New Individualist Review*, Winter, 42–58.

Alchian, A.A. and Allen, W.R. (1968), 'What Price Zero Tuition?' *Michigan Quarterly Review*, October.

Alchian, A.A. and Demsetz, H. (1972), 'Production, Information Costs and Economic Organization', *American Economic Review*, **62** (5), December, 777–95.

American Bar Association (1988), *Policy and Procedures Handbook*, Chicago: ABA Press.

American Bar Association (1990), *ABA Profile General*, Chicago: ABA Press.

American Enterprise Institute (1987), *The New Consensus on Family and Welfare*, Washington, DC.

Anon (1971), 'Legal Services Corporation: Curtailing Political Interference', *Yale Law Journal*, **81**.

Arrow, K.J. (1951, rev. 1963), *Social Choice and Individual Values*, New York: John Wiley.

Arrow, K.J. (1973), 'Some Ordinalist–Utilitarian Notes on Rawls' Theory of Justice', *Journal of Philosophy*, **79**, 245–63.

Barker, M. (1985), 'The Public Interest in Interstate Banking', *American Banker*, June 21.

Barrett, Jane H. (ABA) (1989), *Letters to Timothy B. Shea (LSC)*, Dated April 5, 1989: May 2, 1989.

Barry, N.P. (1987), *On Classical Liberalism and Libertarianism*, New York: St. Martin's Press.

Barzel, Y. and Silberberg, E. (1973), 'Is the Act of Voting Rational?' *Public Choice*, **16**, 51–8.

Becker, G.S. (1976), 'Comment on Peltzman', *Journal of Law and Economics*, **XIX** (2), August, 245–8.

Becker, G.S. (1983), 'A theory of competition among pressure groups for political influence', *Quarterly Journal of Economics*, **96** (3), 371–400.

Becker, G.S. (1985), 'Public policies, pressure groups and deadweight costs', *Journal of Public Economics*, **28**, 325–47.

Beckwith, J.P. (1986), 'What Should Lawyers Do?' *North Carolina Law Journal*, **16**, 1–27.

Bellow, G. (1980), 'Legal Aid in the United States', *Clearinghouse Review*, 343–4.

Bennett, J.T. and DiLorenzo, T.J. (1984), *Underground Government: The Off-Budget Public Sector*, Washington, DC: The Cato Institute.

Bennett, J.T. and DiLorenzo, T.J. (1985a), 'Poverty, Politics and Jurisprudence: Illegalities at the Legal Services Corporation', in *The Robber Barons of the Poor?* Washington, DC.: Washington Legal Foundation, 113–32.

Bennett, J.T. and DiLorenzo, T.J. (1985b), *Destroying Democracy: How Government Funds Partisan Politics*, Washington, DC: The Cato Institute.

Bennett, J.T. and DiLorenzo, T.J. (1989), *Unfair Competition: The Profits of Nonprofits*, New York: Hamilton Press.

Benson, B.L. (1981), 'Why are Congressional Committees Dominated by High-Demand Legislators?' *Southern Economic Journal*, **47** (1), 68–77.

Benston, G.J. (1981), 'Mortgage Redlining Research: A Review and Critical Analysis', *Journal of Bank Research*, June.

Bentham, J. (1789), *An Introduction to the Principles of Morals and Legislation*.

Bentley, A. (1907), *The Process of Government*, Evanston: Principia Press.

Berlin, I. (1969), *Four Essays on Liberty*, Oxford: Oxford University Press.

Besharov, D.J. (ed.) (1990), *Legal Services for the Poor: Time for Reform*, Washington, DC: American Enterprise Institute.

Besharov, D.J. and Tramontozzi, P.N. (1990), 'Background Information on the Legal Services Corporation', in Besharov (1990), 209–27.

Bidinotto, R.J. (1989), 'Crime and Consequences: II The Criminal System', *The Freeman*, **39** (8), 294–304.

Black, D. (1948), 'On the rationale of group decision-making', *Journal of Political Economy*, **56**, 23–34.

Black, R.D.C. (1972), 'Jevons, Bentham and Demorgan', *Economica*, **XXXIX** (154), 119–34.

Blanchard, R.D. (1982), *Litigation and Trial Practice for the Legal Paraprofessional*, New York: The West Publishing Company.

Blaug, M. (1976), 'Kuhn versus Lakatos or Paradigms versus Research Programs in the History of Economics' in S. Latsis (1976), 149–80.

Blaug, M. (1985), *Economic Theory in Retrospect* (4th Edition), Cambridge: Cambridge University Press.

Bleiburg, R.A. (1987), 'Shades of Willie Sutton: Federal Banking Law Gives Activists a License to Steal', *Barrons*, August 10.

Borosage, R., Brown, B., Friedman, P., Gerwitz, P., Jeffries, W. and Kelly, W. (1979), 'The New Public Interest Lawyers', *Yale Law Review*, **79** (6), 1069–151.

Bradford, C. and Schersten, P. (1985), *A Tool for Community Capital: Home Mortgage Disclosure Act*.

Breit, W. (1986), *Creating the Virginia School: Charlottesville as an Academic Environment in the 1960's*, Fairfax: Center for Study of Public Choice, George Mason University.

Brennan, H.G. and Buchanan, J.M. (1980), *The Power to Tax*, Cambridge: Cambridge University Press.

Brennan, H.G. and Buchanan, J.M. (1981), 'The Normative Purpose of Economic Science: Rediscovery of an Eighteenth Century Method', *International Review of Law and Economics*, **1** (2), 155–66.

Brennan, H.G. and Buchanan, J.M. (1983), 'Predictive Power and the Choice Among Regimes', *Economic Journal*, **93** (1), 89–105.

Brennan, H.G. and Buchanan, J.M. (1985), *The Reason of Rules*, Cambridge and New York: Cambridge University Press.

Breton, A. (1974), *The Economic Theory of Representative Government*, Chicago: Aldine Publishing Company.

Breton, A. and Wintrobe, R. (1975), 'The Equilibrium Size of a Budget-Maximizing Bureau', *Journal of Political Economy*, **83**, 195–207.

Breton, A. and Wintrobe, R. (1982), *The Logic of Bureaucratic Conduct*, Cambridge: Cambridge University Press.

Brough, W.T. and Elgin, R.S. (1987), *An Economic Analysis of Public Interest Law*, Legal Services Corporation Working Paper, Washington, DC.

Brough, W.T. and Kimenyi, M.S. (1987), *Rites of Passage: The Bar Exam as Central Enforcement Mechanism*, Legal Services Corporation Working Paper, Washington, DC.

Browning, E.K. (1988), *The Efficiency and Equity Costs of Redistribution*, Texas A. and M. Working Paper, College Station, Texas.

Browning, E.K. (1989), 'Inequality and Poverty', *Southern Economic Journal*, **55** (4), 819–30.

Browning, E.K. and Johnson, W.R. (1984), 'The Trade-Off Between Equality and Efficiency', *Journal of Political Economy*, **82**, 175–203.

Browning, E.K. and Johnson, W.R. (1986), 'The Cost of Reducing Inequality', *The Cato Journal*, 85–109.

Buchanan, J.M. (1959), 'Positive Economics, Welfare Economics, and Political Economy', *Journal of Law and Economics*, **II**, 134–8.

Buchanan, J.M. (1964), 'What Should Economists Do?' *Southern Economic Journal*, **30**, 213–22.

Buchanan, J.M. (1969), *Cost and Choice; an inquiry in economic theory*, Chicago: Markham Publishing Company.

Buchanan, J.M. (1971), 'Equality as Fact and Norm', *Ethics*, **81**, 228–40.

Buchanan, J.M. (1972), 'Rawls on justice and fairness', *Public Choice*, **13**, 123–8.

Buchanan, J.M. (1974a), 'Utopia, the minimal state and entitlement', *Public Choice*, **22**, 121–6.

Buchanan, J.M. (1974b), 'Good Economics – Bad Law', *Virginia Law Review*, **60**, 483–92.

Buchanan, J.M. (1975a), *The Limits of Liberty: Between Anarchy and Leviathan*, Chicago: University of Chicago Press.

Buchanan, J.M. (1975b), 'Comment on The Independent Judiciary in an Interest-Group Perspective', *Journal of Law and Economics*, **XVIII** (3), 903–6.

Buchanan, J.M. (1975c), 'A Contractarian Paradigm for Applying Economic Theory', *American Economic Review*, **65** (2), 225–30.

Buchanan, J.M. (1977a), 'A Hobbesian Interpretation of the Rawlsian Difference Principle', in J.M. Buchanan, *Freedom in Constitutional Contract*, College Station: Texas A. & M. University Press, 194–211.

Buchanan, J.M. (1977b), 'Political Constraints on Contractual Redistribution', in J.M. Buchanan, *Freedom in Constitutional Contract*, College Station: Texas A. & M. University Press, 273–86.

Buchanan, J.M. (1977c), 'Pragmatic Reform and Constitutional Revolution', in J. M. Buchanan, *Freedom in Constitutional Contract*, College Station: Texas A. & M. University Press, 181–93.

Buchanan, J.M. (1980a), 'Rent Seeking and Profit-Seeking', in J.M. Buchanan, R.D. Tollison and G. Tullock (eds), *Toward a Theory of the Rent-Seeking Society*, College Station: Texas A. & M. University Press, 3–15.

Buchanan, J.M. (1980b), 'The Rent-Seeking Society in a Constitutional Perspective', in J.M. Buchanan, R.D. Tollison and G. Tullock (eds), *Toward a Theory of the Rent-Seeking Society*, College Station: Texas A. & M. University Press, 359–67.

Buchanan, J.M. (1983), 'The Public Choice Perspective', *Economia delte scelte pubbliche*, **1**, 7–15.

Buchanan, J.M. (1986a), 'Rights, Efficiency and Exchange', in J.M. Buchanan, *Liberty, Market and State: Political Economy in the 1980s*, Brighton: Harvester Press.

Buchanan, J.M. (1986b), 'Quest for a Tempered utopia', *The Wall Street Journal*, November 14.

Buchanan, J.M. (1989), 'The Achievements and Failures of Public Choice in Diagnosing Government Failure and in Offering Bases for Constructive

Reform', in J.M. Buchanan, *Explorations in Constitutional Economics*, College Station: Texas A. & M. University Press, 24–36.

Buchanan, J.M. and Devletoglou, N.E. (1970), *Academia in Anarchy: An Economic Diagnosis*, New York: Basic Books.

Buchanan, J.M. and Faith, R.L. (1980), 'Subjective elements in Rawlsian contractual agreement on distributional rules', *Economic Inquiry*, **18**, 23–38.

Buchanan, J.M. and Tullock, G. (1962), *The Calculus of Consent*, Ann Arbor: University of Michigan Press.

Bullock, C.S. (1979), 'Freshman Committee Assignments and Re-Election in the US House of Representatives', *American Political Science Review*, 996–1007.

Cahn, E.S. and Cahn, J.C. (1964), 'The War on Poverty: A Civilian Perspective', *Yale Law Journal*, **73**.

Cahn, E.S. and Cahn, J.C. (1970), 'Power to the People or the Profession? The Public Interest in Public Interest Law', *Yale Law Journal*, **79**, 1005–47.

Carter, J.R. and Schap, D. (1987), 'Executive Veto, Legislative Override and Structure-Induced Equilibrium', *Public Choice*, **52**, 227–44.

Chappell, H.W. (1982), 'Campaign Contributions and Congressional Voting', *Review of Economics and Statistics*, **64** (1), 177–83.

Cigler, A.J. and Loomis, B.A. (1986), *Interest Group Politics*, Washington, DC: C.Q. Press.

Clark, B. and Gintis, H. (1978), 'Rawlsian justice and economic systems', *Philosophy and Public Affairs*, **7**, 302–25.

Coase, R.H. (1937), 'The Nature of the Firm', *Economica*, **4**, 386–405.

Coase, R.H. (1960), 'The Problem of Social Cost', *Journal of Law and Economics*, **III**, 1–44.

Coker, D.C. and Crain, W.M. (1990), *Legislative Committees as Loyalty-Generating Institutions*, Fairfax: Center for Study of Public Choice Working Paper.

Collette, W. (1982), 'Going to Court: A Research Guide', *The Organizer*.

Congressional Quarterly (1989), *Congress Again Scrutinizes Legal Services Programs*, Washington, DC, May 13.

Congressional Record (1984), H. 8585-8591, Washington, DC, June 28.

Congressional Record (1985), H. 8570-8597, Washington, DC, August 8.

Congressional Record (1987), S. 17841-17845, Washington, DC, December 11.

Cooper, J. (1983), *Public Legal Services: A Comparative Study of Policy, Politics and Practice*, London: Sweet and Maxwell.

Cooter, R. and Kornhauser, L. (1980), 'Can Litigation Improve the Law Without the Help of Judges?' *Journal of Legal Studies*, **IX**, 139–63.

Cooter, R. and Ulen, T. (1988), *Law and Economics*, Glenview: Scott, Foresman and Company.

Cowart, S. (1981), 'Representation of High Demand Constituencies on Review Committees', *Public Choice*, **37**, 337–42.

Cox, S. (1988), *San Antonio Voucher Project Report*, Washington, DC: Legal Services Corporation.

Crain, W.M. (1977), 'On the Structure and Stability of Political Markets', *Journal of Political Economy*, **85**, 829–42.

Crain, W.M. (1988), 'The House Dynasty: A Public Choice Analysis', in G.S. Jones and J.A. Marini (eds), *The Imperial Congress*, Washington, DC: Phanos Books, 183–203.

Crain, W.M. (1990), 'Legislative Committees: A Filtering Theory', in Crain and Tollison (1990), 149–66.

Crain, W.M., Davis, M.N. and Tollison, R.D. (1990), 'An Economic Theory of Redistricting', in Crain and Tollison (1990), 183–96.

Crain, W.M., Leavens, D.R. and Tollison, R.D. (1986), 'Final Voting in Legislatures', *American Economic Review*, **76**, 833–41.

Crain, W.M., Shughart, W.F. and Tollison, R.D. (1988), 'Legislative Majorities as Nonsalvageable Assets', *Southern Economic Journal*, **55** (2), 303–14.

Crain, W.M. and Tollison, R.D. (1979a), 'Constitutional Change in an Interest-Group Perspective', *Journal of Legal Studies*, **8**, 165–75.

Crain, W.M. and Tollison, R.D. (1979b), 'The Executive Branch in an Interest-Group Perspective', *Journal of Legal Studies*, **8**, 555–67.

Crain, W.M. and Tollison, R.D. (eds) (1990), *Predicting Politics*, Ann Arbor: University of Michigan Press.

Crew, M.A. and Rowley, C.K. (1988), 'Toward Public Choice Theory of Regulation', *Public Choice*, **57** (1), 49–68.

Crew, M.A. and Rowley, C.K. (1989), 'Feasibility of Deregulation: A Public Choice Analysis', in M.A. Crew (ed.), *Deregulation and Diversification of Utilities*, Boston: Kluwer Academic Publishers, 5–20.

Davidson, R.H. (1984), 'The Presidency and Congress', in Nelson (1984).

Davidson, R.H., Oleszek, W.J., and Klephart, T. (1988), 'One Bill, Many Committees: Multiple Referrals in the US House of Representatives', *Legislative Studies Quarterly*, February.

de Alessi, L. (1983), 'Property Rights, Transaction Costs and X-Efficiency', *American Economic Review*, **73** (1), 64–81.

de Bettencourt, K.B. (1988), *The Legal Services Corporation and the Impact on the Family*, Washington, DC: Legal Services Corporation.

de Jasay, A. (1985), *The State*, Oxford: Basil Blackwell.

Denton, J. (1985), 'Survival Campaign: Manipulating the Mandate', in *Robber Barons of the Poor?* Washington, DC: Washington Legal Foundation, 21–92.

Diamond, P.A. (1976), 'Cardinal Welfare, Individualistic Ethics and Inter-personal Comparisons of Utility', *Journal of Political Economy*, **75**, 765–6.

DiLorenzo, T.J. (1988), *The Anti-Business Campaign of The Legal Services Corporation*, St. Louis: Center for Study of American Business, Washington University.

Donahue, W.A. (1985), *The Politics of the American Civil Liberties Union*, New York: Transaction Books.

Dooley, J.A. and Houseman, A. (1984), *Legal Services History*, Washington, DC: NLADA Management Project.

Downs, A. (1957), *An Economic Theory of Democracy*, New York: Harper and Row.

Downs, A. (1967), *Inside Bureaucracy*, Boston: Little Brown and Company.

Duncan, G. (1984), *Years of Poverty, Years of Plenty*, Ann Arbor: University of Michigan Press.

Durant, W.C. (1988), *Remarks on Resignation*, Washington, DC: Legal Services Corporation, December 10.

Dworkin, R. (1985), *A Matter of Principle*, Cambridge: Harvard University Press.

Dworkin, R. (1986), *Law's Empire*, Cambridge: Harvard University Press.

Eisenberg, M.A. (1988), *The Nature of the Common Law*, Cambridge: Harvard University Press.

Enelow, J.M. and Hinich, M.J. (eds) (1984), *The Spatial Theory of Voting: An Introduction*, Cambridge: Cambridge University Press.

Enelow, J.M. and Hinich, M.J. (eds) (1990), *Advances in the Spatial Theory of Voting*, Cambridge: Cambridge University Press.

Epstein, R.A. (1979), *Medical Malpractice: The Case For Contract*, New York: The Center for Libertarian Studies.

Epstein, R.A. (1980), *A Theory of Strict Liability*, Washington, DC: The Cato Institute.

Epstein, R.A. (1985), *Takings: Private Property and the Power of Eminent Domain*, Cambridge: Harvard University Press.

Epstein, R.A. (1986), 'Past and Future: The Temporal Dimension in the Law of Property', *Washington University Law Quarterly*, **64** (3), 667–722.

Faith, R.L., Higgins, R.S. and Tollison, R.D. (1984), 'Managerial Rents and Outside Recruitment in the Coasian Firm', *American Economic Review*, **74**, 660–72.

Fama, E.F. (1980), 'Agency Problems and the Theory of the Firm', *Journal of Political Economy*, **88**, 288–307.

Fama, E.F. and Jensen, M.C. (1983), 'Separation of Ownership and Control', *Journal of Law and Economics*, **26**, 301–25.

Fama, E.F. and Jensen, M.C. (1983), 'Agency Problems and Residual Claims', *Journal of Law and Economics*, **26**, 327–49.

Farber, D.A. and Frickey, P.P. (1991), *Law and Public Choice: A Critical Introduction*, Chicago: University of Chicago Press.

Federal Financial Institutions Examination Council (1986), *A Citizens Guide to the Community Reinvestment Act*, Washington, DC.

Fenno, R.F. (1973), *Congressmen in Committees*, Boston: Little Brown.

Ferejohn, J. (1974), *Pork-Barrel Politics: Rivers and Harbors Legislation 1947–1968*, Stanford: Stanford University Press.

Feyerabend, P. (1975), *Against Method: Outline of an Anarchistic Theory of Knowledge*, London: Verso Press.

Fiorina, M.P. (1977), *Congress: Keystone of Washington Establishment*, New Haven: Yale University Press.

Fisher, L. (1984), *The Politics of Shared Power*, Washington, DC: CQ Press.

Frey, B.S. (1971), 'Why Do High Income People Participate More in Politics?' *Public Choice*, **11**, 101–5.

Friedman, M. (1953), 'The Methodology of Positive Economics', in *Essays in Positive Economics*, Chicago: University of Chicago Press.

Friedman, M. (1962), *Capitalism and Freedom*, Chicago: University of Chicago Press.

Galbraith, J.K. (1973), 'Power and the Useful Economist', *American Economic Review*, **63**, 1–11.

General Accounting Office (1985), *The Establishment of Alternative Corporations by Selected Legal Services Corporation Grant Recipients*, Washington, DC:GAO/HRD-85-51.

Gintis, H. (1972), 'A Radical Analysis of Welfare Economics and Individual Development', *Quarterly Journal of Economics*, November.

Goetz, C.J. (1987), 'Public Choice and the Law: The Paradox of Tullock', in C.K. Rowley (ed.), *Democracy and Public Choice: Essays in Honor of Gordon Tullock*, Oxford: Basil Blackwell, 171–80.

Goodman, J.C. (1978), 'An Economic theory of the Evolution of Common Law', *Journal of Legal Studies*, **VII**, 393–406.

Goodman, J.C. (1984), 'Poverty and Welfare', in J.H. Moore (ed.) *To Promote Prosperity: US Domestic Policy in the Mid-1980s*, Stanford: Hoover Institution Press.

Gordon, S. (1976), 'The New Contractarians', *Journal of Political Economy*, **84**, 573–90.

Gordon, S. (1980), *Welfare, Justice and Freedom*, New York: Columbia University Press.

Greco, M. (1988), 'Unmet Legal Needs of the Poor are Staggering', *Legal Services Crises and Concerns*, **3** (1).

Grier, K. (1990), 'Congressional Influence on US Monetary Policy: An Empirical Test', *Journal of Monetary Economics* (forthcoming).

Gwartney, J. and Wagner, R.E. (eds) (1988), *Public Choice and Constitutional Economics*, Greenwich, Connecticut: JAI Press Inc.

Hally, J. (1988), *The Community Reinvestment Act*, Fairfax: Center for Study of Public Choice Working Paper.

Hamlin, A.P. (1986), *Ethics, Economics and the State*, New York: St. Martin's Press.

Harberger, A.C. (1971), 'Three Basic Postulates for Applied Welfare Economics', *Journal of Economic Literature*, **IX** (3), 781–97.

Hardy, D. (1986), *Teenage Pregnancy and Welfare Dependency*, Washington, DC: Health and Human Services.

Harvey, W.F. (1988), 'Legal Services Corp's Attack on Banks', *Wall Street Journal*, January 19.

Hatch, O. (1985), 'Myth and Reality of the Legal Services Corporation', in *The Robber Barons of the Poor?* Washington, DC: Washington Legal Foundation.

Hayek, F.A. (1960), *The Constitution of Liberty*, London: Routledge and Kegan Paul.

Hayek, F.A. (1988), *The Fatal Conceit: The Errors of Socialism*, Chicago: University of Chicago Press.

Hazard, G.C. (1969), 'Social Justice Through Civil Justice', *University of Chicago Law Review*, **36**, 699–711.

Hearings (1984), *U.S. Senate Committee on Labor and Human Resources*, 98th Congress, Washington, DC: April 11, May 4, July 12 and 15.

Heber Smith, R. (1919), *Justice and the Poor*, New York: Carnegie Foundation.

Heclo, H. (1977), *A Government of Strangers*, Washington, DC: The Brookings Institute.

Higgins, R.S. and Rubin, P.H. (1980), 'Judicial Discretion', *Journal of Legal Studies*, **IX**, 129–39.

Higgs, R. (1987), *Crisis and Leviathan: Critical Episodes in the Growth of American Government*, Oxford: Oxford University Press.

Hills, J.S. (1985), 'Why so much stability? The Impact of Agency Determined Stability', *Public Choice*, **46**, 275–87.

Hobbes, T. (1651), *Leviathan*, reprinted in *The English Philosophers*, New York: Modern Library, 1939.

Hochman, H.M. and Rodgers, J.D. (1969), 'Pareto Optimal Redistribution', *American Economic Review*, **59**, 542–57.

Hoffman, S.D. and Podder, N. (1976), 'Income Inequality', in G.J. Duncan and J.N. Morgan (eds), *Five Thousand American Families: Patterns of Progress*, Ann Arbor: Institute for Social Research.

Hogue, A.R. (1985), *Origins of the Common Law*, Indianapolis: Liberty Press.

Houseman, A. (1978), *Legal Services and Equal Justice for the Poor*, Washington, DC: NLADA Brief Case 44.

Houseman, A. (1986), *Philosophical History*, Washington, DC: NLADA Draft Paper.

Houseman, A. and Riggs, Jr (1977), *Support Needs and Options: A Discussion Document*, Washington, DC: NLADA.

Huber, P.W. (1988), *Liability: The Legal Revolution and its Consequences*, New York: Basic Books.

Hume, D. (1739), *Treatise of Human Nature*, Oxford: Oxford University Press, 1941.

Hume, D. (1777), *Essays, Moral, Political and Literary*, Indianapolis: Liberty Press, 1985.

Inman, R.P. (1978), 'Testing Political Economy's "As If" Proposition: Is the Median Income Voter Really Decisive?' *Public Choice*, **33** (4), 45–65.

Ireland, T.R. and Johnson, D.B. (1970), *The Economics of Charity*, Blacksburg: Center for Study of Public Choice.

Isaac, R.J. (1985), 'Bringing Down the System Through Training: The LSC Manuals and Training Materials', in *The Robber Barons of the Poor?* Washington, DC: Washington Legal Foundation, 93–119.

Jensen, M. and Meckling, W.H. (1976), 'The Theory of the Firm: Managerial Behavior, Agency Costs and Ownership Structure', *Journal of Financial Economics*, **3**, 305–60.

Johnson, D.B. (1991), *Public Choice: An Introduction to the New Political Economy*, Mountain View, California: Mayfield Publishing Company.

Johnson, E. Jr (1978), *Justice and Reform: The Formative Years of the OEO Legal Services Program*, New York: Russell Sage.

Kalt, J.P. and Zupan, M.A. (1984), 'Capture and Ideology in the Economic Theory of Politics', *American Economic Review*, **74** (3), 279–300.

Kant, I. (1797), *The Metaphysical Elements of Justice* (translated by J. Ladd, 1965), Indianapolis: The Liberty Press.

Kaplan, D.A. (1985), 'Bar Exam: The Rites of Passage are Getting Tougher', *National Law Journal*, June 3.

Kau, J.B., Keenan, D. and Rubin, P.H. (1982), 'A General Equilibrium Model of Congressional Voting', *Quarterly Journal of Economics*, **97**, 271–93.

Kau, J.B. and Rubin, P.H. (1979), 'Self-Interest, Ideology and Logrolling in Congressional Voting', *Journal of Law and Economics*, **22**, 365–84.

Kau, J.B. and Rubin, P.H. (1982), *Congressmen, Constituents and Contributors: Determinants of Roll Call Voting in the House of Representatives*, Boston: Martinus Nijhoff Publishing.

Kelman, M. (1987), *A Guide to Critical Legal Studies*, Cambridge: Harvard University Press.

Kennedy, D. (1981), 'Cost-Benefit Analysis of Entitlement Problems: A Critique', *Stanford Law Review*, **33**.

Kibbe, M.E. (1988), *The Legal Services Corporation – Who Needs It?* Fairfax: Center for Study of Market Processes.

Kimenyi, M.S., Shughart, W.F. and Tollison, R.D. (1985), 'What Do Judges Maximize?' *Journal of Public Finance and Public Choice*, **3**.

King, A. (ed.) (1983), *Both Ends of the Avenue*, Washington, DC: American Enterprise Institute.

Knight, F.H. (1921), *Risk, Uncertainty and Profit*, New York: Harper and Row.

Kuhn, T. (1970), *The Structure of Scientific Revolutions* (2nd Edition), Chicago: University of Chicago Press.

Laband, D.N. and Sophocleus, J.P. (1988), 'The Social Cost of Rent-Seeking: First Estimates, *Public Choice*, **58** (3), 269–76.

Lakatos, I. and Musgrave, A. (eds) (1970), *Criticism and the Growth of Knowledge*, Cambridge: Cambridge University Press.

Lakatos, I. (1978), *The Methodology of Scientific Research Programs*, Cambridge: Cambridge University Press.

Landes, W.M. and Posner, R.A. (1975), 'The Independent Judiciary in an Interest-Group Perspective', *Journal of Law and Economics*, **XVIII** (3), 875–902.

Landes, W.M. and Posner, R.A. (1987), *The Economic Structure of Tort Law*, Cambridge: Harvard University Press.

Lang, C. (1981), 'Poor Women and Health Care', *Clearinghouse Review*, **14**.

Langley, L.D. and Oleszek, W.J. (1989), *Bicameral Politics: Conference Committees in Congress*, New Haven: Yale University Press.

Latsis, S. (ed.) (1976), *Method and Appraisal in Economics*, Cambridge: Cambridge University Press.

Lee, D. (1988), 'Politics, Ideology and the Power of Public Choice, *Virginia Law Review*, **74**, 191–8.

Lee, D. and McKenzie, R.B. (1988), 'Helping the Poor Through Governmental Poverty Programs: The Triumph of Rhetoric Over Reality', in Gwartney and R.E. Wagner (1988).

Legal Aid Board (1989), *Legal Aid Handbook, 1989*, London: HMSO.

Legal Services Corporation, *Act and Regulations, 1874 and 1977*, Washington, DC.

Legal Services Corporation, *Annual Reports 1976–1990*, Washington, DC.

Legal Services Corporation (1977), *Ad Hoc Committee Report*, Washington, DC.

Legal Services Corporation (1980), *The Delivery Systems Study: A Report to the Congress and the President of the United States*, Washington, DC.

Legal Services Corporation (1984), *Final Report on the National Legal Aid and Defender Association*, Washington, DC.

Legal Services Corporation (1986), *Preliminary Findings on the National Support Centers*, Washington, DC.

Legal Services Corporation (1988a), *Legal Services Opposition to Banking Activities*, Washington, DC.

Legal Services Corporation (1988b), *Federally-Funded Legal Services and Public Utilities*, Washington, DC.

Legal Services Corporation (1988c), *Legal Services Programs Involvement in Housing Law*, Washington, DC.

Legal Services Corporation (1988d), *Legal Services Corporation and Agriculture*, Washington, DC.

Legal Services Corporation (1988e), *Legal Services Program Involvement in Agricultural Labor Markets*, Washington, DC.

Legal Services Corporation (1988f), *Legal Services Activities in the Banking Sector*, Washington, DC.

Legal Services Corporation (1989), 'Comments and Correspondence on *The American Bar Association's May 5, 1989 San Antonio Study of Legal Services Delivery Systems*', Washington, DC.

Leibenstein, H. (1966), 'Allocative efficiency versus X-efficiency', *American Economic Review*, **56**, 392–415.

Leibowitz, A. and Tollison, R.D. (1980), 'A Theory of Legislative Organization: Making the Most of your Majority', *Quarterly Journal of Economics*, **XXXXV**.

LeLoup, L.T. (1988), *Budgetary Politics*, Brunswick, Ohio: King's Court Communications Inc.

Leube, K.R. and Moore, T.G. (eds) (1986), *The Essence of Stigler*, Stanford: Hoover Institution Press.

Levy, F. (1987), *Dollars and Dreams: The Changing American Income Distribution*, New York: Basic Books.

Lewis, I.A. and Schneider, W. (1985), 'Hard Times: The Public on Poverty', *Public Opinion*.

Lindbeck, A. (1971), *The Political Economy of the New Left: An Outsider's View*, New York: Harper and Row.

Locke, J. (1690), *Two Treatises of Government*, New York: Hafner Press, 1947.

Madison, J. (1786), *The Federalist, No. 51*, New York: The Modern Library, 1937.

Mandel, E. (1968), 'Marxist Economic Theory', *Monthly Review Press*.

Marcuse, H. (1964), *One Dimensional Man*, New York: Beacon Press.

Marcuse, H. (1969), *An Essay on Liberation*, New York: Beacon Press.

Margolis, M. and Mauser, G.A. (1989), *Manipulating Public Opinion*, Pacific Grove: Brooks/Cole Publishing Company.

Massachusetts Legal Services Corporation (1987), *Plan for Action*, Boston.

Maurizi, A. (1974), 'Occupational Licensing and the Public Interest', *Journal of Political Economy*, **82**, 399–413.

McClean, I. (1987), *Public Choice: An Introduction*, Oxford: Basil Blackwell.

McChesney, F.S. (1987), 'Rent Extraction and Rent Creation in the Economic Theory of Regulation', *Journal of Legal Studies*, **12** (1), 101–18.

McChesney, F.S. (1989), 'Extortion for Not Passing Laws is a Political "Big Easy"', *The Independent*, **1** (1).

McChesney, F.S. (1991), 'Rent Extraction and Interest-Group Organization in a Coasean Model of Regulation', *Journal of Legal Studies*, **20** (1), 73–90.

McCloskey, D.M. (1985), *The Rhetoric of Economics*, Madison: University of Wisconsin Press.

McCormick, R.E. and Tollison, R.D. (1981), *Politicians, Legislation and the Economy*, Boston: Martinus Nijhoff Publishing.

Mermin, L. (1973), *Law and the Legal System*, Boston: Little Brown.

Merrill, T.W. (1986), 'Introduction to Epstein Symposium', *Washington Law Quarterly*, **64** (3), 661–5.

Mill, J.S. (1859), *On Liberty*, Cambridge: Cambridge University Press, 1989.

Miller, D. (1979), 'Joint Custody', *Family Law Quarterly*, **13** (364).

Mises, L. von (1944), *Bureaucracy*, New Haven: Yale University Press.

Mises, L. von (1949), *Human Action: A Treatise on Economics*, New Haven: Yale University Press.

Mirrlees, J.A. (1982), 'The economic uses of utilitarianism', in Sen and Williams (1982).

Mitchell, W.C. (1988a), *Government As It Is*, London: Institute of Economic Affairs, Hobart Paper 109.

Mitchell, W.C. (1988b), 'Virginia, Rochester and Bloomington: Twenty-Five Years of Public Choice', *Public Choice*, **56** (2), 101–20.

Mitchell, W.C. (1989), 'Chicago Political Economy: A Public Choice Perspective', *Public Choice*, **63** (3), 282–92.

Moe, T.M. (1987), 'An Assessment of the Positive Theory of Congressional Dominance', *Legislative Studies Quarterly*, **12** (4), 475–520.

Mueller, D.C. (1985), *The Virginia School and Public Choice*, Fairfax: Center for Study of Public Choice.

Mueller, D.C. (1989), *Public Choice II*, Cambridge: Cambridge University Press.

Muris, T.J. (1986), 'Regulatory Policymaking at the Federal Trade Commission: The Extent of Congressional Control', *Journal of Political Economy*, **94**, 884–9.

Murray, C. (1984), *Losing Ground: American Social Policy, 1950–1980*, New York: Basic Books.

Murray, C.L. (1986), 'Losing Ground: Two Years Later', *Cato Journal*, **6** (1), 19–29.

Murray, C.L. (1987), 'In Search of the Working Poor', *The Public Interest*, Fall, 3–19.

Murray, C.L. (1988), *In Pursuit of Happiness and Good Government*, New York: Simon and Schuster.

National Conference of Catholic Bishops (1986), *Economic Justice for All*, Washington, DC: United States Catholic Conference.

Nelson, D.E. and Silberberg, E. (1987), 'Ideology and Legislator Shirking', *Economic Inquiry*, **25**, 15–25.

Nelson, M. (ed.) (1984), *The Presidency and the Political System*, Washington, DC: Congressional Quarterly Press.

Nelson, R.R. and Winter, S.G. (1982), *An Evolving Theory of Economic Change*, Cambridge: Harvard University Press.

Newcomer, S. and Udry, S. (1987), 'Parental Marital Status Effects on Adolescent Sexual Behavior', *Journal of Marriage and Family*, May.

Niskanen, W.A. (1971), *Bureaucracy and Representative Government*, Chicago: Aldine Press.

Niskanen, W.A. (1975), 'Bureaucrats and Politicians', *Journal of Law and Economics*, **XVIII** (3), 617–44.

Norell, N. (1983), *Oversight of the Legal Services Corporation*, Washington, DC: Committee on Labor and Human Resources, United States Senate.

North, D.C. (1984), 'Transaction Costs, Institutions and Economic History', *Journal of Institutional and Theoretical Economics*, Band **140** (1), 7–17.

North, D.C. (1990), *Institutions, Institutional Change and Economic Performance*, Cambridge: Cambridge University Press.

Nozick, R. (1973), 'Distributive Justice', *Philosophy and Public Affairs*, **3**, 45–126.

Nozick, R. (1974), *Anarchy, State and Utopia*, New York: Basic Books.

Office of Economic Opportunity (1965), *Community Action Guide*, Washington, DC.

Office of Economic Opportunity (1966), *Guidelines for Legal Services Programs*, Washington, DC.

Olson, M. (1965), *The Logic of Collective Action*, Cambridge: Harvard University Press.

Olson, M. (1982), *The Rise and Decline of Nations*, New Haven: Yale University Press.

O'Neill, J. (1986), 'Transfers and Poverty: Cause and/or Effect', *The Cato Journal*, Spring/Summer, 55–76.

Ordeshook, P.C. (1986), *Game Theory and Political Theory*, Cambridge: Cambridge University Press.

Ordeshook, P.C. and Shepsle, K.A. (1982), *Political Equilibrium*, Boston: Kluwer-Nijhoff Publishing.

Orzechowski, W. (1977), 'Economic Models of Bureaucracy', in T.E. Borcherding (ed.), *Budgets and Bureaucrats: The Sources of Government Growth*, Durham, N.C.: Duke University Press.

Parkinson, C.N. (1957), *Parkinson's Law and Other Studies in Administration*, New York: Ballantine Books.

Peacock, A.T. (1979a), *The Economic Analysis of Government and Related Themes*, Oxford: Martin Robertson.

Peacock, A.T. (1979b), 'Public X-inefficiency: Informational and Institutional Constraints', in H. Hanosch (ed.), *Anatomy of Government Deficiencies*, Berlin: Springer.

Peltzman, S. (1976), 'Towards a More General Theory of Regulation', *Journal of Law and Economics*, **19**, 211–40.

Peltzman, S. (1984), 'Constituent Interest and Congressional Voting', *Journal of Law and Economics*, **27**, 181–210.

Peltzman, S. (1985), 'An Economic Interpretation of Congressional Voting in the Twentieth Century', *American Economic Review*, **75**, 656–75.

Peltzman, S. (1990), 'How Efficient is the Voting Market?' *Journal of Law and Economics*, **33** (1), 27–64.

Polikoff Report (1976), *The Support Center Study*, Washington, DC: Legal Services Corporation.

Ponce, L. (1988), 'Bar Associations Keep Fighting to bar non-lawyers', *Washington Times*, July 18.

Popper, K.R. (1959), *The Logic of Scientific Discovery*, New York: Basic Books.

Popper, K.R. (1962), *The Open Society and Its Enemies*, Princeton: Princeton University Press.

Posner, R.A. (1979), 'Some uses and abuses of economics in law', *University of Chicago Law Review*, **46**, 281–306.

Posner, R.A. (1981a), 'A Reply to Some Recent Criticisms of the Efficiency Theory of the Common Law', *Hofstra Law Review*, **9**.

Posner, R.A. (1981b), *The Economics of Justice*, Cambridge: Harvard University Press.

Posner, R.A. (1984), 'Wealth Maximization and Judicial Decision-Making', *International Review of Law and Economics*, **4** (2), 131–6.

Posner, R.A. (1985), *The Federal Courts: Crisis and Reform*, Cambridge: Harvard University Press.

Posner, R.A. (1986), *Economic Analysis of Law*, 3rd Edn, Boston: Little Brown.

Posner, R.A. (1990), *The Problems of Jurisprudence*, Cambridge: Harvard University Press.

Price, D.A. (1986), 'Pulling the Reins on Legal Services Lobbying', *Harvard Journal of Law and Public Policy*, **9** (1).

Project Advisory Group and NLADA (1989), *Preliminary Comment on Proposed Regulation on Competitive Bidding for Grants and Competition Manual*, Washington, DC.

Rabin, R.L. (1976), 'Lawyers for Social Change: Perspectives on Public Interest Law', *Stanford Law Review*, **28**, January.

Raven, R.D. (1989a), *Statement on behalf of the American Bar Association before the Subcommittee on Commerce, Justice, State, the Judiciary and Related Agencies*, Chicago: American Bar Association, May 2.

Raven, R.D. (1989b), *Statement on behalf of the American Bar Association before the Subcommittee on Administrative Law and Government Relations*, Chicago: American Bar Association, July 19.

Rawls, J. (1971), *A Theory of Justice*, Cambridge: Belknap Press.

Rawls, J. (1974), 'Some Reasons for the Maximin Criterion', *American Economic Review*, **64**, 141–6.

Rawls, J. (1980), 'Kantian constructivism in moral theory', *Journal of Philosophy*, **77**.

Rawls, J. (1985), 'Justice as fairness: political not metaphysical', *Philosophy and Public Affairs*, **14**.

Rayack, E. (1976), *An Economic Analysis of Occupation Licensure*, Washington, DC: US Department of Labor.

Reder, M.W. (1982), 'Chicago Economics: Permanence and Change', *Journal of Economic Literature*, **20**, 1–38.

Riker, W.H. (1962), *The Theory of Political Coalitions*, New Haven: Yale University Press.

Riker, W.H. and Ordeshook, P.C. (1973), *Introduction to Positive Political Theory*, Englewood Cliffs, N.J.: Prentice-Hall.

Roberts, P. (1986), 'Ameliorating the Feminization of Poverty: Whose Responsibility?' *Clearinghouse Review*, **18**.

Roberts, R.D. (1984), 'A Positive Model of Private Charity and Public Transfers', *Journal of Political Economy*, **92**, 136–48.

Roche, T. (1987a), 'The National Commitment to Civil Legal Services for the Poor', *Legal Services Crises and Concerns*, **3** (1).

Roche, T. (1987b), 'What's Really Happening With LSC Monitoring?' *Legal Services Cases and Concerns*, **2** (2).

Roche, T. (1988), 'Assessing and Meeting the Legal Needs of the Poor', *Legal Services Crises and Concerns*, **3** (1).

Roemer, J.E. (1982), *A General Theory of Exploitation and Class*, Cambridge: Harvard University Press.

Romer, T. (1988), 'On James Buchanan's Contributions to Public Economics, *Journal of Economic Perspectives*, **2** (4), 165–79.

Romer, T. and Rosenthal, H. (1979), 'The Elusive Median Voter', *Journal of Public Economics*, **12**, 143–70.

Rose-Ackerman, S. (1978), *Corruption*, New York: Academic Press.

Rorty, R. (1979), *Philosophy and the Mirror of Nature*, Princeton, Princeton University Press.

Ross, L.J. (1987), 'Bar Leaders Have Duty to Protect Legal Services and to Preserve Justice', *Legal Crises and Concerns*, **2** (2).

Roten, M. and Webster, C. (1986), *Some Notes on Negotiating CRA Agreements*, Washington, DC: NCLSC/CFLS.

Rowley, C.K. (1969), 'The Political Economy of British Education', *Scottish Journal of Political Economy*, **XVI**, 152–76.

Rowley, C.K. (1978a), 'Market Failure and Government Failure', in *The Economics of Politics*, IEA Readings 18, London: Institute of Economic Affairs, 29–43.

Rowley, C.K. (1978b), 'Liberalism and Collective Choice: A Return to Reality?' *Manchester School*, September, 224–52.

Rowley, C.K. (1979), 'Collective Choice and Individual Liberty', *Ordo*, **30**, 107–16.

Rowley, C.K. (1981), 'Social Sciences and Law: The Relevance of Economic Theories', *Oxford Journal of Legal Studies*, **1** (3), 391–405.

Rowley, C.K. (1984), The Relevance of the Median Voter Theorem', *Journal of Institutional and Theoretical Economics*, March, 104–35.

Rowley, C.K. (1985a), 'Rules versus Discretion in Constitutional Design', in D. Laidler (ed.), *Responses to Economic Change*, Toronto: University of Toronto Press, 75–106.

Rowley, C.K. (1985b), 'The Relationship between Economics, Politics and Law in the Formation of Public Policy', in R.C. Matthews (ed.), *Economy and Democracy*, London: Macmillan, 127–150.

Rowley, C.K. (1986), 'The Law of Property in Virginia School Perspective', *Washington University Quarterly*, **64** (3), 759–74.

Rowley, C.K. (1987), 'A Public Choice Perspective on Judicial Pragmactivism', in J. Dorn and H. Manne (eds), *Economic Liberties and the Judiciary*, Fairfax: George Mason University Press, 219–24.

Rowley, C.K. (1988a), 'The Economic Philosophy of James M. Buchanan', *Journal of Public Finance and Public Choice*, **3**, 171–87.

Rowley, C.K. (1988b), 'Rent-Seeking in Constitutional Perspective', in C. K. Rowley, R.D. Tollison and G. Tullock (eds), *The Political Economy of Rent-Seeking*, Boston: Kluwer Academic Publishers, 447–64.

Rowley, C.K. (1989a), 'Public Choice and the Economic Analysis of Law', in N. Mercuro (ed.), *Law and Economics*, Boston: Kluwer Academic Publishers, 123–74.

Rowley, C.K. (1989b), 'Competition and the Right to Justice', *Legal Services Record*, March/April, **11**.

Rowley, C.K. (1989c), 'The Common Law in Public Choice Perspective', *Hamline Law Review*, **12**, 355–83.

Rowley, C.K. (1991a), 'A Changing of the Guard', *Public Choice*, **71** (1).

Rowley, C.K. (1991b), 'The Supreme Court and the Constitution', in N. Mercuro (ed.), *Legal Economic Perspectives of the Takings Issue*, Boston: Kluwer Academic Publishers.

Rowley, C.K. and Brough, W. (1987), 'The Efficiency of the Common Law: A New Institutional Economics Perspective', in R. Pethig and U. Schlieper (eds), *Efficiency, Institutions and Economic Policy*, Berlin: Springer-Verlag.

Rowley, C.K. and Elgin, R.S. (1985), 'Towards a Theory of Bureaucratic Behavior', in D. Greenaway and G. K. Shaw (eds), *Public Choice, Public Finance and Public Policy*, Oxford: Basil Blackwell, 31–50.

Rowley, C.K. and Peacock, A.T. (1972), 'Pareto Optimality and the Political Economy of Liberalism', *Journal of Political Economy*, **80**, 476–90.

Rowley, C.K. and Peacock, A.T. (1975), *Welfare Economics: A Liberal Restatement*, Oxford: Martin Robertson.

Rowley, C.K., Shughart, W.F. and Tollison, R.D. (1987), 'Interest Groups and Deficits', in J. M. Buchanan, C.K. Rowley and R.D. Tollison (eds), *Deficits*, Oxford: Basil Blackwell, 263–80.

Rowley, C.K., Tollison, R.D. and Tullock, G. (eds) (1988), *The Political Economy of Rent-Seeking*, Boston: Kluwer Academic Publishers, 447–64.

Rowley, C.K. and Vachris, M. (1990), *Why Democracy in the US Does Not Produce Efficient Results*, Fairfax: Center for Study of Public Choice.

Rowley, C.K. and Wagner, R.E. (1990), 'Choosing Freedom: Public Choice and the Libertarian Idea', *Liberty*, **3** (3), 43–5.

Rubin, P.H. (1977), 'Why Is the Common Law Efficient?' *Journal of Legal Studies*, 51–63.

Rudman, W.B. (1987), 'Rudman Takes on Durrant Logic', *Legal Services Crisis and Concerns*, **2**.

Samuels, W.J. and Mercuro, N. (1984), 'Posnerian Law and Economics on the Bench', *International Review of Law and Economics*, **4** (2), 107–30.

Sandel, J.E. (1982), *A General Theory of Exploitation and Class*, Cambridge: Harvard University Press.

Sandel, M.J. (1982), *Liberalism and the Limits of Justice*, Cambridge: Cambridge University Press.

Sandmo, A. (1990), 'Buchanan on Political Economy: A Review Article', *Journal of Economic Literature*, **28** (1), 50–65.

Sawhill, I.V. (1988), 'Poverty in the US: Why Is It So Persistent?' *Journal of Economic Literature*, **XXVI** (3), 1073–1119.

Scheibler, S. (1977), 'Bar Sinister – The Legal Services Corporation Sketches Its Mandate', *Barrons*.

Scheingold, S.A. (1984), 'The Dilemma of Legal Services', *Stanford Law Review*, **36**, 879–93.

Schelling, T.C. (1963), *The Strategy of Conflict*, New York: Oxford University Press.

Schelling, T.C. (1984), *Choice and Consequence*, Cambridge: Harvard University Press.

Schick, A.E.J. (1983), *Making Economic Policy in Congress*, Washington, DC: American Enterprise Institute.

Schmid, A.A. (1987), *Property, Power and Public Choice*, New York: Proeger.

Schmitt, R.B. (1987), 'Public Service or Blackmail: Banks Pressed to Finance Local Projects', *Wall Street Journal*, September 10.

Schwarz, B. and Houseman, A.W. (1984), *Legislative and Administrative Representation – Permissible Activity Under the LSC Regulations and Applicable Law*, Washington, DC: NLADA.

Seldon, A. (1986), *The Riddle of the Voucher*, London: Institute of Economic Affairs, Hobart Paper 21.

Seldon, A. (1990), *Capitalism*, Oxford: Basil Blackwell.

Sen, A.K. (1970), 'The impossibility of a Paretian liberal', *Journal of Political Economy*, **78**, 152–7.

Sen, A.K. (1976), 'Liberty, Unanimity and Rights', *Economica*, **43**, 217–45.

Sen, A.K. (1987), *On Ethics and Economics*, Oxford: Basil Blackwell.

Sen, A.K. and Williams, B.A.O. (eds) (1982), *Utilitarianism and Beyond*, Cambridge: Cambridge University Press.

Senate Committee on Labor and Human Resources (1983), *Oversight of the Legal Services Corporation*, Washington, DC.

Shavell, S. (1987), *Economic Analysis of Accident Law*, Cambridge: Harvard University Press.

Shepsle, K.A. (1978), *The Giant Jigsaw Puzzle*, Chicago: University of Chicago Press.

Shepsle, K.A. and Weingast, B.R. (1981), 'Structure-induced equilibrium and legislative choice', *Public Choice*, **37**, 189–202.

Shughart, W.F., Tollison, R.D. and Goff, B.L. (1986), 'Bureaucratic Structure and Congressional Control', *Southern Economic Journal*, 962–972.

Siegen, B.H. (1980), *Economic Liberties and the Constitution*, Chicago: University of Chicago Press.

Siegen, B.H. (1987), *The Supreme Court's Constitution*, New Brunswick: Transation Books.

Simon, H. (1972), 'Theories of Bounded Rationality', in C.B. McGuire and R. Radner (eds), *Decision and Organization*, New York: Elsevier Press.

Smith, A. (1776), *The Wealth of Nations*, Edinburgh: Thomas Nelson.

Spangenburg Group (1984), *American Bar Association National Civil Legal Needs Survey*, Chicago: American Bar Association.

Stigler, G.J. (1970), 'Director's Law of Public Income Redistribution', *Journal of Law and Economics*, XIII (1), 1–10.

Stigler, G.J. (1971), 'The theory of economic regulation', *Bell Journal of Economics and Management Science*, 2, 3–21.

Stigler, G.J. (1976), 'Xistence of X-efficiency?' *Bell Journal of Economics and Management Science*, 2, 3–21.

Stigler, G.J. (1982), *The Economist as Preacher*, Oxford: Basil Blackwell.

Stigler, G.J. (1988a), *Memoirs of an Unregulated Economist*, New York: Basic Books.

Stigler, G.J. (ed.) (1988b), *Chicago Studies in Political Economy*, Chicago: University of Chicago Press.

Sugden, R. (1985), 'Liberty, Preference and Choice', *Economics and Philosophy*, 1, 213–30.

Terrebonne, P.A. (1981), 'Strictly Evolutionary Model of Common Law', *Journal of Legal Studies*, X, 397–407.

Thomas, E.C. (1987), 'Legal Services Corporation Board Chairman Should Resign', *Legal Services Crises and Concerns*, February 12.

Tollison, R.D. (1982), 'Rent-Seeking: A Survey', *Kyklos*, fasc. 4, 575–602.

Tollison, R.D. (1987), 'Public Choice and Legislation', *Virginia Law Review*, 74, 339–71.

Tollison, R.D. (1989), 'Chicago Political Economy', *Public Choice*, 63 (3), 293–8.

Tollison, R.D. and Wagner, R. E. (1990), 'Romance, Reality and Economic Reform', *Kyklos*.

Tribe, L.H. (1985), *Constitutional Choices*, Cambridge: Harvard University Press.

Tullock, G. (1965), *The Politics of Bureaucracy*, Washington, DC: Public Affairs Press.

Tullock, G. (1966), 'Information without profit', *Papers in Non-Market Decision Making*, 1.

Tullock, G. (1967a), *Toward a Mathematics of Politics*, Ann Arbor: University of Michigan Press.

Tullock, G. (1967b), 'The welfare costs of tariffs, monopolies and theft', *Western Economic Journal*, 5, 224–32.

Tullock, G. (1971), 'The Charity of the Uncharitable', *Western Economic Journal*, 9, 379–92.

Tullock, G. (1975), 'The transitional gains traps', *Bell Journal of Economics and Management Science*, 6, 671–8.

Tullock, G. (1980), *Trials on Trial*, New York: Columbia University Press.

Tullock, G. (1981a), 'Why so much stability?' *Public Choice*, 37, 189–203.

Tullock, G. (1981b), 'The Rhetoric and Reality of Redistribution', *Southern Economic Journal*, **47** (4), 895–907.

Tullock, G. (1981c), 'Negligence Again', *International Review of Law and Economics*, **1** (1), 51–62.

Tullock, G. (1983a), *Welfare for the Well-To-Do*, Dallas: The Fisher Institute.

Tullock, G. (1983b), *Economics of Income Redistribution*, Boston: Kluwer Academic Publishing.

Tullock, G. (1984), 'How to do well while doing good!', in D. Colander (ed.), *Neoclassical Political Economy*, Cambridge: Ballinger Publishing.

Tullock, G. (1986), *The Economics of Wealth and Poverty*, New York: New York University Press.

Tullock, G. (1989), *The Economics of Special Privilege and Rent Seeking*, Boston: Kluwer Academic Publishing.

Unger, R.M. (1983), *The Critical Legal Studies Movement*, Cambridge: Harvard University Press.

Vorenberg, Black, Brest, Calabresi and Stone (Law Deans) (1989), *Letter to President Bush*, June 16.

Wagner, R.E. (1987), 'Parchment, Guns and the Maintenance of Constitutional Contract', in C.K. Rowley (ed.), *Democracy and Public Choice: Essays in Honor of Gordon Tullock*, Oxford: Basil Blackwell.

Wagner, R.E. (1988), 'Agency, Economic Calculation and Constitutional Construction', in C.K. Rowley, R.D. Tollison and G. Tullock (eds), *The Political Economy of Rent-Seeking*, Kluwer Academic Publishing.

Wagner, R.E. (1989a), *To Promote the General Welfare*, San Francisco: Pacific Research Institute for Public Policy.

Wagner, R.E. (1989b), *Efficiency and Inefficiency in Political Process: Zenoistic Variations on Austrian and Neoclassical Themes*, Fairfax: Center for Study of Public Choice.

Weber, M. (1947), *The Theory of Social and Economic Organization*, New York: The Free Press.

Weicher, J.L. (1987), 'Mismeasuring Poverty and Progress', *The Cato Journal*, Winter.

Weingast, B.R. (1981), 'Republican Reregulation and Deregulation: The Political Foundations of Agency – Clientele Relationships', *Journal of Law and Contemporary Problems*, **44**, 147–73.

Weingast, B.R. (1984), 'The Congressional – Bureaucratic System: A Principal–Agent Perspective, *Public Choice*, **44**, 147–91.

Weingast, B.R. and Marshall, W.J. (1988), 'The Industrial Organization of Congress: of Why Legislatures, Firms, Are Not Organized as Markets', *Journal of Political Economy*, **96**, 132–63.

Weingast, B.R. and Moran, M.J. (1983), 'Bureaucratic Discretion or Congressional Control: Regulatory Policy Making by the Federal Trade Commission', *Journal of Political Economy*, **91**, 765–800.

Weisbrod, B.A. (1988), *The Nonprofit Economy*, Cambridge: Harvard University Press.

Weitzman, L. (1981), 'The Economics of Divorce: Social and Economic Consequences', *UCLA Law Review*, **28**.

West, E.G. (1969), 'The Political Economy of Alienation', *Oxford Economic Papers*, **21**.

Wicksell, K. (1896), *Finanztheoretische Untersuchungen*, Jena.

Williams, W. (1984), *The State Against Blacks*, New York: Laissez Faire Books.

Williamson, O.E. (1985a), 'Assessing Contract', *Journal of Law, Economics and Organization*, **1**, 177–208.

Williamson, O.E. (1985b), *The Economic Institutions of Capitalism*, New York: The Free Press.

Williamson, O.E. (1988), 'The Logic of Economic organization', *Journal of Law, Economics and Organization*, **4** (1), 65–94.

Wittman, D. (1989), 'Why Democracies Produce Efficient Results', *Journal of Political Economy*, **97** (6), 1395–1424.

Wood, A.W. (1972), 'The Marxian critique of justice', *Philosophy and Public Affairs*, **1**, 244–82.

Woods, L. (1985), 'Mediation: A backlash to women's progress on family law issues', *Clearinghouse Review*, **19**.

Selected newspaper articles on legal services

'Indians on the Warpath', *The New Republic*, April 30, 1977, pp. 16–21.

Reginald Stewart, 'Court to decide if Black English is a learning barrier', *New York Times*, June 12, 1979.

'City asked to pay for man's sex change', *The Washington Post*, January 15, 1981, p. B3.

R. Carelli, 'There Isn't a Governor in America we Haven't Sued', *Associated Press*, April 4, 1981.

'More Legal Insults for the Poor', *New York Times*, December 5 1982.

'Legal Services Head's Contract is Sweet', *The Washington Post*, December 16, 1982, pp. A1, A8.

'Recovery of Legal Fees Paid Legal Officials Demanded', *The Washington Post*, December 18, 1982, pp. A1, A5.

'Legal Disservice', *The Washington Post*, December 19, 1982, p. C6.

'Defending the Wreckers', *New York Times*, December 28, 1982, p. A22.

'The Dubious Deals of Reagan's Crowd', *The Washington Post*, January 2, 1983, p. A1.

David Ranii, 'Lawyers to Lobby for Poor in Illinois', *National Law Journal*, April 4, 1983, p. 22.

G. Lardner Jr, 'Legal Services Agency Lobbied Hard to Save It', *National Law Journal*, April 4, 1983, p. 22.

'Ruling Books Fees Paid to Legal Services Board', *The New York Times*, April 12, 1983.

'Put Legal Back into Legal Services', *The New York Times*, April 14, 1983, p. A30.

H. Kurtz, 'No violations found in Legal Services fees', *The Washington Post*, September 8, 1983, p. A6.

Tom Seppy, 'Auditors Accuse Legal Services Corporation of Illegal Spending', *The Washington Post*, September 20, 1983.

Mary Thornton, 'Former Employees of Legal Services Faulted GAO Funds Spending Violations', *The Washington Post*, September 23, 1983.

'Illegal Services', *The Washington Post*, September 23, 1983.

M.S. Serrill, 'An Organization at War With Itself', *Time*, October 3, 1983, p. 83.

'The Law, the Poor and the Torpedoes', *The New York Times*, November 17, 1983, p. A26.

'More Lawlessness in Legal Services', *The New York Times*, November 29, 1983.

S. Taylor, Jr, 'Legal Aid for the Poor: Reagan's Largest Brawl', *New York Times*, June 8, 1984, p. A16.

'LSC Official Irks Senator', *National Law Journal*, August 13, 1984.

'FTC Official to Head Legal Services', *The Washington Post*, June 29, 1985.

R. Carelli, 'Three Lawmakers Accuse Legal Services Chief of Playing Politics', *Associated Press*, October 30, 1985.

Mary Thornton, 'Legal Services Audits Assailed as Witch Hunt', *The Washington Post*, November 30, 1985, p. A3.

'Civil War at Legal Services', *Newsweek*, January 20, 1986, p. 24.

Lawrence Feinberg, '"U.S. Agency Lashes Antioch Law School", End $447,000 Grant', *The Washington Post*, September 10, 1986, p. C1.

Becky Dickinson, 'Support Center Pathetic Legal Services Says', *Legal Times*, September 22, 1986.

Ed Bruske, 'Chief of Legal Services Corporation Identified in Store Incident', *The Washington Post*, November 18, 1986, p. B1.

Saundra Saperstein, 'Legal Services Weighs Action On Wentzel', *The Washington Post*, November 18, 1986, p. B1.

'Antioch v. LSC?' *Legal Times*, December 1, 1986, p. 3.

'LSC Pinch', *The National Law Journal*, December 8, 1986, p. 45.

Aaron Friwald, 'LSC Officials Said to Wage Campaign Against Senator', *Legal Times*, December 22, 1986.

'New Era at LSC?' *Legal Times*, January 19, 1987.

Fred Strasser, 'New Agency Head', *National Law Journal*, January 19, 1987.

Nancy Belane, 'Reagan's Legal Services Chairman Takes on American Bar Association', *Associated Press*, March 8, 1987.

Richard Carelli, 'Rudman Accuses Legal Services Corporation Employees of Working Against Re-election', *Associated Press*, May 20, 1987.

Jonathan Ross, 'Bar Leaders Have Duty to Protect Legal Services and to Preserve Justice', *Legal Services Crises and Concerns*, Summer 1987 Update.

'Unregulated Entrepreneurs to Serve Poor?' *Legal Services Crises and Concerns*, Summer 1987 Update.

'Rudman Takes on Durant Logic', *Legal Services Crises and Concerns*, Summer 1987 Update.

'LSC Head Pushes for Unlicensed Legal Entrepreneurs to Serve Poor', *Legal Services Crises and Concerns*, Summer 1987. Update, August 1, 1987.

Anne Kornhauser, 'LSC Under Fire for Monitoring Program', *Legal Times*, August 24, 1987, p. 2.

Anne Kornhauser, 'LSC Under Fire for Monitoring Program', *Legal Times*, October 26, 1987.

Anne Kornhauser, 'Suit Hits Congressional Limits on LSC', *Legal Times*, October 26, 1987.

'Legal Services Corporation Board Chairman Should Resign', *Legal Services Crises and Concerns*, Fall 1987. Update, November 30, 1987.

'Bar Sinister: It's Time to Set Federally Funded Legal Services Straight', *Barron's*, September 26, 1988, p. 11.

Chris Adams, 'Churning Waters at Legal Services', *The Wall Street Journal*, September 28, 1988.

'Last Chance on Legal Services', *The Wall Street Journal*, September 28, 1988.

'Last Chance to Reform Legal Services', *The National Conservative Weekly*, October 1, 1988, p. 1, 7.

Law cases cited

Bowen v. *Guillard*, 107 S.Ct. 3008 (1987).

Brown v. *Board of Education* (1955), 2347 US 483 (1954), 349 US (1955).

Cash v. *Kirk*, No. C–C–87–9817 (W.D.N.c. May 21, 1987).

Committee to Defend Reproductive Rights v. *Myers*, 29 Cal. 3d 252, 172 Cal, Rpts.866, 625 P.wd 785 (1984).

Curry v. *Dempsey*, 701 F. 2d 580 (6th Cir. 1983).

Curtis v. *Commissioner of Human Services*, 507 A. 2d 566 (Me 1986).

Davidson v. *Duval County School Board*, No. 82–31 Ap. Fla. Cir. Ct., Duval County Sept. 29, 1982.

Doe v. *Zimmerman*, 405 F. Supp. 534 (M.D. Penn 1975).

Goldberg v. *Kelly*, 397 US 254 (1970).

H. L. v. *Matheson*, 450 US 398 (1981).

Hypolite v. *Carleson*, 32 Cal. App. 3d,979,108 Col. Rptr. 7511 (1973).

Isaac v. *Outgamie County*, E.D. Wisc. filed Jan. 6, 1983.

Jiminez v. *Cohen*, No. 85–5285 (E.D. Pa. July 1986).

Johnson v. *Mattison*, PS–30 (Boston, Mass. Mun, Ct. April 9, 1987).

King v. *Smith*, 392 US 309 (1968).

Lady Jane v. *Maher*, 420 F. Supp. 318 (D. Conn. 1976).

Lopez-Rivas v. *Donovan*, 629 F. Supp. 564 (D. Puerto Rico 1986).

Lyng v. *Castillo*, 106 S. Ct. 2727.

Malloy v. *Eicher*, No. 85–398 LON (D. Del. filed October 29, 1985).

Nafsinger v. *Blum*, No. 80–CU–623 (N.D.N.Y. June 2, 1982).

New Jersey Welfare Rights Organization v. *Cahill*, 411 US 619 622 (1973).

Northern States Power Company v. *Hagen* 314 N.S. 2d 278 (Supreme Ct. N.D. 1987).

Parham v. *J.R.*, 442 US 584 (1979).

Payless Drug Stores Northwest Inc. v. *Brown*, No. A309085 Cor. Ct. App. Nov. 5, 1985.

Planned Parenthood Affiliates of California v. *Van de Kamp*, 226 Cal Rptr.361C Cal, App. 1 Dist. (1986).

Planned Parenthood Association Inc. v. *Department of Human Services*, 297 Or. 562, 687 P.wd 785 (1984).

Roe v. *Casey*, 723 F.2d 829 (3d. Cir. 1980).

Shapiro v. *Thompson*, 396 US 618 (1969).

Thompson v. *Smith* (Cal. Super, Ct. San Francisco County, filed Aug. 6, 1981).

Two Associates v. *Brown* No. 8491/86 (N.Y. Sup. Ct. April 22, 1986).

US Dept. of Agriculture v. *Moreno* 413 US 528 (1973).

Williams v. *Zbarez*, 448 US 358 (1980).

Woe v. *Perales*, No. CIV 87–646 T (W.D.N.Y. filed June 12, 1987).

Wort v. *Vierling*, No. 82–3169 (C.D.III Sept. 4, 1984).

Index

poverty and absence of, 270–71
VPE perspective on, 78, 82–4, 196–7
in US Congress, 109–18
local programs *see under* Legal Services
Corporation
Locke, John, 26, 28, 29, 51
Lopez-Rivas v. *Donovan* (1986), 341
Lorenz, James D., 344
Lucas, Robert, 38
Lyng v. *Castillo*, 333
Lyons, Clinton, 212, 213, 220, 223, 298,
299

McCalpin, William, 8
McChesney, F. S., 40, 69, 84, 339
McCloskey, D. M., 38, 43–4
McCormick, R. E., 42, 110, 111, 112,
168
McKenzie, R. B., 231, 239, 240
McKinsey Report, 201
Madison, James, 82, 124, 182, 267–8
Magna Carta, 3
Mandel, E., 34
Mao Tse-Tung, 325
Marcuse, H., 35
market share liability, 65
Marshall, W. J., 117, 198
Marxism, 23, 34–6, 104, 249, 250–51
Maurizi, A., 273
Max, Steve, 308
Meckling, W. H., 117
media persuasion, 165–6
median voter theorem, 79, 109
Mercuro, N., 21
merit goods, 33
Mermin, L., 324
Merrill, T. W., 50–51
Migrant Legal Action Program, 312
Miller, D., 334
Miller, Melvin D., 298
minimum access issue, 172, 260
Mirrlees, J. A., 20
'mirror corporations', 209–10
Mises, L. von, 36, 159
Mitchell, W. C., 39, 41, 42, 113, 356,
357
Mondale-Steiger Bill, 14
Moore, T. G., 69
Moorhead, Representative, 173, 203
Moorhead Amendment, 202–3

moral hazard, 66
Moran, M. J., 114–21 *passim*, 198
Morris v. *Williams* (1967), 12
Morrison, Alan, 292
Morrison, Bruce A., 169, 180, 188, 216–
17, 222, 226
Moya, Jesus, 341
Mueller, D. C., 31, 41, 42
Muris, T. J., 118
Murphy, George, 12
Murray, Charles L., 237–45 *passim*, 264,
331, 332, 365, 375
Musgrave, A., 45

Nafzinger v. *Blum,* 333
National Association of Legal Aid Or-
ganizations, 5
National Center on Women and Family
Law, 334, 337
National Center for Youth Law, 334, 336
National Clients' Council (NCC), 202,
295, 297, 299–300
National Conference on Law and Pov-
erty, 8
National Consumer Law Center, 342
National Lawyers' Guild, 174, 276, 295
National Legal Aid and Defender Asso-
ciation (NLADA), 5, 8, 202, 212,
218, 252, 295–9, 312
National Social Science and Law Center,
311–12
national support centers, 140–41, 154, 206–
8, 210–11, 218, 308–14, 334, 373
National Training and Information
Center, 347
Native Americans, 204
negative freedom, 23–5
Nelson, M., 123
Nelson, R. R., 158
New Haven Legal Assistance Associa-
tion, 210
New Jersey Welfare Rights Organization
v. *Cahill* (1973), 331
New York Times, 165
Newman, Paul, 306
Niskanen, W. A., 84, 85, 97, 101, 102,
118, 119, 126, 166, 179, 182, 316,
358, 362
Nixon, Richard M., 14–16, 91, 157–8,
206, 309